07/2015

THE BOOK OF DAYS

THE
BOOK OF
DAYS

ANTHONY FREWIN

Wood engravings by Yvonne Skargon

COLLINS
ST JAMES'S PLACE, LONDON
1979

William Collins Sons & Co Ltd
London · Glasgow · Sydney · Auckland
Toronto · Johannesburg

First published 1979
© Anthony Frewin 1979
© Illustrations William Collins Sons and Co Ltd,
and Yvonne Skargon
ISBN 0 00 216085 4
Set in 11 on 12pt Bembo type
Made and Printed in Great Britain by
W & J Mackay Limited, Chatham

R
902.02
F897b

For
Nicky and Charlene
and to the *Manes* of
Richard Aldington
1892–1962

Oblivion is not to be hired.

SIR THOMAS BROWNE, *Hydriotaphia* (1658)

CONTENTS

PREFACE AND ACKNOWLEDGEMENTS

This is not the first 'Book of Days' to be published and it certainly will not be the last. The Day Book has a high history and derives ultimately from the annotated religious and civil calendars that reminded priest and prince, as much as populace, who was to be commemorated, what was to be observed and accomplished (and sometimes why), and when important lunar, solar and sidereal changes were to be expected. Its lineage could be traced with little difficulty back to Babylonian stone calendars and, perhaps, even beyond: in other words, like its close companions the diary and almanack, the Day Book shares the ancestry of the calendar.

In the literary sense, Day Books, that is works listing the events that have occurred on each of the year's days, together with religious and other associations, and births, deaths and so on, really date only from the early years of the nineteenth century, notably from the publication of the volumes edited by that worthy satirist and jobbing-journalist, William Hone.

Hone and the authors of other contemporary Day collections, John Brady, Robert Chambers (see Section V of the Bibliography), were not principally concerned with historical, biographical and celebratory listings so much as hanging discursive and anecdotal essays and articles upon the 365/6 pegs. For instance, Chambers in *A Book of Days* (1863), under 10 March, prints a long piece on 'Honeycombs in Timber' because, as we learn, on that day in 1858 'some workmen employed by Mr Brumfitt, of Preston, while sawing up a large solid log of baywood, twenty feet long by two feet square, discovered a cavity in it about eight feet long, containing a full-formed honeycomb.' This is very worthy, but essentially it belongs in a 'Cabinet of Curiosities' or a book on bees. By saying this I am not decrying the work of Chambers or his colleagues, neither am I misunderstanding the principles and purpose of their ventures, but merely drawing the reader's attention to my own dissatisfaction with them, a dissatisfaction that produced the book now before you. What was previously only presented tantalizingly – namely a trinity of items, historical, biographical and celebratory – is here the sole concern and substance.

Originally, when I thought this book was going to be completed in a quarter of the time it actually took, I was going to include a lengthy bibliographical essay on Day Books and their relatives. As it is I list only seven in the last section of the Bibliography. I am aware that many others exist, but of those known to me I can unhesitatingly recommend only those included, and I have reservations about Darling's, it seems never to have been edited and contains a great many inaccuracies.

And talking of inaccuracies, there may well be a residue (reservoir?) of errata in the pages that follow, in fact chance and the human element are firmly in favour of it. For corrections I will be both sad and glad. And details of omissions would also be warmly welcomed.

Finally, it gives me great pleasure to be able to thank the many people who have helped in the preparation of this book.

My good friend Dick Brewis of Brighton and Camden Town supplied and confirmed a number of dates at a moment's notice. Sally Whitaker unwittingly gave me much encouragement at a time when it was most needed, as did Susan Hill, and Eileen Gallagher, an assiduous library sleuth, kindly loaned a book that I would not otherwise have seen.

Lucinda Campbell assisted with the verification of biographical dates and I am most deeply indebted to her. I am also indebted to Jan Hutton for re-typing many pages of notes with great speed and accuracy, and Stanley Noble, antiquarian bookseller, for supplying an important set of books and advising on numerous others.

Thanks must also go to Philip Ziegler who readily responded to the suggestion for a new Book of Days and waited patiently as it became long overdue.

Neville Adlam of the Johannesburg *Star* sent a good many dates in his country's history that were not included in the first draft, and his great pains are much appreciated.

Yvonne Skargon's woodcuts are a delight. Thanks to her and Ronald Clark for making this such an attractive volume.

David Massel, Clerk to the Board of Deputies of British Jews was most helpful in sharing his profound knowledge of the calendar with me.

Brother Alan of the Friars of Atonement, Librarian of the Catholic Central Library, was unfailingly obliging in many ways, including operating a Xerox machine at 7 a.m. so that material might be ready when I arrived.

I would also like to register gratitude to Arnold W. L. Nayler of the Royal Aeronautical Society, the Librarian of the Royal Astronomical Society, a young lady at the Nautical Almanac Office, and the staffs of the London Library, University College Library and the Westminster Central Reference Library.

Jean and Eddie Frewin gave me considerable support. Mark Frewin must be thanked for his innumerable kindnesses, along with Ruby Weeks who also reminded me of two commemorations I had forgotten.

Like all writers who have cause to mention the *sancti* I owe a very great debt to the work of Herbert Thurston SJ and Donald Attwater. Their editions of *Butler's Lives of the Saints* are fitting examples of the rigorous and magisterial scholarship sometimes associated with the Society of Jesus and could be studied rewardingly by anyone at all interested in historical method.

Lastly, a very special debt of thanks to Charlene whose contributions to this book were considerable, and without whom it would have taken much longer to complete. To her, as ever, I owe much.

ANTHONY FREWIN

Anno Mundi MCMLXXXIII

INTRODUCTION

Each day is divided into three main sections:

A. *Celebratory*: the italic matter at the head, comprising fixed religious feasts, civil commemorations and holidays from around the world, together with some customs and associations from folk-lore and mythology.
B. *Historical*: Events and occurrences from history generally.
C. *Biographical*: Births, deaths.

I have largely avoided the use of abbreviations and those that do appear will be readily recognized, UN for United Nations, US for United States of America, and so on. But BCP, perhaps not familiar, stands for *The Book of Common Prayer*, SS is the plural of saint.

All dates are AD unless suffixed with BC.

Julian dates have not been reduced to the Gregorian reckoning.

I have quietly accepted a number of *factoids*, Norman Mailer's lovely term for statements of dubious certainty that have been repeated and passed on so many times they have garnered an aura of truth. These are chiefly to be found in the births section. As an example, Shakespeare's birthday. While we know that he was baptized on 26 April 1564 we do not know for sure on what day he was born. But a tradition sprung up that it was on the same day that he died, 23 April, the day accepted for his birth herein.

The *Historical* and *Biographical* sections are arranged chronologically, first dates first.

Celebratory
The entries in this section are *fixed* in the *Gregorian* calendar. Thus the absence of immovable Jewish, Muslim and other celebrations; while fixed in their own calendar systems the days do not always correspond with the same day in the Gregorian year. All saints are 'confessors' unless the contrary is stated.

Historical
Here are included the chief dates of world history and also a selection from the arts, science, discovery and exploration, and human achievement generally.

Events of only a few days' duration, like some battles, are usually entered under the final day. If they continued for longer and are sufficiently important I have entered the first and last days and cross-referenced both. But this depends very much on the importance of the entry and it is hard to generalize.

Biographical
The general styling adopted for the births is name, a word or two of description, followed by, wherever possible, examples of the subject's work or achievement

and the place of birth, and concluding with the year. The entries in the deaths section are the same except that I have not usually given the place.

A NOTE ON THE GREGORIAN CALENDAR AND THE CHRISTIAN ERA

The major system of date reckoning used throughout the world is the Gregorian Calendar (the New Style), named after Pope Gregory XIII who promulgated it in a Bull dated 24 February 1582. It was introduced because the earlier reckoning, the Julian or Old Style Calendar, was becoming increasingly out of step with the seasons, but particularly because the date of the vernal equinox was receding in the calendar and the observance of Easter, the most important Christian feast, computed from its occurrence was moving further and further away from the time within which it should, historically, fall. When the Council of Nicaea fixed the rules for Easter in 325, the vernal equinox was on 21 March, by 1582 it had moved back to 12 March. Pope Gregory therefore introduced a reckoning, drawn up largely by Christopher Clavius, that kept the calendrial year 'in time' with the equinoxes and thus with the Equinoctial or Tropical Year, the time taken by the Earth to revolve around the sun from equinox to equinox, namely 365.24 solar days.

The Gregorian Calendar was adopted in France, Italy, Portugal and Spain in the year of its promulgation, by the German Protestant states in 1700, by England and her possessions in 1752, by Russia not until after the Revolution, 1918, and by Greece as late as 1923.

The Julian Calendar takes its name from Julius Caesar who abandoned the Roman Republican Calendar in 42BC to institute the proposals put forward by Sosigenes, an Alexandrian astronomer whom he had employed for the purpose.

We have *twelve* months essentially because many of the earliest calendars were lunar, that is based upon the phases of the moon, and there are approximately twelve lunations in a year; a lunation is the time taken by the moon to return to 'full' or any phase. The names of the months, as will be seen, originated in classical Rome, as too did their varying lengths, partly from the Romans regarding even numbers as being unlucky and partly from the Emperor Augustus wishing the month named after him to have as many days as that named in honour of Caesar (July).

The nearest to a standard, universal year reckoning is the Christian Era. That is years are reckoned as so many before or after the birth of Christ (BC and AD); the styling was introduced by Dionysius Exiguus in 533, rapidly gained acceptance throughout the Christian world and replaced the era that had previously been in use, the Mundane Era, *Anno Mundi*, reckoned from 4004BC the supposed year of Creation.

And there are many other eras. Muslims, for instance, reckon from the Hegira, the flight of the Prophet Muhammad from Mecca to Medina, that corresponds with AD622 (16 July). The ancient Greeks used the Era of the Olympiads (776BC) whilst the Romans dated from the Foundation of Rome (743BC).

JANUARY

THIRTY-ONE DAYS

January, like February, was introduced into the
Roman calendar by a legendary King of Rome,
Numa Pompilius (*c.* 715–673BC), who named it
in honour of Janus, the god of doors and openings
(Latin *janus*, a door). Janus is represented in
Roman art as a man with two faces, one looking
forwards and one looking backwards, implying
as Robert Chambers has noted, 'that he stood
between the old and the new year, with a regard
to both.'

*New Year's Day, a legal holiday in many countries. The Feast of the
Circumcision of Our Lord Jesus Christ, celebrating Christ receiving the
sacrament of circumcision (and the name Jesus); the feast was first recorded in a
lectionary of the year 546 and its observance soon spread throughout the church;
the Octave* of Christmas. The Roman festival of Janus, the god of doors and
openings. 'Yule Girth (see 18 December). The Festival of Fools, observed in
Paris from about 1198 until 1438, a day of licensed jesting and amusement.
Celebration of the Anniversary of the Revolution, Cuba (1959). Independence
Day, Sudan (1956). Feasts of SS: Concordius, martyr; Almachius, or
Telemachus, martyr; Euphrosyne, virgin; Eugendus, or Oyend, abbot;
Fulgentius, bishop; Felix of Bourges, bishop; Clarus, abbot; Peter of Atroa,
abbot; William of Saint Benignus, abbot; Odilo, abbot.*

The two Roman legions at Mainz refuse to swear the oath of allegiance to the
Emperor, Servias Sulpicius Galba (of whom Tacitus wrote, *Capax imperii nisi
imperasset* – 'Worthy of empire if he had never been emperor'), 69. ¶ Helvius
Pertinax is proclaimed emperor in Rome upon the death of Lucius Aelius
Aurelius Commodus (Pertinax is subsequently slain by the Praetorian Guard on
28 March), 193. ¶ The Gregorian calendar introduced by Swiss Catholics, 1583.
¶ The Gregorian calendar introduced by the Catholic states in Germany, 1583.
¶ For Swiss Protestants this day became 12 January with the introduction of the
Gregorian calendar in 1701. ¶ John Walter publishes the first issue of the *Daily
Universal Register* on his Logographic Press, 1785. ¶ The name of the *Daily
Universal Register* is changed to *The Times*, 1788. ¶ Ceres (Asteroid I) discovered
by Piazzi, 1801. ¶ The Act of Union between England and Ireland becomes
operative, 1801. ¶ Sovereignty over the Falkland Isles is proclaimed by Britain,
1833. ¶ Capitulation of British forces to the Afghans at Kabul, 1842. ¶ London
is divided into ten postal districts, 1858. ¶ Abraham Lincoln's Emancipation
Proclamation (proclaimed on 22 September 1862) comes into effect regarding
slavery in the US, 1863. ¶ The Church of Ireland is disestablished, 1871. ¶ The
State of New York adopts the electric chair for capital punishment, 1889.
¶ Queen Victoria is made the Empress of India, 1877. ¶ The Michigan–Mississippi Canal opened, 1900. ¶ The Commonwealth of Australia is formally
established, with Edmund Barton as Prime Minister, 1901. ¶ Port Arthur is surrendered by the Russians to Japan, 1905. ¶ Old-age pensions for all British
subjects over the age of 70 become payable, 1909. ¶ HMS *Formidable* is sunk in
the English Channel by German actions, 1915. ¶ The capital of Norway,
Christiania, resumes the name Oslo, 1925. ¶ Mustapha Kemal adopts the name

* The seventh day after a feast, but the *eighth* counting from the feast itself. Called also
the *Utas*.

of Kemal Atatürk after family names are made obligatory in Turkey by the National Assembly, 1935. ¶ British Fourteenth Army offensive in Burma begins, 1945. ¶ Nationalization of the coal industry in Britain, 1947. ¶ Proclamation of independence by the Republic of the Cameroons, 1960. ¶ Farthings cease to be legal tender in Britain, 1961. ¶ Britain's entry into the European Common Market, 1973. ¶ New Year's Day is a national public holiday in Britain from 1974. ¶ John Ehrlichman, H. R. Haldeman and John Mitchell are found guilty in Washington of obstructing the course of justice in the Watergate Affair, 1975. ¶ The fishing limits of the United Kingdom are extended to 200 miles around the coast, 1977. ¶ Control of the Panama Canal will revert to Panama itself (as agreed by treaty signed by President Jimmy Carter and General Torrijos in Washington on 7 September 1977), 2000.

BORN: Edmund Burke, politician and writer, *Reflections on the French Revolution*, Dublin, 1729. Paul Revere, American patriot, Boston, Massachusetts, 1735. Maria Edgeworth, Irish novelist, *The Absentee*, Oxfordshire, 1767. Sándor Petöfi, poet, Hungary, 1823. Sir James Frazer, scholar and anthropologist, *The Golden Bough*, Glasgow, 1854. Henry Handel Richardson (Henrietta Richardson), Australian novelist, *The Fortunes of Richard Mahony* (a trilogy), Melbourne, 1870. E. M. Forster, novelist and critic, *A Passage to India*, London, 1879. William Fox, film impresario, a founder of 20th Century Fox, Hungary, 1879. Ernest Jones, psychoanalyst; popularizer, translator and biographer of Sigmund Freud, Glamorgan, Wales, 1879. Martin Niemoller, priest, open opponent of Hitler in the 1930s, President of the World Council of Churches, Lippstadt, Germany, 1892. J. Edgar Hoover, founder and head of the Federal Bureau of Investigation, Washington, D.C., 1895. Harold 'Kim' Philby, Russian master-spy in the British intelligence organization from 1933–63, India, 1912. Jerome David Salinger, novelist, *Catcher in the Rye, Franny and Zooey*, New York City, 1919.

DIED: William Wycherley, dramatist, *The Gentleman Dancing-master*, *The Plain Dealer*, London, 1716. Johann Bernoulli, mathematician, Switzerland, 1748. Johann Christian Bach, composer, a son of J. S. Bach, 1782. Martin Klaproth, chemist, Germany, 1817. Louis Auguste Blanqui, revolutionary socialist, 1881. Heinrich Rudolph Hertz, physicist, discovered electro-magnetic (radio) waves, Germany, 1894. August von Wassermann, physician and bacteriologist, Austria, 1925. Sir Edwin Landseer Lutyens, architect, London, 1944. Maurice Chevalier, French singer and entertainer, 1972.

JANUARY 2

The Feast of the Holy Name of Jesus, originally granted as a special feast to the Franciscan Order in 1530, not extended to the church generally until 1751 (7 August BCP). 'Yule Girth' (see 18 December). Day of the Glorification of the Heroes of Independence, Haiti. Feasts of SS: Macarius of Alexandria; Munchin, bishop; Vincentian; Adalhard, or Adelard, abbot; Caspar del Bufalo.

Cardinal Richelieu establishes the *Académie Française*, 1635. ¶ Calcutta taken by Clive of India, 1757. ¶ Georgia enters the Union (4th), 1788. ¶ The state of Georgia ratifies the Constitution of the United States of America, 1788. ¶ Napoleon Bonaparte advances into Syria, 1799. ¶ Britain joins the alliance of Russia and Turkey, 1799. ¶ The battle of Nashville, 1863. ¶ Sir Robert Napier leads a British expedition to Ethiopia as a result of the resident Consul being abducted, 1868. ¶ Britain recognizes Colombia and Mexico, 1875. ¶ First municipal crematorium opened in England, at Hull, by the Lord Mayor, 1901. ¶ *Lunik I* spacecraft launched by USSR, 1959. ¶ A barrier collapses at Ibrox Park football ground in Glasgow and 66 people are crushed to death, 1971.

BORN: Nathaniel Bacon, Virginian rebel, Suffolk, 1647. John Manners, Marquis of Granby, British military commander, principally in the Seven Years War, 1721. Gilbert Murray, classicist and translator, Professor of Greek at Oxford; Sydney, Australia, 1866.

DIED: Fabian Gottlieb Bellingshausen, polar explorer and naval commander, Russia, 1852. General Tom Thumb (Charles Sherwood Stratton), famous dwarf, 31 inches tall, 1883. Alexander William Kinglake, historian, *History of the War in the Crimea*, Somerset, 1891. Sir George Biddell Airy, Astronomer Royal, Alnwick, 1892. Léon Philippe Teisserenc de Bort, meteorologist, experimented with balloons and discovered the stratosphere, Cannes, France, 1913. Sir Edward Burnett Tylor, anthropologist, *Researches into the Early History of Mankind,* Wellington, Somerset, 1917.

'Yule Girth' (see 18 December). National Holiday, Republic of Upper Volta.
Feasts of SS: Antherus, pope and martyr; Peter Balsam, martyr; Genevieve,
or Genovefa, virgin; Bertilia of Mareuil, widow.

British forces defeated at Princeton, New Jersey, by George Washington, 1777. ¶ Russia and Austria agree treaty for third partition of Poland, 1795. ¶ Construction begins of the Brooklyn–New York Bridge, 1870. ¶ Oscar Wilde's *An Ideal Husband* opens at the Haymarket Theatre. Wilde is at the height of his success, 1895. ¶ First Parliament in India meets, 1921. ¶ Alaska made a US state (49th), 1959. ¶ Diplomatic relations with Cuba severed by US, 1961. ¶ Jack Ruby, who shot Lee Harvey Oswald, alleged assassin of President John F. Kennedy, dies in a hospital in Dallas, 1967. ¶ The International Monetary Fund in Washington approves the loan of £2,300 million ($3,900 million) to Britain, 1977.

BORN: Pietro Antonio Metastasio, poet and dramatist, *Attilio Regolo*, Rome, 1698. Robert Whitehead, engineer, invented the naval torpedo, Bolton-le-Moors, Lancashire, 1823. Clement Attlee, British Labour Prime Minister and statesman, Putney, London, 1883. James Bridie, dramatist and physician, *The Anatomist*, Glasgow, 1888. John Ronald Reuel Tolkien, philologist and writer, *The Lord of the Rings*, Bloemfontein, South Africa, 1892.

DIED: George Monck, 1st Duke of Albemarle, military commander, fought on both sides in the English Civil War, Whitehall, London, 1670. Luca Giordano, Italian painter, decorated the Escorial in Madrid for Charles II of Spain, 1705. Josiah Wedgewood, potter and industrialist, Etruria, Staffordshire, 1795. Rachel (Elisa Felix), actress, Cannes, France, 1858. Pierre Larousse, French editor and lexicographer, 1875. William Harrison Ainsworth, popular novelist, Reigate, Surrey, 1882. James Elroy Flecker, dramatist and poet, 1915. Jaroslav Hašek, Czech novelist, *The Good Soldier Schweik*, 1923. William Joyce, 'Lord Haw-haw', Nazi collaborator, hanged, London, 1946. Edwin Muir, Scottish poet, translator and critic, *First Poems, The Story and the Fable, Poor Tom*, Cambridge, 1959.

JANUARY 4

'Yule Girth' (see 18 December). Independence Day, Burma (Britain relinquished authority in 1948). Martyrs of Independence Day, Zaire. Feasts of SS: Gregory of Langres, bishop; Pharaildis, virgin; Rigobert, archbishop.

Napoleon defeats the Austrians at Rivoli, 1797. ¶ Semele (Asteroid 86) discovered by F. Tietjen, 1866. ¶ Koronis (Asteroid 158) discovered by V. Knorre, 1876. ¶ Utah is made a US state (45th), 1896. ¶ Riga is captured by the Bolsheviks, 1919. ¶ Seoul taken from United Nations' forces by Chinese communists and North Koreans, 1951. ¶ Pope Paul VI begins a tour of the Holy Land and visits Jordan and Jerusalem, 1964. ¶ President Richard M. Nixon ignores the Federal Court deadline to hand over the White House tapes (Watergate affair), 1974.

BORN: James Usher (or Ussher), Archbishop of Armagh, divine and scholar, *Annales Veteris et Novi Testamenti*, Dublin, 1581. Giovanni Pergolesi, composer, Italy, 1710. Jacob Grimm, philologist, historian and folk-lore collector, *Fairy Tales* (with his brother Wilhelm), Hanau, Germany, 1785. Louis Braille, invented the Braille system of reading for the blind, Paris, 1809. Sir Isaac Pitman, printer and publisher, devised one of the most successful short-hand systems, Trowbridge, Wiltshire, 1813. Emile Cohl, pioneer French film animator, Paris, 1857. Augustus John, artist, Wales, 1878. Jan Lenica, film animator, *Le Labyrinthe*, Poznan, Poland, 1928.

DIED: Stephen Hales, clergyman, inventor and chemist, pioneered the study of plant physiology, *Vegetable Staticks*, Teddington, Middlesex, 1761. Clarence Dutton, geologist, 1912. Benito Perez Galdos, novelist and dramatist, *Episodios nacionales* (a series of 46 novels), Madrid, 1920. Henri Bergson, French philosopher and writer, *Creative Evolution*, 1941. Donald Malcolm Campbell, killed whilst attempting the water speed record, 1948. Albert Camus, novelist, *The Outsider*, 1960. Erwin Schrödinger, physicist, Nobel Prize winner, Vienna, 1961. T. S. Eliot, poet and critic, *The Waste Land*, 1965.

JANUARY 5

Twelfth Day Eve.   Twelfth Night (5/6 January). 'Yule Girth' (see 18 December).
Feasts of SS: Telesphorus, pope and martyr; Apollinaris, virgin; Syncletica,
virgin; Simeon the Stylite; Convoyon, abbot; Dorotheus the Younger, abbot;
Gerlac.

Charles the Bold killed by the Swiss at the battle of Nancy, 1477. ¶ The Treaty of the Dardanelles is concluded by Britain and Turkey, 1809. ¶ Bishop Colenso is publicly excommunicated at Maritzburg Cathedral by Dr Gray, Bishop of Capetown, for his heretical study of *The Pentateuch*, 1866. ¶ German National Socialist Party is formed, 1919. ¶ Mrs Nellie Tayloe Ross in Wyoming becomes first US woman Governor, 1925. ¶ Billie Holiday records *When You're Smiling (The Whole World Smiles with You)* with Teddy Wilson and his Orchestra in New York, 1938. ¶ Pope Paul VI meets the Ecumenical Patriarch Athenagoras I of Constantinople in Jerusalem, the first meeting between leaders of the Roman Catholic and Orthodox churches since the 1400s, 1964.

BORN: Jean-Baptiste Say, political economist, Lyons, France, 1767. Khristo Botev, poet and revolutionary, Bulgaria, 1848. King Camp Gillette, American inventor of the safety razor, 1855. Konstantin Sergeyevich Stanislavsky, actor and drama teacher, Moscow, 1863. Joseph Erlanger, neuro-physiologist, 1874. Konrad Adenauer, German statesman, 1876. Humbert Wolfe, diplomat and poet, 1885. Kathleen Kenyon, archaeologist, used radio-carbon to date the remains of Jericho, London, 1906. Jack Lovelock, New Zealand athlete, 1910. Friedrich Dürrenmatt, dramatist and novelist, *The Visit*, Switzerland, 1921.

DIED: Catherine de Medici, wife of Henry II of France, intriguer, Blois, France, 1589. Joseph Gillot, perfected the steel writing pen, Edgbaston, Birmingham, 1873. Sir Ernest Henry Shackleton, Antarctic explorer, Falkland Islands, 1922. Calvin Coolidge, President of the USA, 1933. Humbert Wolf, diplomat and poet, 1940.

JANUARY 6

*Twelfth Day (after Christmas). The feast of the Epiphany of Our Lord
Jesus Christ, or the Adoration of the Magi, celebrating the appearance (epiphany)
of Christ to the Three Wise Men, or Magi; the feast probably originated
in the Eastern church, recognized in the West by the early 5th century;
known in Scotland as Uphaliday or Uphalimas. 'Yule Girth' (see 18 December).
Old Christmas Day in England (prior to the introduction of the Gregorian
calendar in 1752). Public Holiday, Andorra. Christmas Day, Ethiopia. Army
Day, Iraq. Children's Day, Uruguay. Three Kings Day, Virgin Islands
(Epiphany). Feasts of SS: Wiltrudis, widow; Erminold, abbot; Guarinus,
or Guerin, bishop.*

Sir Edward Coke is sent to prison, 1622. ¶ The Committee of Inquiry on the
South Sea Bubble publishes its findings, 1720. ¶ Cyclone in Georgia and neigh-
bouring states causes many deaths, 1892. ¶ New Mexico made a US state (47th),
1912. ¶ The New Sadler's Wells Theatre is opened in London, 1931. ¶ President
Roosevelt submits the Lend-Lease Bill (for Allied aid) to Congress, 1941. ¶ The
German offensive in the Ardennes ends, the 'Battle of the Bulge' (began 16
December 1944), 1945. ¶ Communist China is recognized by Britain, 1950.
¶ After being held captive for over eight months Lindsay Tyler, a British
veterinary doctor, and his wife and two children are released by rebel guerillas
in Ethiopia, 1977.

BORN: Jacques Etienne Montgolfier, balloonist and paper manufacturer,
Annonay, France, 1745. Heinrich Schliemann, a pioneer of modern archaeology,
excavated at Mycenae and Troy, Neubuckow (now in East Germany), 1822.
Gustave Doré, artist and illustrator, France, 1832. Clarence King, geologist,
founder of the US Geological Survey, Rhode Island, 1842. Fred Niblo, film
director, *The Sign of Zorro*, Nebraska, 1874. Carl Sandburg, poet and biographer,
Smoke and Steel, *Abraham Lincoln*, Galesburg, Illinois, 1878. Khalil Gibran,
writer of worthless 'mystical' tracts, *The Prophet*, Lebanon, 1883.

DIED: Baldassare Peruzzi, Renaissance architect, Rome, 1536. Jean-Etienne
Guettard, naturalist and geologist, 1786. Fanny Burney, diarist and novelist,
Cecilia, 1840. Louis Braille, invented the Braille system of reading for the
blind, 1852. Richard Henry Dana, American novelist, *Two Years Before the Mast*,
1882. Gregor Mendel, Augustine monk, pioneered the study of heredity by
crossing garden peas, Brünn, Austria, 1884. Philip Armour, food industrialist,
founder of the Armour Company, 1901. Georg Cantor, mathematician, worked
on the theory of infinity, Germany, 1918. Theodore Roosevelt, President of the
US, Oyster Bay, New York, 1919. Victor Fleming, film director, *The Wizard
of Oz*, Phoenix, Arizona, 1949.

JANUARY 7

The final day of the Yule Girth celebrations (see 18 December). Popularly known in England as St Distaff's Day or Rock Day until the 19th century, supposedly because it was the custom of women to return to the spinning wheel (or distaff or rock). Feasts of SS: Lucian of Antioch, martyr; Valentine, bishop; Tillo; Aldric, bishop; Reinold; Canute Lavard, martyr.

Foundation of the University of Glasgow, 1450. ¶ Calais is retaken by the French, 1558. ¶ Four satellites of Jupiter discovered by Galileo, (I) Io, (II) Europa, (III) Ganymede, (IV) Callisto, 1610. ¶ Blanchard and Jeffries ascend at Dover, cross the English Channel and descend near Calais, by hot-air balloon, 1785. ¶ Blockade of the French coast by the British, 1807. ¶ First services run by the London General Omnibus Company, 1857.

BORN: Millard Fillmore, thirteenth President of the USA, New York, 1800. Saint Bernadette, received visions of the Virgin Mary at her birthplace, Lourdes, France, 1844. Carl Laemmle, film producer, founder of Universal Pictures, Germany, 1867. Charles Péguy, poet and socialist, Orleans, France, 1873. François Poulenc, composer and pianist, Paris, 1899. Charles Addams, *New Yorker* cartoonist and author, New Jersey, 1912. Gerald Durrell, author and naturalist, India, 1925.

DIED: Catherine of Aragon, wife of Henry VIII, 1536. Nicholas Hillyarde, miniaturist, London, 1619. François de Salignac de la Mothe Fénelon, theologian and writer, 1715. Andrei Bely, novelist and poet, 1934. Nikola Tesla, inventor and engineer, worked with Thomas Edison, New York City, 1943.

JANUARY 8

Battle of New Orleans Day, Louisiana, USA (1815). Feasts of SS: Apollinaris of Hierapolis, bishop; Lucian of Beauvais, martyr; Severinus of Noricum; Severinus of Septempeda, bishop; Erhard, bishop; Gudula, virgin; Pega, virgin; Wulsin, bishop; Thorfinn, bishop.

Accession of Alexander I of Scotland (reigned until 27 April 1124), 1106. ¶ 11th Amendment (Article XI) to the Constitution of the US becomes effective, 1798. ¶ The first soup kitchens are opened in London for the relief of the poor, 1800. ¶ Britain occupies the Cape of Good Hope, 1806. ¶ In Rome the Pope is deprived of his temporal power, 1849. ¶ Gallipoli evacuated by the British, 1916. ¶ Lord Lee of Fareham presents 'Chequers' to the nation and it becomes the official country residence for British prime ministers, 1921. ¶ Rationing of sugar and certain farm produce began in Britain, 1940. ¶ General Charles de Gaulle becomes President of the Fifth Republic, 1959. ¶ The British Ambassador in Uruguay, Geoffrey Jackson, is kidnapped by guerillas (released unharmed on 9 September), 1971.

BORN: Alfred Wallace, naturalist and explorer, *Travels on the Amazon and Rio Negro, Contributions to the Theory of Natural Selection*, Usk, Monmouthshire, Wales, 1823. Wilkie Collins, novelist, *The Woman in White*, London, 1824. Hans Guido von Bülow, pianist and conductor, Dresden, 1830. Frank Doubleday, publisher and editor, New York, 1862. Solomon Bandaranaike, Ceylonese Prime Minister, Colombo, 1899. Georgi Malenkov, Soviet politician, Orenburg, 1902. Elvis Presley, popular singer, Mississippi, 1935.

DIED: Giotto, Florentine artist, 1337. Galileo Galilei, astronomer and physicist, 1642. Arcangelo Corelli, Italian composer and violinist, 1713. John Baskerville, printer and type designer, 1775. Jean Marie Collot d'Herbois, French revolutionary, 1796. Eli Whitney, inventor, perfected the cotton gin and pioneered industrial mass production, New Haven, Connecticut, 1825. Paul Verlaine, French Symbolist poet, *Poèmes Saturniens, Sagesse*, Paris, 1896. Robert Baden-Powell, defended Mafeking, founded the Boy Scout movement, 1941. Kurt Schwitters, painter and collagist, Westmorland, England, 1948.

JANUARY 9

Day of National Mourning, Panama. Feasts of SS: Marciana, virgin and martyr; Julian and Basilissa, and Companions, martyrs; Peter of Sebastea, bishop; Waningus, or Vaneng; Adrian of Canterbury, abbot; Berhtwald of Canterbury, archbishop.

The state of Connecticut ratifies the Constitution of the United States of America, 1788. ¶ The first human ascent in a balloon in America, by the Frenchman Jean Pierre Blanchard, near Woodbury, New Jersey, 1793. ¶ Lord Nelson is buried at St Paul's Cathedral, London, 1806. ¶ Mississippi secedes from the Union (readmitted 23 February 1870), 1861. ¶ The unarmed ship *Star of the West* fails to relieve Fort Sumter (turns back after being fired upon by batteries on the South Carolina coast), 1861. ¶ Resignation of the British Prime Minister Anthony Eden, 1957. ¶ The British tanker *Haustrom* is fired upon by the Vietcong as she proceeds up the Saigon River, 1967. ¶ First trial flight of the *Concorde*, at Bristol, 1969. ¶ Serious earthquakes in Los Angeles and surrounding area, 1971. ¶ The *Queen Elizabeth* gutted by fire in Hong Kong, 1972.

BORN: Hayyim Nahman Bialik, Hebrew writer, Russia, 1873. John Watson, behaviourist psychologist, Greenville, South Carolina, 1878. Lascelles Abercrombie, writer and critic, Cheshire, 1881. Wolfgang Köhler, *Gestalt* psychologist, Russia, 1887. Karel Capek, dramatist, *Rossum's Universal Robots*, Bohemia, 1890. Gracie Fields, popular singer and entertainer, Lancashire, 1898. Rudolph Bing, conductor, Vienna, 1902. George Balanchine, American choreographer, St Petersburg, Russia, 1904. Simone de Beauvoir, novelist and critic, companion of Jean-Paul Sartre, *The Second Sex*, Paris, 1908. Richard Nixon, Republican US President, California, 1913. Joan Baez, folk-singer, Staten Island, New York, 1941.

DIED: Bernard Le Bovier Sieur de Fontenelle, philosopher, 1757. Napoleon III, Emperor of France; in exile, Chiselhurst, Kent, 1873. Wilhelm Busch, cartoonist, *Max und Moritz*, 1908. Katherine Mansfield, writer, *Bliss, The Garden Party*, Fontainebleau, France, 1923. Karl Mannheim, sociologist and philosopher, *Ideology and Utopia*, London, 1947.

JANUARY 10

Feasts of SS: Marcian; John the Good, bishop; Agatho, pope; Peter Orseolo; William of Bourges, archbishop.

The first section of the first polyglot Bible is printed at Alcalá de Henares in Spain by Arnold Guillen de Brocar, 1514. ¶ Bishop Pompallier arrives at Hokianga in New Zealand and establishes a mission, 1838. ¶ The 'Penny Post' is introduced in Britain by Rowland Hill, 1840. ¶ Florida secedes from the Union (readmitted 25 June 1868), 1861. ¶ Formal establishment of the League of Nations, 1920. ¶ Beginning of the war trials in Leipzig before German Supreme Court, 1921. ¶ Beginning of the communist-inspired Red Revolt on the Witwatersrand in the Union of South Africa (later crushed by General Smuts), 1922. ¶ Juan de la Cierva demonstrates the first autogyro, in Spain, 1923. ¶ Hood and Moncrieff are lost whilst attempting the first flight from Australia to New Zealand across the Tasman Sea, 1928. ¶ First meeting of the United Nations General Assembly, in London, 1946. ¶ Harold Macmillan becomes Prime Minister after the resignation of Anthony Eden (9 January), 1957. ¶ Food riots in Gujarat in India, 1974.

BORN: Niels Stensen, anatomist and physiologist, Copenhagen, Denmark, 1638. Michel Ney, Napoleonic military commander, commanded the Old Guard at Waterloo, Saarlouis, Germany, 1769. Lord Acton, statesman and writer, Naples, 1834. Manuel Azaña, president of the Spanish Republic at the time of the Civil War, 1880. Grock (Adrien Wettach), clown and entertainer, Switzerland, 1880. Alexsei Tolstoy, novelist and dramatist, *The Road to Calvary, Aelita*, Russia, 1883. Robinson Jeffers, poet, *Tamar and Other Poems*, Pennsylvania, 1887. Dame Barbara Hepworth, sculptress, Wakefield, Yorkshire, 1903. Galina Ulanova, ballerina, St Petersburg, Russia, 1910.

DIED: William Laud, Archbishop of Canterbury, supporter of Charles I; beheaded, Tower Hill, London, 1645. Carolus Linnaeus, botanist and taxonomist, Uppsala, Sweden, 1778. Adrien Marie Legendre, mathematician, Paris, 1833. Samuel Colt, American gunsmith and inventor, Hartford, Connecticut, 1862. William Frederick Cody (Buffalo Bill), frontiersman and impresario, 1917. Sinclair Lewis, American novelist, *Main Street, Babbitt, Elmer Gantry*, near Rome, 1951. Gabriela Mistral, Chilean poet, Nobel Prize for Literature, diplomat, New York, 1957. Coco Chanel, fashion designer, 1971.

JANUARY 11

Sacrifices were offered by the Romans on this day to Juturna, nymph of the fountain in Latium, the waters of which were famous for their healing powers. Proclamation of the Republic Day, Albania (1946). Hostos's Birthday, Puerto Rico (Eugenio Maria Hostos, 1839–1903, educator and reformer). Feasts of SS: Hyginus, pope; Theodosius the Cenobiarch; Salvius, or Sauve, bishop.

Trincomalee in Ceylon surrendered by the Dutch to the British, 1782. ¶ Murat deserts Napoleon and the French forces, 1814. ¶ Alabama secedes from the Union (readmitted 13 July 1868), 1861. ¶ Charing Cross Station in London is formally opened, 1864. ¶ Major Esterházy is acquitted of forging documents for the trial of Alfred Dreyfus (Zola's letter, *J'accuse*, 13 January), 1898. ¶ Neville Chamberlain and Lord Halifax meet Benito Mussolini in Rome, 1939. ¶ Owerri in Biafra is taken by federal Nigerian troops; the Biafran leader General Ojukwu leaves the country, 1970.

BORN: Il Parmigianino (Francesco Mazzola), painter, Parma, Italy, 1503. Alexander Hamilton, statesman and lawyer, Nevis, West Indies, 1755. Ezra Cornell, founder of Cornell University, New York, 1807. Sir John A. Macdonald, first Prime Minister of Canada, Glasgow, Scotland, 1815. William James, psychologist and philosopher, *Principles of Psychology*, *The Varieties of Religious Experience*, New York City, 1842. Lord Curzon, statesman, Viceroy of India, Derbyshire, 1859. Harry Gordon Selfridge, American founder of the Oxford Street (London) department store, Ripon, Wisconsin, 1864. Alan Paton, South African novelist and humanitarian, *Cry, The Beloved Country*, Pietermaritzburg, Natal, 1903.

DIED: Yemelyan Pugachev, Cossack, leader of the revolt against Catherine II of Russia, Zimoveyskaya, Russia, 1726. Sir Hans Sloane, physician and naturalist, his museum and library formed the basis of the British Museum, London, 1753. Louis François Roubiliac, French-born sculptor, London, 1762. Domenico Cimarosa, composer, *The Secret Marriage*, 1801. Theodor Schwann, physiologist, Cologne, Germany, 1882. Georges Eugene Haussmann, architect and civil servant, responsible for the re-planning of Paris; in great poverty, Paris, 1891. Thomas Hardy, poet and novelist, *Tess of the D'Urbervilles*, *The Mayor of Casterbridge*, Dorset, 1928. Alberto Giacometti, sculptor, 1966. Shri Lal Bahadur Shastri, statesman, Indian Prime Minister, 1966. Padraic Colum, poet, a founder of the Irish National Theatre, 1972.

JANUARY 12

Zanzibar Revolutionary Day, Tanzania (1964). Feasts of SS: Arcadius, martyr; Tigrius and Eutropius, martyrs; Caesaria, virgin; Victorian, abbot; Benedict, or Benet, abbot.

The Gregorian calendar introduced by Swiss Protestants, 1701. ¶ Leda (Asteroid 38) discovered by Chacornac, 1856. ¶ The Aeronautical Society of Great Britain is formed in London, 1866. ¶ Kwang-su is made Emperor of China, 1875. ¶ Proposals for women's enfranchisement are defeated in the US House of Representatives, 1915. ¶ Parliament in New Zealand first opened by a reigning monarch, Queen Elizabeth II, 1954. ¶ The *Boeing 747* jumbo-jet touches down at Heathrow Airport after its first trans-Atlantic proving flight from New York, 1970. ¶ Two bombs explode at the home of Robert Carr, Secretary of State for Employment and Productivity, at Hadley, near Barnet, on the outskirts of London ('Angry Brigade' responsible), 1971.

BORN: Jean Baptiste van Helmont, chemist and natural scientist, coined the word *gas*, Brussels, 1580. Lazzaro Spallanzani, physiologist and chemist, disproved the theory of 'spontaneous generation', Modena, Italy, 1729. Johann Heinrich Pestalozzi, educator and teacher, Zurich, 1746. Erik Gustaf Geijer, poet and historian, *Swedish Ballads*, Sweden, 1783. John Singer Sargent, portrait painter, Florence, 1856. Jack London, novelist, *Call of the Wild*, *The Iron Heel*, San Francisco, 1876. Ferenc Molnár, Hungarian dramatist, *The Guardsman*, Budapest, 1878, Curbastro Gregorio Ricci, mathematician, Italy, 1883. Hermann Goering, Nazi leader, creator of the Luftwaffe, Germany, 1893. Paul Müller, chemist, formulated dichlorodiphenyltichloroethane (DDT), Switzerland, 1899. Igor Vasilevich Kurchatov, Soviet nuclear physicist, Russia, 1903.

DIED: Maximillian I, King of Germany, Holy Roman Emperor, 1519. Pierre de Fermat, mathematician, 1665. Georg Forster, explorer, scientist and writer, 1794. Sir Isaac Pitman, printer and publisher, devised one of the most successful shorthand systems, Somerset, 1897. Dame Agatha Christie, popular detective novelist, 1976.

JANUARY 13

Redemption Day, Ghana (commemorating the military government seizing power in 1972). Liberation Day, Togo.
Feasts of SS: Agrecius, bishop; Berno, abbot.

Cremation Societies founded in London and Vienna, 1874. ¶ Lumen (Asteroid 141) discovered by Paul Henry, 1875. ¶ The Independent Labour Party is formed in Britain under the auspices of Keir Hardie, 1893. ¶ Zola writes *J'accuse*, an open letter to the French President after the acquittal of Major Esterházy, 1898. ¶ Admission of Argentina to the League of Nations granted, 1920. ¶ The Inter-Governmental Maritime Consultative Organization (IMCO) established as an agency of the United Nations, 1959. ¶ Great cut-backs in the US space programme are announced, 1970. ¶ The Court of Appeal in London rules that the mere possession of leaves from a cannabis plant is not an offence under English law, 1977.

BORN: Jan van Goyen, Dutch landscape painter, Netherlands, 1596. Charles Pérrault, writer and critic, collector and publisher of fairy tales, *Les Contes de Ma Mère L'Oye*, Paris, 1628. Louis de Rochemont, film producer and director, *The House on 92nd Street*, Boston, Massachusetts, 1899. Albert Lamorisse, film director, *The Red Balloon*, Paris, 1922. Sir Brian Barratt Boyes, New Zealand heart surgeon, 1924.

DIED: Edmund Spenser, poet, *The Shepheards Calendar, The Faerie Queene*, London, 1599. George Fox, founder of the Society of Friends, 1691. Stephen Collins Foster, popular song writer, *Swanee River*, 1864. Jean Baptiste Marchand, soldier and explorer, Paris, 1934. James Joyce, novelist, *Ulysses, Finnegan's Wake*, 1941. Hubert Horatio Humphrey, US senator and Vice-President (under Lyndon B. Johnson); of cancer, 1978.

JANUARY 14

*The Festival of the Ass, a popular theatrical representation of the Biblical
'Flight into Egypt' performed in the Middle Ages. Feasts of SS: Hilary
of Poitiers, bishop and doctor; Felix of Nola; Macrina the Elder, widow;
Barbasymas and his Companions, martyrs; The Martyrs of Mount Sinai;
Datius, bishop; Kentigern, or Mungo, bishop; Sava, archbishop.*

Attempted assassination of Napoleon III by Orsini, 1858. ¶ The *Boston Weekly
Journal* is printed on paper derived from wood-pulp, the first recorded instance
in the US of a newspaper using the material, 1863. ¶ War declared on Spain by
Peru, 1866. ¶ First demonstration of Alexander Graham Bell's telephone to
Queen Victoria, by W. H. Preece at Osborne House on the Isle of Wight, 1878.
¶ Winston Churchill becomes Secretary of State for Air, 1919. ¶ The *Enterprise*,
a US nuclear-powered aircraft carrier, suffers several explosions off the coast of
Hawaii, over 10 men are killed and many injured, 1969.

BORN: Waldemar the Great, King of Denmark, Denmark, 1131. Benedict
Arnold, soldier and spy, Connecticut, 1741. Matthew Fontaine Maury, hydrographer, *The Physical Geography of the Sea*, Virginia, 1806. Henri Fantin-Latour,
artist, lithographer, Grenoble, France, 1836. Pierre Loti, novelist, *Iceland
Fisherman, Disenchanted*, Rochefort, France, 1850. Albert Schweitzer, philosopher,
musician and missionary, *The Quest of the Historical Jesus, On the Edge of the
Primeval Forest*, Alsace, 1875. Hal Roach, film producer and director, with Mack
Sennett and Laurel and Hardy, Elmira, New York, 1892. John Dos Passos,
novelist, *USA* trilogy, Chicago, 1896. Cecil Beaton, photographer and writer,
London, 1904. Joseph Losey, film director, *The Servant*, La Crosse, Wisconsin,
1909. Yukio Mishima, novelist, *Confessions of a Mask*, Tokyo, 1925.

DIED: Odoric of Pordenone, Franciscan and traveller, visited China, India and
Ceylon; Udine, Italy, 1331. Edmond Halley, mathematician and astronomer, a
comet whose return he predicted bears his name, Greenwich, London, 1742.
Jean Ingres, artist, Paris, 1867. Lewis Carroll, writer, *The Hunting of the Snark,
Alice in Wonderland*, 1898. Humphrey Bogart, film actor, *The Maltese Falcon,
Casablanca*, 1957. Peter Finch, actor, *Network*, 1977.

JANUARY 15

Martin Luther King's Birthday, observed in some states only of USA.
Feasts of SS: Paul the Hermit; Macarius the Elder; Isidore of Alexandria;
John Calybites; Ita, virgin; Maurus, abbot; Bonitus, or Bonet, bishop; Ceolwulf.

After the murder of Servias Sulpicius Galba the Praetorian Guard hail M. Salvius Otho as Emperor, 69. ¶ The Confederate cruiser *Florida* leaves Mobile for the beginning of its raiding operations on Union shipping, 1863. ¶ Severe frost in London, over 40 people perish when the ice on the lake in Regent's Park collapses, 1867. ¶ The railway tunnel between Dover and Folkestone collapses owing to great rains, 1877. ¶ *Savoy Shout* and *Call of the Freaks* recorded by Luis Russell and his Burning Eight (with Louis Metcalf, Charlie Holmes, etc.), New York, 1929. ¶ American troops force the Japanese off Guadalcanal, 1943. ¶ A violent earthquake in the west of Sicily, over 300 people lose their lives, 1968. ¶ General Gowon of Nigeria accepts unconditional surrender from Biafran commanders and officers, 1970. ¶ President Sadat of Egypt and President Podgorny of the USSR officially open the Aswan High Dam, 1971. ¶ President Richard M. Nixon calls a halt to American offensives in Vietnam, 1973.

BORN: Louis de Rouvroy, Duc de Saint-Simon, nobleman (at the Court of Louis XIV) and memoirist, Paris, 1675. Franz Grillparzer, dramatist, *The Ancestress*, Vienna, 1791. Pierre Proudhon, socialist and anarchist, *What is Property?*, Besançon, France, 1809. Mihail Eminescu, poet, 'The Evening Star', Rumania, 1850. Lewis Terman, psychologist, pioneered the devising of intelligence tests, Johnson County, Indiana, 1877. Ion Antonescu, Rumanian dictator, 1882. Mazo De La Roche, popular novelist, *Whiteoaks*, Ontario, 1885. Edward Teller, US physicist, developed the hydrogen bomb, Budapest, Hungary, 1908. Gene Krupa, drummer and bandleader, Chicago, Illinois, 1909. Michel Debré, statesman, Paris, 1912. Gamal Abdul Nasser, politician, President of Egypt, Alexandria, 1918. Martin Luther King, civil rights leader, Nobel Prize for Peace, Georgia, 1929.

DIED: Fra Paolo Sarpi, philosopher and scholar, excommunicated by Pope Paul V, 1623. Fanny Kemble, actress and writer, London, 1893. Matthew Brady, photographer, chiefly remembered for the pictures taken during the American Civil War; destitute, New York, 1896. Rosa Luxembourg, socialist, a founder of the Spartacus League; murdered, Berlin, 1919.

JANUARY 16

Feasts of SS: Marcellus I, pope and martyr; Priscilla, matron;
Honoratus of Arles, bishop; Fursey, abbot; Henry of Cocket; Berard and
his Companions, martyrs.

The Spanish are defeated at Cape St Vincent by Admiral Rodney, 1780.
¶ Corunna and the death of Sir John Moore, 1809. ¶ Brazil becomes an Empire
under the Prince Regent of Portugal, 1816. ¶ Final ratification of Prohibition
Amendment to US Constitution, 1919. ¶ The Council of the League of Nations
meets for the first time in Paris, 1920. ¶ 18th Amendment (Article XVIII) to the
Constitution of the US becomes effective, Prohibition instituted (repealed by the
21st Amendment on 5 December 1933), 1920. ¶ Senate in the US votes against
America joining the League of Nations, 1920. ¶ Dismissal of Trotsky as Chairman of Russian Revolution Military Council, 1925. ¶ *It don't mean a thing*
recorded by Duke Ellington and his Orchestra, 1932.

BORN: Franz Brentano, German philosopher, 1838. Sir Johnston Forbes-
Robertson, theatrical actor-manager, London, 1853. André Michelin, industrialist, built the first factories for the mass-production of rubber motor tyres, Paris,
1853. Gordon Craig, stage designer and director, Stevenage, Hertfordshire,
1872. Robert Service, Canadian poet, *Trail of '98*, Preston, Lancashire, England,
1874. Karl Freund, cinematographer, *Metropolis*, *Camille*, Bohemia, 1890.
Fulgencio Batista y Zaldivar, Cuban dictator, was deposed by Fidel Castro in
1959, Cuba, 1901. Ethel Merman, singer, Astoria, New York, 1909. Eduardo
Frei, Chilean politician, Chile, 1911.

DIED: Edward Gibbon, writer, historian, *Decline and Fall of the Roman Empire*,
1794. Léo Delibes, ballet composer, *Coppelia*, 1891. Arnold Böcklin, painter,
The Isle of the Dead, Sweden, 1901. Marshall Field, founder of the modern
department store, 1906. Arturo Toscanini, musician and conductor, New York,
1957. Robert Van de Graaff, physicist, inventor of the Van de Graaff nuclear
accelerator, Boston, Massachusetts, 1967.

JANUARY 17

Feasts of SS: Antony the Abbot; Speusippus, Eleusippus and Meleusippus, martyrs; Genulf, or Genou, bishop; Julian Sabas; Sabinus of Piacenza, bishop; Sulpicius II, or Sulpice, bishop; Richimir, abbot.

Johann Gutenberg, the German printer, is appointed the servant and courier of Archbishop Adolf of Mainz in recognition for his services to printing and to the city of Mainz, 1465. ¶ The Scottish rebels defeat Hawley at Falkirk, 1746. ¶ The first ship crosses the Antarctic Circle, Captain James Cook's *Resolution*, 1773. ¶ The Duke of Wellington is appointed Commander-in-Chief of the British Army, 1827. ¶ Captain Jack and the Modoc Indians defeat US troops who are sent to expel them from their tribal lands in Oregon, 1873. ¶ Conviction of Grigori Zinoviev and others after treason trials in the USSR, 1935. ¶ Gary Gilmore, a convicted murderer, is shot by a firing squad in Nevada, as he had requested, 1977.

BORN: Leonnard Fuchs, physician and botanist, Germany, 1501. Thomas Fairfax, 3rd Baron Fairfax of Cameron, commander of the Parliamentarian army in the English Civil War, Yorkshire, 1612. Benjamin Franklin, statesman and scientist, Boston, 1706. Stanislaw II, King of Poland, Poland, 1732. Sir James Hall, founder of experimental geology, East Lothian, Scotland, 1761. August Weismann, biologist and geneticist, Frankfurt, Germany, 1834. Anton Chekhov, dramatist and writer, *The Seagull*, *The Three Sisters*, 1860. David Lloyd George, statesman and British Prime Minister, Manchester, 1863. Mack Sennett, film comedian and producer, Richmond, Canada, 1880. Ronald Firbank, novelist, *Vainglory*, *Valmouth*, London, 1886.

DIED: Murad III, Sultan of Turkey, Constantinople (Istanbul), 1595. George Bancroft, diplomat, historian, *History of the United States*, 1891. Rutherford B. Hayes, US President, Fremont, Ohio, 1893. Charles Marie Leconte de Lisle, Parnassian poet, *Poèmes barbares*, Paris, 1894. Frederic William Henry Myers, poet, scholar and psychical researcher, *The Renewal of Youth and Other Poems*, *Phantasms of the Living* (with Edmund Gurney and Frank Podmore), *Human Personality and its Survival of Bodily Death*, Rome, 1901. Sir Francis Galton, explorer and geneticist, *Hereditary Genius*, 1911. Terence Hanbury White, novelist, *The Sword in the Stone*, 1964.

JANUARY 18

Old Twelfth Day in England (prior to the introduction of the Gregorian calendar in 1752). Feast of St Peter's Chair at Rome, commemorating the first Pope. Feasts of SS: Prisca, virgin and martyr; Volusian, bishop; Deicolus, or Desle, abbot.

The Houses of Lancaster and York are united with the marriage of Henry VII to Elizabeth, eldest daughter of Edward IV, 1485. ¶ William of Prussia is proclaimed the first German Emperor, 1871. ¶ General Gordon leaves London for Khartoum, 1884. ¶ Oil first discovered in Taranaki, New Zealand, 1886. ¶ Lieutenant Eugene Ely of the US Navy becomes the first man to take off from land in an aeroplane and touch down on a ship, the cruiser *Pennsylvania* in San Francisco Bay, 1911. ¶ Captain Robert F. Scott and his expedition arrive at the South Pole, 1912. ¶ The Versailles Peace Conference begins with Georges Clémenceau as chairman, 1919.

BORN: Charles Louis de Secondat, Baron de Montesquieu, lawyer and philosopher, *Lettres persanes, Considérations sur la grandeur et la décadence des Romains*, near Bordeaux, France, 1689. Joseph Farwell Glidden, farmer, devised a machine for making barbed wire, New Hampshire, 1813. Sir Edward Frankland, chemist, proposed the theory of valence, Lancashire, 1825. Alexis Emmanuel Chabrier, composer, France, 1841. Rubén Darío, Nicaraguan poet, *Songs of Life and Hope*, 1867. Alan Alexander Milne, children's writer, *Winnie-the-Pooh, The House at Pooh Corner*, London, 1882. Antoine Pevsner, Constructivist sculptor, Russia, 1886. Cary Grant, actor, Bristol, England, 1904.

DIED: Marquis de Louvois, French statesman and Minister of War, Paris, 1639. Jan van Riebeck, naval surgeon, founder of Cape Town; Batavia, Java (now Djakarta, Indonesia), 1677. John Tyler, US President, Richmond, Virginia 1862. Rudyard Kipling, novelist and poet, *The Jungle Book*, 1936. Hugh Gaitskell, politician, leader of the British Labour Party, 1963. Malcolm H. Ellis, Australian historian and biographer, 1964.

JANUARY 19

The Epiphany of Jesus Christ, Ethiopia. Robert E. Lee's Birthday, celebrated in some southern states only of USA. Confederate Heroes Day, Texas, USA. Lee–Jackson Day, Virginia, USA. Feasts of SS: Marius, Martha, Audifax and Abachum, martyrs; Germanicus, martyr; Nathalan, bishop; Albert of Cashel, bishop; Fillan, or Foelan, abbot; Canute of Denmark, martyr; Wulfstan, bishop; Henry of Uppsala, bishop and martyr.

John Wilkes is expelled from the House of Commons for seditious libel, 1764. ¶ The first balloon ascent in Ireland, at Ranelagh Gardens in Dublin, 1785. ¶ Ciudad Rodrigo taken by the Duke of Wellington, 1812. ¶ Georgia secedes from the Union (readmitted 21 July 1868, but the representatives are unseated, second readmission 15 July 1870), 1861. ¶ President Roosevelt in Washington sends greetings to King Edward in London by 'wireless telegraphy' (probably the first 'greetings telegram'), 1903. ¶ Several ports on the East Coast of Britain are bombed by a German airship, 1915. ¶ *Echoes of Harlem* recorded by Cootie Williams and his Rug Cutters in New York City, 1938. ¶ Kassala in the Sudan is taken by British troops, 1941. ¶ Burma is invaded by the Japanese, 1942.

BORN: James Watt, engineer, inventor and industrialist, perfected the steam engine, Greenock, Renfrewshire, Scotland, 1736. Johann Bode, astronomer, Germany, 1747. General Robert E. Lee, Confederate Commander-in-Chief during the American Civil War, Stratford House, Virginia, 1807. Edgar Allan Poe, short-story writer, poet and critic, *Murders in the Rue Morgue, The Raven*, Boston, Massachusetts, 1809. Sir Henry Bessemer, metallurgist, a pioneer of the mass production of cheap steel, Hertfordshire, 1813. Paul Cézanne, Impressionist painter, France, 1839.

DIED: Henry Howard, Earl of Surrey, poet and courtier, translated Virgil's *Aeneid*, London, 1547. William Congreve, Restoration dramatist, 1729. Isaac D'Israeli, writer, father of Benjamin D'Israeli, *Curiosities of Literature*, Buckinghamshire, 1848. Joseph Hayden, writer, *Dictionary of Dates and Universal Information*, London, 1856. Pierre Proudhon, socialist and anarchist, *What is Property?*, Paris, 1865.

JANUARY 20

*St Agnes Eve, popularly the day upon which a woman could divine her
future husband; subject of a poem by John Keats. Rio de Janiero Foundation Day,
Brazil. National Heroes Day, Cape Verde Islands. National Heroes Day,
Guinea-Bissau. Army Day, Republic of Mali. Presidential Inauguration Day,
USA (every four years). Feasts of SS: Fabian, pope and martyr;
Sebastian, martyr; Euthymius the Great, abbot; Fechin, abbot.*

First assembly of the Commons as an agreed representational body (according
to Sir William Dugdale), 1265. ¶ The first Secretary of State for the Colonies is
appointed in Britain, 1768. ¶ The London Docks are opened, 1805. ¶ Chile
victorious over Peru and Bolivia at the battle of Yungay, 1839. ¶ Adrianople is
taken by the Russians, 1878. ¶ British–Chinese Treaty of Peking, 1925. ¶ Edward
VIII ascends the throne in Britain upon the death of George V, 1936. ¶ Assassination of Mahatma Gandi in India, 1948. ¶ Inauguration of Dwight D. Eisenhower
as US President, 1953. ¶ The South Pole is reached by the British contingent of
the Commonwealth Transantarctic Expedition under the leadership of Vivian
Fuchs, 1958. ¶ Inauguration of John F. Kennedy as US President, 1961.
¶ Inauguration of L. B. Johnson as 36th President of US, 1965. ¶ Inauguration of
Richard M. Nixon as President of the US, 1969. ¶ Four members of the RAF's
Red Arrow aerial display team are killed in a mid-air collision in Gloucestershire,
1971. ¶ British and French authorities abandon the Channel Tunnel proposal,
1975. ¶ Press censorship is brought to an end in India and many political
prisoners are released, 1977. ¶ Inauguration of Jimmy Carter as President of
US, 1977.

BORN: Theobald Wolfe Tone, Irish Nationalist, fought against British rule in
Ireland and enlisted French support, Dublin, 1763. André-Marie Ampère,
physicist, Lyon, 1775. Johannes Jensen, poet and novelist, *The Long Journey*,
Denmark, 1873. Federico Fellini, film director, *La Dolce Vita*, Italy, 1920.
Edwin 'Buzz' Aldrin, US astronaut, New Jersey, 1930.

DIED: David Garrick, actor and theatre manager, 1779. Sir John Soane,
architect, London, 1837, John Ruskin, art critic, teacher and reformer, *The
Stones of Venice, Modern Painters*, near Coniston, Lancashire, 1900. Dmitri
Mendeleyev, chemist, formulated the periodic table of chemical elements,
St Petersburg, Russia, 1907. Charles Doughty, writer, *Travels in Arabia Deserta*,
1926. King George V of England (reigned 1910–36), 1936. Robinson Jeffers, poet,
Tamar and Other Poems, 1962. Edmund Blunden, poet and literary critic,
Undertones of War, 1974.

JANUARY 21

Altagracia Day, Dominican Republic. Feasts of SS: Agnes, virgin and martyr;
Fructuosus of Tarragona, bishop and martyr; Patroclus, martyr;
Epiphanius of Pavia, bishop; Meinrad, martyr.

Louis XVI is executed in Paris, 1792. ¶ First publication of the *Daily News* in London, 1846. ¶ General Zuloaga assumes control of the government in Mexico after a successful *coup d'état* (Comonfort deposed), 1858. ¶ The *Daily Worker* is suppressed in London, 1941. ¶ *One O'Clock Jump* is recorded by Count Basie and his Orchestra, 1942. ¶ Disarmament conference in Geneva resumed by 17 nations, 1964. ¶ The inaugural flight of British Airways' *Concorde* to Bahrain, 1976.

BORN: John Charles Frémont, explorer, US senator, Savannah, Georgia, 1813. Thomas Jonathan 'Stonewall' Jackson, Confederate general in the American Civil War, Clarksburg, West Virginia, 1824. Joseph Achille Le Bel, chemist, France, 1847. Field-Marshall Sir Thomas Blamey, Australian soldier, 1884.

DIED: Louis XVI of France, Paris, 1793. Alexander Ivanovich Herzen, journalist and political theorist, *From the Other Shore*, Paris, 1870. Franz Grillparzer, dramatist, *The Ancestress*, Vienna, 1872. John Couch Adams, astronomer, co-discoverer of the planet Neptune, 1892. Vladimir Ilyich Lenin, leader of the Bolshevik Revolution, Soviet politician and theorist, 1924. Lytton Strachey, writer, a member of the Bloomsbury Group, *Eminent Victorians, Elizabeth and Essex*, near Hungerford, Berkshire, 1932. George Moore, novelist, dramatist and critic, *Confessions of a Young Man, The Brook Kerith, The Bending of the Bough*, London, 1933. George Orwell (Eric Blair), novelist, critic and essayist, *Coming up for Air, 1984, Animal Farm*, 1950. Cecil B. de Mille, Hollywood film producer, California, 1959.

JANUARY 22

*Feasts of SS: Vincent of Saragossa, martyr; Blesilla, widow;
Anastasius the Persian, martyr; Dominic of Sora, abbot;
Berhtwald of Ramsbury, bishop.*

Johann Gutenberg and his one-time partner, Andres Heilman, are amongst the goldsmiths mentioned in a roll as living in Strasbourg and eligible for military service, 1444. ¶ Assembly of a Convention Parliament (subsequently offers the crown to William and Mary on 13 February), 1689. ¶ The Elector of Bavaria becomes the Emperor Charles VII, 1742. ¶ The Falkland Isles ceded to Britain by Spain, 1771. ¶ Nemausa (Asteroid 52) discovered by Laurent, 1858. ¶ Massacre of British troops at Isandhlwana by Zulus, 1879. ¶ Edward VII's accession upon the death of Queen Victoria, 1901. ¶ Successful experiments by Marconi transmitting from Poldhu Station at the Lizard (Cornwall) to St Catherine's on the Isle of Wight, 1902. ¶ Insurgent workers are fired upon in St Petersburg resulting in 'Bloody Sunday', 1905. ¶ Resignation of the British Prime Minister Stanley Baldwin, 1924. ¶ Second USSR Five-Year Plan begins, 1932. ¶ Guyana is proclaimed a republic (but stays within the British Commonwealth), 1970.

BORN: Ivan III (Ivan the Great), Grand Duke of Muscovy, Moscow, 1440. Francis Bacon, philosopher and statesman, London, 1561. Pierre Gassendi, scientist and philosopher, France, 1592. Gotthold Lessing, dramatist, *Minna von Barnhem*, Germany, 1729. Lord George Gordon Byron, poet, *Don Juan*, London, 1788. Paul Vidal de la Blache, geographer, Pezenas, France, 1845. August Strindberg, dramatist, novelist and poet, *Miss Julie, The Red Room*, Stockholm, 1849. David Wark Griffith, film director and producer, *The Birth of a Nation*, Kentucky, 1875. Hjalmar Schacht, Hitler's Minister of Economics, imprisoned after Stauffenberg's abortive assassination attempt, Tinglev, Sleswick (now Denmark), 1877. Lev Davidovitch Landau, physicist, Russia, 1908. U Thant, Secretary-General of the United Nations, Burma, 1909.

DIED: William Paterson, financier, involved with the establishment of the Bank of England, London, 1719. Horace Benedict de Saussure, physicist and natural historian, Geneva, 1799. Sir Joseph Whitworth, industrialist and engineer, Monte-Carlo, 1887. Carlo Pellegrini, the cartoonist 'Ape', London, 1889. David Edward Hughes, inventor of the teleprinter and the microphone, 1900. Victoria I, Queen of the United Kingdom of Great Britain and Ireland and Empress of India, Osborne House, Isle of Wight, 1901. Lord James Bryce, historian and diplomat, *The Holy Roman Empire*, 1922. Walter Sickert, artist, Bath, England, 1942. Lyndon B. Johnson, US President, 1973.

JANUARY 23

Feasts of SS: Raymund of Peñafort; Asclas, martyr; Emerentiana, virgin and martyr; Clement and Agathangelus, martyrs; John, the Almsgiver, bishop; Ildephonsus, archbishop; Bernard of Vienne, archbishop; Lufthildis, virgin; Maimbod, martyr.

Second partition of Poland agreed by Russia and Prussia, 1793. ¶ First Labour Government formed in Britain, under Ramsay McDonald, 1924. ¶ Beginning of the trial of Karl Radek and others in the Moscow purges, 1937. ¶ Tripoli entered by the British Eighth Army, 1943. ¶ The US Navy bathyscape *Trieste* descends to a depth of over 35,000 feet in the Challenger Deep (Pacific Ocean), 1960. ¶ The USS *Pueblo* is seized by the North Koreans, 1968. ¶ President Richard M. Nixon announces that fighting in Vietnam will stop at midnight on 27 January, 1973.

BORN: Philipp Jakob Spener, Protestant theologian and founder of Pietism, Alsace, 1635. Stendhal (Marie Henri Beyle), novelist, *The Red and the Black, The Charterhouse of Parma*, Grenoble, France, 1783. Edouard Manet, Impressionist painter, *Dejeuner sur l'Herbe*, Paris, 1832. Subhas Chandra Bose, Indian nationalist, 1897. Sergei Eisenstein, Soviet film director, *Ivan the Terrible*, 1898.

DIED: William Baffin, navigator and explorer, 1622. Giambattista Vico, philosopher and jurist, *The New Science*, Naples, 1744. William Caslon, English typefounder, 1766. William Pitt ('the Younger'), Prime Minister, London, 1806. John Field, Irish composer and pianist, 1837. Thomas Love Peacock, novelist and poet, *Headlong Hall, Nightmare Abbey, Crotchet Castle*, near London, 1866. Charles Kingsley, novelist, *The Water Babies*, London, 1875. Gustave Doré, artist and illustrator, 1883. Eugène Labiche, French dramatist, 1888. Anna Pavlova, ballerina, The Hague, Holland, 1931. Edvard Munch, painter and lithographer, Oslo, Norway, 1944. Pierre Bonnard, French painter, 1947. Sir Alexander Korda, film producer, *The Private Life of Henry VIII, Four Feathers*, London, 1956. Paul Robeson, singer, 1976.

JANUARY 24

Feasts of SS: Timothy, bishop and martyr; Babylas, bishop and martyr; Felician, bishop and martyr; Macedonius.

Supreme Court in US rules that income tax is unconstitutional, 1916. ¶ Trade unions not aligned to the Fascist cause are abolished in Italy, 1924. ¶ An Air India Boeing 707 crashes into Mont Blanc and all 117 people on board are killed, 1966. ¶ Resignation of Brian Faulkner, Deputy Prime Minister of Northern Ireland, 1969. ¶ Dr Donald Coggan enthroned as the Archbishop of Canterbury at the Cathedral, 1975. ¶ A bomb outrage in New York City by extremist Puerto Ricans kills three people, 1975. ¶ The *Olympic Bravery*, a tanker, runs aground off the coast of France and is wrecked; at over 270,000 tons deadweight it is the largest shipwreck hitherto recorded (she breaks in two on 13 March), 1976. ¶ An orbiting Russian satellite crashes near Yellow Knife, North West Territory, Canada, 1978.

BORN: Hadrian (Publius Aelius Hadrianus), Roman emperor, Italica, Spain, 76. William Congreve, Restoration dramatist, Yorkshire, 1670. Farinelli (Carlo Broschi), castrati singer, Italy, 1705. Frederick (II) the Great, King of Prussia, Berlin, 1712. Pierre de Beaumarchais, dramatist, *The Barber of Seville* (later made into an opera by Rossini), Paris, 1732. Charles James Fox, liberal statesman, London, 1749. Ernst Theodor Amadeus Hoffmann, author and composer, *The Devil's Elixirs*, Königsberg, Germany, 1776. Sir Edwin Chadwick, social reformer, *Report on the General Sanitary Conditions of the Labouring Classes in Britain*, Lancashire, 1800. Henry King, US film director, *Stella Dallas, Tol'able David*, Denmark, 1892. Robert Motherwell, writer and abstract painter, *The Dada Painters and Poets*, Aberdeen, Washington, 1915.

DIED: Jan Kollár, Slavonic poet and scholar, 1852. Lord Randolph Churchill, Conservative statesman, 1895. Amedeo Modigliani, painter and sculptor, Paris, 1920, Paul Walden, chemist, Germany, 1957. Sir Winston Churchill, statesman and historian, 1965.

JANUARY 25

Dies Mala or 'Egyptian Day', considered unlucky in the Middle Ages.
Burns Day or Burns Night in Scotland, commemorating the birth of
Robert Burns, the 'national' poet, in 1759. Feast of the Conversion of St Paul.
Feasts of SS: Artemas, martyr; Juventinus and Maximinus, martyrs;
Publius, abbot; Apollo, abbot; Praejectus, or Prix, bishop and martyr;
Poppo, abbot.

Accession of Edward III of England (reigned until 21 June 1377), 1327. ¶ The Confession of Augsburg is published, 1530. ¶ Joseph E. Hooker replaces Ambrose E. Burnside as Commander of the Army of the Potomac, 1863. ¶ First meeting of the London Chamber of Commerce, 1882. ¶ *Bughouse* recorded by Red Norvo in New York, 1935. ¶ In the US Alger Hiss is found guilty of perjury in not declaring his membership of the Communist Party, 1950. ¶ Russian proclaims end of belligerency with Germany, 1955. ¶ Soviet authorities release close-up pictures of Venus taken by *Venus 7* spacecraft, 1971. ¶ Charles Manson and three of his 'family' are found guilty in Los Angeles of murder on several counts (he is sentenced to death on 29 March), 1971. ¶ President Obote and his government are deposed in Uganda by Major-General Idi Amin, 1971.

BORN: Edmund Campion, scholar and Jesuit, London, 1540. Robert Boyle, chemist and physicist, County Cavan, Ireland, 1627. Joseph Lagrange, mathematician and physicist, Turin, 1736. Robert Burns, poet, Ayrshire, 1759. Somerset Maugham, novelist and dramatist, *Of Human Bondage, Cakes and Ale,* Paris, 1874. Virginia Woolf, novelist and critic, *To the Lighthouse, The Waves,* London, 1882. Wilhelm Furtwängler, conductor and musician, Berlin, 1886. Witold Lutoslawski, composer, Warsaw, 1913.

DIED: Marcus Cocceius Nerva, Roman Emperor, 98. Robert Burton, scholar, *Anatomy of Melancholy,* 1640. Dorothy Wordsworth, writer, sister of William Wordsworth, 1855.

JANUARY 26

Australia Day, Australia. Duarte's Day, Dominican Republic (Juan Pablo Duarte, liberator, 1813–76). Republic Day, India (proclaimed in 1950).
Feasts of SS: Polycarp, bishop and martyr; Paula, widow; Conan, bishop; Alberic, abbot; Eystein, archbishop; Margaret of Hungary, virgin.

Vicente Yañez Pinzon discovers Brazil, 1500. ¶ Governor Arthur Phillip founds Sydney near Port Jackson, with 1030 persons, 1788. ¶ Napoleon Bonaparte is made the President of the Italian Republic, 1802. ¶ The Grand Duke Constantine renounces the right of succession in Russia, 1822. ¶ Michigan made a US state (26th), 1837. ¶ Hong Kong proclaimed a British sovereign territory, 1841. ¶ Louisiana secedes from the Union (readmitted 9 July 1868), 1861. ¶ An announcement is made in London that transportation to Australia will cease in three years' time, 1865. ¶ Virginia readmitted to the Union (seceded 17 April 1861), 1870. ¶ Aemilia (Asteroid 159) discovered by Paul Henry, 1876. ¶ Captain Wells discovers the largest diamond in the world, at the Premier Mines in Pretoria, South Africa (it weighs over $1\frac{1}{4}$lb), 1905. ¶ Mahatma Gandhi is released from prison for discussions with the British government, in India, 1931. ¶ Italian aid helps General Franco and rebel forces take Barcelona, 1939. ¶ Hindi becomes the official language of India, 1965.

BORN: Claude Helvetius, philosopher and encyclopedist, Paris, 1715. Douglas MacArthur, military commander, Supreme Allied Commander in Japan after the Second World War, Little Rock, Arkansas, 1880. Edward Sapir, American linguist and anthropologist, Poland, 1884. Paul Newman, film actor, *Hud*, *The Hustler*, Cleveland, Ohio, 1925. Jules Feiffer, cartoonist and playwright, New York City, 1929.

DIED: Edward Jenner, physician, discovered vaccination, Berkeley, Gloucestershire, 1823. Théodore Géricault, painter, *Raft of the Medusa*, 1824. Gérard de Nerval, poet and writer, *Les Chimères*, Paris, 1855. General Charles George Gordon, soldier, defended Khartoum, 1885. Nicholaus Otto, invented and produced the first four-stroke internal combustion engine, Cologne, 1891. Arthur Cayley, mathematician, 1895. Nikolai Ivanovich Vavilov, geneticist and horticulturist; in a labour camp, Siberia, 1943.

JANUARY 27

Feasts of SS: John Chrysostom, archbishop and doctor;
Julian of Le Mans, bishop; Marius, or May, abbot; Vitalian, pope.

Independence in Greece proclaimed, 1822. ¶ US marines land in Haiti to preserve law and order after President Oreste abdicates during insurgency, 1914. ¶ The world's first public demonstration of television is given by John Logie Baird in London, 1926. ¶ First bombing raid on Germany by US, 1943. ¶ Final relief of Leningrad (besieged by German forces since 1941), 1944. ¶ Three members of the US Apollo space-craft crew are killed by fire in the craft during a simulated launch, 1967. ¶ Great flooding in Southern California, many deaths, several thousands made homeless, 1969. ¶ Ceasefire begins in Vietnam, as announced on 23 January by President Richard M. Nixon, 1973.

BORN: Wolfgang Amadeus Mozart, harpsichordist and composer, *The Marriage of Figaro*, *Don Giovanni*, *The Magic Flute*, Salzburg, Austria, 1756. Samuel Palmer, landscape painter, London, 1805. Eugène-Emmanuel Viollet-le-Duc, architect, Paris, 1814. Lewis Carroll, writer, *The Hunting of the Snark*, *Alice in Wonderland*, Cheshire, 1832. Dmitri Mendeleyev, chemist, formulated the periodic table of chemical elements, Tobolsk, Russia, 1834. William II, King of Prussia, Emperor of Germany, Berlin, 1859. Ilya Grigoryevich Ehrenburg, novelist and poet, Kiev, Russia, 1891. Hyman Rickover, US admiral, chiefly responsible for the development of atomic submarines, Makov, Russia, 1900.

DIED: Bartolommeo Cristofori, craftsman, developed the first pianos, 1731. Philippe Buache, geographer and cartographer, devised contour lines for maps and charts, 1773. Johann Gottlieb Fichte, German philosopher of 'ethical, idealism', 1814. John James Audubon, naturalist and artist, 1851. Janos Bolyail, mathematician, Hungary, 1860. John Gibson, sculptor, member of the Royal Academy, 1866. Giuseppe Verdi, composer, *Rigoletto*, *Il Trovatore*, *La Traviata*, Milan, 1901. Endre Ady, Hungarian poet, 1919. Giovanni Verga, novelist and dramatist, *The Vanquished*, *Mastro Don Gesualdo*, Catania, Sicily, 1922. Emile Cohl, pioneer French film animator, Orly, France, 1938. Baron Carl Gustaf Emil von Mannerheim, military commander and statesman, secured the independence of Finland from Russia, Lausanne, 1951. Mahalia Jackson, US jazz and gospel singer, 1972.

JANUARY 28

Feasts of SS: Peter Nolasco; John of Reomay, abbot;
Paulinus of Aquileia, bishop; Amadeus of Lausanne, bishop;
Peter Thomas, bishop.

Accession of Edward VI of England (reigned until 6 July 1553), 1547. ¶ Execution of Sir John Fenwick (by attainder) for attempted assassination of William III of England, 1696. ¶ First penal colony in Australia founded at Botany Bay by the British, 1788. ¶ Execution in Edinburgh of William Burke ('burking'), 1829. ¶ Sikhs defeated at Aliwal by East India Company forces under the command of Harry Smith, 1846. ¶ Polana (Asteroid 142) discovered by J. Palisa, 1875. ¶ Arrival of the British relief forces at Khartoum, 1885. ¶ Widespread suffragette demonstrations in London, 1913. ¶ The Ruhr is fully under the control of French forces, 1923. ¶ Miguel Primo de Rivera's dictatorship ends in Spain, 1930. ¶ States of emergency are declared in New Jersey, New York, and Ohio after severe blizzards and freezing, several other states are declared disaster areas, 1977.

BORN: Henry VII, King of England, Pembroke Castle, Wales, 1457. Giovanni Borelli, mathematician and astronomer, Naples, 1608. John Baskerville, printer and type designer, Worcester, 1706. General Charles George Gordon, soldier, defended Khartoum, 1833. Sir Henry Stanley, explorer and journalist, Denbigh, Wales, 1841. José Marti, revolutionary and poet, leader of the revolt against Spanish rule in Cuba; Havana, 1853. William Seward Burroughs, inventor of the first popular adding machine, New York, 1855. Colette, novelist, *Gigi, La Chatte,* France, 1873. Vsevolod Meyerhold, actor and stage director, Periza, Russia, 1874. Auguste Piccard, deep-sea explorer and balloonist, Basel, Switzerland, 1884. Artur Rubinstein, virtuoso pianist, Warsaw, 1889. Ernst Lubitsch, film director, *Ninotchka, That Uncertain Feeling,* Berlin, 1892. Sir Grenfell Price, Australian historian and geographer, 1892. Jackson Pollock, Abstract Expressionist painter, Cody, Wyoming, 1912. Claes Oldenburg, Pop artist, Stockholm, 1929.

DIED: Charlemagne, Holy Roman Emperor, 814. Henry VIII, King of England, 1547. Sir Francis Drake, adventurer and explorer, 1596. Peter the Great, Tsar of Russia, St Petersburg, 1725. William Burke, of Burke and Hare, body-snatchers, executed in Edinburgh, 1829. William Prescott, historian, *The History of the Conquest of Mexico, The History of the Conquest of Peru,* Boston, Massachusetts, 1859. Adalbert Stifter, novelist, *Indian Summer,* Linz, Austria, 1868. Fyodor Dostoyevsky, novelist, *Crime and Punishment,* 1881. Vicente Blasco Ibañez, writer and politician, *The Four Horsemen of the Apocalypse,* 1928.

Feasts of SS: Francis de Sales, bishop and doctor; Sabinian, martyr; Gildas the Wise, abbot; Sulpicius 'Severus', bishop.

The Death Warrant for Charles I of England is issued, 1649. ¶ John Gay's *The Beggar's Opera* is first performed, in London, 1728. ¶ Accession of George IV of England (as Regent from 6 February 1811), 1820. ¶ Greenwich Mean Time adopted by Scotland, 1848. ¶ At the Tuileries Napoleon III marries Eugénie de Montijo, 1853. ¶ The Victoria Cross is instituted by Queen Victoria, 1856. ¶ Kansas made a US state (34th), 1861. ¶ Karl-Friedrich Benz patents the first petrol-driven motor car (*Motor-wagen*), 1886. ¶ First bombing of Paris by Zeppelins, 1916. ¶ First trials of tanks in Britain, at Hatfield, Hertfordshire, 1916. ¶ Britain refused entry into Common Market, 1963.

BORN: Emmanuel Swedenborg, scientist, philosopher and mystic, *Heaven and Hell, Divine Love and Divine Wisdom*, Stockholm, 1688. Daniel Bernoulli, mathematician, studied the motions of fluids, Switzerland, 1700. Thomas Paine, writer, reformer and propagandist, *The Rights of Man, Common Sense*, Thetford, Norfolk, 1737. Ernst Eduard Kummer, mathematician, Poland, 1810. William McKinley, US President, Niles, Ohio, 1843. Frederick Delius, composer, Bradford, Yorkshire, 1862. Romain Rolland, novelist and biographer, Nobel Prize for Literature, *Jean Christophe*, Clamecy, France, 1866. Vicente Blasco Ibañez, writer and politician, *The Four Horsemen of the Apocalypse*, Spain, 1867. Havergal Brian, composer, *Gothic Symphony*, Staffordshire, 1876. W. C. Fields, film comedian, *Never Give a Sucker an Even Break*, Pennsylavnia, 1880. Paddy Chayefsky, dramatist and scriptwriter, *Marty*, New York, 1923. Luigi Nono, composer, Venice, 1924.

DIED: Vicomte Paul François Barras, statesman and member of the Directory, France, 1829. Aleksandr Sergeyevich Pushkin, novelist, dramatist and poet, *Eugene Onegin, Boris Godunov*, St Petersburg, 1837. Edward Lear, artist and poet, *The Book of Nonsense*, San Remo, Italy, 1888. Alfred Sisley, Impressionist painter, France, 1899. Earl Haig, officer and soldier, British Commander-in-Chief during the First World War, Dryburgh, Scotland, 1928. William Butler Yeats, Irish poet and dramatist, *Easter 1916, The Countess Cathleen*, France, 1939. James Bridie, dramatist and physician, *The Anatomist*, 1951. Henry Louis Mencken, journalist, editor, critic and scholar, *The American Language, A Treatise on the Gods*, Baltimore, Maryland, 1956. Fritz Kreisler, Austrian virtuoso violinist, 1962. Robert Frost, American poet, 1963.

JANUARY 30

Franklin D. Roosevelt's Birthday, USA.
Feasts of SS: Martina, virgin and martyr; Barsimaeus, bishop;
Bathildis, widow; Aldegundis, virgin; Adelemus, or Aleaume abbot;
Hyacintha Mariscotti, virgin.

Execution in London of Digby, Winter, Grant, and Bates, Gunpowder Plot conspirators, 1606. ¶ The Commonwealth of England established upon the execution of Charles I, 1649. ¶ Mungo Park sets sail from Portsmouth on his second voyage to Africa, 1805. ¶ First submarine attack without warning by Germany occurs off the French coast near Le Havre, 1915. ¶ The first jazz recordings, made by the Original Dixieland Jazz Band in Camden, New Jersey (some authorities dispute the date, and others would describe the O.D.J.B.'s music as 'dixieland', *not* jazz), 1917. ¶ Hitler becomes Chancellor of Germany and forms a Nazi cabinet with Göring, Frick and others, 1933. ¶ The British Eighth Army under Wavell captures Derna, 1941. ¶ Vietcong attack Saigon and capture the US Embassy, President Thieu's palace is fired upon, 1968. ¶ Pakistan leaves the British Commonwealth, 1972. ¶ Violent rioting in Londonderry, Northern Ireland, during a banned civil rights march, troops shoot dead thirteen people, 1972.

BORN: Walter Savage Landor, poet and writer, *Imaginary Conversations*, Warwick, 1775. Francis Herbert Bradley, philosopher, *Appearance and Reality*, London, 1846. Ion Caragiale, dramatist, Rumania, 1852. Franklin Roosevelt, lawyer, President of the US, Hyde Park, New York, 1882. Roy Eldridge, jazz trumpeter and composer, Pittsburgh, 1911.

DIED: Charles I, King of Great Britain and Ireland; beheaded, Whitehall, London, 1649. Georges de La Tour, French painter, 1652. Charles Bradlaugh, British politician and free-thinker, an early advocate of birth control, 1891. Frank Doubleday, US publisher and editor, 1934. Orville Wright, aviation pioneer, Dayton, Ohio, 1945. Mahatma Gandhi, architect of India's independence; assassinated, 1948. François Poulenc, composer and pianist, Paris, 1963.

JANUARY 31

Feasts of SS: John Bosco; Cyrus and John, martyrs; Marcella, widow;
Aidan, or Maedoc, of Ferns, bishop; Adamnan of Coldingham;
Ulphia, virgin; Eusebius, martyr; Nicetas of Novgorod, bishop;
Francis Xavier Bianchi.

Execution in London of Winter, Rookwood, Keys, and Guy Fawkes, Gunpowder Plot conspirators, 1606. ¶ The Ashantee tribesmen are defeated at Amoaful, near Coomassie in West Africa, by British troops under the command of Sir Garnet Wolseley, 1874. ¶ The Sydney *Bulletin* is published for the first time, 1880. ¶ The USSR expels Leon Trotsky and he goes into exile, 1929. ¶ The US Atomic Energy Commission is instructed to proceed with developing the H-bomb by President Truman, 1950. ¶ Completion of the Trans-Iranian pipeline, 1957. ¶ *Explorer I* launched by the US at Cape Canaveral, 1958. ¶ *Apollo 14* launched from Cape Kennedy on Moon mission, 1971. ¶ Eritrean rebels attack Asmara in the north of Ethiopia, 1975.

BORN: Arnold Geulinex, Flemish philosopher, 1624. André Jacques Garnerin, balloonist, Paris, 1769. Franz Peter Schubert, composer, Vienna, 1797. Zane Grey, writer of cowboy and western stories, Ohio, 1872. Irving Langmuir, physicist, responsible for extending the life of electric lamps by replacing the vacuum with an inert gas, New York, 1881. Anna Pavlova, ballerina, St Petersburg, 1882. Tallulah Bankhead, actress, Huntsville, Alabama, 1903. Norman Mailer, novelist, *The Naked and the Dead, Advertisements for Myself*, New Jersey, 1923. Rudolph Mossbauer, atomic physicist, Munich, 1929. Jean Simmons, actress, London, 1929.

DIED: Guy Fawkes, Catholic co-conspirator in the Gunpowder plot, 1606. Charles Edward Stuart, 'Bonnie Prince Charlie', leader of the Jacobite Rebellion to depose George II of England, Rome, 1788. John Galsworthy, novelist, *The Forsyte Saga*, 1933. Jean Giraudoux, dramatist, *Siegfried*, 1944. Sir C. B. Cochran, theatrical producer and impresario, 1951. Alan Alexander Milne, children's writer, *Winnie-the-Pooh, The House at Pooh Corner*, Hartfield, Sussex, 1956. Samuel Goldwyn, film producer, a founder of Metro-Goldwyn-Mayer, 1974.

FEBRUARY

TWENTY-EIGHT DAYS
BUT IN LEAP YEARS TWENTY-NINE

Like January, the month of February was introduced
into the Roman calendar by Numa Pompilius
(*c.* 715–673BC), a legendary King of Rome. Its
name comes from the Roman festival of
purification and religious expiation observed
during this month, the *Februa* (Latin *februare*,
to purify).

FEBRUARY 1

Federal Territory Holiday, Malaysia. Feasts of SS:
Ignatius of Antioch, bishop and martyr; Pionuis, martyr;
Brigid, or Bride, of Kildare, virgin; Sigebert III of Austrasia;
John 'of the Grating', bishop.

France declares war on Holland and Britain, 1793. ¶ Pogrom against the Jews in Damascus after the disappearance of a Greek priest, 1840. ¶ A violent eruption of Mount Etna in Sicily begins (lasts until June), 1865. ¶ Beginning of General Sherman's march through North and South Carolina, 1865. ¶ Washington Conference agrees treaties restricting poison gas and submarine warfare, 1922. ¶ USSR formally recognized by the British government, 1924. ¶ Vidkun Quisling is made the Norwegian premier, 1942. ¶ Major Vietcong offensive, fierce attack upon Hué, 1968. ¶ Blizzards throughout north-eastern area of the US, over 100 deaths, 1977.

BORN: Sir Edward Coke, jurist and statesman, Norfolk, 1552. Emile Littré, lexicographer and philosopher, *Auguste Comte and Positivist Philosophy*, Paris, 1801. Louis Auguste Blanqui, revolutionary socialist, France, 1805. Feodor Ivanovich Chaliapin, operatic bass, Russia, 1873. Hugo von Hofmannsthal, dramatist and poet, *Everyman, The Tower*, Vienna, 1874. Louis St Laurent, Canadian Prime Minister, Compton, Quebec, 1882. Yevgeny Vakhtangov, early Expressionist theatrical director, Vladikavkaz, Russia, 1883. John Ford, film director, *Stagecoach, The Informer*, Maine, 1895. Clark Gable, film actor, *The Misfits*, Ohio, 1901. Langston Hughes, poet, *Weary Blues*, Missouri, 1902. S. J. Perelman, humorous writer, Brooklyn, New York, 1904. George Pal, film and special-effects director, *The War of the Worlds*, Hungary, 1908.

DIED: René Descartes, philosopher, *Discourse on Method*, 1650. Augustus II, Elector of Saxony and King of Poland, 1733. Mary Wollstonecraft Shelley, novelist, wife of Percy Bysshe Shelley, *Frankenstein, The Last Man*, London, 1851. Matthew Fontaine Maury, hydrographer, *The Physical Geography of the Sea*, Lexington, 1873. George Cruikshank, caricaturist and illustrator, 1878. Prince Aritomo Yamagata, military leader and minister, Prime Minister of Japan, Japan, 1922. Piet Mondrian, abstract painter, co-founder of the De Stijl group, New York City, 1944. Buster Keaton, film comedian, *The Navigator, The General*, 1966.

FEBRUARY 2

*The Feast of the Purification of the Blessed Virgin Mary, when after
the birth of Christ Mary was ritually cleansed in the Temple,
commonly known as Candlemas Day after the penitential procession held with
torches or candles in Rome. The Fortieth Day of Christmas.
Candlemas is a Scottish Quarter Day. Known as Wives' Feast Day in
the north of England. Feasts of SS: Adalbald of Ostrevant, martyr;
The Martyrs of Ebsdorf; Joan de Lestonnac, widow.*

King Stephen defeated at the battle of Lincoln, 1141. ¶ Lancastrians defeated by the Yorkists at Mortimer's Cross, 1461. ¶ First assembly of the parliament of the United Kingdom of Great Britain and Ireland, 1801. ¶ War between Mexico and US ends with the Treaty of Guadaloupe Hidalgo, 1848. ¶ War declared on Turkey by Greece, 1878. ¶ Bread is rationed in Britain, 1917. ¶ Heavy fighting between Israel and Syria, 1970. ¶ Major-General Idi Amin declares himself absolute ruler for 'ever and ever' in Uganda, 1971. ¶ The British Embassy in Dublin is burnt by besieging crowds, 1972.

BORN: James I, King of Aragon, France, 1208. Lodovico Ferrari, mathematician, Italy, 1522. Nell Gwynn, actress, King Charles II's mistress, London, 1650. Charles Maurice de Talleyrand-Périgord, statesman and politician, Périgord, France, 1754. Havelock Ellis, psychologist and writer, *Studies in the Psychology of Sex*, Croydon, near London, 1859. Fritz Kreisler, virtuoso violinist, Vienna, 1875. James Joyce, novelist, *Ulysses, Finnegan's Wake*, Dublin, 1882. James Stephens, novelist and poet, *Insurrection*, Dublin, 1882.

DIED: Baldassarre Castiglione, aristocrat and courtier, 1529. Francis Hayman, painter, 1776. John L. Sullivan, champion heavy-weight boxer, Massachusetts, 1918. Sir Owen Seaman, poet, editor of *Punch* magazine, London, 1936. Bertrand Russell, philosopher, mathematician and reformer, *An Introduction to Mathematical Philosophy, The Analysis of Mind*, Merioneth, Wales, 1970.

FEBRUARY 3

Heroes Day, People's Republic of Mozambique. Feasts of SS:
Blaise, bishop and martyr; Laurence of Spoleto, bishop; Ia, virgin;
Laurence of Canterbury, archbishop; Werburga, virgin;
Anskar, archbishop; Margaret 'of England', virgin.

Bartholomew Diaz lands at Mossal Bay in the Cape – the first white man known to have landed on the southern extremity of Africa, 1488. ¶ Illinois organized as a territory (statehood on 3 December 1818), 1809. ¶ Germany and US sever diplomatic relations, 1917, ¶ The first League of Nations meeting, in Paris with President Woodrow Wilson as 'chairman', 1919. ¶ Severe earthquake in Napier and Hastings, New Zealand, with 256 deaths, 1931. ¶ Signing of the Benelux economic treaty, 1958. ¶ The first rocket-assisted, controlled landing on the Moon by a space vehicle, the Soviet *Luna IX*, 1966. ¶ Assassination of Teferi Bante, the Ethiopian premier, in a military *coup*, 1977.

BORN: Sweyn I, King of Denmark, Lincolnshire, England, 1014. Felix Mendelssohn, Romantic composer, *Midsummer Night's Dream*, Hamburg, 1809. Horace Greeley, journalist and editor, Amherst, New Hampshire, 1811. Lord Robert Cecil, 3rd Marquess of Salisbury, statesman and Prime Minister, Hatfield House, Hertfordshire, 1830. Gertrude Stein, poet, novelist and critic, *The Making of Americans*, Allegheny, Pennsylvania, 1874. Carl Dreyer, film director, *La Passion de Jeanne d'Arc*, Copenhagen, Denmark, 1889. Alvar Aalto, Finnish architect, 1898. Luigi Dallapiccola, Italian composer, Austria, 1904.

DIED: Germain Pilon, sculptor, Paris, 1590. George Crabbe, poet and writer, 1832. Mikhail Glinka, Russian composer, *A Life for the Tsar*, 1857. Sir Henry Maine, jurist and historian, *Ancient Law*, Cannes, France, 1888. Christoph Buys Ballot, meteorologist, Netherlands, 1890. Sir Morell Mackenzie, physician, a founder of laryngology, London, 1892. Edward Pickering, astronomer, Cambridge, Massachusetts, 1919. Oliver Heaviside, physicist, London, 1925. Boris Karloff, actor, played Baron Frankenstein's monster in numerous films, 1969.

Dies Mala or 'Egyptian Day', considered unlucky in the Middle Ages.
Celebration of the Beginning of the Struggle for Liberation, Angola.
National Day, Socialist Republic of Sri Lanka (Independence Day prior to 1978).
Feasts of SS: Andrew Corsini, bishop; Theophilus the Penitent;
Phileas, bishop and martyr; Isidore of Pelusium, abbot; Modan, abbot;
Nicholas Studites, abbot; Rembert, archbishop; Joan of France, matron;
Joseph of Leonessa; John de Britto, martyr.

Alabama, Georgia, Florida, Louisiana, Mississippi and South Carolina decide, at the Montgomery convention, to elect Jefferson Davis President of the Confederate States of America, 1861. ¶ Japan lays siege to Port Arthur on the outbreak of the Russo–Japanese War, 1904. ¶ Hitler takes office as War Minister, von Ribbentrop is appointed Foreign Minister, 1938. ¶ Roosevelt, Churchill and Stalin meet at Yalta, 1945. ¶ First issue in Great Britain of a 'colour supplement', by the *Sunday Times*, 1962. ¶ The Rolls-Royce company goes into voluntary self-liquidation, 1971.

BORN: Pierre Marivaux, novelist and playwright, *The Poor Peasant*, *The Game of Love and Chance*, Paris, 1688. Carl Bellman, song-writer, Stockholm, 1740. Tadeusz Kosciuszko, Polish patriot and fighter, 1746. William Harrison Ainsworth, popular novelist, Manchester, 1805. Fernand Léger, Cubist painter, France, 1881. Edwin Pratt, Canadian poet, *Brébeuf and His Brethren*, *Towards the Last Spike*, Western Bay, Newfoundland, 1883. Ugo Betti, dramatist, *The Joker*, Italy, 1892. Ludwig Erhard, economist and statesman, Germany, 1897. Jacques Prevert, poet, scriptwriter and novelist, Paris, 1900. Charles Lindbergh, aviator, the first man to fly the Atlantic solo, Detroit, 1902. Dietrich Bonhoeffer, Protestant theologian, Prussia, 1906. Ida Lupino, actress and director, London, 1918.

DIED: Lucius Septimius Severus, Roman emperor, Eburacum (York in England), 211. Antonio Pollaiuolo, sculptor, Rome, 1498. Robert Koldewey, German archaeologist, excavated Babylon, 1925. Edward Sapir, American linguist and anthropologist, New Haven, Connecticut, 1939. Sir William Darling, soldier and civic dignitary, Lord Provost of Edinburgh, *A Book of Days*, Edinburgh, 1962.

FEBRUARY 5

CCM Day, Tanzania (commemorating the foundation of the Chama Cha Mapinduzi party in 1976). Feasts of SS: Agatha, virgin and martyr; Avitus of Vienne, bishop; Bertulf, or Bertoul; Indractus and Dominica, martyrs; Vodalus, or Voel; Adelaide of Bellich, virgin; The Martyrs of Japan, I.

Minorca captured by the Spanish from British forces, 1782. ¶ The insanity of George III leads to the Regency Act and the Prince of Wales becomes the Prince Regent, 1811. ¶ Antigone (Asteroid 129) discovered by C. H. F. Peters, 1873. ¶ Formal separation of Church and State is enacted in Russia, 1918. ¶ Glenn Miller records *Tuxedo Junction* with his Orchestra, 1940. ¶ *Jammin' in Four* and *Celestial Express* recorded by the Edmond Hall Celeste Quartet in New York City, 1941. ¶ US troops under the command of General MacArthur enter Manila, 1945. ¶ Conjunction of the Sun, Moon, Mercury, Venus, Mars, Jupiter and Saturn, as viewed from the Pacific during an eclipse, 1962.

BORN: Madame de Sévigné, lady-of-fashion and writer, *Lettres*, Paris, 1629. James Otis, lawyer, prominent in resisting the British government in Massachusetts, New Barnstable, Massachusetts, 1725. Sir Robert Peel, Prime Minster and founder of the Metropolitan Police Force, Bury, Lancashire, 1788. John Boyd Dunlop, inventor of the pneumatic tyre, Ayrshire, Scotland, 1840. Sir Hiram Stevens Maxim, inventor, perfected the machine gun, Maine, 1840. Joris Karl Huysman, novelist, *Là-Bas, The Oblate*, Paris, 1848, Adlai Ewing Stevenson, US Democratic statesman and politician, Ambassador at the UN, Los Angeles, 1900. William Burroughs, American novelist, *Naked Lunch, Dead Fingers Talk*, St Louis, 1914.

DIED: Joost van den Vondel, poet and playwright, *Lucifer*, Amsterdam, 1679. Philipp Jakob Spener, Protestant theologian and founder of Pietism, Berlin, 1705. Thomas Carlyle, historian and essayist, *The French Revolution*, 1881. William Morris Davis, founder of modern geomorphology, 1934. A. B. 'Banjo' Peterson, Australian folk poet and journalist, 1941. George Arliss, stage and film actor, 1946. Henry Major Tomlinson, maritime novelist and essayist, *The Sea and the Jungle, The Turn of the Tide*, London, 1958. Marianne Moore, poet, *Observations, The Pangolin and Other Verse*, New York City, 1972.

FEBRUARY 6

New Zealand Day, New Zealand. Feasts of SS: Titus, bishop;
Dorothy, virgin and martyr; Mel and Melchu, bishops; Vedast, or Vaast, bishop;
Amand, bishop; Guarinus, bishop; Hildegund, widow.

Gaius Julius Caesar's victory at Thapsus, in north Africa, over the Pompeians under Cato, Metellus Scipio and King Juba II, 46BC. ¶ Accession of James II of Great Britain (abdicated by flight on 11 December 1688), 1685. ¶ Britain declares war on France, 1778. ¶ Massachusetts joins the Union (6th), 1788. ¶ The state of Massachusetts ratifies the Constitution of the United States of America, 1788. ¶ Beginning of the *Regency*, by the Prince of Wales, 1811. ¶ Treaty of Waitangi concluded in New Zealand, 1840. ¶ First storm-warnings sent to the coast by the Meteorological Department of the Board of Trade in England, 1861. ¶ General Robert E. Lee is appointed Commander-in-Chief of the Confederate armies, 1865, ¶ Union with Greece proclaimed by Crete, 1897. ¶ Ramsay MacDonald is elected chairman of the British Labour Party, 1911. ¶ Cardinal Achille Ratti becomes Pope Pius XI, 1922. ¶ Accession of Queen Elizabeth II of Great Britain upon the death of George VI, 1952. ¶ Independence of Grenada proclaimed, 1974.

BORN: António Vieira, Jesuit priest and missionary in Brazil, writer, Lisbon, Portugal, 1608. Antoine Arnauld, Jansenist theologian, France, 1612. Queen Anne of Great Britain and Ireland, the last Stuart ruler, London, 1665. Ugo Foscolo, Italian novelist and poet, 1778. Sir Charles Wheatstone, inventor and physicist, perfected and developed the electric telegraph, Gloucester, 1802. Sir Henry Irving, theatrical actor and manager, near Glastonbury, Somerset, 1838. Frederic William Henry Myers, poet, scholar and psychical researcher, *The Renewal of Youth and Other Poems, Human Personality and its Survival of Bodily Death*, Keswick, Cumberland, 1843. William Murphy, physician and medical researcher, Nobel Prize winner, Stoughton, Wisconsin, 1892. 'Babe' Ruth, champion baseball player, Baltimore, Maryland, 1895. Alberto Cavalcanti, documentary film maker, *Night Mail* (as producer), Rio de Janiero, Brazil, 1897. Wladyslaw Gomulka, Communist statesman, Poland, 1905. Ronald Reagan, actor and Governor of California, Illinois, 1911. Eva Braun, Hitler's mistress, Bavaria, 1912. François Truffaut, film director, *Jules et Jim*, Paris, 1932.

DIED: Aldus Manutius, printer, author and type-designer, Venice, 1515. Charles II, King of Great Britain and Ireland, 1685. Lancelot 'Capability' Brown, landscape gardener, 1783. Carlo Goldoni, Italian dramatist, Belisario, 1793. Vuk Stefanović Karadžić, folklorist and scholar, Serbia, 1864. Rubén Darío, Nicaraguan poet, *Songs of Life and Hope*, 1916. Gustav Klimt, Art Nouveau painter, 1918. Edward Emerson Barnard, American astronomer, 1923.

FEBRUARY 7

Independence Day, Grenada, West Indies. Feasts of SS: Romuald, abbot;
Adaucus, martyr; Theodore of Heraclea, martyr; Moses, bishop;
Richard, 'King'; Luke the Younger.

Austria and Prussia form alliance against France, 1792. ¶ HMS *Orpheus* is wrecked on the coast of New Zealand, 185 soldiers and sailors lose their lives, 1863. ¶ First meeting of the Irish Nationalist League, 1883. ¶ Severe blizzards in Nebraska, South Dakota and other American states result in many deaths (blizzards last for several days), 1891. ¶ British railways are taken over by the government, 1940. ¶ Beginning of the German offensive on the Anzio bridgehead, 1944.

BORN: Sir Thomas More, humanist, statesman and writer, *Utopia, The History of Richard III*, canonized in 1935 by Pope Pius XI; London, 1478. Philippe Buache, geographer and cartographer, devised contour lines for maps and charts, Paris, 1700. Charles Dickens, novelist, *David Copperfield*, Portsmouth, Hampshire, 1812. Sir William Huggins, astronomer, London, 1824. Sir James Murray, philologist, editor of the Oxford *New English Dictionary*, Denholm, Roxburghshire, 1837. Alfred Adler, Austrian psychologist, 1870. Sinclair Lewis, novelist, *Main Street, Babbitt, Elmer Gantry*, Sauk Centre, Minnesota, 1885.

DIED: William Boyce, organist and composer, London, 1779. Ch'ien Lung, Chinese Emperor, 1799. Joseph Sheridan Le Fanu, novelist, *Uncle Silas, In a Glass Darkly*, Dublin, 1873. Adolphe Sax, instrument maker, invented the saxophone and the sax-horn, Paris, 1894. Daniel François Malan, architect of South Africa's apartheid policy, Stellenbosch, South Africa, 1959. Igor Vasilevich Kuchatov, Soviet nuclear physicist, 1960.

FEBRUARY 8

Anniversary of the Ramadan Revolution, Iraq (1963). Feasts of SS:
John of Matha; Nicetius, or Nizier, of Besançon, bishop; Elfleda, virgin;
Meingold, martyr; Cuthman; Stephen of Muret, abbot.

The 'Great Frost' of London ends (began 25 December 1739), 1740. ¶ Laetitia
(Asteroid 39) discovered by Chacornac, 1856. ¶ The Union takes Roanoke
Island, North Carolina, from the Confederacy, 1862. ¶ The Viceroy of India,
Earl Mayo, is murdered, 1872. ¶ Great rioting, looting and violence in Oxford
Street and Pall Mall after a peaceable demonstration by the unemployed in
Trafalgar Square, 1886. ¶ Odessa is taken by Bolshevik forces, 1920. ¶ The first
man to be executed in a gas chamber, at Nevada State Prison, Carson City,
Nevada, 1924. ¶ Malaga is taken by Spanish rebels with assistance from Italian
forces, 1937. ¶ US astronauts return to Earth after 85 days in *Skylab* space
station, 1974.

BORN: Robert Burton, scholar, *Anatomy of Melancholy*, 1577. John Ruskin, art
critic, teacher and reformer, *The Stones of Venice, Modern Painters*, Dulwich,
London, 1819. William Sherman, Union general and military commander in
the US Civil War, Lancaster, Ohio, 1820. Henry Walter Bates, naturalist,
explorer of South America, *The Naturalist on the Amazon*, Leicester, 1825. Jules
Verne, writer of scientific romances, *Journey to the Centre of the Earth, Twenty-
thousand Leagues under the Sea*, Nantes, France, 1828. Martin Buber, philosopher
and theologian, *I and Thou*, Vienna, 1878. Dame Edith Evans, actress, London,
1888. King Vidor, film director, *Duel in the Sun*, Galveston, Texas, 1894.
Chester Carlson, inventor of the Xerox copying process, Washington, 1906.
Jack Lemmon, actor, Boston, Massachusetts, 1925. James Dean, film actor,
Rebel Without a Cause, Indiana, 1931.

DIED: Mary Stuart, Queen of Scots; beheaded, Fotheringay Castle, Northamptonshire, 1587. Gustaf Fröding, poet, *Guitar and Concertina*, 1911. Prince Peter
Kropotkin, anarchist and geographer, *Mutual Aid*, 1921. William Bateson,
biologist, originated the term *genetics*, 1926.

FEBRUARY 9

Feasts of SS: Cyril of Alexandria, archbishop and doctor;
Apollonia, virgin and martyr; Nicephorus, martyr; Sabinus of Canosa, bishop;
Teilo, bishop; Ansbert, bishop; Alto, abbot.

Bishop Hooper is burned at the stake in Gloucester, 1555. ¶ Murder of Lord Darnley, consort of Mary, Queen of Scots, 1567. ¶ The Peace of Lunéville between France and Austria signals the end of the Holy Roman Empire,1801. ¶ Rome is proclaimed a Republic by Mazzini, 1849. ¶ Formal founding of the Confederate States of America, 1861. ¶ Lieutenant Dawson's expedition in search of Dr Livingstone begins, 1872. ¶ Soap rationing begins in Britain, 1942. ¶ The French liner *Normandie* is burned, 1942. ¶ The next appearance of Halley's Comet, 1986.

BORN: William Henry Harrison, US President, Charles City, Virginia, 1773. Edward Carson, Anglo-Irish politician, Dublin, 1854. Mrs Patrick Campbell, actress and friend of G. B. Shaw, London, 1865. George Ade, humorous writer, *Fables in Slang*, Indiana, 1866. Amy Lowell, Imagist poet, Massachusetts, 1874. Alban Berg, composer, *Wozzeck*, Vienna, 1885. Pietro Nenni, Italian Socialist politician, Faenza, Italy, 1891. Brendan Behan, playwright and novelist, *The Quare Fellow*, Dublin, 1923.

DIED: Agnes Sorel, mistress of Charles VII of France, 1450. Dr John Gregory, physician, Professor of Medicine at Aberdeen University, 1773. Johan Barthold Jongkind, artist, Netherlands, 1891. Norman Douglas, Scottish writer, *Siren Land*, 1952. Alexandre Benois, painter and theatrical designer, 1960.

FEBRUARY 10

Anniversary of Oruro, a department of Bolivia. Feasts of SS:
Scholastica, virgin; Soteris, virgin and martyr; Trumwin, bishop;
Austreberta, virgin; William of Maleval.

The Seven Years' War between Britain and Spain ends with the signing of the Treaty of Paris, 1763. ¶ Queen Victoria of England marries Francis-Albert-Augustus-Charles-Emmanuel, Duke of Saxe, Prince of Saxe-Coburg and Gotha (ordered to be styled Prince Consort on 20 June 1857), 1840. ¶ Lord Sydenham proclaims the Union of Upper and Lower Canada, 1841. ¶ Ausonia (Asteroid 63) is discovered by de Gasparis, 1861. ¶ The use of the revised version of the *Bible* in church services is authorized by the Church of England, 1899. ¶ PAYE (Pay-as-you-earn) system of income tax is introduced in Britain, 1944. ¶ The Eritrean Liberation Front launches new offensives in northern Ethiopia, 1975.

BORN: Honoré d'Urfé, author, *Astrée*, Marseilles, 1568. Charles Lamb, essayist and writer, *Essays of Elia*, Temple, London, 1775. Samuel Plimsoll, reformer, devised the Plimsoll line for ships, Bristol, 1824. William Pember Reeves, politician and poet, *The Long White Cloud*, Lyttelton, New Zealand, 1857. Boris Pasternak, novelist and poet, *Doctor Zhivago*, Moscow, 1890. Harold Macmillan, Conservative politician, Prime Minister, London, 1894. John Enders, microbiologist, Connecticut, 1897. Dame Judith Anderson, Australian actress, 1898. Bertolt Brecht, dramatist and theatrical director, *The Caucasian Chalk Circle, Mother Courage*, Bavaria, 1898. Henri Alekan, cinematographer, *La Belle et La Bête*, Paris, 1909. Larry Adler, harmonica-player and composer, Baltimore, Maryland, 1914. Sir Stanley Matthews, footballer, near Stoke-on-Trent, 1915.

DIED: Charles Louis de Secondat, Baron de Montesquieu, lawyer and philosopher, *Lettres persanes, Considérations sur la grandeur et la décadance des Romains*, Paris, 1755. David Thompson, explored western Canada and produced the first accurate maps of the area, near Montreal, 1857. Sir David Brewster, physicist, *Letters on Natural Magic*, 1868. Claude Bernard, physiologist, discovered vaso-motor nerves, 1878. Joseph Lister, surgeon, campaigned for antiseptic surgery, Walmer, Kent, 1912. Wilhelm Konrad von Röntgen, physicist, discovered X-rays, Munich, 1923. Sir Truby King, founder of the Plunket Society, New Zealand, 1938.

FEBRUARY 11

*Youth Day, Republic of Cameroun. National Founding Day, Japan
(commemorating the Imperial House Law of 1889 regulating the descent of the
throne). Armed Forces Day, Liberia. Anniversary of the Agreement
between the Vatican and Italy, Vatican City State (1929).
The Feast of the Appearing of Our Lady at Lourdes, celebrating the
appearances of the Virgin to Bernadette Soubirous, her sister and a friend in 1858.
Feasts of SS: Saturninus, Dativus and other Martyrs;
Lucius, bishop and martyr; Lazarus, bishop; Severinus, abbot;
Caedmon; Gregory II, pope; Benedict of Aniane, abbot; Paschal I, pope.*

Severndroog and other strongholds on the coast of India held by the pirate
Angria are taken by British forces, 1755. ¶ The marriage of Napoleon and Marie-
Louise of Austria, 1810. ¶ London University is chartered, 1826. ¶ The Virgin
Mary is said to have appeared to three young girls at Lourdes in France, 1858.
¶ Benito Juarez declared constitutional president of Mexico by an assembly at
Vera Cruz, 1858. ¶ Riots in Chatham after convicts break-out of prison, finally
suppressed by troops, 1861. ¶ First 'Weekly Weather Report' published by
Meteorological Office, 1878. ¶ Honduras declared an independent republic,
1922. ¶ USSR offensive on the Mannerheim Line, 1940. ¶ *Linger Awhile* and
Mobile Bay recorded in New York City by Rex Stewart and his Orchestra, 1940.
¶ North Vietnam releases first American prisoners after ceasefire, 1973. ¶ Mrs
Margaret Thatcher becomes the first woman leader of a British political party
(Conservatives), 1975.

BORN: Bernard Le Bovier Sieur de Fontenelle, philospher, 1657. William
Henry Fox Talbot, photographic pioneer, published the first book with photographic illustrations, in 1846, *The Pencil of Nature*, Lacock Abbey, Wiltshire,
1800. J. Willard Gibbs, physicist, Connecticut, 1839. Thomas Alva Edison,
inventor, Milan, Ohio, 1847. Joseph Mankiewicz, film producer and writer,
All about Eve, Wilkes-Barre, Pennsylvania, 1909. Farouk I, King of Egypt,
Cairo, 1920.

DIED: Lazzaro Spallanzani, physiologist and chemist, disproved the theory of
'spontaneous generation', Pavia, Italy, 1799. Leon Foucault, physicist, 1868.
Honoré Daumier, caricaturist and artist, 1879. Sir Charles Parsons, engineer,
inventor of the steam turbine, Kingston, Surrey, 1931. John Buchan (Lord
Tweedsmuir), novelist, *The 39 Steps, Prester John*, 1940. Sergei Eisenstein, Soviet
director, *Ivan the Terrible*, 1948. Ernest Jones, psychoanalyst; popularizer,
translator and biographer of Freud, 1958.

FEBRUARY 12

Union Day, Burma. Anniversary of Abraham Lincoln's Birthday, USA
and its territories (a legal holiday, celebrated since 1866).
The Feast of the Seven Founders of the Servite Order.
Feasts of SS: Marina, virgin; Julian the Hospitaller;
Meletius of Antioch, archbishop; Ethelwald of Lindisfarne, bishop;
Antony Kauleas, bishop; Ludan.

French defeated by the English at Herrings, 1429. ¶ General Tate lands at Pembrokeshire on the coast of Wales with over 1,000 French troops (subsequently surrenders), 1797. ¶ Independence proclaimed by Chile, 1818. ¶ First public demonstrations of Alexander Graham Bell's 'articulating telephone', between Boston and Salem, 1877. ¶ Formation of the London County Council, 1889. ¶ Winston Churchill is made Colonial Secretary, 1921. ¶ *Rhythm Lullaby* and *Bubbling Over* recorded in New York City by Earl Hines and his Orchestra, 1935. ¶ Bomb outrages throughout San Francisco by the New World Liberation Front, 1977.

BORN: Thomas Campion, musician and poet, London, 1567. John Winthrop, Puritan and lawyer, the first Governor of the Massachusetts Bay Colony, Groton, Suffolk, 1588. Jan Swammerdam, entomologist and microscopist, Amsterdam, 1637. Cotton Mather, writer and Puritan, Boston, 1663. George Hadley, meteorologist, London, 1685. Charles Darwin, naturalist and writer, *On the Origin of the Species*, Shropshire, 1809. Abraham Lincoln, President of the United States, Kentucky, 1809. George Meredith, novelist, poet and critic, *Ballads and Poems of Tragic Life, The Ordeal of Richard Feverel, The Egoist*, Portsmouth, 1828. John Llewellyn Lewis, US labour leader, Iowa, 1880. Max Beckmann, Expressionist painter, Leipzig, 1884. Roy Harris, composer, *Folksong Symphony*, Oklahoma, 1898.

DIED: Lady Jane Grey, Queen of England; executed, Tower Hill, London, 1554. Gianbattista Marino, poet, Naples, 1625. Charles Le Brun, painter, Versailles, France, 1690. Ts'ao Hsueh-ch'in, novelist, *The Dream of the Red Chamber*, Peking, 1763. Pierre Marivaux, novelist and playwright, *The Poor Peasant, The Game of Love and Chance*, Paris, 1763. Stanislaw II, King of Poland, 1798. Immanuel Kant, philosopher, *Critique of Pure Reason*, Königsberg, Germany, 1804. Friedrich Ernst Daniel Schleiermacher, philosopher and Protestant theologian, *Introduction to Plato's Dialogues*, Berlin, 1834. Nikolai Ivanovich Lobachevsky, mathematician, 1856. Hans Guido von Bülow, pianist and conductor, 1894. Julius Dedekind, German mathematician, 1916. Lillie Langtry, actress and entertainer, 1929. Charles Voysey, architect, Winchester, Hampshire, 1941.

St Valentine's Eve. Feasts of SS: Polyeuctus, martyr; Martinian the Hermit;
Stephen of Rieti, abbot; Modomnoc; Licinius, or Lésin, bishop;
Ermengild, or Ermenilda, widow; Catherine dei Ricci, virgin.

Accession of William III and Mary II of Great Britain (reigned *together* until 27 December 1694), 1689. ¶ Massacre of the Macdonalds at Glencoe in Scotland, 1692. ¶ Coalition against France formed by Prussia, Austria, Holland, Britain, Sardinia, and Spain, 1793. ¶ First appearance of the Asiatic cholera in London, at Limehouse and Rotherhithe, 1832. ¶ Fenian outrages and disturbances at Kerry, 1867. ¶ The League of Nations admits Switzerland, 1920. ¶ Alexander Solzhenitsyn is expelled from Russia, 1974.

BORN: John Hunter, physiologist, surgeon and dentist, *A Treatise on the Blood and Gunshot Wounds*, East Kilbride, Scotland, 1728. Lord Randolph Churchill, Conservative statesman, 1849. Georges Simenon, writer, creator of Inspector Maigret, Liège, Belgium, 1903.

DIED: Catherine Howard, wife of Henry VIII; beheaded, 1542. Benevenuto Cellini, sculptor and autobiographer, 1571. Jacopo Bassano, Venetian painter, 1592. Cotton Mather, writer and Puritan, Boston, 1728. Richard Wagner, composer, *The Flying Dutchman, Lohengrin, The Ring of the Nibelung*, Venice, 1883. Georges Rouault, Expressionist painter, Paris, 1958.

FEBRUARY 14

St Valentine's Day: Valentine cards have been a popular custom since the late 17th century. Feasts of SS: Abraham, bishop; Maro, abbot; Auxentius; Conran, bishop; Antoninus of Sorrento, abbot; Adolf of Osnabrück, bishop.

Attempted assassination of William III at Turnham Green ('Assassination Plot'), 1696. ¶ Spanish fleet defeated off Cape St Vincent by Horatio Nelson and John Jervis, 1797. ¶ Oregon is made a US state (33rd), 1859. ¶ Temporary annexation of Hawaii by US, 1893. ¶ Rising 43 minutes before the Sun, and setting 43 minutes after it, the planet Venus is both a morning star and evening star, 1894. ¶ Arizona made a US state (48th), 1912. ¶ The first regular broadcasting transmissions in Britain, by Guglielmo Marconi in Essex, 1922. ¶ Nationalization of the Bank of England, 1946.

BORN: Nicolaus Copernicus, astronomer, proposed the heliocentric theory of the Solar System, Poland, 1473. Thomas Robert Malthus, economist, *An Essay on the Principles of Population*, Surrey, 1766. Christopher Latham Sholes, inventor of the modern typewriter, near Mooresburg, Pennsylvania, 1819. Frank Harris, writer, journalist and editor, County Galway, Ireland, 1856. Jack Benny, comedian and actor, Illinois, 1894. John Longden, American jockey, Wakefield, Yorkshire, 1907.

DIED: Captain James Cook, explorer; murdered by natives in Hawaii, 1779. Sir William Blackstone, jurist, *Commentaries on the Laws of England*, 1780. Henry Maudslay, engineer and inventor, London, 1831. William Dyce, Scottish artist, *Pegwell Bay*, 1864. William Sherman, Union general and military commander in the US Civil War, New York City, 1891. Hendrick Antoon Lorentz, physicist, Haarlem, 1928. P. G. Wodehouse, novelist, creator of Jeeves, 1975.

FEBRUARY 15

*The Roman Lupercalia, a festival of purification honouring Lycaean Pan
(or Faunus). Feasts of SS: Faustinus and Jovita, martyrs; Agape, virgin and
martyr; Walfrid, abbot; Tanco, bishop and martyr; Sigfrid, bishop.*

Antony offers Gaius Julius Caesar the diadem in public at Rome on the festival
of Lupercalia, but Caesar declines it, 44BC. ¶ Prussia and Austria sign peace
Treaty of Hubertusburg, 1763. ¶ The first shipment of frozen meat leaves New
Zealand for England, on the SS *Dunedin*, 1882. ¶ The USS *Maine* is destroyed in
Havana, 1898. ¶ The Permanent Court of International Justice holds its first
sitting at The Hague, 1922. ¶ Mayor Anton J. Cermak of Chicago assassinated
in Miami by Giuseppe Zangara; President-elect Franklin D. Roosevelt escapes
unhurt, 1933. ¶ Rebel forces under General Franco take Teruel, 1938. ¶ *Take the
'A' Train* recorded by Duke Ellington and his Orchestra, 1941. ¶ Surrender of
Singapore to Japanese army, 1942. ¶ Allied bombing of the Monte Cassino
monastery, 1944. ¶ Heavy fighting between Israel and Jordan in the Jordan
Valley, 1968. ¶ Fierce battles on the Golan Heights between Israel and Syria,
1974. ¶ A state of emergency was declared by Ethiopian authorities in Eritrea
and martial law is imposed, 1975.

BORN: Philipp Melanchthon, theologian, colleague of Martin Luther's, Bretten,
Germany, 1497. Pedro Menendez de Aviles, soldier and navigator, settled
Florida as a Spanish colony, Aviles, Spain, 1519. Galileo Galilei, astronomer and
physicist, Pisa, 1564. Michael Praetorius, composer, historian of music, Thur-
ingia, Germany, 1571. Louis XV of France, Versailles, 1710. Jeremy Bentham,
Utilitarian philosopher, London, 1748. Cyrus Hall McCormick, engineer,
perfected the mechanical harvester, Virginia, 1809. Sir Halford John Mackinder,
political geographer, *The Geographical Pivot of History*, Gainsborough, Lincolnshire, 1861. Alfred North Whitehead, philosopher and mathematician, *Science
and the Modern World*, *Principia Mathematica* (with Bertrand Russell), Ramsgate,
Isle of Thanet, Kent, 1861. Sir Ernest Henry Shackleton, Antarctic explorer,
Kilkee, County Clare, Ireland, 1874. John Barrymore, actor, 1882. Graham Hill,
racing driver, London, 1929. Claire Bloom, actress, London, 1931.

DIED: Michael Praetorius, composer, historian of music, Wolfenbüttel,
Germany, 1621. Jan Swammerdam, entomologist and microscopist, Amsterdam,
1680. Gotthold Lessing, dramatist, *Minna von Barnhem*, 1781. Aleksandr Borodin,
chemist and composer, *Prince Igor*, 1887. Herbert Henry Asquith, Liberal
politician and Prime Minister, 1928.

FEBRUARY 16

Feasts of SS: Onesimus, martyr; Juliana, virgin and martyr;
Elias, Jeremy and their Companions, martyrs; Gilbert of Sempringham.

Resignation of Pitt as Prime Minister, 1801. ¶ France invades Spain, 1808. ¶ The Confederates surrender Fort Grant to General Ulysses S. Grant, 1862. ¶ The tomb of Tutankhamen is opened, 1923. ¶ Fidel Castro becomes Cuban premier, 1959.

BORN: Giambattista Bodoni, printer and type designer, Italy, 1740. Heinrich Barth, explorer in North Africa, Hamburg, 1821. Sir Francis Galton, geneticist, Birmingham, 1822. Nikolai Semyonovich Leskov, novelist, *Cathedral Folk*, Gorokhova, Russia, 1831. Ernst Haeckel, biologist, Potsdam, Germany, 1834. Henry Brooks Adams, historian, *America's Economic Supremacy*, 1838. Hugo de Vries, geneticist, Haarlem, Netherlands, 1848. Robert Flaherty, film maker, *Nanook of the North*, Michigan, 1884. Hal Porter, Australian writer, 1911. Peter Porter, Australian poet, *After Martial*, 1929.

DIED: Alphonso III, King of Portugal, 1279. Henry Deane, Archbishop of Canterbury, Bishop of Bangor, 1502. Lionel Lukin, inventor of the lifeboat, 1834. Henry Walter Bates, naturalist, explorer in South America, *The Naturalist on the Amazon*, 1892. Giosuè Carducci, poet, Nobel Prize for Literature, 1907. James Harvey Robinson, historian, *The New History*, New York City, 1936.

FEBRUARY 17

Feasts of SS: Theodulus and Julian, martyrs; Loman, bishop;
Fintan of Cloneenagh, abbot; Finan, bishop; Silvin, bishop; Evermod, bishop.

The Lancastrians defeat the Yorkists at the second battle of St Albans, 1461. ¶ The USS *Housatonic* is sunk by the *Hunley*, a Confederate submarine, 1864. ¶ Columbia in South Carolina is burnt by supporters of the advancing Union army, 1865. ¶ Aegle (Asteroid 96) discovered by M. Coggia, and Clotho (Asteroid 97) by M. Tempel, 1868. ¶ Electra (Asteroid 130) discovered by C. H. F. Peters, 1873. ¶ Attempted assassination of Czar Alexander II of Russia by an explosion in the Winter Palace, St Petersburg, 1880. ¶ President Richard M. Nixon leaves Washington for China, 1972.

BORN: Arcangelo Corelli, composer and violinist, Italy, 1653. Horace Benedict de Saussure, physicist and natural historian, Geneva, 1740. René Laënnec, army doctor and physician, invented the stethoscope, Brittany, France, 1781. Frederick Eugene Ives, inventor, perfected the half-tone printing process, Connecticut, 1856. A. B. 'Banjo' Paterson, Australian folk poet and journalist, 1864. Sir Ernest Davis, New Zealand businessman and philanthropist, 1872.

DIED: Giordano Bruno, Dominican philosopher, 1600. James Macpherson, poet, *The Ossian Poems*, Inverness, 1796. Johann Heinrich Pestalozzi, educator and teacher, Switzerland, 1827. Heinrich Heine, poet, journalist and satirist, *Travel Sketches, On the History of Religion and Philosophy in Germany*, Paris, 1856. Adolphe Quételet, Belgian statistician, 1874. Christopher Lathan Sholes, inventor of the modern typewriter, Milwaukee, Wisconsin, 1890. Henry Olcott, co-founder, with Helena Blavatsky, of the Theosophical Society, Madras, 1907. Geronimo, Apache chief, 1908. Sir Wilfred Laurier, Canadian Prime Minister, 1919. Hans Hofmann, Abstract Expressionist painter, 1966. Samuel Agnon, Hebrew novelist, *The Bridal Canopy*, 1970.

FEBRUARY 18

Republic Day, The Gambia (1965). Democracy Day, Nepal
(commemorating the constitutional monarchy established in 1951).
Feasts of SS: Simeon, bishop and martyr; Leo and Paregorius, martyrs;
Flavian, bishop and martyr; Helladius, archbishop;
Colman of Lindisfarne, bishop; Angilbert, abbot; Theotonius.

Beginning of a naval engagement between the British under Admiral Blake and the Dutch under Van Tromp off Portsmouth (British victorious by 20 February), 1653. ¶ After a lengthy siege Charleston is taken by the Union fleet, 1865. ¶ Hertha (Asteroid 135) discovered by C. H. F. Peters, 1874. ¶ Direct telegraphic line between London and New Zealand established, 1876. ¶ General Gordon reaches Khartoum, 1884. ¶ Surrender of the last German garrisons in the Cameroons, 1916. ¶ Discovery of the planet Pluto, by Clyde Tombaugh (from photographs taken the previous month), at Lowell Observatory in the US, 1930.

BORN: Mary Tudor, Queen of England, popularly known as 'Bloody Mary', Greenwich, 1516. Alessandro Volta, physicist, investigated electricity and made the first battery, Como, Lombardy (now Italy), 1745. Marshall Hall, physician and physiologist, *Respiration and Irritability*, Basford, Nottinghamshire, 1790. Ramakrishna, Hindu teacher and writer, Bengal, 1836. Ernst Mach, physicist, philosopher of science, Austria, 1838. Sholem Aleichem (Solomon J. Rabinowitz), Yiddish writer, Ukraine, 1859. Wendell Louis Wilkie, Republican politician and presidential candidate, Elwood, Indiana, 1892. Andres Segovia, virtuoso classical guitarist, Linares, Spain, 1894. André Breton, founder of the Surrealist movement, art critic, poet, *Nadja*, France, 1896.

DIED: Fra Angelico, Dominican, painter, 1455. Cornelius Agrippa, scholar and astrologer, *The Three Books on Occult Philosophy*, 1535. Michelangelo Buonarroti, Renaissance painter, sculptor and poet, Rome, 1564. Nicholas I, Tsar of Russia, St Petersburg, 1855. James Corbett (Gentleman Jim), pugilist and prize fighter, 1933. Robert Oppenheimer, physicist, developed the US atomic bomb at Los Alamos, Princeton, New Jersey, 1967.

FEBRUARY 19

Feasts of SS: Mesrop, bishop; Barbatus, bishop; Beatus of Liebana;
Boniface of Lausanne, bishop; Conrad of Piacenza.

Albinus is defeated near Lyons, 197. ¶ Henry IV defeats the rebels at Bramham Moor, 1408. ¶ Napoleon Bonaparte establishes himself in the Tuileries as First Consul, 1800. ¶ The British fleet forces a passage through the Dardanelles to support Russia against Turkey, 1807. ¶ Bread riots in Liverpool, 1855. ¶ Thomas Alva Edison patents the first gramophone (demonstrated on 7 December 1877), 1878. ¶ Dardanelles shelled by British and French ships, 1915. ¶ Darwin in Australia is bombed by Japanese planes, 1942. ¶ Beginning of the battle of Iwo Jima, a tiny island in the West Pacific, with the invasion of US troops (lasts until 17 March), 1945. ¶ Independence of Cyprus established with an agreement signed in London by Britain, Turkey and Greece, 1959.

BORN: David Garrick, actor and theatre manager, Hereford, 1717. Luigi Boccherini, composer and cellist, perfected the art of string quartets and quintets, Italy, 1743. Sir Roderick Murchison, geologist, Tarradale, Ross and Cromarty, 1792. Svante August Arrhenius, chemist, Nobel Prize winner, Sweden, 1859. Sven Anders Hedin, cartographer and traveller, chiefly in Central Asia, Stockholm, 1865. Alvaro Obregon, revolutionary, reformer and President of Mexico, Alamos, Mexico, 1880. Merle Oberon, actress, Tasmania, 1911. Carson McCullers, novelist, *The Heart is a Lonely Hunter, Member of the Wedding*, Columbus, Georgia, 1917. HRH Prince Andrew Albert Christian Edward, second son of Queen Elizabeth II, 1960.

DIED: Elizabeth Carter, writer and translator, *Poems on several occasions*. Deal, Kent, 1806. Georg Büchner, dramatist, *Danton's Death*, 1837. Charles Blondin, tightrope walker who crossed Niagara Falls many times, 1897. Ernst Mach, physicist, philosopher of science, Austria, 1916. André Gide, novelist and critic, *L'Immoraliste*, 1951. Knut Hamsun, Norwegian novelist and poet, *The Growth of the Soil*, 1952. John Grierson, documentary film maker, founded the Canadian National Film Board, *Drifters*, Scotland, 1972.

Feasts of SS: Tyrannio, Zenobius and other Martyrs; Sadoth, bishop and martyr; Eleutherius of Tournai, bishop; Eucherius of Orleans, bishop; Wulfric.

Edward VI of England crowned (reign had begun 28 January), 1547. ¶ Admiral Blake defeats the Dutch fleet under Admiral Van Tromp off Portsmouth (began 18 February), 1653. ¶ Leopold II of Austria becomes the Holy Roman Emperor, 1790. ¶ Austria announces itself to be bankrupt, 1811. ¶ Great storm in England, much damage to the Crystal Palace, and the steeple of Chichester Cathedral is blown off, 1861. ¶ Una (Asteroid 160) discovered by C. H. F. Peters, 1876.

BORN: Karl Czerny, composer and pianist, Vienna, 1791. Bela Kun, Hungarian Communist, 1886. Georges Bernanos, novelist, Paris, 1888. Carl Mayer, film director, *The Cabinet of Dr Caligari*, Gratz, Germany, 1892. Alexei Kosygin, Soviet politician and Premier, Leningrad, 1904.

DIED: Aurangzeb, last Mogul emperor of India, 1707. Joseph II, King of Germany and Holy Roman Emperor, 1790. Robert Edwin Peary, Arctic explorer, supposedly the first man to reach the North Pole, Washington D.C., 1920. Sir Leonard Woolley, archaeologist, excavated Ur of the Chaldees, London, 1960. Percy Grainger, composer and pianist, 1961. Chester William Nimitz, US Commander-in-Chief of the Pacific Fleet during the Second World War, San Francisco, 1966.

FEBRUARY 21

*Feasts of SS: Germanus of Granfel, martyr; George of Amastris, bishop;
Severian, bishop and martyr.*

James I of Scotland murdered by nobles, 1436. ¶ Accession of James II of
Scotland (reigns until 3 August 1460), 1436. ¶ Freedom of worship established in
France, 1795. ¶ The first demonstration of a self-powered railway locomotive is
accomplished by Richard Trevithick, in Glamorgan, Wales, 1804. ¶ Inauguration of the Memorial Obelisk to George Washington in Washington, D.C.,
(555 feet high), 1885. ¶ Beginning of the battle of Verdun (ends 16 December),
1916. ¶ Ending of British Protectorate in Egypt, 1922. ¶ Allied forces in North
Africa are placed under the supreme command of General Eisenhower, 1943.
¶ The SS *Exilona* arrives at Odessa with the first American wheat for USSR,
1964. ¶ Black Muslim leader Malcolm X is murdered in Manhattan, 1965. ¶ John
Ehrlichman, H. R. Haldeman and John Mitchell are sentenced in Washington
for their part in the Watergate cover-up, 1975.

BORN: Antonio Lopez de Santa-Anna, revolutionary, military commander and
President of Mexico, Jalapa, Mexico, 1794. John Henry Newman, Cardinal,
theologian and writer, *Apologia pro Vita Sua*, London, 1801. Léo Delibes, ballet
composer, *Coppelia*, France, 1836. George Lansbury, British Labour Party
politician, near Lowestoft, Suffolk, 1859. August von Wassermann, physician
and bacteriologist, Bamberg, Germany, 1866. Constantin Brancusi, sculptor,
Bird in Space, Rumania, 1876. Sacha Guitry, actor, playwright and film director,
The Story of a Cheat, Leningrad, 1885. Raymond Queneau, novelist and critic,
Exercises du Style, Zazie, Le Havre, France, 1903. W. H. Auden, poet and writer,
York, 1907.

DIED: Jethro Tull, agriculturist, near Hungerford, Berkshire, 1741. Nikolay
Gogol, novelist and dramatist, *Dead Souls*, 1852. George Ellery Hale, American
astronomer, founded the Yerkes and Mount Palomar Observatories, 1938.
Jacques Becker, film director, *Le Trou*, Paris, 1960. Malcolm X (Malcolm Little),
US Black Muslim leader; assassinated by persons unknown, New York City
1965.

FEBRUARY 22

*George Washington's Birthday, USA and its territories (a legal holiday
in many states, observed since 1796). The Feast of St Peter's Chair at Antioch.
Feasts of SS: Thalassius and Limnaeus; Baradates; Margaret of Cortona.*

Accession of Robert II of Scotland (reigns until 19 April 1390), 1370. ¶ The
Mexicans are defeated at the battle of Buena Vista by US forces led by General
Taylor, 1847. ¶ Benjamin Disraeli is made leader of the Conservative Party,
1849. ¶ Jefferson Davis is formally inaugurated as President of the Confederacy,
1862. ¶ Dizzy Gillespie records *Anthropology* in New York City with Al Haig
and Milt Jackson, 1946. ¶ Pakistan recognizes the independence of Bangladesh,
1974.

BORN: George Washington, first US President, Bridges Creek, Westmoreland
County, Virginia, 1732. Arthur Schopenhauer, pessimist philosopher, *The
World as Will and Idea*, Danzig, Poland, 1788. James Lowell, poet and diplomat,
Biglow Papers, first editor of the *Atlantic Monthly,* Cambridge, Massachusetts,
1819. Robert Baden-Powell, founder of the Boy Scout movement, defended
Mafeking, London, 1857. Heinrich Rudolph Hertz, physicist, discovered electro-
magnetic (radio) waves, Hamburg, Germany, 1857. Norman Lindsay, Australian
artist and novelist, *Age of Consent*, 1879. Eric Gill, sculptor and type designer,
Brighton, 1882. Edna St Vincent Millay, poet, *A Few Figs from Thistles, The
Harp-Weaver and Other Poems*, Rockland, Maine, 1892. Luis Buñuel, film
director, *Viridiana, Nazarin*, Spain, 1900. Romulo Betancourt, statesman and
President of Venezuela, 1908.

DIED: Jean Baptiste Corot, classical landscape painter, 1875. Sir Charles Lyell,
geologist, *Principles of Geology*, London, 1875. Hugo Wolf, *Lieder* composer,
Vienna, 1903. Francisco Idalecio Madero, politician, led the revolution against
the Mexican dictator Diaz, Mexico City, 1913. Elizabeth Bowen, novelist,
Death of the Heart, 1973.

FEBRUARY 23

The Roman Terminalia, the festival of Terminus, god of boundaries.
Republic Day, Guyana (the Co-Operative republic was proclaimed in 1970).
Feasts of SS: Peter Damian, bishop and doctor; Serenus the Gardener, martyr;
Alexander Akimetes; Dositheus; Boisil, or Boswell, abbot;
Milburga, virgin; Willigis, archbishop.

The Cato Street Conspiracy is uncovered in London, 1820. ¶ Captains Speke and Grant announce the discovery of the source of the River Nile to be in Lake Victoria, 1863. ¶ Mississippi readmitted to the Union (seceded 9 January 1861), 1870. ¶ Adria (Asteroid 143) discovered by J. Palisa, 1875. ¶ Zola is imprisoned for writing *J'accuse*, an open letter to the French President concerning the Dreyfus affair, 1898. ¶ Beginning of the 'February Revolution' in Russia (ends 1 March), 1917.[1] ¶ The Fasci del Combattimento founded in Italy by Benito Mussolini, 1919.

BORN: Samuel Pepys, civil servant and diarist, London, 1633. George Frederick Handel, composer, violinist and organist, *The Messiah, Water Music*, Halle, Germany, 1685. Meyer Amschel Rothschild, banker and founder of a dynasty, Frankfurt, Germany, 1743. George Watts, painter, London, 1817. Victor Fleming, film director, *The Wizard of Oz*, Pasadena, California, 1883. Karl Jaspers, existentialist philosopher, *Man in the Modern Age*, Germany, 1883. Erich Kastner, writer, *Emil and the Detectives*, Germany, 1899.

DIED: Sir Joshua Reynolds, painter, London, 1792. John Keats, poet, *On First Looking into Chapman's Homer, Ode to a Nightingale*, Rome, 1821. John Quincy Adams, sixth President of the US (1825–9), 1848. Carl Friedrich Gauss, mathematician and astronomer, 1855. William Butterfield, architect of the Gothic Revival in England, 1900. Thomas Woodrow Wilson, US President, a founder of the League of Nations, Washington D.C., 1924. Dame Nellie Melba, Australian operatic singer, 1931. Sir Edward Elgar, composer, *The Enigma Variations*, 1934. Leo Hendrik Baekeland, inventor of Bakelite, 1944. Paul Claudel, dramatist and poet, 1955. Stan Laurel, film comedian (with Oliver Hardy), 1965. L. S. Lowry, painter of industrial landscapes, Glossop, Derbyshire, 1976.

[1] These are the Old Style dates. Russia did not adopt the Gregorian calendar until 1918, but had it done so earlier than 1917 the Revolution's dates would have been 8–14 March.

FEBRUARY 24

Feasts of SS: Matthias, apostle; Montanus, Lucius, and their Companions, martyrs; Praetextatus, or Prix, bishop and martyr.

Galerius Valerius Maximianus issues the first edict of persecution against the Christians, in Rome, 303. ¶ Francis I defeated at Pavia, 1525. ¶ Pope Gregory's Papal Bull announces the New (Gregorian) Calendar and the rules governing its implementation, 1582. ¶ The US Supreme Court declares for the first time an act of Congress to be unconstitutional, 1803. ¶ Abdication of Louis-Philippe of France, 1848. ¶ Argentina elects Juan Perón as President, 1946. ¶ Dr Nkrumah ousted by Ghanain army, 1966.

BORN: Matthias Corvinus, King of Hungary, Cluj, Rumania, 1443. John of Austria, defeated the Turks at Lepanto, Ratisbon, Germany, 1547. Charles Le Brun, painter, Paris, 1619. Wilhelm Grimm, historian and folklore collector, *Fairy Tales* (with his brother Jacob), Hanau, Germany, 1786. Winslow Homer, painter, Boston, Massachusetts, 1836. George Moore, novelist, dramatist and critic, *Confessions of a Young Man, The Brook Kerith, The Bending of the Bough,* Ballyglass, County Mayo, Ireland, 1852. Arnold Dolmetsch, musical instrument maker, France, 1858. Chester William Nimitz, US Commander-in-Chief of the Pacific Fleet during the Second World War, Fredericksburg, Texas, 1885.

DIED: Francis, Duke of Guise, French military commander; assassinated by a Huguenot whilst besieging Orleans, 1563. Sir Edmund Andros, diplomat, Governor of Virginia, 1714. Henry Cavendish, physicist, 1810. Robert Fulton, inventor of the first steam boat, 1815. Thomas Bowdler, censor and prude, edited the 'Family Shakespeare' and an edition of Gibbon, Swansea, Wales, 1825. Pierre Janet, psychologist, Paris, 1947.

Feasts of SS: Victorinus and his Companions, martyrs; Caesarius of Nazianzus;
Ethelbert of Kent; Walburga, virgin; Tarasius, bishop;
Gerland, bishop; Bd Robert of Arbrissel, abbot.

Edward II of England crowned (reign began 8 July 1307), 1308. ¶ The Treason
of Wallenstein and his assassination, in Germany, 1634. ¶ The 'Oxford Declaration', ascribed to Archdeacon Denison and Dr Pusey, sent to clery throughout
Britain for signature, 1864. ¶ Impeachment of President Andrew Johnson for
violation of the Tenure of Office Act (acquitted in May), 1868. ¶ Meat, butter
and other foodstuffs are rationed in the southern counties of Britain, 1918.
¶ *Mariner 6,* for Mars fly-by, launched from Cape Kennedy, 1969.

BORN: Giovanni Morgagni, physician, a pioneer of pathology, Forli, Italy,
1682. Carlo Goldoni, dramatist, *Belisario*, Venice, 1707. José de San Martin,
Argentinian revolutionary, Yapeyu, Argentina, 1778. Pierre Renoir, Impression-
ist painter, Limoges, France, 1841. Enrico Caruso, operatic tenor, Naples, 1873.
John Foster Dulles, American Secretary of State, Washington D.C., 1888. Dame
Myra Hess, pianist, London, 1890. Jed Harris, theatrical producer and director,
Vienna, 1900.

DIED: Robert Devereux, 2nd Earl of Essex, English soldier and statesman, 1601.
Albrecht von Wallenstein, Austrian general and military commander, Egar,
Germany, 1634. Sir Christopher Wren, astronomer and architect, London, 1723.
Thomas Moore, poet and song writer, *Lalla Rookh, Loves of the Angels*, Wiltshire,
1852. Paul Julius von Reuter, founder of the news agency, Nice, France, 1899.
Sir John Tenniel, artist, illustrated *Alice's Adventures in Wonderland* and *Through
the Looking Glass*, cartoonist for *Punch* magazine, London, 1914. George Minot,
physician and medical researcher, Nobel Prize winner, Brookline, Massachusetts, 1950. Alexander Archipenko, sculptor, 1965. Mark Rothko, painter,
New York City, 1970.

FEBRUARY 26

Dies Mala or 'Egyptian Day', considered unlucky in the Middle Ages.
National Day, Kuwait. Feasts of SS: Nestor, bishop and martyr;
Alexander of Alexandria, bishop; Porphyry, bishop; Victor the Hermit.

Manfred defeated by Charles of Anjou at Benevento, 1266. ¶ Severe earthquake in Lisbon results in an estimated 20,000 people losing their lives, 1531. ¶ First issue of £1 and £2 bank-notes in England, 1797. ¶ Napoleon Bonaparte escapes from Elba, 1815. ¶ Poland annexed by Russia, 1832. ¶ The French Republic is proclaimed, 1848. ¶ A state of emergency is declared in Southern Rhodesia, 1959.

BORN: Victor Hugo, novelist and poet, *The Hunchback of Notre Dame, The Man Who Laughs*, Besançon, France, 1802. Honoré Daumier, caricaturist and artist, France, 1808. William Frederick Cody (Buffalo Bill), frontiersman and impresario, Iowa, 1846. Johnny Cash, American country singer, Arkansas, 1932.

DIED: Roger II, King of Sicily, Palermo, 1154. Alois Senefelder, inventor of lithography, Munich, 1834. Émile Coué, psychologist, *Suggestion and Auto-Suggestion*, France, 1857. Richard Gatling, inventor of the Gatling gun, 1903. Sir Harry Lauder, Scottish entertainer, 1950. Levi Eshkol, Israeli statesman, 1969. Karl Jaspers, existentialist philosopher, *Man in the Modern Age*, Germany, 1969.

FEBRUARY 27

Independence Day, Dominican Republic (1844). Statehood Day, St Kitts,
West Indies (1967). Feasts of SS: Gabriel Possenti; Julian, Cronion and
Besas, martyrs; Thalelaeus the Hermit; Leander of Seville, bishop;
Baldomerus, or Galmier; Alnoth; John of Gorze, abbot.

First Russian embassy to Britain, 1557. ¶ Pitt the Younger resigns his commission in the army rather than fight America, 1776. ¶ The British are defeated by the Boers at the battle of Majuba, South Africa, 1881. ¶ Foundation of the British Labour Party, 1900. ¶ The first major British victory in the Boer War, General Cronje surrenders at Peerdebarg, 1900. ¶ The Reichstag Fire is engineered by the Nazis, Hitler subsequently suspends all civil liberties and the freedom of the press, 1933. ¶ Both Britain and France recognize General Franco's rebel government in Spain, 1939.

BORN: Constantine the Great, Roman Emperor and Christian, Yugoslavia, 280. Henry Wadsworth Longfellow, poet, *Hiawatha*, Portland, Maine, 1807. Dame Ellen Terry, actress, Coventry, Warwickshire, 1847. Rudolph Steiner, educationalist and writer, Austria, 1861. Charles Best, co-discoverer of the treatment for diabetes, Maine, 1899. Marino Marini, sculptor, Italy, 1901. John Steinbeck, novelist, *The Grapes of Wrath*, Salinas, California, 1902. Lawrence Durrell, novelist, *Justine*, India, 1912. Elizabeth Taylor, actress, London, 1929.

DIED: John Evelyn, diarist and writer, *Sylvana*, 1706. John Arbuthnot, satirist, creator of 'John Bull', 1735. Samuel Pierpont Langley, US astronomer and aeronautical pioneer, 1906. Adam Sedgwick, geologist, London, 1913. Ivan Pavlov, physiologist and psychologist, Leningrad, 1936. Peter Behrens, architect and industrialist, 1940.

FEBRUARY 28

*Feast of the Martyrs in the Plague of Alexandria. Feasts of SS: Proterius,
bishop and martyr; Romanus and Lupicinus, abbots; Hilarus, pope;
Oswald of Worcester, bishop.*

Threatened secession from Britain by the Boston Assembly unless all rights of the colonies are maintained, 1772. ¶ Re-introduction of the silver standard in the US, 1878. ¶ Ladysmith is relieved by Redvers Buller, 1900. ¶ US forces land in Honduras, 1924. ¶ Forty-two people die as a result of a London Underground train crashing into a siding at Moorgate, 1975. ¶ Spain withdraws from Spanish Sahara. 1976.

BORN: René Reamur, inventor, naturalist and writer, La Rochelle, France, 1683. Marquis de Montcalm de Saint-Véran, commander of French forces in Canada, France, 1712. Rachel, actress, Switzerland, 1820. Sir John Tenniel, artist, illustrated *Alice's Adventures in Wonderland* and *Through the Looking Glass*, cartoonist for *Punch* magazine, London, 1820. Charles Blondin, tightrope walker who crossed Niagara Falls many times, France, 1824. Henri Breuil, archaeologist and priest, France, 1877. Ben Hecht, journalist and screenplay writer, *Scarface, Front Page, A Child of the Century* (autobiography), New York City, 1894. Linus Pauling, chemist and physicist, Portland, Oregon, 1901. Stephen Spender, poet and writer, editor of *Encounter* magazine, *World Within World, The Creative Element*, London, 1909. Vicente Minelli, film director, *An American in Paris*, Chicago, 1913. Sir Peter Medawar, immunologist, Nobel Prize winner, Rio de Janiero, Brazil, 1915.

DIED: Alphonse de Lamartine, poet and statesman, *Jocelyn*, Passy, France, 1869. Henry James, novelist and man of letters, *The Portrait of a Lady, The Ambassadors*, Rye, Sussex, 1916. Arnold Dolmetsch, musical instrument maker, 1940. Maxwell Anderson, dramatist, 1959. Rajendra Prasad, Indian politician, Patna, India, 1963. Henry Luce, founded *Time, Fortune* and *Life* magazines, Phoenix, Arizona, 1967.

FEBRUARY 29

Leap Year Day, intercalated once every four years, that is if the year is exactly
divisible by four, and in centurial years only if they are exactly divisible by
400 (1800 and 1900 were not leap years, but 2000 will be). Were it not
for this intercalation the seasons and other natural periodic events would move
slowly backwards through the calendar year: 365 days is the length of
our calendar year, yet the Equinoctial or Tropical Year, the time the Earth
takes to complete a revolution of the Sun from equinox to equinox, is actually
365.242199 days. Thus a Leap Year makes up for the
discrepancy and keeps us 'on time.'
People born on 29 February celebrate their birthday on 28 February in Common
or non-Leap Years. The theory of the Julian Calendar is that a Leap Year
contains only 365 days, but the intercalated day comprises 'two natural days
in one civil day.' The statute of 21 Henry III, De Anno bissextili, shares
this thinking, 'the day of the leap year and the day before should be holden as
one day,' as do most government departments, insurance companies and other
agencies today. The Feast of St Oswald of Worcester, AD992. The only saint
ever to grace today's date, but it was not to last, his feast day was removed
to 28 February in the 1930s.

First ministry of Benjamin Disraeli begins, 1868. ¶ Cutting of the St Gothard
Tunnel completed, 1880. ¶ German fleet, is instructed to attack armed merchant
shipping without pre-warning, 1916. ¶ Nazi revolts in Finland begin, 1932.
¶ Heavy Allied bombing raids on Berlin, 1944. ¶ Islamic Republic proclaimed in
Pakistan, 1956. ¶ Dr Jocelyn Burnell announces the discovery of the first
pulsating radio source, or 'pulsar', at Cambridge, England, 1968.

BORN: Edward Cave, printer and publisher, began the *Gentleman's Magazine*,
near Rugby, 1692. Ann Lee, religious teacher, founded a colony of Shakers in
the US, Manchester, England, 1736. Karl von Baer, embryologist, Estonia, 1792.
Gioacchino Antonio Rossini, composer, *The Barber of Seville*, Pesaro, Italy, 1792.
John Philip Holland, US inventor, pioneered the modern submarine, County
Clare, 1840. William A. Wellman, film director, *The Ox-Bow Incident*, Brooklyn,
New York, 1896.

DIED: Archbishop John Whitgift, divine, London (?), 1604. Adolph Appia,
theatrical designer, 1928. Edward Frederic Benson, novelist, *The Dodo, The
Vintage*, 1940.

MARCH

In the pre-Julian Roman Calendar March was the
first month of the year, but Julius Caesar's calendar
reforms in 46BC made it the third. To the
Romans it was *Martius*, named in honour of the
god of war and battle, Mars.

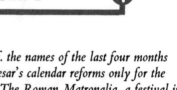

*The old Roman New Year's Day (cf. the names of the last four months
of the year), retained after Julius Caesar's calendar reforms only for the
computation of Roman military service. The Roman Matronalia, a festival in
honour of Juno, the queen of heaven and patroness of womanhood.
Dies Mala or 'Egyptian Day', considered unlucky in the Middle Ages.
St David's Day in Wales, the patron saint. Independence Movement Day,
Republic of Korea (1919). Heroes Day, Paraguay. Neuchâtel Independence Day,
Neuchâtel canton, Switzerland. Feasts of SS: David, or Dewi, bishop;
Felix II (III), pope; Albinus, or Aubin, of Angers, bishop; Swithbert, bishop;
Rudesind, or Rosendo, bishop.*

Massacre of Protestants at Vassy in France, 1562. ¶ The Jesuits are expelled from
Spain by Charles I, 1767. ¶ Francis II of Austria becomes Holy Roman Emperor,
1792. ¶ Ohio is made a US state (17th), 1803. ¶ Mehemet Ali massacres the
Mamelukes in Egypt and obtains supreme power throughout the kingdom,
1811. ¶ Annexation of Texas and admission into the Union agreed by US
Congress, 1845. ¶ Bellona (Asteroid 28) discovered by R. Luther and Amphitrite
(Asteroid 29) by Marth, 1854. ¶ Nebraska made a US state (37th), 1867. ¶ Oscar
Wilde applies for a warrant against the Marquis of Queensberry for alleged
criminal libel, 1895. ¶ Defeat of the Italians at Adowa by Ethiopian forces ends
Italian occupation, 1896. ¶ The 'February Revolution' in Russia ends, 1917.
¶ Woody Herman and his Orchestra record *Apple Honey* in New York, 1945.
¶ The International Monetary Fund begins operations, 1947. ¶ Hydrogen bomb
tests at Bikini Atoll by US, 1954. ¶ The exile of Archbishop Makarios ends with
his return to Cyprus, 1959. ¶ President Kennedy forms the Peace Corps of
Young Americans for overseas aid and service, 1961. ¶ The Soviet *Venus 3*
spacecraft touches down on Venus, 1966.

BORN: Sir Samuel Romilly, lawyer and reformer, London, 1747. Frederic
François Chopin, composer, Poland, 1810. Augustus Welby Pugin, Victorian
Gothic architect, London, 1812. Georg Simnel, philosopher and sociologist,
Berlin, 1858. Lytton Strachey, writer, a member of the Bloomsbury Group,
Eminent Victorians, Elizabeth and Essex, London, 1880. Roger Martin du Gard,
dramatist, novelist, Neuilly-sur-Seine, France, 1881. Oscar Kokoschka, Expres-
sionist artist, Austria, 1886. David Niven, actor, Kirriemuir, Scotland, 1910.
Robert Lowell, poet, Boston, Massachusetts, 1917.

DIED: Thomas Campion, musician and poet, 1620. George Herbert, poet and
clergyman, *The Temple*, near Salisbury, Wiltshire, 1633. Girolamo Frescobaldi,
organist and composer, 1643. Hermann Reimarus, philosopher, Germany, 1768.
George Grossmith, humorist, *The Diary of a Nobody* (with Weedon Grossmith),
London, 1912. Gabriele D'Annunzio, Italian writer, 'The Warrior Poet', 1938.

MARCH 2

Anniversary of the Battle of Adowa, Ethiopia (defeat of the Italian invaders in 1886).
Texas Independence Day, Texas, USA (a legal holiday).
Feast of the Martyrs under the Lombards. Feast of St Chad, or Caedda, bishop.

Spain declares the 'War of Oranges' with Portugal, 1801. ¶ Texas proclaims independence from Mexico, 1836. ¶ Texas secedes from the Union (readmitted 30 March 1870), 1861. ¶ Attempted assassination of Queen Victoria at Windsor by R. Maclean, 1882. ¶ Oil is nationalized in Mexico, 1937. ¶ Captain James Gallagher of the US Air Force and his crew of 13 complete the first round-the-world non-stop flight, in a little over 94 hours, 1949. ¶ The first crossing of the Antarctic, completed by (Sir) Vivian Fuchs and a British team (began the trek on 24 November 1957), 1958. ¶ Rhodesia is proclaimed a republic, 1970.

BORN: William Murray, 1st Earl of Mansfield, jurist, authority on commercial law, Scone, Perthshire, 1705. Samuel Houston, soldier, first President of the Republic of Texas, Rockbridge County, Virginia, 1793. Bedřich Smetana, composer, *The Bartered Bride*, Leitomischl, Bohemia (Czechoslovakia), 1824. Pope Pius XII, Rome, 1876. Ivar Kreuger, industrialist and forger, Sweden, 1880. Kurt Weill, composer, *The Threepenny Opera* (with Brecht), Dessau, Germany, 1900. Martin Ritt, film director, *Edge of the City*, New York City, 1920.

DIED: Louis de Rouvroy, Duc de Saint-Simon, nobleman and memoirist, Paris, 1755. John Wesley, evangelist and theologian, founder of Methodism, London, 1791. Horace Walpole, novelist and historian, *The Castle of Otranto, Anecdotes of Painting in England*, Twickenham, Middlesex, 1797. Heinrich Olbers, astronomer, discovered several comets and asteroids, Bremen, 1840. Ismail Pasha, Khedive of Egypt, responsible for selling shares in the Suez Canal to Britain, Constantinople (Istanbul), Turkey, 1895. David Herbert Lawrence, novelist and critic, *Sons and Lovers, The Rainbow*, 1930. Howard Carter, Egyptologist, discovered the tomb of Tutankhamun, 1939. Azorin, novelist, *The Villages*, Spain, 1967.

MARCH 3

Martyrs Day, Malawi (1959). Celebration of the Throne Day, Morocco.
Unity Day, Sudan. Feasts of SS: Marinus and Astyrius, martyrs;
Emeterius and Chelidonius, martyrs; Arthelais, virgin; Non, or Nonnita;
Winwaloe, or Guénolé, abbot; Anselm of Nonantola, abbot;
Cunegund, widow; Gervinus, abbot; Aelred, abbot.

Swiss defeat Charles the Bold at Granson, 1476. ¶ Fighting between civilians and soldiers in Boston (the 'Boston Massacre'), 1770. ¶ Florida made a US state (27th), 1845. ¶ Proposals to join the International Court of Justice are rejected by the US Senate, 1923. ¶ *Frenesi* recorded by Artie Shaw and his Orchestra in New York, 1940. ¶ Stalin is replaced by Bulganin as Defence Minister in the USSR, 1947. ¶ *Apollo 9* spacecraft launched from Cape Kennedy, 1969.

BORN: Edmund Waller, poet, *Go, Lovely Rose*, Coleshill, Hertfordshire, 1606. Thomas Otway, dramatist, *Venice Preserved*, Sussex, 1652. John Austin, jurist, Suffolk, 1790. William Macready, actor and theatrical manager, London, 1793. George Mortimer Pullman, industrialist and inventor of railway Pullman carriages, Brocton, New York, 1831. George Cantor, mathematician, worked on the theory of infinity, Germany, 1845. Alexander Graham Bell, inventor of the telephone and wax cyclindrical recording, Edinburgh, 1847. Alain, philosopher, *Les Propos d'Alain*, France, 1868. Sir Henry Wood, conductor and composer, co-founder of the Promenade Concerts, London, 1869. Edward Thomas, poet and writer, *Collected Poems, A Literary Pilgrimage through England*, Lambeth, London, 1878. Alexander Oparin, biologist, near Moscow, 1894. Jean Harlow, actress, Kansas City, 1911. Manning Clark, Australian historian and writer, *Short History of Australia*, 1915.

DIED: Robert Hooke, physicist, 1703. William Stukelye, antiquary and 'Arch-Druid', London, 1765. Robert Adam, architect and designer, 1792.

MARCH 4

Feasts of SS: Casimir of Poland; Lucius I, pope;
Adrian and his Companions, martyrs; Peter of Cava, bishop.

Henry VI of England deposed (Restored 9 October 1470), 1461. ¶ Accession of Edward IV of England (reigns, with interruptions, until 8 April 1483), 1461. ¶ First meeting of Congress in New York, 1789. ¶ Vermont enters the Union (14th), 1791. ¶ Angelina (Asteroid 64) discovered by M. Tempel, 1861. ¶ First electric tramcars run in London, at Leytonstone, 1882. ¶ The *Nautilus*, US atomic submarine, passes under the North Pole ice cap, 1958. ¶ The National Liberation Council is recognized by Britain as rightful government of Ghana, 1966. ¶ The first North Sea gas arrives ashore in Britain, off Durham, 1967. ¶ The *Eurydice*, a French submarine, is lost off the coast of Toulon in the Mediterranean, the whole crew of 57 perishes, 1970. ¶ Presidents of the United States of America were originally inaugurated on this day until Article XX, the 'Lame Duck Amendment', to the US Constitution became effective on 15 October 1933, after which 20 January was the appointed day.

BORN: Antonio Vivaldi, composer and violinist, *The Four Seasons, Concerto for flute, oboe and bassoon*, Venice, 1678. Giovanni Virginio Schiaparelli, astronomer and writer, Savigliano, Piedmont, 1835. Fritz Graebner, German sociologist, Berlin, 1877. Marlon Brando, actor, Omaha, Nebraska, 1924. James Clark, British racing driver, 1936.

DIED: Saladin, Muslim commander, Sultan of Egypt and Syria, Damascus, 1193. Jean François Champollion, Egyptologist, deciphered the Rosetta Stone, 1832. Antonin Artaud, stage director and dramatist, 1948. Sir Charles Sherrington, neurologist and physician, Eastbourne, Sussex, 1952. William Carlos Williams, physician and poet, *Journey to Love, Paterson*, Rutherford, New Jersey, 1963.

MARCH 5

National Day, Equatorial Guinea. Feasts of SS: Adrian and Eubulus, martyrs;
Phocas of Antioch, martyr; Eusebius of Cremona; Gerasimus, abbot;
Kieran, or Ciaran, of Saighir, bishop; Piran, abbot; Virgil of Arles, archbishop;
John Joseph of the Cross.

An uprising by Irish convicts at Castle Hill, New South Wales, is crushed by government troops, 1804. ¶ Covent Garden Theatre is destroyed by fire, 1856. ¶ Unsuccessful Fenian risings throughout Ireland, 1867. ¶ The railway line between Bombay and Calcutta is completed, 1870. ¶ German elections result in Nazi party winning nearly half of the seats, 1933.

BORN: Gerhardus Mercator, cartographer, Rupelmonde, Flanders, 1512. William Oughtred, mathematician and probable inventor of the slide rule, Eton, Buckinghamshire, 1575. Antoine de la Mothe Cadillac, soldier, founded the city of Detroit, Governor of Louisiana, France, 1658. Giovanni Battista Tiepolo, Venetian painter, Venice, 1696. James Madison, fourth President of the US (1809–17), Port Conway, Virginia, 1751. Sir Austen Henry Layard, archaeologist, excavated Nineveh, Paris, 1817. Sir Charles Wyville Thomson, zoologist, *The Depths of the Sea*, West Lothian, Scotland, 1830. Frank Norris, novelist, *McTeague*, *The Octopus*, Chicago, 1870. Rosa Luxembourg, socialist, Poland, 1871. William Henry Beveridge, wrote the Beveridge Report on social services, India, 1879. Laszlo Benedek, film director, *The Wild One*, Budapest, Hungary, 1907.

DIED: Antonio Corregio, Italian painter, 1534. Thomas Augustine Arne, composer of *Rule Brittania*, 1778. Flora Macdonald, Jacobite, Skye, 1790. Franz Mesmer, physician, hypnotist, Austria, 1815. Pierre Simon, Marquis de Laplace, astronomer and mathematician, Paris, 1827. Alessandro Volta, physicist, investigated electricity, Como, Lombardy (now Italy), 1827. Hippolyte Adolphe Taine, philosopher, historian and critic, *The Philosophy of Art*, *History of English Literature*, Paris, 1893. Edgar Lee Masters, poet and novelist, *Spoon River Anthology*, *Mirage*, Philadelphia, 1950. Sergei Prokofiev, composer, *Peter and the Wolf*, Moscow, 1953. Joseph Stalin, Soviet dictator, Moscow, 1953. William Cameron Menzies, film director and designer, *Things to Come*, California, 1957. Anna Akhmatova, Russian poet, 1966. Mohammed Mossadegh, Persian statesman and politician, Tehrán, 1967.

MARCH 6

Independence Day, Ghana (1951). Feasts of SS: Perpetua, Felicity and their Companions, martyrs; Fridolin, abbot; Cyneburga, Cyneswide and Tibba; Chrodegang, bishop; Balred and Bilfrid; Cadroe, or Cadroel, abbot; Ollegarius, or Oldegar, archbishop; Cyril of Constantinople; Colette, virgin.

York in Upper Canada is incorporated as a city under the name of Toronto, with W. L. Mackenzie as the first mayor, 1834. ¶ The Alamo in Texas falls to Mexican forces commanded by Santa Anna (Texas War of Independence), 1836. ¶ Servia is proclaimed a kingdom, 1882. ¶ From bases in Britain American bombers begin daytime attacks on Berlin, 1944. ¶ Cologne is taken by the Allies, 1945.

BORN: Michelangelo Buonarroti, Renaissance painter, sculptor and poet, Italy, 1475. Francesco Guicciardini diplomat, statesman and historian *History of Italy*, Florence, Italy, 1483. Cyrano de Bergerac, dramatist, model for a play by Rostand, Paris, 1619. Joseph von Fraunhofer, physicist and optician, Germany, 1787. Elizabeth Barrett Browning, poet, Durham, 1806. George Du Maurier, artist and novelist, *Trilby*, Paris, 1834. Nikolai Rimsky-Korsakov, composer and teacher, *Scheherazade, Russian Easter*, Tikhvin, Russia, 1844. Obafemi Awolowo, Nigerian politician, 1909.

DIED: Heliogabalus (Varius Avitus), Roman emperor; murdered with his mother, Julia Soaemias (some authorities insist that 11 March is a more likely date), 222. Hongi Hika, Ngapuhi War Chief of New Zealand, 1828. Davy Crockett, frontiersman; fell at the Alamo in Texas, 1836. John Stevens, lawyer, inventor and early US railway builder, Hoboken, New Jersey, 1838. Jean-Baptiste Girard, priest and educator, 1850. William Whewell, philosopher and writer, *History of the Inductive Sciences, Elements of Morality*, Cambridge, 1866. Artemus Ward (Charles Farrar Browne), US humorist and writer, *Babes in the Woods, Artemus Ward: His Book*, Southampton, Hampshire, England, 1867. Louisa May Alcott, novelist, 1888. Gottlieb Daimler, engineer and inventor, Germany, 1900. William Worrell Mayo, surgeon, a founder of the Mayo Clinic, Minnesota, 1911. John Philip Sousa, bandmaster and composer, *The Stars and Stripes Forever*, Reading, Pennsylvania, 1932. Oliver Wendell Holmes, Jr., jurist, US Supreme Court, *The Common Law*, 1935. Sir Halford John Mackinder, political geographer, *The Geographical Pivot of History*, Dorset, 1947. Zoltan Kodály, Hungarian composer, *The Peacock*, 1967. Pearl Buck, novelist, *The Good Earth, A House Divided*, 1973.

MARCH 7

'Feasts of SS: Thomas Aquinas, doctor; Paul the Simple; Drausius, or Drausin, bishop; Esterwine, abbot; Ardo; Theophylact, bishop.

War with Spain declared by France, 1793. ¶ Germany violates the Treaty of Versailles in occupying demilitarized zones in the Rhineland, 1936. ¶ *Things Ain't What They Used To Be* and *Squaty Roo* recorded by Johnny Hodges and his Orchestra in New York City, 1941. ¶ Abyssinia is entered by British forces, 1941. ¶ Flare-up of racial violence in Selma, Alabama, 1965.

BORN: Joseph Nicéphone Niepce, photographic inventor and pioneer, Châlons-sur-Marne, France, 1765. Alessandro Francesco Manzoni, poet and novelist, *The Betrothed*, Milan, 1785. Sir John Herschel, astronomer, Slough, Buckinghamshire, 1792. Sir Edwin Henry Landseer, painter, London, 1802. Henry Draper, astronomer, Virginia, 1837. Thomáš Masaryk, Czech statesman and philosopher, Hodonín, 1850. Piet Mondrian, abstract painter, co-founder of the De Stijl group, Netherlands, 1872. Maurice Ravel, composer, *Bolero, Daphnis et Chloé*, France, 1875.

DIED: Antonius Pius, Roman Emperor, 161. Jean Pierre Blanchard, balloonist and early aeronaut, the first man to cross the English Channel by air (with John Jeffries), 1809. Aristide Briand, French statesman, Nobel Prize for Peace, 1932. Herman Mankiewicz, scenarist, collaborated with Orson Welles on *Citizen Kane*, New York City, 1953. Percy Wyndham Lewis, painter and novelist, a founder of Vorticism, *The Apes of God*, London, 1957.

MARCH 8

Woman's Day, Cape Verde Islands. Syrian Revolution Anniversary,
Arab Republic of Egypt. Woman's Day, Guinea-Bissau. Decoration Day, Liberia.
National Day, Arab Republic of Libya. Sultan's Birthday,
Selangor State, Malaysia. International Woman's Day, People's
Republic of Mongolia. International Woman's Day, USSR.
International Woman's Day, Socialist Republic of Vietnam.
Feasts of SS: John of God; Pontius; Philemon and Apollonius, martyrs;
Senan, bishop; Felix of Dunwich, bishop; Julian of Toledo, archbishop;
Humphrey, or Hunfrid, bishop; Duthac, bishop; Veremund, abbot;
Stephen of Obazine, abbot.

Accession of Queen Anne of Great Britain (reigns until 1 August 1714), 1702. ¶ Cybele (Asteroid 65), originally named Maximiliana, discovered by M. Tempel, 1861. ¶ The *Merrimack*, a Confederate frigate, sinks the Union's *Cumberland* in Hampton Roads, 1862. ¶ Without the authority of Congress, President Woodrow Wilson orders arming of US merchant ships, 1917. ¶ Beginning of the 'February Revolution' in Russia (ends on 14 March), 1917.[1] ¶ Dusseldorf and other towns on the Ruhr occupied by French troops after Germany fails to make first reparation payments, 1921. ¶ Nearly 4,000 US Marines lands in South Vietnam, 1965.

BORN: Carl Philipp Emanuel Bach, German composer, a son of J. S. Bach, Weimar, 1714. Oliver Wendell Holmes, Jr., jurist, US Supreme Court, *The Common Law*, Boston, Massachusetts, 1841. Kenneth Grahame, author, *The Wind in the Willows*, Edinburgh, 1859. Frederic William Goudy, printer and type designer, Illinois, 1865. Otto Hahn, chemist and physicist, discovered nuclear fission, Germany, 1879.

DIED: Francesco Sforza, *condottiere* (soldier of fortune), fought against and for Venice, Milan and the Pope, Milan, 1466. William III, Prince of Orange, King of England, London, 1702. Abraham Darby, iron founder and industrialist, Worcester, 1717. Sir William Chambers, architect, designed Somerset House in London, *A Treatise on Civil Architecture*, 1796. Hector Berlioz, composer, *Harold in Italy*, 1869. Millard Fillmore, thirteenth President of the US, New York, 1874. John Ericsson, inventor of the screw propeller, 1889. Graf Ferdinand von Zeppelin, airship pioneer, an officer in the German Army, Charlottenburg, near Berlin, 1917. Sherwood Anderson, novelist, *Winesburg, Ohio, Dark Laughter*, 1941.

[1] These are the Gregorian, or New Style dates. It was not until 1918 that Russia reformed its (Julian) calendar and adopted the system that is now used by most nations throughout the world. The Old Style dates are 23 February — 1 March, hence the '*February* Revolution'.

MARCH 9

Baron Bliss Day, Belize. Feasts of SS: Frances of Rome, widow;
Pacian, bishop; Gregory of Nyssa, bishop; Bosa, bishop;
Catherine of Bologna, virgin; Dominic Savio.

Napoleon Bonaparte marries Joséphine de Beauharnais, 1796. ¶ The war between Mexico and France is ended, 1839. ¶ The Confederate *Merrimack* is forced to withdraw at Hampton Roads by the Union's vessel *Monitor*, 1862. ¶ General Ulysses S. Grant is appointed General-in-Chief of Union forces, 1864. ¶ Great snow storms throughout southern England, many wrecks and a great loss of life in the Channel, near-hurricanes off Dover and Plymouth, about 14 ships lost in total, over 60 people perish (storms last until 13 March), 1891. ¶ The Russians are defeated at Mukden by the Japanese, 1905. ¶ Éamon de Valéra is elected President of Ireland, 1932. ¶ Deportation by the British of Archbishop Makarios from Cyprus, 1956.

BORN: Honoré Mirabeau, politician, a member of the National Assembly at the beginning of the French Revolution, France, 1749. William Cobbett, writer and politician, *Rural Rides*, Surrey, 1763. Modest Petrovich Mussorgsky, composer, *Pictures from an Exhibition*, *Night on the Bare Mountain*, Karevo, Russia, 1839. Edward Goodrich Acheson, US industrial chemist, discovered 'Carborundum', 1856. Ernest Bevin, politician and Minister of Labour during World War Two, Somerset, 1881. Vyacheslav Molotov, Bolshevik and politician, co-founder of *Pravda*, Vyatka Province, Russia, 1890. Victoria Sackville-West, novelist, poet and critic, *All Passion Spent*, *The Land*, Knole Castle, Kent, 1892. David Smith, sculptor, Decatur, Indiana, 1906. Samuel Barber, composer, *Adagio for Strings*, West Chester, Pennsylvania, 1910. Mickey Spillane, popular novelist, Brooklyn, New York, 1918. Yury Gagarin, Soviet test-pilot and cosmonaut, 1934. Bobby Fischer, American chess champion, 1943.

DIED: Jules Mazarin, cardinal and statesman, Vincennes, France, 1661. William I, King of Prussia, Emperor of Germany, Berlin, 1888. Frank Wedekind, dramatist and actor, *Spring's Awakening*, *Pandora's Box*, Munich, Germany, 1918.

Labour Day, Republic of Korea. Governor's Birthday, Malacca State, Malaysia.
Feast of the Forty Martyrs of Sebastea. Feasts of SS: Codratus and his
Companions, martyrs; Macarius of Jerusalem, bishop; Simplicius, pope;
Kessog, bishop and martyr; Anastasia Patricia, virgin;
Droctoveus, or Drotté, abbot; Himelin.

Completion of the re-building of the temple at Jerusalem after the Jewish captivity, 515BC. ¶ Zanzibar recognized by France and Britain, 1862. ¶ Velasquez's painting known as the 'Rokeby Venus' is damaged in the National Gallery by suffragettes, 1914. ¶ The conviction of the syndicalist Eugene Debs for espionage is upheld by the US Supreme Court, 1919. ¶ James Earl Ray (alias Eric Starvo Galt) pleads guilty to the murder of Martin Luther King, in Memphis, 1969. ¶ A Japanese soldier is discovered on Lubang Island in the Philippines who believed that World War II was still continuing, 1974.

BORN: Ferdinand I, Austrian Holy Roman Emperor, 1503. Marcello Malpighi, physiologist, microscopist, 1628. Tamara Karsavina, ballerina, St Petersburg, 1885. Arthur Honegger, composer, *King David, Pacific 231*, France, 1892. Bix Beiderbecke, early jazz cornetist and composer, *In a mist*, Iowa, 1903. HRH Prince Edward Antony Richard Louis, third son of Queen Elizabeth II, 1964.

DIED: Giuseppe Mazzini, Italian patriot, Pisa, Italy, 1872. Sir Charles Wyville Thomson, zoologist, scientific director of the *Challenger* voyage, *The Depths of the Sea,* West Lothian, Scotland, 1882. Mikhail Afanasyevich Bulgakov, dramatist and novelist, *The White Guard*, Moscow, 1940. Jan Masaryk, Czech Foreign Secretary, Prague, 1948. Frank O'Connor (Michael O'Donovan), short-story writer, *Guests of the Nation, An Only Child*, Dublin, 1966.

MARCH 11

Feasts of SS: Constantine, martyr; Sophronius, bishop; Vindician, bishop; Benedict of Milan, archbishop; Oengus, abbot-bishop; Eulogius of Cordova, martyr; Aurea, virgin; Teresa Margaret Redi, virgin.

Peace Treaty with Tippoo of Mysore signed by Britain, 1784. ¶ Maori risings in New Zealand against the British, 1845. ¶ The southern states assembled at the Montgomery Convention approve a draft of the permanent Confederate constitution, 1861. ¶ The Bradfield reservoir in Sheffield bursts and over 250 people are drowned in the flooding, 1864. ¶ British blockade of Germany begins, 1915. ¶ Éamon de Valéra resigns as head of the Sinn Fein, 1926. ¶ Foundation of the Bank of Canada, 1935. ¶ The Lend-Lease Bill is finally passed by Congress and signed, 1941. ¶ Eruptions of Mount Etna in Sicily, 1974.

BORN: Torquato Tasso, poet, *Jerusalem Delivered, Aminta*, Sorrento, Italy, 1544. Urbain Le Verrier, astronomer, co-discoverer of Neptune, Saint Lô, France, 1811. Marius Petipa, choreographer and ballet director, Marseilles, France, 1819. Sir Malcolm Campbell, set land and water speed records, Kent, 1885. Henry Cowell, experimental modern composer, California, 1887. Raoul Walsh, film director, *High Sierra, White Heat*, New York City, 1892. Dorothy Gish, actress, Ohio, 1898. Lawrence Welk, bandleader, North Dakota, 1903. Harold Wilson, British Labour politician and Prime Minister, Huddersfield, Yorkshire, 1916. Geoffrey Blainey, Australian historian and writer, *Tyranny of Distance*, 1930.

DIED: Heliogabalus (Varius Avitus), Roman Emperor; murdered with his mother, Julia Soaemias (some authorities insist that 6 March is a more likely date), 222. Sir Alexander Mackenzie, explorer in Canada, the Mackenzie River is named after him, Perth, Scotland, 1820. Benjamin West, American painter, President of the Royal Academy, London, 1820. Rolf Boldrewood (pseudonym of T. A. Browne), popular writer, *Robbery Under Arms*, 1915. Frederich Wilhelm Murnau, film director, *Nosferatu, Sunrise*; in a road accident, California, 1931. Sir Alexander Fleming, Scottish bacteriologist, 1955. Richard Byrd, aviator and polar explorer, the first man to fly across the North Pole, 1957. Erle Stanley Gardner, popular writer, creator of Perry Mason, 1970.

MARCH 12

*Feast of the Renovation, Gabon Republic (commemorating the founding
of the Democratic Party in 1968). Independence Day, Mauritius (gained from
Britain, 1968). Feasts of SS: Gregory the Great, pope and doctor;
Maximilian, martyr; Peter, Gorgonius and Dorotheus, martyrs;
Paul Aurelian, bishop; Theophanes the Chronicler, abbot;
Alphege of Winchester, bishop; Bernard of Capua, bishop; Fina, or Seraphina, virgin.*

Johann Gutenberg, the German printer, pays a wine tax of one guilder on his
extensive cellar (in 1439 it is recorded that he had over 400 gallons of wine),
1444. ¶ James II lands in Scotland, 1689. ¶ A Provincial Committee of Cor-
respondence for action against the British is appointed by the Virginia House of
Burgesses, 1773. ¶ Bordeaux taken by the Duke of Wellington, 1814. ¶ The
Sikhs surrender to the British at Rawalpindi, 1849. ¶ Annexation of Basutoland
by Britain, 1868. ¶ Amalthoea (Asteroid 113) discovered by R. Luther, 1871.
¶ Mahatma Gandhi begins a campaign of civil disobedience in India, 1930.
¶ A speed limit of 30mph is introduced for towns and other built-up areas in
Britain, 1935. ¶ The 'Truman Doctrine' (for US aid to countries threatened by
communism) delivered to Congress by President Truman, 1947. ¶ Independence
of Mauritius declared, 1968.

BORN: John Aubrey, antiquary and writer, *Brief Lives*, 1626. Thomas Augustine
Arne, composer of *Rule Brittania*, London, 1710. John Frederic Daniell, chemist,
inventor of an electric cell, London, 1790. Gustav Robert Kirchoff, physicist,
made the first spectroscope, Prussia, 1824. Sir William Henry Perkin, chemist,
discovered the first artificial dye, London, 1838. Adolph Simon Ochs, newspaper
proprietor, bought the *New York Times*, Cincinnati, Ohio, 1858. Gabriele
D'Annunzio, writer, 'The Warrior Poet', Italy, 1863. William Rivers, anthropologist, *History of Melanesian Society*, near Chatham, Kent, 1864. Vaslav
Nijinsky, ballet dancer and choreographer, associated with Diaghilev, Kiev,
Russia, 1890. Jack Kerouac, novelist, *On the Road*, Lowell, Massachusetts, 1922.

DIED: St Gregory the Great, Church Father and Pope, Rome, 604. Alessandro
Magnasco, Genoese painter, 1749. Bedřich Smetana, composer, *The Bartered
Bride*, Prague, 1884. George Westinghouse, inventor, mechanic and industrialist,
patented the Westinghouse railway brake, New York City, 1914. Hilaire,
Comte de Chardonnet, invented rayon, 1924. Sun Yat-Sen, Chinese nationalist
and revolutionary, founded the Kuomintang Party, Peking, China, 1925.
Edward Scripps, journalist, founded the US newspaper chain; at sea, off Liberia,
1926. Ivar Kreuger, industrialist and forger, 1932.

Feasts of SS: Euphrasia, or Eupraxia, virgin; Mochoemoc, abbot;
Gerald of Mayo, abbot; Nicephorus of Constantinople, bishop; Ansovinus, bishop;
Heldrad, abbot; Roderic and Solomon, martyrs.

Lancastrians defeated by the Yorkists at the battle of Stamford, 1470.
¶ Huguenots defeated at Jarnac, 1569. ¶ The planet Uranus discovered by Sir
William Hershel (who originally named it Georgium Sidus, after George III),
1781. ¶ The Confederate Congress agrees to the recruitment of slaves into the
army, 1865. ¶ Assassination of Czar Alexander II of Russia by a bomb, 1881.
¶ Bloemfontein taken by forces under the command of Frederick Roberts,
1900. ¶ Dr Lee de Forest demonstrates a sound motion-picture system, in
New York, 1923. ¶ The Popular Front ministry is formed in France by Léon
Blum (it lasts until 10 April), 1938. ¶ The *Olympic Bravery* breaks in two on the
French coast near Brest, 1976.

BORN: Joseph II, King of Germany and Holy Roman Emperor, Vienna, 1741.
Charles, Earl Grey, Whig statesman and Prime Minister, Falloden, Northumber-
land, 1764. Percival Lowell, astronomer, *Mars and its Canals*, Boston, 1855.
Hugo Wolf, *Lieder* composer, Windischgraz, Austria, 1860. Ramón Menéndez
Pidal, literary historian and linguist, *The Cid and his Spain*, La Coruña, Spain,
1869. Henry Hathaway, film director, *Lives of a Bengal Lancer*, Sacramento,
California, 1898. George Seferis, poet and critic, Turkey, 1900.

DIED: Nicolas Boileau-Despréaux, poet and critic, *Le Lutrin*, 1711. John
Frederic Daniell, English chemist, inventor of an electric cell, 1845. Benjamin
Harrison, US President, San Francisco, 1901. Lucien Lévy-Bruhl, philosopher
and psychologist, Paris, 1939. Stephen Vincent Benet, poet, 'John Brown's
Body', 1943. Karl Haushofer, German officer and geographer; suicide, 1946.

MARCH 14

Feasts of SS: Leobinus, or Lubin, bishop;
Eutychius, or Eustathius, martyr; Matilda, widow.

Peter of Castile defeated at Montiel, 1369. ¶ Henry IV defeats the League at Ivry (Yvres), 1590. ¶ First appearance of the Asiatic cholera in Ireland, at Belfast, 1832. ¶ (Sir) Samuel Baker discovers and names Lake Albert (Nyanza), assumed to be another source of the River Nile, 1864. ¶ The *Monarch* lays the first submarine telephone line across the English Channel, 1891. ¶ The 'February Revolution' in Russia ends (began 8 March. *See* Footnote for 8 March above), 1917. ¶ The *New English Bible* New Testament was published by Oxford and Cambridge University Presses, 1961. ¶ Jack Ruby is convicted of murdering Lee Harvey Oswald (presumed assassin of President John F. Kennedy) and is sentenced to death, by jury in Dallas, Texas, 1964.

BORN: Sir Lander Brunton, pharmacologist and physician, *The Action of Medicines*, Roxburgh, 1844. Paul Ehrlich, German bacteriologist, 1854. Vilhelm Bjerknes, meteorologist, Oslo, 1862. Albert Einstein, physicist, formulated Relativity Theory, Germany, 1879.

DIED: John Byng, British Admiral; shot for allegedly neglecting his duty, 1757. Friedrich Klopstock, German poet and dramatist, 1803. Karl Marx, philosopher and economist, *The Communist Manifesto, Das Kapital*, London, 1883. George Eastman, photographic pioneer, 1932. Nikolai Ivanovic Bukharin, Soviet journalist and politician; executed in Moscow, 1938. Klement Gottwald, Czech Communist dictator, 1953. Busby Berkeley, film choreographer, *Gold-diggers of 1933, 42nd Street*, 1976.

*The Roman festival of Anna Perenna, the goddess of the circle of the year,
celebrated near the first milestone on the Via Flaminia. The Birthday of
J. J. Roberts, Liberia (first President, 1809–65). Youth Day, Zambia.
Feasts of SS: Longinus, martyr; Matrona, virgin and martyr;
Zachary, pope; Leocritia, or Lucretia, virgin and martyr;
Louisa de Marillac, widow; Clement Hofbauer.*

Assassination of Julius Caesar by Brutus and others in Rome, 44BC. ¶ Columbus returns to Spain after his first expedition, 1493. ¶ Americans defeated at Battle of Guilford Court House, North Carolina, by Cornwallis, 1781. ¶ Maine joins the Union (23rd), 1820. ¶ An annular eclipse, observed well at Oundle, 1858. ¶ Diana (Asteroid 78) discovered by R. Luther, 1863. ¶ Peitho (Asteroid 118) discovered by R. Luther, 1872. ¶ The office of *The Times* in London is nearly blown up by Irish-American terrorists, 1883. ¶ German forces occupy Moravia and Bohemia, 1939. ¶ *Expo '70* is formally opened in Japan, 1970. ¶ Asylum is granted in Brazil to ex-President Spinola of Portugal, 1975.

BORN: Andrew Jackson, army general and US President, Waxhaw, North Carolina, 1767. William Lamb, 2nd Viscount Melbourne, Victorian statesman and Prime Minister, London, 1779. Lady Augusta Gregory, dramatist and writer, County Galway, Ireland, 1852. Emil von Behring, physician and immunologist, Nobel Prize winner, Germany, 1854.

DIED: Gaius Julius Caesar, Emperor, writer and soldier; assassinated, 44BC. Odoacer, German barbarian leader, Ravenna, Italy, 493. Luigi Cherubini, operatic composer, 1842. James Sylvester, mathematician, London, 1897. Sir Henry Bessemer, metallurgist, a pioneer of the mass production of cheap steel, 1898. Howard Phillips Lovecraft, writer of ghost and horror stories, Providence, Rhode Island, 1937. Nevil Sidgwick, chemist, Oxford, 1952. Arthur Holly Compton, American physicist, 1962. Aristotle Onassis, Greek ship-owner, 1975.

MARCH 16

Feasts of SS: Julian of Antioch, martyr; Abraham Kidunaia;
Finnian Lobhar, abbot; Eusebia, abbess; Gregory Makar, bishop;
Heribert, archbishop.

Accession of Queen Margaret of Scotland (some authorities favour 19 March. Reigns until the end of September 1290), 1285. ¶ Edward II defeats the Barons at Boroughbridge, 1322. ¶ First launching of a liquid-fuelled rocket, by Dr Robert Goddard in the US, 1926. ¶ Reintroduction of compulsory military service in Germany, 1935. ¶ The *New English Bible* Old Testament is published by the Oxford and Cambridge University Presses, 1961. ¶ $350-million bill to fight poverty is presented to Congress by President Johnson, 1964.

BORN: Pieter Hooft, historian and poet, Amsterdam, 1581. Georg Ohm, physicist, chiefly remembered for his work on electricity, Bavaria, 1787. Camilo Castelo Branco, Portuguese novelist, Lisbon, 1825. Friedrich Brugmann, philologist, Germany, 1849. Maksim Gorky, Russian novelist and dramatist, *The Lower Depths*, 1868. Robert Rossen, film director, *All the Kings' Men*, New York City, 1908.

DIED: Tiberius Claudius Nero, Roman emperor, Capri, 37. Giovanni Pergolesi, composer, Italy, 1736. Robert Surtees, novelist and sports writer, *Jorrocks' Jaunts and Jollities*, *Mr Sponge's Sporting Tours*, Brighton, Sussex, 1864. Modest Petrovich Mussorgsky, composer, *Pictures from an Exhibition*, *Night on the Bare Mountain*, St Petersburg, 1881. Aubrey Beardsley, artist and illustrator, 1898. J. J. R. Macleod, discoverer of the insulin treatment for diabetes, Aberdeen, 1935. Selma Lagerlöf, novelist, *The Wonderful Adventures of Nils*, Sweden, 1940. Constantin Brancusi, sculptor, *Bird in Space*, 1957. William Henry Beveridge, established labour exchanges in Britain and wrote the Beveridge Report on social services, 1963. Thomas Dewey, American Republican politician, 1971.

Popularly regarded in the Middle Ages as the day Noah entered the Ark.
World Maritime Day, commemorating the founding of the Inter-Governmental
Maritime Consultancy Organization of the UN in 1978.
St Patrick's Day, Ireland (patron saint); celebrated too in parts of USA,
New York has an annual parade down Fifth Avenue. Evacuation Day,
Massachusetts, USA. Feasts of SS: Joseph of Arimathea; The Martyrs
of the Serapeum; Agricola bishop; Gertrude of Nivelles, virgin;
Paul of Cyprus.

Caesar defeats Pompey's supporters at Munda, 45BC. ¶ The British are forced to evacuate Boston by George Washington, 1776. ¶ Venetian Republic declared, 1848. ¶ Psyche (Asteroid 16) discovered by de Gasparis, 1852. ¶ The Second Maori War begins in New Zealand, 1860. ¶ Germany is prevented from gaining membership of the League of Nations by Spain and Brazil, 1926. ¶ End of the battle for Iwo Jima with US victory (began 19 February), 1945 ¶ *Vanguard I* spacecraft launched at Cape Canaveral by US, 1958. ¶ Tibetans rise against the occupying Chinese. The Dalai Lama escapes to India, 1959. ¶ Violent anti-Vietnam demonstrations outside the American Embassy in London, over 300 people are arrested, 1968. ¶ The *Amoco Cadiz* oil-tanker runs aground on the coast of Brittany (a total of 220,000 tons of crude oil are subsequently disgorged), 1978.

BORN: Jean Nattier, portrait painter, Paris, 1685. Roger Brooke Taney, politician and jurist, Chief Justice of the US Supreme Court, Calvert County, Maryland, 1777. Gottlieb Daimler, engineer and inventor, Germany, 1834. Kate Greenaway, writer and illustrator of children's books, London, 1846. Charles Francis Brush, devised the arc lamp, Ohio, 1849. Margaret Grace Bondfield, the first woman Cabinet member in Britain (1929), Somerset, 1873. Bobby Jones, champion golfer, Georgia, 1902. Nat King Cole, jazz pianist and singer, Montgomery, Alabama, 1919. Rudolf Nureyev, ballet dancer, defected to the West in 1961, Irkutsk, Russia, 1938.

DIED: Marcus Aurelius (Aurelius Antoninus Marcus Aelius), Roman Emperor and military commander, wrote the *Meditations*, Sirmium, Vindobona, 180. Ibn Khaldun, Arab historian, Tunis (?), 1406. François, Duc De La Rochefoucauld, courtier and writer, *Maximes*, France, 1680. Daniel Bernoulli, mathematician, studied the motions of fluids, 1782. Friedrich Bessel, astronomer and mathematician, 1846. Christian Doppler, physicist (the 'Doppler effect'), 1853. Robert Chambers, publisher and author, *A Book of Days*, St Andrews, Scotland, 1871. Franz Brentano, German philosopher, 1917. Isaak Babel, novelist, *Red Cavalry*, 1941.

*The Feast of King Edward of the West Saxons, BCP, not retained in
the 1928 revision. Feasts of SS: Cyril of Jerusalem, archbishop and doctor;
Alexander of Jerusalem, bishop and martyr; Frigidian, or Frediano,
bishop; Edward the Martyr; Anselm of Lucca, bishop; Salvator of Horta.*

Murder of King Edward the Martyr, 979. ¶ Execution of Charnock, King, and
Keyes for attempted assassination of William III of England, 1696. ¶ The
Tolpuddle labourers are sentenced to transportation for swearing oath to
Robert Owen's Grand National Consolidated Trades Union, 1834. ¶ The
synagogue in Great Portland Street, London, founded by Baron Rothschild,
1869. ¶ Beginning of the Commune rising in Paris, 1871. ¶ Austria (Asteroid
136) discovered by J. Palisa, 1874. ¶ First communications over the London-
Paris telephone line, by the Prince of Wales and President Carnot of France,
1891. ¶ Winnecke's Comet observed in Europe, 1892. ¶ Phoebe (IX), a
satellite of Saturn, discovered by Professor Pickering, in Arizona, 1899. ¶ French
religious orders are dissolved, 1903. ¶ Assassination of King George I of Greece
at Salonika, 1913. ¶ Gandhi is sentenced to six years' imprisonment as a result of
civil disobedience, 1922. ¶ Papal Encyclical on the theme of Atheistic Communism, 1937. ¶ The first walk in space, by Lieutenant-Colonel Leonov of the
USSR from the satellite *Voshkod*, 1965. ¶ The *Torrey Canyon* wrecked on the
Pollard Rock between Cornwall and the Scilly Isles, it subsequently disgorges
over 30,000 tons of crude oil, 1967. ¶ *Apollo 10* spacecraft launched from Cape
Kennedy for rehearsal of Moon landing, 1969. ¶ British troops parachuted on to
St John's Island, Antigua, in the Caribbean, 1969. ¶ Assassination of President
Ngouabi of the Republic of the Congo, 1977.

BORN: Marie, Comtesse de La Fayette, novelist, *La Princesse de Clèves*, Paris,
1634. Grover Cleveland, US President, New Jersey, 1837. Stéphane Mallarmé,
Symbolist poet, *L'Après-midi d'un faune*, Paris, 1842. Rudolf Diesel, German
inventor and engineer, Paris, 1858. Neville Chamberlain, statesman and Prime
Minister, signatory of the Munich Agreement, Birmingham, 1869. Kurt Koffka,
Gestalt psychologist, Berlin, 1886. Wilfred Owen, poet of the First World War,
Poems, Oswestry, Shropshire, 1893. Lavrenti Beria, secret-police chief under
Stalin, Russia, 1899.

DIED: Ivan IV (Ivan the Terrible), Tsar of Russia, 1584. Sir Robert Walpole,
Whig statesman and British 'prime minister', London, 1745. Laurence Sterne,
novelist and clergyman, *The Life and Opinions of Tristram Shandy, A Sentimental
Journey through France and Italy*, London, 1768. Pierre Berthelot, organic chemist,
1907. Eleutherios Venizelos, statesman and Prime Minister of Greece, Paris,
1936. William De Mille, film and theatre producer, writer, *Hollywood Saga*,
California, 1955. Farouk I, King of Egypt, in exile, Italy, 1965.

*First day of the Roman festival of Minerva, goddess of wisdom and
good counsel, that lasted until 23 March. Feasts of SS: Joseph;
John of Panaca; Landoald and his Companions; Alcmund, martyr.*

The first eclipse recorded in history, it was lunar and was observed by the
Babylonians (according to Ptolemy), 721BC. ¶ Napoleon lays siege to Acre,
1799. ¶ Second Maori War ends in New Zealand, 1861. ¶ The British Syndicalist
Tom Mann is arrested for sedition, 1912. ¶ The Versailles Treaty is rejected by
the US Senate, 1920. ¶ Fletcher Henderson and his Orchestra record *Sugar Foot
Stomp*, 1931. ¶ British and US oil sources expropriated by Mexico, 1938.

BORN: Georges de La Tour, painter, France, 1593. Nikolay Gogol, novelist and
dramatist, *Dead Souls*, Russia, 1809. Sir Richard Burton, explorer and writer,
discovered Lake Tanganyika, Devon, 1821. Sergei Diaghilev, ballet and theatre
impresario, Russia, 1872. Sir John Hubert Marshall, archaeologist, discovered
the Indus Valley Civilization, Cheshire, 1876. Joseph Albers, German abstract
painter, 1888. Earl Warren, Chief Justice of the US Supreme Court, chairman of
the President's Commission on the Assassination of President John F. Kennedy
(the 'Warren Report'), Los Angeles, California, 1891.

DIED: Robert Cavelier de La Salle, explorer of the Mississippi; murdered, New
Mexico (?), 1687. Arthur James Balfour, British statesman, 1930. Edgar Rice
Burroughs, popular writer, creator of Tarzan, 1950. Gheorghe Gheorghiu-Dej,
Rumanian Premier, 1965.

MARCH 20

Vernal Equinox (or 21 March). The Roman festival of Minerva (see 19 March). Independence Day, Tunisia. Feasts of SS: Photina and her Companions, martyrs; Martin of Braga, archbishop; Cuthbert, bishop; Herbert; Wulfram, archbishop; The Martyrs of Mar Saba.

The French proclaim the Republic in Rome, 1798. ¶ The Burlington Arcade in London is opened, 1819. ¶ The anniversary of the first revolution of Uranus since its discovery is celebrated by astronomers throughout the world (84 years and 7 days to complete one orbit), 1865. ¶ Patricia Hearst is found guilty of armed bank robbery, 1976.

BORN: Publius Ovidius Naso (Ovid), Latin poet, *Ars Amatoria* (*The Art of Love*), Sulmo, 43BC. Jean Antoine Houdon, sculptor, Versailles, France, 1741. Johann Friedrich Holderlin, poet, Lauffen, Germany, 1770. Henrik Ibsen, poet and dramatist, *The Wild Duck*, *Hedda Gabler*, Skien, Norway, 1828. Sergei Rachmaninov, composer and virtuoso pianist, *Rhapsody on a Theme of Paganini*, Onega, Russia, 1873. Hugh MacLennan, novelist, *Two Solitudes, The Watch that Ends the Night*, Nova Scotia, 1907. Sir Michael Redgrave, actor, Bristol, 1908.

DIED: Sir Isaac Newton, mathematician, physicist and astronomer, *Philosophiae Naturalis Principia Mathematica*, London, 1727. William Murray, 1st Earl of Mansfield, jurist, authority on commercial law, 1793. Lajos Kossuth, Hungarian revolutionary and leader, Turin, Italy, 1894. Lord Curzon, statesman, Viceroy of India, 1925. Ferdinand Foch, military commander, Marshall of France, 1929. Henry Handel Richardson (Henrietta Richardson), Australian novelist, *The Fortunes of Richard Mahony* (a trilogy), 1946. C. Wright Mills, Marxist sociologist, *The Power Elite*, 1962. Brendan Behan, playwright and novelist, *The Quare Fellow*, 1964.

Vernal Equinox (or 20 March). The Roman festival of Minerva (see 19 March). New Year's Day, Afghanistan. Discovery Day, Guam. New Year's Day and Feast of Nowrooz, Iran (Spring Festival). National Tree Planting Day, Lesotho. Feasts of SS: Benedict, abbot; Serapion of Thmuis, bishop; Enda, abbot, and Fanchea, virgin.

Accession of Henry V of England (reigned until 31 August 1422), 1413. ¶ Abercromby defeats the French at Alexandria, 1801. ¶ Great earthquakes in Spain, 1829. ¶ Second battle of the Somme begins with German offensive, 1918. ¶ *All of Me* is recorded by Billie Holiday and her Orchestra in New York City, 1941. ¶ Massacre of Africans at Sharpeville by South African police, 1961. ¶ Major Israeli assault on Jordan, Karameh is taken, 1968.

BORN: Johann Sebastian Bach, 'Genesis: 1, 1' (H. L. Mencken's description of Bach's musical importance), 1685. Claude-Nicolas Ledoux, architect, France, 1736. Jean Baptiste Fourier, mathematician and physicist, France, 1768. Benito Juarez, revolutionary, President of Mexico, Oajaca, Mexico, 1806. Sir John Abbott, Canadian Prime Minister, St Andrews, Lower Canada, 1821. Florenz Ziegfeld, theatrical producer and impresario, Chicago, 1869. Hans Hofmann, American Abstract Expressionist painter, Germany, 1880. Erich Mendelsohn, architect, Allenstein (now Olsztyn, Poland), 1887. Sir Bernard Freyberg, Governor-General of New Zealand, 1889. Peter Brook, stage director, director of the Royal Shakespeare Company, London, 1925.

DIED: Thomas Cranmer archbishop and liturgist; burnt at the stake, Oxford, 1556. James Usher (or Ussher) Archbishop of Armagh, divine and scholar, *Annales Veteris et Novi Testamenti*, Reigate, Surrey, 1656. Jean Baptiste Greuze, artist, France, 1805. Robert Southey, poet and writer, *The Curse of Kehama*, *Thalaba*, *Life of Nelson*, Keswick, Cumberland, 1843. Michael Todd, American film producer, *Around the World in 80 Days*, 1958.

The Roman festival of Minerva (see 19 March). Arab League Day,
observed by numerous Arab states. Emancipation Day, Puerto Rico
(abolition of slavery, 1873). Feasts of SS: Paul of Narbonne;
Basil of Ancyra, martyr; Deogratias, bishop;
Benvenuto of Osimo, bishop; Nicholas von Flue.

The English defeated by the Scots at Anjou, 1421. ¶ First demonstration of cinematograph film, by Lumière in Paris (claims for earlier dates have been made but not verified), 1895. ¶ *East St Louis Toodle-oo* is recorded by Duke Ellington and his Orchestra, 1927. ¶ Attempted abduction of Princess Anne in The Mall, London, 1973.

BORN: Maximillian I, King of Germany, Holy Roman Emperor, Austria, 1459. William I, King of Prussia, Emperor of Germany, Berlin, 1797. Robert Andrews Millikan, physicist, measured the charge of the electron, Illinois, 1868. Marcel Marceau, mime and actor, Strasbourg, 1923.

DIED: Jean-Baptiste Lully, composer, Paris, 1687. John Canton, experimented with electricity, a fellow of the Royal Society, London, 1772. Johann Wolfgang von Goethe, German poet, novelist, dramatist, 1832.

MARCH 23

The Roman festival of Minerva (see 19 March). Pakistan Day, Pakistan (republic proclaimed in 1956). Feasts of SS: Victorian and his Companions, martyrs; Benedict the Hermit; Ethelwald the Hermit; Joseph Oriol.

The first known example of printing in Canada, the *Halifax Gazette*, produced by John Bushell in Nova Scotia, 1752. ¶ The Stamp Act is passed by Parliament for taxing the American Colonies, 1765. ¶ First tram-cars in London at Bayswater go into operation (designed by Mr Train of New York), 1861. ¶ Bishop Lee executed by firing squad in Utah for his part in a massacre of settlers at Mountain Meadows by members of the Mormon Church (on 18 September 1857), 1877. ¶ The free steam-ferry at Woolwich in London is opened by Lord Rosebery, 1889. ¶ Paris is shelled by Germans from a distance of over 70 miles, 1918. ¶ Adolf Hitler is granted dictatorial powers until April 1937, 1933. ¶ The *Savannah* was launched at Camden in New Jersey, the world's first nuclear-powered merchant vessel, 1962. ¶ Astronauts Virgil Grissom and John Young manoeuvre US spaceship *Gemini III* while orbiting, 1965. ¶ The Pope meets the Archbishop of Canterbury in the Sistine Chapel, the first meeting between the leaders of their two respective churches in 400 years, 1966.

BORN: Pierre Simon, Marquis de Laplace, astronomer and mathematician, near Trouville, France, 1749. William Smith, geologist and surveyor, *Observations on the Strata of England and Wales*, Churchill, Oxfordshire, 1769. Franklin Giddings, sociologist, *Studies in the Theory of Human Society*, Connecticut, 1855. Michael Joseph Savage, first Labour Prime Minister of New Zealand, 1872. Juan Gris, Cubist painter, Madrid, 1887. Cedric Gibbons, film designer, *Ben Hur*, Dublin, 1893. Erich Fromm, American psychoanalyst and writer, *Fear of Freedom*, Germany, 1900. Frank Sargeson, novelist, *I Saw in My Dreams*, Hamilton, New Zealand, 1903. Joan Crawford, motion-picture actress, Texas, 1908. Akira Kurosawa, Japanese film director, *The Seven Samurai, Throne of Blood*, Tokyo, 1910. Wernher von Braun, rocket engineer for Germany and America, 1912. Donald Malcolm Campbell, winner of water speed records, 1921. Roger Bannister, athlete, doctor, ran the mile in 3 minutes, 59.4 seconds (in 1954), Harrow, 1929.

DIED: Elizabeth I of England (reigned 1558–1603), 1603. Stendhal (Marie Henri Beyle), novelist, *The Red and the Black, The Charterhouse of Parma*, Paris, 1842. Raoul Dufy, Fauvist artist, 1953.

MARCH 24

Feasts of SS: Gabriel the Archangel; Irenaeus of Sirmium, bishop and martyr; Aldemar, abbot; Catherine of Vadstena, virgin; Simon of Trent and William of Norwich.

Accession of James I of England (James VI of Scotland), 1603. ¶ Murder of Czar Paul of Russia (after lengthy mental derangement), 1801. ¶ Concordia (Asteroid 58) discovered by R. Luther, 1860. ¶ Dr Livingstone appointed British Consul for the African Interior, 1865. ¶ Greece is formally declared a Republic, 1924.

BORN: Michael Adrianszoom de Ruyter, Dutch naval commander, Flushing, Netherlands, 1607. Joseph Lioville, mathematician, discovered transcendental numbers, Saint Omer, France, 1809. William Morris, painter, poet, printer and designer, *News from Nowhere*, Walthamstow, Essex, 1834. Olive Schreiner, novelist, *The Story of an African Farm*, Cape Colony (now in South Africa), 1855. Ub Iwerks, film animator, the man who *drew* Mickey Mouse, Kansas City, 1901. Thomas Dewey, US Republican politician, Michigan, 1902.

DIED: John Harrison, watch-maker, invented the chronometer, London, 1776. Bertel Thorwaldsen, sculptor, Copenhagen, 1844. Henry Wadsworth Long-fellow, poet, *Hiawatha*, Cambridge, Massachusetts, 1882. Sir Edwin Arnold, poet and scholar, 1904. Jules Verne, writer of Scientific romances, *Journey to the Centre of the Earth, Twenty-thousand Leagues under the Sea*, Amiens, France, 1905. John Millington Synge, dramatist, *The Playboy of the Western World, The Tinker's Wedding*, Dublin, 1909. Enrique Granados, composer and pianist, 1916. Mrs Humphry Ward (Mary Augustus Arnold), novelist, *Robert Elsmere, The Marriage of Robert Elsmere*, London, 1920. Auguste Piccard, deep-sea explorer and balloonist, Lausanne, 1962.

MARCH 25

The Feast of the Annunciation of the Blessed Virgin Mary,
celebrating the angel Gabriel visiting the Virgin and telling her that
the Word of God has become flesh, 'the begetting of Christ';
liturgically celebrated in Rome since the 7th century, but much earlier in origin;
known also as Our Lady's Day or Lady Day, and in England it is a
Quarter Day. New Year's Day in England (and some Catholic countries)
from the 12th century until 1752. Anniversary of Chuquisaca,
a department of Bolivia. Independence Day, Greece. Maryland Day, Maryland,
USA (a legal holiday). The Feast of the Good Thief, the thief who was
crucified with Christ, known as Gestas or Dismas. Feasts of SS:
Barontius; Hermenland, abbot; Alfwold, bishop; Lucy Filippini, virgin.

Accession of Robert I of Scotland (reigns until 7 June 1329), 1306. ¶ Titan (VI), a satellite of Saturn, discovered by Christian Huyghens, 1655. ¶ Tuscany occupied by French troops, 1799. ¶ I. K. Brunel's Thames Tunnel for pedestrians, linking Rotherhithe with Wapping, is formally opened, 1843. ¶ Italian troops enter Ethiopia, 1895. ¶ Treaties signed in Rome for the Common Market and Euratom by the 'Six', 1957. ¶ An acre of Runnymede, where the Magna Carta was signed in 1215 (15 June), is set aside by the British government as a memorial to President John F. Kennedy, 1964. ¶ Resignation of Field Marshall Ayub Khan as President of Pakistan, replaced by General Yahya Khan who declares martial law, 1969. ¶ Assassination of King Faisal of Saudi Arabia in Riyadh, by his nephew, Prince Museid, 1975.

BORN: Giovanni Amici, astronomer and optician, Italy, 1786. Alexander Ivanovich Herzen, journalist and political theorist, *From the Other Shore*, Moscow, 1812. Béla Bartok, composer, *Bluebeard's Castle*, Hungary, 1881. David Lean, film director, *The Bridge on the River Kwai*, Croydon, near London, 1908. Simone Signoret, actress, Germany, 1921.

DIED: Novalis (Friedrich Leopold Freiherr von Hardenburg), German Romantic poet and novelist, *Hymnen an die Nacht*, *Heinrich von Ofterdingen*, Weissenfels, Germany, 1801. Caroline Chisholm, Australian social worker and reformer, 1877. Frédéric Mistral, Provençal poet, *Lou Pouème dou Rose, Lis Isclo d'or*, Nobel Prize for Literature, France, 1914. Claude Debussy, Impressionist composer, 1918. John Drinkwater, poet and critic, *Abraham Lincoln*, London, 1937.

Independence Day, Bangladesh (1971). Feasts of SS: Castalus, martyr;
Felix of Trier, bishop; Macartan, bishop; Braulio, bishop;
Ludger, bishop; Basil the Younger.

The first British Sunday newspaper published, *The British Gazette and Sunday Monitor*, 1780. ¶ Consecration of the synagogue in Duke's Place, London, 1790. ¶ The Holy Roman Empire formally declares war on France, 1793. ¶ First sighting of Vulcan, a supposed inter-Mercurial planet (reported several times over the next twenty years, now believed to have been a 'rogue asteroid'), 1859. ¶ The Paris Commune is formally established, 1871. ¶ First cremation in England, at Woking, 1886. ¶ Adrianople in Turkey taken by the Bulgarians, 1913. ¶ The British Road Traffic Act introduces driving tests for motor owners, 1934. ¶ The seven men accused of the £2½ million 'Great Train Robbery' (8 August 1963) are found guilty in London, 1964. ¶ Hué falls to the North Vietnamese, 1975.

BORN: Konrad von Gesner, physician, writer, *A Catalogue of Animals*, Zurich, 1516. Sir Benjamin Thompson Rumford, physicist and inventor, founded the Royal Institution in London, Woburn, Massachusetts, 1753. William Edward Hartpole Lecky, historian, *History of the Rise and Influence of the Spirit of Rationalism in Europe*, Dublin, 1838. George Smith, Assyriologist, deciphered many cuneiform scripts, originally a bank-note engraver, *Assyrian Discoveries*, London, 1840. Alfred Edward Housman, poet, classical scholar and translator, *A Shropshire Lad*, Worcestershire, 1859. Sir Gerald Du Maurier, theatrical actor-manager, London, 1873. Robert Frost, American poet, 1874. Wilhelm Backhaus, classical pianist, Leipzig, 1884. Palmiro Togliatti, leader of the Italian Communist Party, Genoa, 1893. Jean Epstein, film director, *L'Or des Mers*, *La Chute de la Maison Usher*, Warsaw, Poland, 1897. Tennessee Williams, dramatist and short story writer, *A Streetcar Named Desire*, *Cat on a Hot Tin Roof*, Columbus, Mississippi, 1911. Pierre Boulez, French composer and conductor, 1925.

DIED: Sir John Vanbrugh, soldier and architect, designed Blenheim Palace, playwright, *The Relapse*, *The Provok'd Wife*, Whitehall, London, 1726. Ludwig van Beethoven, composer, Bonn, Germany, 1827. Thomas Hancock, British inventor, made notable developments in the production and application of elastic and rubber, 1865. Walt Whitman, poet and essayist, *Leaves of Grass*, Camden, New Jersey, 1892. Cecil John Rhodes, colonialist, founder of Rhodesia, Premier of Cape Colony, Muizenberg, Cape Colony, 1902. Sarah Bernhardt, actress, 1923. David Lloyd George, statesman and British Prime Minister, Wales, 1945. Max Ophüls, film director, *Lola Montès*, Hamburg, 1957. Raymond Chandler, detective novelist, *The Big Sleep*, 1959. Sir Noel Coward, actor, entertainer, playwright, 1973.

MARCH 27

Resistance Day, Burma. Feasts of SS: John Damascene, doctor; John of Egypt.

Accession of Charles I of Great Britain (beheaded at Whitehall, 30 January 1649), 1625. ¶ The Peace of Amiens is signed by Britain and France, 1802. ¶ France declares war on Russia, 1854. ¶ Violent earthquakes in Alaska and tidal waves along the Pacific coast of the US, 1964. ¶ France introduces 'summer time', to be two hours ahead of Greenwich Mean Time, and one hour ahead of European Standard Time, 1976. ¶ Two Boeing 747 jumbo-jets collide on the runway of the airport at Tenerife in the Canary Islands, and over 550 people are killed, 1977.

BORN: Alfred de Vigny, poet, novelist and playwright, *Les Destinées, Chatterton*, Loches, France, 1797. George Eugene Haussmann, architect and civil servant responsible for the re-planning of Paris, Paris, 1809. Wilhelm Konrad von Röntgen, physicist, discovered X-rays, Lennep, Rhenish Prussia, 1845. Heinrich Mann, novelist, *Man of Straw*, Germany, 1871. James Cruze, film director, *The Covered Wagon*, Ogden, Iowa, 1884. Ludwig Mies van der Rohe, architect, Aarchen, Germany, 1886. Ferdé Grofe, composer and arranger, *Grand Canyon Suite*, New York City, 1892. Karl Mannheim, sociologist and philosopher, *Ideology and Utopia*, Budapest, 1893. Draža Mikhailović, Serbian nationalist and guerrilla, Serbia, 1893. Budd Schulberg, scenarist and novelist, *What makes Sammy run?*, New York City, 1914.

DIED: James I, King of England, Theobalds, Hertfordshire, 1625. Giovanni Battista Tiepolo, Venetian painter, Madrid, 1770. Sir George Gilbert Scott, architect, designed St Pancras Station (London), London, 1878. John Bright, statesman and reformer, 1889. Henry Brooks Adams, historian, *America's Economic Supremacy*, 1918. Sir James Dewar, physicist, inventor of the vacuum flask, 1923. Arnold Bennett, novelist and critic, *Anna of the Five Towns*, 1931. Michael Joseph Savage, first Labour Prime Minister of New Zealand, 1940.

MARCH 28

Dies Mala or *'Egyptian Day'*, *considered unlucky in the Middle Ages.*
Evacuation Day, Arab Republic of Libya (celebrating the withdrawal of
British troops in 1951).
Feasts of SS: John of Capistrano; Guntramnus; Tutilo.

John Wilkes becomes Member of Parliament for Middlesex, 1768. ¶ The
Coercive Acts against Massachusetts are passed by Parliament in London, 1774.
¶ Irish Parliament passes Act of Union with England, 1800. ¶ Pallas (Asteroid 2)
discovered by Olbers, 1802. ¶ Britain declares war on Russia, 1854. ¶ First
electric lights installed in Westminster Palace, 1878. ¶ Great storm and a tidal
wave in Wellington, New Zealand, cause considerable damage, 1888.
¶ Constantinople to be known as Istanbul and Angora as Ankara after Turkish
proclamation, 1930. ¶ The surrender of Madrid to the rebel forces under General
Franco signals the end of the Spanish Civil War, 1939. ¶ The raid on St Nazaire
on the French coast by British commandos, 1942. ¶ Last German V rocket lands
in Britain, 1945. ¶ Archbishop Makarios is released by the British on the condition that he will not return to Cyrpus, 1957. ¶ Devastating earthquake in Chile,
1965. ¶ Colonel Yuri Gagarin is killed in a jet aeroplane crash, to the north of
Moscow, 1968. ¶ A great earthquake in western Turkey, over 1000 deaths, 1970.

BORN: Raphael, Renaissance artist, Urbino, Italy, 1483. St Teresa of Avila,
Carmelite nun and mystic, *El castillo interior* (*The Interior Castle*), *Life*, Avila,
Castile (Spain), 1515. Johann Amos Comenius, Moravian theologist and writer,
Czechoslovakia, 1592. Alexandre Herculano, poet, historian and politician,
Lisbon, Portugal, 1810. Aristide Briand, French statesman, Nobel Prize for
Peace, 1862. Corneille Heymans, physician, Nobel Prize winner, Ghent,
Belgium, 1892. Dame Flora Robeson, actress, South Shields, Northumberland,
1902. Dirk Bogarde, actor, Hampstead, London, 1921.

DIED: Helvius Pertinax, Roman emperor; murdered by the Praetorian Guard,
193. Waldemar the Victorious, King of Denmark, Denmark, 1241. Peg
Woffington, Irish actress, London, 1760. William Thornton, architect, designed
the Capitol building in Washington, Washington D.C., 1828. Virginia Woolf,
novelist and critic, *To the Lighthouse*, *The Waves*; suicide by drowning, near
Rodmell, Sussex, 1941. Sergei Rachmaninov, composer and virtuoso pianist,
Rhapsody on a Theme of Paganini, Beverly Hills, California, 1943. Stephen
Leacock, economist and humorous writer, *Moonbeams from the Larger Lunacy*,
Canada, 1944. Dwight David Eisenhower, American statesman and soldier,
1969.

*A 'Borrowed Day'; a folk belief was that the last three days of March
had been taken from April. Memorial Day, Malagasy Republic.
Youth Day, Taiwan. Feasts of SS: Jonas and Barachisius, martyrs;
Mark of Arethusa, bishop, and Cyril, martyr; Armogastes, Archinimus
and Saturus, martyrs; Gundleus and Gwladys; Rupert, bishop;
Berthold; Ludolf, bishop.*

The Yorkist defeat the Lancastrians at Towton, 1461. ¶ The Helvetian Republic
is proclaimed, 1798. ¶ After a proclamation by Dessalines many thousands of
white people are massacred on San Domingo, 1804. ¶ Vesta (Asteroid 4)
discovered by Olbers, 1807. ¶ Annexation of the Punjab by Britain, 1849.
¶ President Abraham Lincoln orders the preparation of an expedition to relieve
Fort Sumter, 1861. ¶ Britain cedes the Ionian Island to Greece, 1864. ¶ The
Royal Albert Hall in London is opened by Queen Victoria, 1871. ¶ Over-
whelming support for the Nazi candidates in the German elections, 1936.
¶ President de Gaulle launches the first French nuclear submarine, 1967.
¶ Charles Manson and three of his 'family' are sentenced to death for murder on
several counts, 1971. ¶ Lieutenant William Calley is found guilty of massacring
the villagers of My Lai in South Vietnam (in March 1968), 1971. ¶ The last US
troops leave Vietnam, 1973.

BORN: John Tyler, US President, Charles City County, Virginia, 1790. Arturo
Toscanini, musician and conductor, Parma, Italy, 1867. Sir Edwin Landseer
Lutyens, architect, London, 1869.

DIED: Emmanuel Swedenborg, scientist, philosopher and mystic, *Heaven and
Hell, Divine Love and Divine Wisdom*, London, 1772. Jean, Marquis de Condorcet,
French philosopher, politician; in prison, 1794. John Jacob Astor, millionaire,
1848. John Keble, poet and clergyman, a founder of the Oxford Movement,
Bournemouth, 1866. Paul Emile Botta, archaeologist in Mesopotamia, 1870.
Georges Seurat, 'pointillist' painter, Paris, 1891. Robert Falcon Scott, Antarctic
explorer; returning from the South Pole, Antarctica, 1912.

MARCH 30

A 'Borrowed Day' (see 29 March). Feasts of SS: Regulus, or Rieul, bishop; John Climacus, abbot; Zosimus, bishop; Osburga, virgin.

Joseph Bonaparte is made King of Naples, 1806. ¶ Allied forces enter Paris, 1814. ¶ Alaska is sold by Russia to the US, 1867. ¶ Texas readmitted to the Union (ceded 2 March 1861), 1870. ¶ 15th Amendment (Article XV) to the Constitution of the US becomes effective, 1870. ¶ Ethiopia and Somali meet and agree on a cease-fire in the border dispute, 1964. ¶ The first Chinese civilian airliner to land in the US arrives at Kennedy Airport from Peking, 1974. ¶ Da Nang falls to the North Vietnamese, 1975.

BORN: Maimonides, Jewish philosopher, *Guide of the Perplexed*, Cordoba, 1135. Francisco José Goya y Lucientes, painter, Spain, 1746. Charles Booth, social reformer, *Life and Labour of the People in London*, Liverpool, 1840. Vincent Van Gogh, painter, Netherlands, 1853. Sean O'Casey, dramatist and writer, *Juno and the Paycock*, *The Plough and the Stars*, Dublin, 1880. Melanie Klein, child psychologist, Vienna, 1882.

DIED: Sébastien Le Prestre de Vauban, statesman and military engineer, Marshal of France, near Avallon, France, 1707. William Hunter, obstetrician and anatomist, 1783. Rudolph Steiner, educationalist and writer, Switzerland, 1925. Friedrich Bergius, inventor of a process for extracting petrol from coal, 1949. Léon Blum, socialist statesman, French Prime Minister, 1950.

MARCH 31

End of the British Financial Year. A 'Borrowed Day' (see 29 March).
Transfer Day, Virgin Islands (sold to the US by Denmark,
effective on this day in 1917). Feasts of SS: Balbina, virgin;
Acacius, or Achatius, bishop; Benjamin, martyr; Guy of Pomposa, abbot.

The Roman Emperor Gaius Aurelius Valerius Diocletianus (Diocletian) issues an Edict against the Manicheans, 297. ¶ Quebec and Montreal in Canada are incorporated as cities, 1831. ¶ First US–Japan treaty, 1854. ¶ All property of the clergy is sequestrated in Mexico, 1856. ¶ Harmonia (Asteroid 40) discovered by R. Luther, 1856. ¶ The Eiffel Tower is inaugurated at the Universal Exhibition of Arts, Manufactures, etc. in Paris by Premier Tirard, 1889. ¶ Disestablishment of the Church of Wales, 1920. ¶ British miners' strike begins, 1921. ¶ Support for Poland pledged by France and Britain, 1939. ¶ The Marshall Aid Act is passed by US Congress, 1948. ¶ The Dominion of Canada accepts Newfoundland as a province, 1949. ¶ After escaping from Chinese-occupied Tibet the Dalai Lama is granted political asylum by India, 1959.

BORN: René Descartes, philosopher, *Discourse on Method*, 1596. Franz Joseph Haydn, composer, *Creation, Seasons*, Rohrau, Austria, 1732. Edward Fitzgerald, poet, translator of *Omar Khayyám*, Suffolk, 1809. Robert Bunsen, chemist, inventor of the burner named after him, Germany, 1811. Alexander Ostrovsky, dramatist, *The Bankrupt, The Diary of a Scoundrel, The Storm*, Moscow, 1823. Robert Hamer, film director, *Kind Hearts and Coronets*, Kidderminster, Worcestershire, 1911.

DIED: Francis I of France (reigned 1515–47), 1547. Philip of Hesse, Landgrave of Hesse, Hesse, Germany, 1567. John Donne, English poet and divine, London, 1631. John Constable, landscape painter, 1837. Charlotte Brontë, novelist, *Jane Eyre*, 1855. Antoine Cournot, mathematician and economist, 1877. John Pierpont Morgan, industrialist and banker, Rome, 1913. Emil von Behring, physician and immunologist, Nobel Prize winner, 1917. Medardo Rosso, sculptor, Milan, 1928.

APRIL

The Romans called this month *Aprilis*, which is
taken as deriving from *aperire* meaning to open,
an allusion to Spring. Many writers on the calendar
have been unable to accept this, as to do so
means that April would stand alone amongst all
the months in having as an origin a specific
reference to natural conditions. As this month
was dedicated to Venus, the goddess of love, it
has prompted some authorities to see a derivation
from *Aphrilis*, the Romanized form of *Aphrodite*,
the Greek name for the same goddess.

APRIL 1

*The whole of April was sacred to the Roman goddess Venus who is associated
with love and fertility. Beginning of the British Financial Year.
All Fools Day or April Fools Day, popular for practical jokes and conceits
since the 17th century. Youth Day, Popular Republic of Benin.
Feasts of SS: Melito, bishop; Walaricus, or Valéry, abbot;
Macarius the Wonder-worker; Hugh of Grenoble, bishop;
Hugh of Bonnevaux, abbot; Gilbert of Caithness, bishop;
Catherine of Palma, virgin.*

Hanover is seized and Britain declares war on Prussia, 1806. ¶ The title
'Commonwealth of Australia' is adopted by convention, 1891. ¶ The London–
Paris Telephone line is officially opened to the public, 1891. ¶ Founding of the
Air Battalion of the Royal Engineers in Britain, 1911. ¶ The British Royal Air
Force comes into being, absorbing the Royal Flying Corps (formed 1912), 1918.
¶ The persecution of the Jews begins in Germany, 1933. ¶ The London County
Council Green Belt Scheme to protect the countryside around London comes
into operation, 1935. ¶ US recognizes Franco's rebel government in Spain, 1939.
¶ Invasion of Okinawa by US forces begins (lasts until 20 June), 1945. ¶ US
launch *Tiros 1*, the world's first meteorological satellite, 1960. ¶ After 114 days
the New York newspaper strike comes to an end, 1963.

BORN: William Harvey, physician, discovered the circulation of the blood,
Folkestone, Kent, 1578. L'Abbé Prévost (Antoine Prévost d'Exiles), novelist,
journalist and translator, *Manon Lescaut*, Hesdin, France, 1697. Jean Portalis,
jurist, principally responsible for drafting the *Code Napoleon*, Le Beausset,
France, 1746. Prince Otto von Bismarck, militarist and statesman, Brandenburg,
Germany, 1815. Sir Truby King, founder of the Plunket Society, New
Plymouth, New Zealand, 1858. Ferrucio Busoni, pianist and composer, Tuscany,
1866. Edmond Rostand, dramatist, *Cyrano de Bergerac*, *L'Aiglon*, Marseilles,
1868. Lon Chaney, film actor, Colorado, 1883, Leonard Bloomfield, linguistic
scholar, *Language*, Chicago, 1887. Edouard Tissé, cinematographer, worked for
Eisenstein on *Battleship Potemkin* and *Alexander Nevsky*, 1897.

DIED: Eleanor of Aquitaine, Queen of France, 1204. Tamerlane, conqueror of
Persia, Mesopotamia and parts of Russia, 1405. Robert III, King of Scotland,
Paisley, 1406. Dr John Langhorne, writer and translator, Somerset, 1779.
Dr Isaac Milner, theologian and mathematician, Kensington, London, 1820.
Ferenc Molnár, Hungarian dramatist, *The Guardsman*, New York City, 1952.
Lev Davidovitch Landau, Soviet physicist, 1968. Max Ernst, Surrealist painter
and sculptor, 1976.

APRIL 2

Feasts of SS: Francis of Paola; Apphian and Theodosia, martyrs;
Mary of Egypt; Nicetius, or Nizier, bishop.

Charter granted to the Royal Society in London, 1663. ¶ British annexation of the Punjab, 1849. ¶ The first Parliament in Italy meets at Turin, 1860. ¶ Hecuba (Asteroid 108) discovered by R. Luther, 1869. ¶ The first Canadian census records a population of 3,689,257 persons, 1871. ¶ A mail-sack containing $265,000 of American Telephone and Telegraph Corporation stock is stolen in New York City, 1964.

BORN: Charlemagne, Holy Roman Emperor, 742. Hans Christian Anderson, writer, *Fairy Tales*, Denmark, 1805. William Holman Hunt, painter, a member of the Pre-Raphaelite Brotherhood, London, 1827. Emile Zola, novelist and critic, *Nana, Germinal*, Paris, 1840. Max Ernst, Surrealist painter and sculptor, Germany, 1891. Sir Alec Guinness, actor, London, 1914.

DIED: Honoré Mirabeau, politician, a member of the National Assembly at the beginning of the French Revolution, Paris, 1791. Sir James Clark Ross, Polar explorer, discovered the North magnetic pole, *Voyage of Discovery*, Aylesbury, Buckinghamshire, 1862. Richard Cobden, politician, a founder of the Anti-Corn Law League, 1865. Samuel Morse, artist and inventor of the Morse Code, New York City, 1872. Jean Epstein, film director, *L'Or des Mers, La Chute de la Maison Usher*, Paris, 1953, C. S. Forester, popular novelist, *Hornblower* series, 1966. Georges Pompidou, President of France, Paris, 1974.

APRIL 3

*Feasts of SS: Pancras of Taormina, bishop and martyr; Sixtus, or
Xystus, I, pope and martyr; Agape, Chionia and Irene, virgins and martyrs;
Burgundofara, or Fare, virgin; Nicetas, abbot; Richard of Chichester, bishop.*

Accession of Malcolm III of Scotland (reigns until 13 November 1093), 1057.
¶ Execution of Sir John Friend and Sir William Parkyns for attempted assassination of William III of Great Britain, 1696. ¶ The Prussians overrun Hanover, 1801. ¶ Richmond in Virginia falls to General Grant, 1865. ¶ Althoea (Asteroid 119) discovered by J. C. Watson, 1872. ¶ The Suffragette leader Mrs Emily Pankhurst is sentenced for inciting a number of her supporters to place explosives at the London residence of David Lloyd George, 1913. ¶ Two aeroplanes fly over Mount Everest, 1933.

BORN: George Herbert, poet and clergyman, *The Temple*, Montgomery Castle, Wales, 1593. Washington Irving, essayist and historian, *A History of New York*, New York, 1783. James Barry Munnik Hertzog, Afrikaans nationalist, Prime Minister of South Africa; Wellington, Cape Colony, 1866. Allan Dwan, film director, *Robin Hood* (1922), Toronto, 1885. Henry Luce, founded *Time*, *Fortune* and *Life* magazines, China, 1898. Doris Day, singer and actress, Ohio, 1924.

DIED: John Napier, inventor of logarithms, Merchiston Castle, Edinburgh, 1617. Bartolomé Murillo, painter, Seville, Spain, 1682. Erik Johan Stagnelius, poet and writer, Stockholm, Sweden, 1823. Jesse James, cowboy outlaw and robber, 1882. Johannes Brahms, composer, 1897. Kurt Weill, composer, *The Threepenny Opera* (with Brecht), New York City, 1950.

APRIL 4

Liberation Day, Hungary (1945). National Holiday, Senegal.
Commemoration of the Battle of Naefels, Glarus canton, Switzerland (the
Austrian army defeated by the Swiss, 1388). Feasts of SS:
Isidore of Seville, bishop and doctor; Agathopus and Theodulus, martyrs;
Tigernach, bishop; Plato, abbot; Benedict the Black.

Accession of James I of Scotland, 1406. ¶ Sir Francis Drake is knighted by Queen Elizabeth I, 1581. ¶ Calypso (Asteroid 54) discovered by R. Luther, 1858. ¶ The discovery of gold in the Yukon is announced, 1896. ¶ Proclamation of the Chinese Republic in Tibet, 1912. ¶ The International Civil Aviation Organization (ICAO) of the United Nations established, 1947. ¶ The North Atlantic Treaty is signed in Washington by representatives of 11 countries, 1949. ¶ Assassination of Martin Luther King, black civil rights leader, in Memphis (James Earl Ray alias Eric Starvo Galt later arrested in London), 1968.

BORN: Grinling Gibbons, English sculptor, 1648. Sir William Siemens, inventor, scientist and industrialist, Lenthe, Prussia, 1823. Rémy de Gourmont, writer, *A Night in the Luxembourg*, France, 1858. Maurice Vlaminck, Fauvist painter, Paris, 1876. Marguerite Duras, French novelist and scenarist, 1914.

DIED: Alfonso X (the Wise), King of Castile and Leon, 1284. Oliver Goldsmith, author, *The Vicar of Wakefield*, London, 1774. William Henry Harrison, US President, Washington D.C., 1841. Carl Benz, pioneer of early motor cars, 1929. André Michelin, industrialist, built the first factories for the mass-production of rubber motor tyres, Paris, 1941. Martin Luther King, civil rights leader, Nobel Prize for Peace; assassinated, Memphis, Tennessee, 1968.

APRIL 5

End of the British Income Tax Year. Ching Ming Festival, Hong Kong.
Arbor Day, Republic of Korea. Ching Ming Festival, Taiwan.
Feasts of SS: Vincent Ferrer; Derfel Gadarn; Ethelburga of Lyminge, matron;
Gerald of Sauve-Majeure, abbot; Albert of Montecorvino, bishop.

The 'Addled' Parliament remonstrates with James I and is dissolved by him, 1614.
¶ Themis (Asteroid 24) discovered by de Gasparis, 1853. ¶ Oscar Wilde is
arrested for offences arising from his friendship with Lord Alfred Douglas, at
the Cadogan Hotel, Sloane Square, London, 1895. ¶ Attempted assassination of
Albert Edward, Prince of Wales, in Brussels by a 15-year old youth, Sipido,
1900. ¶ Completion of the German withdrawal on the Western Front (began
4 March), 1917. ¶ Éamon de Valéra becomes the Sinn Fein president, 1919.
¶ Major offensive against Batistá's Cuban government by Fidel Castro and his
supporters, 1958. ¶ First trials of driverless, automatic trains on the London
Underground system, 1964. ¶ Rioting by blacks throughout the US following
the assassination of Martin Luther King (4 April), 1968.

BORN: Thomas Hobbes, philosopher, *Leviathan*, Malmesbury, Wiltshire, 1588.
Giovanni Jacopo Casanova, adventurer, lover, romancer, Venice, 1724. Jean
Honoré Fragonard, landscape painter, France, 1739. Joseph Lister, surgeon,
campaigned for antiseptic surgery, London, 1827. Algernon Charles Swinburne,
poet and writer, *Atlanta in Calydon, Songs Before Sunrise*, London, 1837. Spencer
Tracy, actor, Wisconsin, 1900. Bette Davis, motion-picture actress, Massa-
chusetts, 1908. Herbert von Karajan, conductor, Salzburg, Austria, 1908.
Gregory Peck, actor, La Jolla, California, 1916.

DIED: John Winthrop, Puritan and lawyer, the first Governor of the Massachusetts Bay Colony, Boston, Massachusetts, 1649. Georges-Jacques Danton,
French revolutionary; guillotined, 1794. Robert Raikes, founded and promoted
Sunday schools, Gloucester, 1811. Paul Vidal de la Blache, geographer, France,
1918. Douglas MacArthur, military commander, Supreme Allied Commander
in Japan after the Second World War, Washington D.C., 1964. Howard Hughes,
aircraft manufacturer, film director and industrialist, 1976.

APRIL 6

Beginning of the British Income Tax Year. Patriots Victory Day, Ethiopia. Chakri Memorial Day, Thailand. The Feast of the 120 Martyrs of Persia. Feasts of SS: Marcellinus, martyr; Celestine I, pope. Eutychius, bishop; Prudentius, bishop; William of Eskill, abbot.

Earthquake felt in London, St Paul's and other churches badly damaged, 1580. ¶ Jan van Riebeeck lands at the Cape in South Africa to establish a relay station for the Dutch East India Company, 1652. ¶ The establishment of the Committee of Public Safety, under Danton, in France, 1793. ¶ Badajoz falls to British forces, 1812. ¶ Phocaea (Asteroid 25) discovered by Chacornac, 1853. ¶ Circe (Asteroid 34) discovered by Chacornac, 1855. ¶ Vancouver in British Columbia is founded by the Canadian Pacific Railway Company, 1886. ¶ Commander R. E. Peary arrives at the North Pole, 1909. ¶ The US declares war on Germany, 1917. ¶ Britain and US sign agreement on *Polaris* missile, 1963. ¶ I.R.A. bombings throughout London, and in Manchester and Birmingham, 1974.

BORN: Maximilien de Robespierre, lawyer, a leader of the French Revolution, Arras, France, 1758, Harry Houdini, escapologist and magician, exposer of Spiritualist and other fakes, Wisconsin, 1874. Anthony Herman Fokker, aeronautical engineer, Java, 1890. Sir John Betjeman, writer and Poet Laureate, London, 1906. James Watson, geneticist, constructed the first model DNA molecule, with Francis Crick, Nobel Prize winner, Chicago, 1928.

DIED: Matthias Corvinus, King of Hungary, Vienna, 1490. Raphael, Renaissance artist, Rome, 1520. Albrecht Dürer, painter and engraver, Nuremberg, Germany, 1528. Niels Henrik Abel, Norwegian mathematician, 1829. Giovanni Pascoli, poet, *Myricae, Canti di Castelvecchio*, Bologna, Italy, 1912. Edwin Arlington Robinson, poet, *Tilbury Town, Captain Craig*, New York City, 1935. Jules Bordet, bacteriologist, Nobel Prize for Medicine, 1961. Igor Stravinsky, composer, *The Firebird, The Rite of Spring*, New York City, 1971.

APRIL 7

World Health Day (World Health Organization).
Mozambican Woman's Day, People's Republic of Mozambique.
Feasts of SS: Hegesippus; Aphraates; George the Younger of Mitylene, bishop;
Celsus, or Ceallach, archbishop; Aybert.

The Crucifixion of Christ (this seems the most likely of the many dates proposed. *See* Alexander Philip's *The Calendar*, Cambridge, 1921, for a résumé of the evidence), 30. ¶ Richard Turpin the highwayman executed at York, 1739. ¶ General Ulysses S. Grant, despite great losses and unpreparedness, wins and forces the Confederacy to retreat at the battle of Shiloh in Tennessee, 1862. ¶ Clytie (Asteroid 73) discovered by H. P. Tuttle, 1862. ¶ The synagogue in Great Portland Street is consecrated (it was founded on 18 March 1869 by Baron Rothschild), 1870. ¶ Albania invaded by Italy, 1939. ¶ The Japanese battleship *Yamato* sunk by US planes in the Pacific, 1945. ¶ The World Health Organization (WHO) is established, 1948. ¶ Dag Hammarskjöld of Sweden is elected Secretary of the United Nations Assembly, 1953. ¶ After 11 years' detention Sheik Mohammad Abdullah is released by the Indonesia authorities, 1964. ¶ Pierre Trudeau becomes Liberal Party leader in Canada, 1968.

BORN: Francis Xavier, Jesuit missionary, near Sanguesa, Spain, 1506. Charles Burney, musicologist, *A General History of Music*, Shrewsbury, 1726. William Wordsworth, poet and Poet Laureate, *Lyrical Ballads, Ballads and Poems*, Cockermouth, Cumberland, 1770. Bronislaw Malinowski, anthropologist, Poland, 1884. Gabriela Mistral, Chilean poet, Nobel Prize for Literature, diplomat, Chile, 1889. Sir David Low, political cartoonist, New Zealand, 1891. Billie Holliday, jazz singer, Baltimore, Maryland, 1915.

DIED: Richard I Coeur de Lion, King of England, Chaluz, France, 1199. Jean Baptiste, Abbé de La Salle, Canon of Reims, founder of the Christian Brothers, 1719. Phineas T. Barnum, of Barnum and Bailey, 1891. Henry Ford, industrialist and car manufacturer, 1947. Theda Bara, silent-film actress, 1955. James Clark, British racing driver, 1968.

APRIL 8

Feasts of SS: Dionysius of Corinth, bishop; Perpetuus, bishop;
Walter of Pontoise, abbot.

The Apocrypha received as canonical by the Catholic Church at the Council of Trent, 1546. ¶ A great earthquake had been predicted for London on this day and many people spent the previous night in Hyde Park, 1750. ¶ The first Home Rule for Ireland bill is introduced by W. E. Gladstone, 1886. ¶ Victory of Horatio Kitchener in the Sudan at Atbara River, 1898. ¶ The Parliament of the Chinese Republic sits for the first time, 1913. ¶ Abdication of King Zog of Albania, 1939. ¶ British air-borne forces land in Holland, 1945. ¶ Final assembly of the League of Nations, 1946.

BORN: John Loudon, gardener and horticulturist, *Arboretum et Fruticetum Britannicum, or the Trees and Shrubs of Great Britain, Native and Foreign*, Scotland, 1783. Dionysios Solomos, poet, *Hymn to Liberty*, Zante, Greece, 1798. August von Hofmann, chemist, dye technologist, Giessen, Germany, 1818. William Welch, bacteriologist and teacher, Norfolk, Connecticut, 1850. Edmund Husserl, phenomenological philosopher, *Logical Inquiries*, Czechoslovakia, 1859. Harvey Cushing, pioneer neuro-surgeon, Ohio, 1869. Mary Pickford, actress, Toronto, Canada, 1893. Ian Douglas Smith, Premier of Rhodesia, proclaimed Unilateral Declaration of Independence in 1965, Selvkwe, Rhodesia, 1919.

DIED: Caracalla (Marcus Aurelius Antoninus), Roman emperor, 217. El Greco, artist, Spain, 1614. Karl von Humboldt, philologist, Austria, 1835. Elisha Graves Otis, inventor of the modern safety lift, Yonkers, New York, 1861. Roland Eötvös, Hungarian physicist, 1919. Eric Axel Karlfeldt, poet, refused the Nobel Prize for Literature, Sweden, 1931. Adolph Simon Ochs, newspaper proprietor, bought the *New York Times*, Chattanooga, Tennessee, 1935. Vaslav Nijinsky, ballet dancer and choreographer, associated with Diaghilev, London, 1950. Pablo Picasso, painter, sculptor and lithographer, France, 1973.

APRIL 9

Bataan Day, Philippines (1942). Martyrs Day, Tunisia. Feasts of SS:
Mary of Cleophas, matron; Waldetrudis, or Waudru, widow;
Hugh of Rouen, bishop; Gaucherius, abbot.

Henry V of England crowned (reign had begun 21 March), 1413. ¶ Accession of Edward V of England (murdered in the Tower of London 75 days later, 25 June), 1483. ¶ Maia (Asteroid 66) discovered by H. P. Tuttle, 1861. ¶ Robert E. Lee capitulates to General Grant at Appomattox Courthouse, 1865. ¶ Beginning of the advance on Vimy Ridge (ends successfully on 21 April), 1917, ¶ Turkey ceases to recognize Islam as state religion, 1928. ¶ German invasion of Denmark and Norway, 1940. ¶ The Suez Canal is finally cleared for all shipping, 1957. ¶ US makes Winston Churchill an honorary citizen, 1963.

BORN: James Scott, Duke of Monmouth, illegitimate son of Charles II, defeated at the Battle of Sedgemoor; Rotterdam, 1649. Isambard Kingdom Brunel, engineer, designed the Clifton Suspension Bridge, built the *Great Eastern*, Portsmouth, 1806. Charles Baudelaire, poet, *Les Fleurs du Mal*, Paris, 1821. Eadweard Muybridge, motion photographer, Kingston-upon-Thames, Surrey, 1830. Erich Ludendorff, soldier and early member of the Nazi party, Poland, 1865. Léon Blum, socialist statesman, Paris, 1872. Sol Hurok, theatrical impresario and agent, Russia, 1888. Paul Robeson, actor and singer, Princeton, New Jersey, 1898. Hugh Gaitskell, politician, leader of the Labour Party, London, 1906. Sir Robert Helpmann, ballet dancer and choreographer, Australia, 1909. John Presper Eckert, computer designer, 1919.

DIED: Edward IV of England (reigned 1461–70, and 1471–83), 1484. François Rabelais, scholar, physician and writer, *Gargantua and Pantagruel*, Paris, 1553. Francis Bacon, philosopher and statesman, 1626. Dante Gabriel Rossetti, poet and painter, a member of the Pre-Raphaelite Brotherhood, *The Blessed Damozel*, *The House of Life*, Birchington, Kent, 1882. Edward Thomas, poet and writer, *Collected Poems, A Literary Pilgrimage through England*; killed in action, Arras, France, 1917. Mrs Patrick Campbell, actress and friend of G. B. Shaw, 1940. Dietrich Bonhoeffer, Protestant theologian; in a concentration camp, Germany, 1945. Vilhelm Bjerknes, meteorologist, 1951. Frank Lloyd Wright, architect, Phoenix, Arizona, 1959.

APRIL 10

Dies Mala or 'Egyptian Day', considered unlucky in the Middle Ages.
Feasts of SS: Bademus, abbot; The Martyrs under the Danes;
Macarius, or Macaire, of Ghent; Fulbert of Chartres, bishop;
Paternus of Abdinghof; Michael de Sanctis.

The Prussians defeat the Austrians at Molwitz, 1741. ¶ The US Congress inaugurates the first American patent system, 1790. ¶ The first British settlers arrived in South Africa, at Algoa Bay in the Eastern Cape, 1820. ¶ Russia grants a constitution to Finland, 1861. ¶ The Archduke Maximilian of Austria becomes Emperor of Mexico, 1864. ¶ Abyssinians defeated at Arogee by British troops under the command of Sir Robert Napier, 1868. ¶ Lachesis (Asteroid 120) discovered by Alphonse Borelly, 1872. ¶ Paul von Hindenburg re-elected President of Germany with 19 million votes (Hitler—13 million votes), 1932. ¶ Civil Rights Bill passed by US Senate, 1960. ¶ The USS *Thresher* submarine is lost off Cape Cod, the whole crew of over 125 perishes, 1963. ¶ Severe earthquakes in Iran, over 3,000 people are estimated to have been killed, 1972.

BORN: Hugo Grotius, jurist and lawyer, *On the Law of War and Peace*, Delft, Holland, 1583. John Wilmot, 2nd Earl of Rochester, poet and courtier, *A Satire Against Mankind*, Ditchley, Oxfordshire, 1647. Samuel Hahnemann, physician and doctor, the founder of homeopathic medicine, Meissen, Germany, 1755. William Hazlitt, essayist and critic, *Lectures on the Dramatic Literature of the Age of Elizabeth*, Maidstone, Kent, 1778. William Booth, founder of the Salvation Army, Nottinghamshire, 1829. Joseph Pulitzer, journalist and newspaper owner, endowed Columbia University with a School of Journalism (hence the Pulitzer Prize), Makó, Hungary, 1847. George William Russell, writer under the pen-name of 'AE', Armagh, 1867. George Arliss, stage and film actor, London, 1868. Vladimir Ilyich Lenin, leader of the Bolshevik Revolution, Soviet politician and theorist, Russia, 1870. Clair Booth Luce, playwright, *The Women*, New York City, 1903. Robert Woodward, organic chemist, developed the synthesis of quinine and chlorophyll, Boston, 1917.

DIED: Joseph Lagrange, mathematician and physicist, Paris, 1813. Giovanni Amici, Italian astronomer and optician, 1863. Jean Dumas, chemist, 1884. Algernon Charles Swinburne, poet and writer, *Atalanta in Calydon, Songs Before Sunrise*, Putney, London, 1909. Khalil Gibran, writer of 'mystical' tracts, *The Prophet*, 1931. Auguste Marie Louis Lumière, cinema pioneer, with his brother he invented the process whereby a claw pulls down the film in the cinematograph camera, Lyon, 1954. Michael Curtiz, film director, *The Charge of the Light Brigade, Casablanca*, Los Angeles, California, 1962. Evelyn Waugh, novelist, *Decline and Fall, Brideshead Revisited*, Combe Florey, near Taunton, Somerset, 1966.

APRIL 11

Feasts of SS: Leo the Great, pope and doctor; Barsanuphius;
Isaac of Spoleto; Godeberta, virgin; Guthlac; Gemma Galgani, virgin.

William III and Mary II of Great Britain crowned (their joint reign had begun 13 February), 1689. ¶ France cedes Gibraltar, Newfoundland, Acadia (Nova Scotia) and the Hudson Bay Territory to England with the signing of the Treaty of Utrecht, 1713. ¶ The Treaty of Fontainebleau: Napoleon is forced to abdicate and is banished to Elba, 1814. ¶ Garibaldi arrives in London, 1864. ¶ The Modoc Indians ambush and massacre the US Commissioners and General Canby and his troops in Oregon, 1873. ¶ Uganda declared a British Protectorate, 1894. ¶ William K. Vanderbilt's vast house on Long Island, 'Idle Hour', is burnt to the ground; estimated loss of $300,000, 1899. ¶ The International Labour Organisation (ILO) established, 1919. ¶ German blitz on Coventry, 1941. ¶ General MacArthur is relieved of command in the Far East by President Truman, 1951.

BORN: Sir John Eliot, parliamentarian, Cornwall, 1592. George Canning, politician and Prime Minister, London, 1770. Sir Charles Hallé, pianist and conductor, Hagen, Germany, 1819. Dean Gooderham Acheson, American lawyer and statesman, 1893. Norman McLaren, film animator, *Around is Around*, Sterling, Scotland, 1914.

DIED: Llewelyn ab Iorwerth, Welsh prince, Aberconway, Wales, 1240. Donato Bramante, Renaissance architect, Italy, 1514. Sir Thomas Wyatt (the Younger), soldier, led a revolt of Kentish men to London; executed, London, 1554. Thomas Otway, dramatist, *Venice Preserved*, London, 1685. James Bailey, of Barnum and Bailey, 1906. Sir Gerald Du Maurier, theatrical actor-manager, 1934. Sir Archibald McIndoe, New Zealand plastic surgeon, 1960.

APRIL 12

The Roman Cerealia or Ludi Ceriales, the festival of Ceres,
a goddess representing the fertility of the earth in producing corn;
the celebrations began on this day and lasted until 19 April.
Sinhala New Year's Day, Socialist Republic of Sri Lanka.
Halifax Independence Day, North Carolina, USA. Feasts of SS:
Julius I, pope; Zeno of Verona, bishop; Sabas the Goth, martyr;
Alferius and other abbots of La Cava.

Admiral Rodney saves the West Indies by defeating de Grasse in the battle of The Saints, 1782. ¶ Victory for the English settlers against King Dingaan's Zulu warriors at the battle of Tugela, South Africa, 1838. ¶ President Polk sends troops into New Mexico after disagreement with Mexico over the territory, 1846. ¶ Hygeia (Asteroid 10) discovered by de Gasparis, 1849. ¶ Bombardment begins of Fort Sumter (surrenders on 13 April), 1861. ¶ Nathan B. Forrest of the Confederacy takes Fort Pillow in Tennessee from the Union, 1864. ¶ Armentières is taken by German forces, 1918. ¶ Upon the death of Roosevelt, Harry S. Truman is made US President, 1945. ¶ The first successful manned flight in space, by (Colonel) Yuri Gagarin of the USSR in *Vostock I*, 1961. ¶ Palestinian guerillas raid Qiryat Shemeona in Israel and massacre eighteen people (including some children), 1974. ¶ A great blow-out on the Bravo Norwegian Ekofisk oil-rig in the North Sea (finally capped by Red Adair of Texas on 30 April), 1977.

BORN: Edward Bird, painter, Wolverhampton, 1772. John George, Earl of Durham, British statesman and ambassador, Governor General of Canada, Durham, 1792. Georges Frenju, film director, *Les Yeux sans Visage*, Fougères, France, 1912. Maria Callas, operatic singer, New York City, 1923.

DIED: Jacques Bénigne Bossuet, theologian, tutor of the Dauphin, 1704. William Kent, architect, painter and gardener, London, 1748. Pietro Antonio Metastasio, poet and dramatist, *Attilio Regolo*, Vienna, 1782. Charles Burney, musicologist, *A General History of Music*, 1814. Charles-Joseph Messier, astronomer, published the first list of nebulae, Paris, 1817. Feodor Ivanovich Chaliapin, operatic bass, 1938. Franklin Roosevelt, lawyer, President of the US, Warm Springs, Georgia, 1945. Antoine Pevsner, Constructivist sculptor, Paris, 1962.

APRIL 13

The Roman Cerealia (see 12 April). National Day, Republic of Chad.
Tamil New Year's Day, Socialist Republic of Sri Lanka.
Anniversary of Thomas Jefferson's Birthday, some southern states only of USA.
Feasts of SS: Hermenegild, martyr; Carpus, Papylus and Agathonice, martyrs;
Martius, or Mars, abbot.

Marcus Didius Salvius Julianus is proclaimed Emperor in Rome (put to death by order of the Senate on 1 June), 193. ¶ Henry IV of France promulgates the Edict of Nantes, 1598. ¶ Warren Hastings becomes the Governor of Bengal (until 1785), 1772. ¶ Sicily becomes independent of Naples, 1848. ¶ Fort Sumter in Charleston is taken by the Confederacy and the American Civil War begins, 1861. ¶ Robert Napier leading British forces takes Magdala in Ethiopia, 1868. ¶ Foundation of the Anti-Semitic League and the presentation to Bismarck of a petition demanding restrictions on the liberty of Prussian Jews, 1882.

BORN: Thomas Wentworth, Earl of Strafford, statesman and supporter of Charles I, Lord Deputy of Ireland, London, 1593. Frederick North, 2nd Earl of Guildford (Lord North), British Prime Minister, levied the tax on the American colonies that provoked the Boston Tea Party, London, 1732. Thomas Jefferson, US President, Shadwell, Virginia, 1743. Richard Trevithick, engineer and mechanic, developed the steam locomotive, Cornwall, 1771. György Lukacs, critic and philosopher, *History and Class Consciousness*, Budapest, 1885. Samuel Beckett, novelist and dramatist, *Krapp's Last Tape*, Ireland, 1906. Eudora Welty, novelist and short story writer, *A Curtain of Green, Delta Wedding*, Jackson, Mississippi, 1909. John Braine, novelist, *Room at the Top*, Bradford, 1922. Stanley Donen, film director and producer, *Seven Brides for Seven Brothers*, Columbia, 1924.

DIED: Krum, King of Bulgaria, 814. Boris Fyodorovich Godunov, Russian Tsar, 1605. Jean de La Fontaine, writer, *Fables*, France, 1695. Charles Leslie, Irish-born writer, published attacks on Papists, Deists, Jews and just about everyone else, Glaslough, Ireland, 1722. Captain Hugh Clapperton, naval officer and African explorer, Africa, 1827. Lavr Georgievich Kornilov, leader of the Don Cossacks at the beginning of the Russian Civil War, 1918.

The Roman Cerealia (see 12 April). Cuckoo Day in England, traditionally the day upon which the first cuckoo is heard. Feasts of SS: Justin Martyr; Tiburtius, Valerius and Maximus, martyrs; Ardalion, martyr; Lambert of Lyons, archbishop; Bernard of Tiron, abbot; Caradoc; Bénezet; John, Antony and Eustace, martyrs.

Yorkists defeat the Lancastrians at the battle of Barnet, and Henry VI of England is deposed for the second and final time, 1471. ¶ President Abraham Lincoln assassinated at Ford's Theatre in Washington by John Wilkes Booth, at 11pm (he dies at 7.30am on 15 April), 1865. ¶ Attempted assassination of Czar Alexander II of Russia by Alexander Solovieff, 1879. ¶ President Wilson orders US fleet to Tampico, Mexico, 1914. ¶ Arnhem is finally entered by US forces, 1945.

BORN: Ortelius (Abraham Oertel), cartographer and engraver, produced the first atlas, Antwerp, 1527. Christian Huygens, physicist and mathematician, The Hague, Netherlands, 1629. Peter Behrens, architect and industrial designer, Hamburg, 1868. Moritz Schlick, philosopher, Berlin, 1882. Edward Tolman, psychologist, West Newton, Massachusetts, 1886. Vere Gordon Childe, archaeologist, *Man Makes Himself, What Happened in History*, Australia, 1892. Sir John Gielgud, actor, London, 1904. François Duvalier, dictator ('Papa Doc'), Haiti, 1907. Rod Steiger, actor, Westhampton, New York, 1925. Anthony Perkins, actor, *Psycho, The Trial*, New York City, 1932.

DIED: Richard Neville, Earl of Warwick ('Warwick the Kingmaker'), soldier and statesman, fought in the Wars of the Roses, 1471. George Frederick Handel, composer, violinist and organist, *The Messiah, Water Music*, London, 1759. Alexander Scriabin, composer and pianist, *Prometheus*, Moscow, 1915. Louis Henri Sullivan, architect of the 'Chicago school', Chicago, 1924. Vladimir Mayakovsky, Soviet dramatist and novelist, *The Bed Bug*; suicide, Moscow, 1930. Ernest Bevin, British politician and Minister of Labour during World War Two, 1951. Fredric March, actor, 1975.

The Roman Cerealia (see 12 April). Swallow Day, the day on which the chimney swallow was said to arrive back in England. Anniversary of Tarija, a department of Bolivia. Feasts of SS: Basilissa and Anastasia, martyrs; Padarn, or Patern, bishop; Ruadan of Lothra, abbot; Hunna, matron.

Mutiny of the British Navy at Spithead, 1797. ¶ Ariadne (Asteroid 43) discovered by Norman Pogson, 1857. ¶ President Abraham Lincoln calls for 75,000 militia after announcing a state of insurrection, 1861. ¶ Andrew Johnson sworn in as the President of the US upon the death of Abraham Lincoln at 7.30 am (shot the previous night by John Wilkes Booth at Ford's Theatre in Washington), 1865. ¶ The SS *Titanic* sinks on her maiden voyage and over 1500 people are drowned, 1912. ¶ Chiang Kai-shek forms a government in Hankow, 1927.

BORN: Nanak, founder of Sikhism, near Lahore, India, 1469. Leonard Euler, mathematician, *Introduction to the Analysis of Infinite Numbers*, Switzerland, 1707. William Augustus, Duke of Cumberland, military commander, 1721. Wilhelm von Struve, astronomer, Altona, Germany, 1793. Sir James Clark Ross, Polar explorer, discovered the North magnetic pole, *Voyage of Discovery*, London, 1800. Hermann Grassmann, German mathematician, Poland, 1809. Wilhelm Busch, cartoonist, *Max und Moritz*, Germany, 1832. Henry James, novelist, *The Portrait of a Lady*, *The Ambassadors*, New York City, 1843. Bliss Carman, Canadian poet, 1861.

DIED: Richard Mulcaster, early educator, Essex, 1611. Marquise de Pompadour, the mistress of Louis XV of France, Versailles, 1764. Mikhail Lomonosov, poet and scientist, instituted major reforms of the Russian language, St Petersburg, 1765. Hubert Robert, landscape painter, Paris, 1808. Oliver Evans, American inventor, 1819. Abraham Lincoln, President of the United States; assassinated, Washington, 1865. Matthew Arnold, poet and critic, *Culture and Anarchy*, 1888. John Singer Sargent, portrait painter, London, 1925.

APRIL 16

The Roman Cerealia (see 12 April). Anniversary of Diego's Birthday, Puerto Rico (José de Diego, poet and statesman, 1866–1913). Feasts of SS: Optatus and his Companions, and St Encratis, virgin martyrs; Turibius of Astorga, bishop; Paternus, or Pair, bishop; Fructuosus of Braga, archbishop; Magnus of Orkney, martyr; Drogo, or Druon; Contardo; Benedict Joseph Labre; Bernadette, virgin.

The Senate in Rome appoints two new Emperors: D. Caelius Balbinus to run civil affairs, and M. Clodius Pupienus Maximus to command the legions, 238. ¶ Cumberland defeats the Scottish rebels at Culloden, 1746. ¶ Dr. Colenso, Bishop of Natal, deposed by his metropolitan, Dr Gray, Bishop of Capetown, for his work on *The Pentateuch*, 1864. ¶ Attempted assassination of Czar Alexander II of Russia by Karakozow at St Petersburg, 1866. ¶ Paul Kruger is made President of the South African Republic, 1883. ¶ USSR seeks an alliance of defence with Britain, 1939. ¶ Ian Smith announces that diplomatic relations between Britain and Rhodesia will be broken off, 1966.

BORN: Jules Hardouin Mansart, architect, designed the Galerie de Glaces at Versailles, Paris, 1646. Sir Hans Sloane, physician and naturalist, his museum and library formed the basis of the British Museum, *Natural History of Jamaica*, Killyleagh, County Down, Ireland, 1660. Charles Montagu, 1st Earl of Halifax, politician and poet, founder of the Bank of England, Horton, Northamptonshire, 1661. Joseph Black, chemist, formulated the concept of latent heat, 1728. Sir John Franklin, sought the 'North West Passage', Lincolnshire, 1786. Anatole France, novelist and critic, *Penguin Island*, Paris, 1844. Wilbur Wright, aviation pioneer, near Millville, Indiana, 1867. John Millington Synge, dramatist, *The Playboy of the Western World*, *The Tinker's Wedding*, Rathfarnham, near Dublin, 1871. Edward, Lord Halifax, statesman, Devon, 1881. Nadia Boulanger, composer and teacher, Paris, 1887. Charlie Chaplin, actor and comedian, *The Gold Rush*, *Modern Times*, London, 1889. Peter Ustinov, actor and dramatist, London, 1921. Kingsley Amis, novelist and critic, *Lucky Jim*, London, 1922.

DIED: Marcus Salvius Otho, Roman Emperor, suicide, Brixellum, 69. Aphra Behn, novelist and dramatist, *Oronooko*, *The Rover*, 1689. Comte George Louis Buffon, naturalist, Paris, 1788. Mikhail Kutuzov, Prince of Smolensk, Russian military commander, 1813. Francisco José Goya y Lucientes, Spanish painter, 1828. Alexis Charles de Tocqueville, historian, *Democracy in America*, *The Old Regime and the Revolution*, Cannes, France, 1859. Saint Bernadette, received visions of the Virgin Mary at Lourdes, her birthplace, 1879.

APRIL 17

The Roman Cerealia (see 12 April). Evacuation Day, Arab Republic of Syria.
Feasts of SS: Anicetus, pope and martyr; Mappalicus and his Companions,
martyrs; Innocent, bishop; Donnan and his Companions, martyrs;
Robert of Chaise-Dieu, abbot; Stephen Harding, abbot.

The sea broke the banks at Dort in Holland and an estimated 100,000 people are believed to have been drowned, 1421. ¶ Martin Luther is excommunicated by the Diet at Worms, 1521. ¶ Thetis (Asteroid 17) discovered by R. Luther, 1852. ¶ Virginia secedes from the Union (readmitted 26 January 1870), 1861. ¶ Asia (Asteroid 67) discovered by Norman Pogson, 1861. ¶ Premium Savings Bonds introduced in Britain by Harold Macmillan's Budget speech, 1956. ¶ The new India Congress movement is formed by Pandit Nehru, 1957. ¶ Fidel Castro defeats rebels and others in attempted invasion of Cuba at 'The Bay of Pigs', 1961. ¶ Sirhan Sirhan found guilty in Los Angeles of the murder of Senator Robert Kennedy, 1969. ¶ Mr Dubcek is replaced as head of the Czechoslovak Communist Party by Dr Gustav Husak, 1969.

BORN: Henry Vaughan, poet and translator, *Silex Scintillans, The Mount of Olives,* Llansantffraed, Wales, 1622. Edward Gibbon, writer, historian, *Decline and Fall of the Roman Empire,* 1737. John Pierpont Morgan, industrialist and banker, Connecticut, 1835. Constantine Cavafy, modern Greek poet, Egypt, 1863. ¶ Sir Leonard Woolley, archaeologist, excavated Ur of the Chaldees, London, 1880. Nikita Khruschev, Soviet statesman and Premier, Russia, 1894. Thornton Wilder, novelist and playwright, *The Bridge of San Luis Rey, Our Town,* Madison, Wisconsin, 1897. Lindsay Anderson, English film director, *This Sporting Life,* Bangalore, India, 1923.

DIED: Sir Philip Sidney, poet, courtier and soldier, *Arcadia, Astrophel and Stella,* Arnhem, Holland, 1586. Madame de Sévigné, lady-of-fashion and writer, *Lettres,* Grignan, France, 1696. Benjamin Franklin, American statesman and scientist, 1790. Kawabata Yasunari, Japanese novelist, *Snow Country,* 1972.

APRIL 18

*The Roman Cerealia (see 12 April). Feasts of SS: Apollonius
the Apologist, martyr; Eleutherius and his Companions, martyrs;
Laserian, Laisren, or Molaisse, bishop; Idesbald, abbot; Galdinus, archbishop.*

Louis XVI prevented by mob from going to St Cloud, 1791. ¶ General Scott leading US troops defeats the Mexicans at Cerro Gorda, 1847. ¶ Ianthe (Asteroid 98) discovered by C. H. F. Peters, 1868. ¶ Coggia's Comet, observed by M. Coggia at Marseilles, 1874. ¶ Dr Livingstone's remains interred in Westminster Abbey (died in Africa on 1 May 1873), 1874. ¶ Sidney Bechet records *The Sheikh of Araby* on overlaying tapes, playing clarinet, soprano saxophone, tenor saxophone, piano, bass and drums, in New York City, 1941. ¶ Formal dissolving of the League of Nations, 1946. ¶ Formal proclamation of the Republic of Eire, 1949. ¶ Bangladesh is admitted into the British Commonwealth, 1972.

BORN: Lucrezia Borgia, aristocrat and poisoner, Rome, 1480. Sir Francis Baring, banker and merchant, London, 1740. Louis Adolphe Thiers, statesman and President of France, put down the Paris Commune, Marseilles, France, 1797. Antero Tarquínio de Quental, Portuguese poet, *Sonetos Completos, Raios da Extinta Luz*, Porta Delgada, Azores, 1842. Leopold Stokowski, conductor, chiefly associated with the Philadelphia Symphony Orchestra, London, 1882.

DIED: John Leland, antiquary, *The Itinerary*, London, 1552. John Foxe, martyrologist and preacher, *History of the Acts and Monuments of the Church* (popularly known as *Foxe's Book of Martyrs*), London, 1587. Ottorino Respighi, composer, *The Pines of Rome*, Rome, 1936. Sir John Ambrose Fleming, electrical engineer, 1945. Leonard Bloomfield, US linguistics scholar, *Language*, 1949. Albert Einstein, physicist, formulated Relativity Theory, 1955. Ben Hecht, journalist and screenplay writer, *Scarface, Front Page, A Child of the Century* (autobiography), 1964.

*The last day of the Roman Cerealia (see 12 April). Primrose Day,
observed in England by Conservatives sharing the ideals of
Benjamin Disraeli (died 19 April 1881); primrose because it was said to be
the Prime Minister's favourite flower. Republican Anniversary Day,
Sierra Leone (1971). Anniversary of the Landing of the Thirty-three Orientales,
Uruguay (the return of the thirty-three revolutionary patriots in 1825
who fought for independence). Declaration of Independence Day, Venezuela (1811).
Feasts of SS: Leo IX, pope; Expeditus; Ursmar, abbot and bishop;
Geroldus; Alphege, archbishop and martyr.*

Accession of Robert III of Scotland (reigns until 4 April 1406), 1390. ¶ The War of American Independence opens, the British are defeated at Lexington and Concord, 1775. ¶ Leucothea (Asteroid 35) discovered by R. Luther and Atalanta (Asteroid 36) by H. Goldschmidt, 1855. ¶ President Lincoln proclaims the blockade of the Southern coast, 1861. ¶ Lydia (Asteroid 110) discovered by Alphonse Borelly, 1870. ¶ US demands that Spain relinquishes its power in Cuba, 1898. ¶ Halley's Comet re-appeared, 1910. ¶ Literacy is made a condition of entry to the US by the Dillingham Immigration Bill, 1912. ¶ The North Pole is finally reached, by Ralph Plaisted and four others of the US, 1968. ¶ 145 missions flown against North Vietnam by US, 1968. ¶ Russians launch *Salyut*, an unmanned space station, 1971. ¶ US *Apollo 16* spacecraft begins Moon orbit (astronauts land on the surface on 21 April), 1972.

BORN: Christian Ehrenberg, founder of protozoology, Saxony, 1795. Lucien Lévy-Bruhl, philosopher and psychologist, Paris, 1857. Getulio Dornelles Vargas, dictator and President of Brazil, Sao Borja, Brazil, 1883. Richard Hughes, novelist, *A High Wind in Jamaica*, Surrey, 1900.

DIED: Philipp Melanchthon, theologian, colleague of Martin Luther, Wittenburg (?), 1560. Paolo Veronese, Venetian painter, Venice, 1588. Anton Van Dieman, Governor-General of the Dutch East Indies, 1645. Lord George Gordon Byron, poet, *Don Juan;* of fever in Greece, 1824. Benjamin Disraeli, statesman and novelist, 1881. Charles Darwin, naturalist and writer, *On the Origin of the Species*, 1882. Pierre Curie, French chemist, physicist, 1906. Hugo Winkler, archaeologist, Berlin, 1913. Charles Pierce, philosopher and scientist, near Milford, Pennsylvania, 1914. Konrad Adenauer, German statesman, 1967.

APRIL 20

Dies Mala or 'Egyptian Day', considered unlucky in the Middle Ages.
Feasts of SS: Marcellinus of Embrun, bishop; Marcian, or Marian;
Caedwalla; Hildegund, virgin; Agnes of Montepulciano, virgin.

The foundation of Rome by Romulus occurred on this day according to the historian Varro, in the Fourth Year of the Sixth Olympiad, Year 3961 of the Julian Period, otherwise 735BC. ¶ Oliver Cromwell cursorily dissolves the Long Parliament, 1653. ¶ The Spanish fleet is vanquished and burnt in the harbour of Santa Cruz by the English under Admiral Blake, 1657. ¶ General Rommel launches major offensive on Tobruk, 1941. ¶ Massacre by the Germans of the Jews in the Warsaw Ghetto, 1943. ¶ The US warns Cuba against interference with its aerial surveying of that country, 1964.

BORN: Pietro Aretino, satirist, Italy, 1492. Johann Agricola, theologian and reformer, Saxony, 1494. Napoleon III, Emperor of France, Paris, 1808. Charles Maurras, writer and philosopher, founded Action Française, France, 1868. Adolf Hitler, Führer of the Third Reich, Austria, 1889. Harold Lloyd, silent film comedian, 1893. Joan Miro, Surrealist painter, Barcelona, 1893. Lionel Hampton, jazz vibraphonist and bandleader, Birmingham, Alabama, 1914.

DIED: Antonio Canaletto, artist, 1768. Pontiac, Chief of the Ottawa Indians, organised the Indian tribes against the British, Illinois, 1769. Arthur Young, agriculturalist and writer, *A Tour through the Southern Counties*, London, 1820. Bram Stoker, theatrical manager and novelist, *Dracula*, London, 1912. Samuel R. Crockett, novelist, *The Raiders*, Galloway, Scotland, 1914.

The Roman festival of Pales, god of shepherds and their herds.
Independence Heroes National Holiday, parts of Brazil.
Battle of San Jacinto Day, Texas, USA (1836, last battle in the
Texas Revolution). Feasts of SS: Anselm, archbishop and doctor;
Simeon Barsabae, bishop, and his Companions, martyrs;
Anastasius I of Antioch, bishop; Beuno, abbot;
Malrubius, or Maelrubha, abbot; Conrad of Parzham.

¶ Lambert is defeated by General Monk at Daventry, 1660. ¶ Mexico defeated at the battle of San Jacinto by Texas, 1836. ¶ Garibaldi receives the freedom of the City of London, 1864. ¶ Meliboea (Asteroid 137) discovered by J. Palisa, 1874. ¶ Roger Casement lands in Ireland by German submarine, 1916. ¶ Canadians take Vimy Ridge (after assault which began on 9 April), 1917. ¶ BOAC inaugurate the world's first scheduled jet-liner service, between London and Rome using De Havilland Comets, 1952. ¶ US *Apollo 16* astronauts walk on the Moon, 1972. ¶ £1-million was stolen by masked raiders from a firm of bookmakers in Melbourne, the greatest robbery ever in Australia, 1976.

BORN: Jan van Riebeck, naval surgeon, founder of Cape Town, Netherlands, 1634. Catherine the Great, Empress of Russia, 1729. Friedrich Froebel, educator, developed the idea of the *Kindergarten*, Germany, 1782. Charlotte Brontë, novelist, *Jane Eyre*, Yorkshire, 1816. Hippolyte Adolphe Taine, philosopher, historian and critic, *The Philosophy of Art*, *History of English Literature*, Vouziers, France, 1828. Billy Bitzer, pioneer American cinematographer, worked with D. W. Griffith, Boston, Massachusetts, 1874. Henri de Montherlant, novelist and dramatist, *The Bullfighters*, *Chaos and Night*, *Port-Royal*, Paris, 1896. Elizabeth II of England, London, 1926.

DIED: Henry VII, King of England, Richmond, Surrey, 1509. Jean Racine, dramatist and poet, *Alexandre le Grand*, *Andromaque*, Paris, 1699. Eugene of Savoy, Austrian soldier and statesman, 1736. Mark Twain (Samuel Langhorne Clemens), writer, journalist and lecturer, *Tom Sawyer*, *Huckleberry Finn*, Reading, Connecticut, 1910. Eleanora Duse, actress, 1924. Robert Bridges, Poet Laureate, 'A Testament of Beauty', 1930. John Maynard Keynes, economist, *The General Theory of Employment*, Cambridge, 1946. Stafford Cripps, English lawyer and politician, 1952. Sir Edward Appleton, physicist, 1965. François Duvalier, dictator of Haiti ('Papa Doc'), 1971.

APRIL 22

National Sovereignty Day, Turkey (and 23 April). Arbor Day, Nebraska, USA. Feasts of SS: Soter and Caius, popes and martyrs; Epipodius and Alexander, martyrs; Leonides, martyr; Agapitus I, pope; Theodore of Sykeon, bishop; Opportuna, virgin and abbess.

Accession of Henry VIII of England (reigned until 28 January 1547), 1509. ¶ Mme Dubarry becomes Louis XV's official mistress, 1769. ¶ Napoleon defeats Piedmontese at Mondovi, 1796. ¶ Arthur Wellesley embarks at Lisbon to take command in the Peninsular, 1809. ¶ Poison gas used on the Western Front for the first time by German forces, 1915. ¶ Beginning of the second Ypres battle (lasts until 25 May), 1915. ¶ Opening of the New York World's Fair, 1964. ¶ *Coup* by the army in Greece, martial law is declared and many prominent politicians are arrested, 1967. ¶ From the beginning of the year until the end of this day 7,508 US servicemen were killed in Vietnam, 1968.

BORN: Isabella I, Queen of Castile and Aragon, Spain, 1451. Henry Fielding, magistrate and novelist, *Tom Jones*, Somerset, 1707. Immanuel Kant, philosopher, *Critique of Pure Reason*, Königsberg, Germany, 1724. Madame de Staël (Anne Louise Germaine Necker), novelist and critic, *De l'Allemagne, Delphine*, Paris, 1766. Alexander Kerensky, Premier of the Provisional Russian Government in 1917, Simbirsk, Russia, 1881. Otto Rank, psychologist, *The Myth of the Birth of the Hero*, Vienna, 1884. Vladimir Nabokov, novelist, poet and lepidopterist, *Pale Fire, Lolita*, St Petersburg, Russia, 1899. Robert Oppenheimer, physicist, developed the US atomic bomb at Los Alamos, New York City, 1904. Kathleen Ferrier, contralto singer, Lancashire, 1912. Yehudi Menuhin, virtuoso violinist, New York City, 1916. Sidney Nolan, Australian painter, Melbourne, 1917.

DIED: John Tradescant, gardener and naturalist, Lambeth, London, 1662. James Hargreaves, weaver and carpenter, invented the spinning jenny, Nottingham, 1778. John Crome, landscape painter of the 'Norwich School', 1821. Thomas Rowlandson, caricaturist and artist, *Imitations of Modern Drawings*, London, 1827. Richard Trevithick, engineer and mechanic, developed the steam locomotive, Dartford, Kent, 1833. Henry Campbell-Bannerman, Liberal, British Prime Minister, 1908. Roy Campbell, poet, 1957.

APRIL 23

St George's Day in England, the patron saint has been celebrated
since the Conquest. National Sovereignty Day, Turkey (and 22 April).
Feasts of SS: George, martyr; Felix, Fortunatus and Achilleus, martyrs;
Ibar, bishop; Gerard of Toul, bishop; Adalbert of Prague, bishop and martyr.

Danes defeated in Ireland at the battle of Clontarf, 1014. ¶ Charles II of England crowned 1661. ¶ Queen Anne of Great Britain crowned (reign had begun 8 March), 1702. ¶ Acquittal of Warren Hastings for high treason, 1795. ¶ Russians launch *Union 1* manned space-craft, 1967. ¶ Russians launch manned spacecraft *Soyuz 10*, 1971.

BORN: Maarten Harpertszoon Tromp, Dutch admiral and naval commander, Briel, Netherlands, 1598. William Shakespeare, dramatist, *Romeo and Juliet*, Stratford-upon-Avon, Warwickshire, 1564. Admiral George Anson, naval commander and reformer, 1697. Joseph Mallord William Turner, landscape painter, etcher and watercolourist, Covent Garden, London, 1775. James Buchanan, fifteenth President of the US (1857–61), Pennsylvania, 1791. Maria Taglioni, ballerina, Stockholm, 1804. Max Ludwig Planck, physicist, Nobel Prize winner, Kiel, Switzerland, 1858. Edmund, Viscount Allenby, military commander, Nottinghamshire, 1861. Sergei Prokofiev, composer, *Peter and the Wolf*, Ukraine, 1891. Frank Borzage, film director, *A Man's Castle, Moonrise*, Salt Lake City, 1893. Lester Bowles Pearson, Prime Minister of Canada, Nobel Prize for Peace, Toronto, 1897. Dame Ngaio Marsh, writer, *Enter a Murderer*, New Zealand, 1899. J. P. Donleavy, novelist, *The Ginger Man*, New York, 1926.

DIED: Miguel de Cervantes Saavedra, dramatist and novelist, *Don Quixote, Exemplary Novels*, 1616. William Shakespeare, dramatist and poet, Stratford-upon-Avon, 1616. Maurice of Nassau, Prince of Orange, The Hague, 1625. Henry Vaughan, poet and translator, *Silex Scintillans, The Mount of Olives*, Llansantffraed, Wales, 1695. Erik Gustaf Geijer, poet and historian, *Swedish Ballads*, 1847. William Wordsworth, poet and Poet Laureate, *Lyrical Ballads, Ballads and Poems*, near Grasmere, Westmorland, 1850. Auguste Laurent, French chemist, 1853. Karl Ludwig, physiologist, Leipzig, 1895. Rupert Brooke, poet; killed in action, 1915.

APRIL 24

*St Mark's Eve, on which apparitions of those to die in the coming year
are said to appear at midnight in churchyards. Feasts of SS: Fidelis of
Sigmaringen, martyr; Mellitus, archbishop; Ivo, bishop; Egbert, bishop;
William Firmatus; Mary Euphrasia Pelletier, virgin.*

Charles I defeats the Protestants at Mühlberg, 1547. ¶ First publication of the
Daily Express, London, 1900. ¶ Roger Casement is arrested in Ireland after
landing by German submarine three days earlier, 1916. ¶ German National
Socialist Party election successes in Bavaria, Prussia, and Hamburg, 1932.
¶ Gambia proclaimed a republic, 1970. ¶ Chinese launch their first Earth-
orbiting satellite, 1970. ¶ The Russian *Soyuz 10* spacecraft links up with the
orbiting space station *Salyut*, 1971.

BORN: William I, founder of the United Provinces (the Dutch Republic),
Nassau, Germany, 1533. Edmund Cartwright, inventor of the power-driven
loom, Nottinghamshire, 1743. Anthony Trollope, novelist, *Barchester Towers*,
Phineas Finn, London, 1815. Marcus Andrew Hislop Clarke, Australian writer,
For the Term of his Natural Life, 1846. Henry Philippe Pétain, First World War
military leader, puppet governor of France for the Germans in the Second
World War, Cauchy-à-la-Tour, France, 1856. Stafford Cripps, lawyer and
politician, London, 1889. Benjamin Whorf, linguist and anthropologist,
Language, Thought and Reality, Winthrop, Massachusetts, 1897. Robert Penn
Warren, poet and novelist, *All the King's Men*, Guthrie, Kentucky, 1905.
William Joyce, 'Lord Haw-haw', Nazi collaborator, New York City, 1906.
Barbra Streisand, singer, Brooklyn, New York, 1942.

DIED: Jacopo Sannazaro, Neapolitan poet, *Arcadia*, Naples, 1530. Daniel Defoe,
writer, *Robinson Crusoe*, *Moll Flanders*, 1731. Maria Taglioni, ballerina, Marseilles,
France, 1884. Willa Cather, novelist, *My Antonia*, 1947. Gerhard Domagk,
German biochemist, Nobel Prize winner, 1964.

APRIL 25

The Roman festival of Robigalia, honouring the god Robigus who protected cornfields from blight and great heat. Anzac Day, commemorating the contribution of Australian and New Zealand troops in the Gallipoli landing, 1915; a holiday in both countries. Liberation Day, Italy. Portugal Day, Portugal. National Flag Day, Swaziland. Anzac Day, Western Samoa. Feasts of SS: Mark, evangelist; Anianus, bishop; Heribald, bishop.

A decisive victory for the Dutch against the Spanish in the Bay of Gibraltar, 1607. ¶ A Convention Parliament meets and votes the restoration of Charles II, 1660. ¶ Metis (Asteroid 9) discovered by A. Graham, 1848. ¶ The Confederate forces at New Orleans surrender to Admiral David G. Farragut, 1862. ¶ War declared on Spain by the US, 1898. ¶ British and French troops land in Gallipoli, 1915. ¶ Paul von Hindenburg becomes President of Germany after general elections, 1925. ¶ The head of 'The Little Mermaid' statue in Copenhagen harbour is sawn off and stolen, 1964. ¶ First democratic elections in Portugal since 1927 were held, 1976.

BORN: Louis IX of France, 1214. Oliver Cromwell, Lord Protector of England, Huntingdon, 1599. Emerich de Vattel, diplomat and jurist, Couret, Switzerland, 1714. John Keble, poet and clergyman, a founder of the Oxford Movement, Fairford, Gloucestershire, 1792. Peter Ilyich Tchaikovsky, composer, *Romeo and Juliet, Swan Lake*, Votkinsk, Russia, 1840. Walter De la Mare, writer and poet, Kent, 1873. Guglielmo Marconi, inventor, pioneer of the wireless, Bologna, Italy, 1874. Wolfgang Pauli, physicist, Nobel Prize winner, first postulated the existence of the neutrino, Vienna, 1900. Edward R. Morrow, journalist and broadcaster, Director of the US Information Agency, Greensboro, North Carolina, 1908. Ella Fitzgerald, popular jazz singer, Virginia, 1918. Yvette Corlett, New Zealand athlete, 1929.

DIED: Torquato Tasso, poet, *Jerusalem Delivered, Aminta*, Rome, 1595. Anders Celsius, astronomer, devised the centrigade temperature scale, 1744. William Cowper, English poet and writer, East Dereham, Norfolk, 1800. William Beaumont, physiologist, 1853. Vladimir Ivanovich Nemirovich-Danchenko, dramatist and theatrical director, Moscow, 1943.

APRIL 26

*Union Day, Tanzania (commemorating the union of Tanganyika and
Zanzibar in 1964). Confederate Memorial Day, some southern states
only of USA. Feasts of SS: Cletus and Marcellinus, popes and martyrs;
Peter of Braga, bishop; Richarius, or Riquier, abbot; Paschasius Radbertus, abbot:
Franca of Piacenza, virgin and abbess; Stephen of Perm, bishop.*

Beatrix (Asteroid 83) discovered by de Gasparis, 1865. ¶ John Wilkes Booth, the
assassin of Abraham Lincoln (on 14 April), is shot by troops at a farmhouse some
distance from Washington while attempting to escape, his accomplice Harrold
is captured, 1865. ¶ Cuban invasion of Panama begins, 1959. ¶ The largest
underground nuclear device ever to be tested in US is exploded in Nevada, 1968.

BORN: John James Audubon, naturalist and artist, Haiti, 1785. Eugène
Delacroix, Romantic artist, France, 1798. Alfred Krupp, industrialist, Essen,
Germany, 1812. Artemus Ward (Charles Farrar Browne), humorist and writer,
Babes in the Wood, Artemus Ward, His Book, Waterford, Maine, 1834. Syngman
Rhee, the founder of South Korea, Korea, 1875. Michel Fokine, dancer and
choreographer, 1880. Rudolf Hess, Hitler's Deputy, Alexandria, Egypt, 1894.
John Grierson, documentary film maker, *Drifters*, Perth, Scotland, 1898. Jean
Vigo, film director, *Zéro de Conduite*, Paris, 1905. Bernard Malamud, novelist,
The Fixer, Brooklyn, New York, 1914.

DIED: John Wilkes Booth, actor, assassin of President Abraham Lincoln; shot
'whilst trying to escape', 1865. Bjørnstjerne Bjørnson, novelist and dramatist,
The Newly-Married Couple, 1910. Karl Bosch, pioneered the industrial production of nitrogenous fertilizers, Nobel Prize for Chemistry, 1940. Edwin Pratt,
Canadian poet, *Brebeuf and His Brethren, Towards the Last Spike*, Toronto, 1964.

Independence Day, Togo (1960, formerly a German protectorate).
Feasts of SS: Peter Canisius, doctor; Anthimus, bishop; Asicus, or
Tassach, bishop; Maughold, or Maccul, bishop; Floribert, bishop;
Stephen Pechersky, bishop; Zita, virgin; Turibius of Lima, archbishop.

Antony defeated by Hirtius at Mutina, 43 BC. ¶ Accession of David I of Scotland (reigned until 24 May 1153), 1124. ¶ Scots defeated at Dunbar, 1296. ¶ US forces capture Toronto (York), 1813. ¶ Germany's liability is declared to be £6,650-million by the Reparations Commission, 1921. ¶ Guernica in Northern Spain is destroyed in blitz by German planes, 1937. ¶ The state of Israel is recognized by the British government, 1950. ¶ Eight satellites are put into orbit around the Earth by a single Russian rocket, 1970. ¶ Quang Tri is isolated from the rest of South Vietnam by North Vietnamese troops, 1972.

BORN: Samuel Morse, artist and inventor of the Morse Code, Charlestown, Massachusetts, 1791. Herbert Spencer, philosopher and social scientist, *Principles of Psychology*, *Principles of Sociology*, Derby, 1820. Ulysses Simpson Grant, commander of the Union Army, American President, Ohio, 1822. Edward Whymper, artist and mountaineer, the first man to climb the Matterhorn, (Switzerland), *Scrambles Amongst the Alps*, London, 1840. Wallace Carothers, chemist, developed nylon, Iowa, 1896. C. Day Lewis, writer, Poet Laureate, Sligo, Ireland, 1904.

DIED: Jan van Goyen, Dutch landscape painter, 1656. James Bruce, African explorer, rediscovered the source of the Blue Nile, 1794. William Macready, actor and theatrical manager, Cheltenham, 1873. Emile de Girardin, political journalist, 1881. Ralph Waldo Emerson, philosopher and poet, Concord, Massachusetts, 1882. Henry Hobson Richardson, architect, Brookline, Massachusetts, 1886. Hart Crane, poet; committed suicide, 1932. Kwame Nkrumah, Ghanaian politician, Bucharest, Rumania, 1972.

APRIL 28

The Roman Floralia, or festival of Flora the goddess of flowers;
the celebrations began on this day and lasted until 3 May. Feasts of SS:
Paul of the Cross; Vitalis and Valeria, martyrs; Pollio, martyr;
Theodora and Didymus, martyrs; Cronan of Roscrea, abbot;
Pamphilus of Sulmona, bishop; Cyril of Turov, bishop;
Louis Mary of Montfort; Peter Mary Chanel, martyr.

Captain Cook, Sir Joseph Banks and others land at Botany Bay (Australia) and name the country New South Wales, 1770. ¶ The State of Maryland ratifies the Constitution of the United States of America, 1788. ¶ The Rush-Bagot Agreement is concluded between US and Britain, 1817. ¶ Italian partisans kill Benito Mussolini, 1945. ¶ Fidel Castro arrives in USSR on visit, 1963. ¶ President Nasser of Egypt dies of a heart attack in Cairo; the Vice-President, Anwar Sadat, is appointed as acting president, 1970. ¶ The last American civilians are evacuated from South Vietnam, 1975. ¶ Gudrun Ensslin, Andreas Baader, and Jan Raspe, leaders of the Baader-Meinhof terrorist gang, are sentenced to life imprisonment in West Germany, 1977.

BORN: Edward IV of England (reigned 1461–70, and 1471–83), 1442. James Monroe, fifth President of the US, Westmoreland County, Virginia, 1758. Charles Sturt, British officer, explored the Australian interior, Bengal, India, 1795. Lord Shaftesbury (Anthony Ashley Cooper), social reformer and Member of Parliament, responsible for many acts improving the conditions of lunatics and child and women labourers, London, 1801. Frances Hodgkins, New Zealand painter, 1869. Lionel Barrymore, actor, 1878. Antonio de Oliveira Salazar, Prime Minister of Portugal, Vimiero, Portugal, 1889.

DIED: Sweyn II, King of Denmark, Denmark, 1074. Count Johann von Struensee, physician and politician, executed, Copenhagen, 1792. Sir Charles Bell, anatomist, 1842. Johannes Müller, physiologist, Berlin, 1858. Gavrilo Princip, the Bosnian revolutionary who, on 28 June, 1914, assassinated the Archduke Ferdinand at Sarajevo; Austria, 1918. Benito Mussolini, dictator, 'Il Duce'; executed by Italian partisans, near Azzano, Italy, 1945. Richard Hughes, novelist, *A High Wind in Jamaica*, Wales, 1976.

APRIL 29

The Roman Floralia (see 28 April). Popularly regarded in the Middle Ages
as the day Noah quit his Ark. Day of the Emperor's Birthday,
Japan (Hirohito, born 1901). Feasts of SS: Peter of Verona, martyr;
Wilfrid the Younger, bishop; Hugh of Cluny, abbot; Robert of Molesmes,
abbot; Joseph Cottolengo.

The Siege of Orleans relieved, 1429. ¶ Execution of Rookwood, Lowick, and Cranbourne for attempted assassination of William III of England, 1696. ¶ The Corn Law Bill received the Royal Assent, 1842. ¶ Leto (Asteroid 68) discovered by R. Luther, and Hesperia (Asteroid 69) by Schiaparelli, 1861. ¶ Women were first admitted to Oxford University examinations, 1885. ¶ The first cargo of North Sea oil was exported from Britain (crude oil to Germany), 1976. ¶ Trades unions are declared legal in Spain (the first time since 1936), 1977.

BORN: Georges Boulanger, soldier and politician, France, 1837. William Randolph Hearst, newspaper publisher, San Francisco, 1863. Sir Thomas Beecham, composer and conductor, 1879. Sir Malcolm Sargent, conductor, London, 1895. Duke Ellington, jazz composer and pianist, Washington D.C., 1899. Hirohito, Emperor of Japan, Tokyo, 1901. Fred Zinnemann, US film director, *The Nun's Story*, Vienna, 1907.

DIED: John Cleveland, poet and cavalier, London, 1658. Michael Adrianszoom de Ruyter, Dutch naval commander, Italy, 1676. James Montgomery, poet, writer of hymns, Sheffield, 1854. Constantine Cavafy, modern Greek poet, 1933. Wallace Carothers, chemist, developed nylon, 1937.

APRIL 30

The Roman Floralia (see 28 April). Walpurgisnacht in Germany when the Witches' Sabbath is held in the Harz Mountains, a time of great evil generally. Feasts of SS: Catherine of Siena, virgin; Maximus, martyr; Marian and James, martyrs; Eutropius, bishop and martyr; Forannan, abbot; Gualfardus, or Wolfhard.

Christians are given legal recognition by the Roman Empire when Galerius Valerius Maximianus issues an Edict at Nicomedia, 311. ¶ French defeat the Anglo-Hanoverian army under Cumberland at Fontenoy, 1745. ¶ John Wilkes is arrested on a general warrant for attacking the King's Speech, London, 1763. ¶ Inauguration of George Washington as President of US, with John Adams as Vice-President, 1789. ¶ US purchases Louisiana Territory and New Orleans from the French, 1803. ¶ Louisiana made a US state (18th), 1812. ¶ Hawaii becomes a US territory, 1900 ¶ Death of Adolf Hitler in a Berlin bunker, 1945. ¶ Saigon falls to the Vietcong and North Vietnamese and is renamed Ho Chi Minh City, 1975.

BORN: Casimir III, King of Poland, founded Cracow University, 1310. Jean Baptiste, Abbé de La Salle, Canon of Reims, founder of the Christian Brothers, Reims, France, 1651. David Thompson, explored western Canada, London, 1770. Carl Friedrich Gauss, mathematician and astronomer, Germany, 1777. Franz Lehar, composer, *The Merry Widow*, Hungary, 1870. Jaroslav Hasek, novelist, *The Good Soldier Schweik*, Prague, 1883. Joachim von Ribbentrop, diplomat, appointed Foreign Minister by Hitler, Wesel, Germany, 1893.

DIED: Edouard Manet, Impressionist painter, *Dejeuner sur l'Herbe*, Paris, 1883. Jens Peter Jacobsen, poet and novelist, *Niels Lynne*, Denmark, 1885. William Welch, bacteriologist and teacher, Baltimore, Maryland, 1934. Alfred Edward Housman, poet, classical scholar and translator, *A Shropshire Lad*, London, 1936. Edwin S. Porter, pioneer US film director, *The Great Train Robbery*, New York City, 1941. Otto Jespersen, philologist and grammarian, *Growth and Structure of the English Language*, Copenhagen, Denmark, 1943. Eva Braun, Hitler's mistress, 1945. Adolf Hitler, Führer of the Third Reich, Berlin, 1945.

MAY

May is commonly thought to come from the Roman
goddess of growth and increase, Maia, the mother
of Hermes. It has also been suggested that the
name derives from the *Majores* or *Mairoes*, the
Senate of early Rome (and June from *Juniores*,
the lower branch of the legislature).

*The Roman Floralia (see 28 April). May Day. Labour Day in many
countries, often a public holiday. Loyalty Day, USA. Spring Feast, Turkey.
Feasts of SS: Philip and James, apostles; Amator, or Amatre, bishop;
Brieuc, or Briocus, abbot; Sigismund of Burgundy; Marculf, or
Marcoul, abbot; Theodard of Narbonne, archbishop; Peregrine Laziosi.*

Defeat of Maximinus at Tzirallum by Licinius Licinianus, 313. ¶ Union of
Scotland and England proclaimed, 1707. ¶ The first British 'Penny Black' stamps,
bearing the head of Queen Victoria, are made available to the public, 1840.
¶ The London Library, founded by Thomas Carlyle, W. E. Gladstone, Lord
Macaulay and others, is officially opened, 1841. ¶ The Great Exhibition in
London opens (closes 11 October), 1851. ¶ The World's Columbian Exposition
opened in Chicago by President Grover Cleveland, 1893. ¶ US Admiral
George Dewey routs the Spanish Fleet at Manila, 1898. ¶ German submarines
sink the *Gulflight*, a US vessel, without warning, 1915. ¶ Sebastopol occupied by
German troops, 1918. ¶ Beginning of the British miners' strike (lasts until early
November), 1926. ¶ Surrender of the German Army in Italy, 1945. ¶ USSR
shoot down U-2 plane flown by Francis Gary Powers, 1960. ¶ Major offensive
by US and South Vietnam forces into Cambodia, 1970.

BORN: Rudolf I of Hapsburg, Holy Roman Emperor, founder of the Hapsburg
dynasty, Schloss Limburg (Germany), 1218. Sébastien Le Prestre de Vauban,
statesman and military engineer, Marshal of France, Saint Leger, France, 1633.
Joseph Addison, essayist and critic, Wiltshire, 1672. Arthur Wellesley, Duke of
Wellington, military commander and statesman, defeated Napoleon in the
Peninsular and at Waterloo, British Prime Minister, Dublin, 1769. Hilaire,
Comte de Chardonnet, invented rayon, France, 1839.

DIED: Dermot MacMurrough, Irish King of Leinster, 1171. John Dryden, poet,
translator, dramatist, London, 1700. Antonin Dvorák, composer, *Slavonic
Dances*, 1904. José Enrique Rodó, Uruguayan essayist, *Ariel, Los motivos de
Proteo*, Palermo, 1917. Joseph Goebbels, Nazi leader and propagandist; suicide,
1945. William Fox, film impresario, a founder of 20th Century Fox, New
York, 1952.

MAY 2

The Roman Floralia (see 28 April). King's Birthday Celebration,
Lesotho (King Moshoeshoe II). Feasts of SS: Athanasius, archbishop and doctor;
Exsuperius and Zoë, martyrs; Waldebert, abbot; Ultan, abbot;
Wiborada, virgin and martyr; Conrad of Seldenbüren; Mafalda.

The Hudson Bay Company is incorporated as the 'Governor and Company of Adventurers of England trading into Hudson's Bay' under Prince Rupert, 1670. ¶ American mission in Paris succeeds in loaning 1 million livres from the French, 1776. ¶ Mutiny of the British navy at the Nore, 1797. ¶ Sappho (Asteroid 80) discovered by Norman Pogson, 1864. ¶ US forces arrive in Nicaragua to restore order after revolt, 1926. ¶ Suppression of German trades unions, 1933. ¶ Berlin falls and surrenders to Russian forces, 1945. ¶ TV transmissions relayed by US satellite *Early Bird* for the first time, 1965. ¶ Harold Wilson announces in the House of Commons that Britain will apply for membership of the Common Market, 1967. ¶ Spain closes the frontier with Gibraltar, 1968.

BORN: Alessandro Scarlatti, Baroque composer, Palermo, Italy, 1660. Novalis (Friedrich Leopold Freiherr von Hardenburg), German Romantic poet and novelist, *Hymnen an die Nacht, Heinrich von Ofterdingen,* Prussian Saxony, 1772. Theodor Herzl, Zionist, *The Jewish State,* Budapest, Hungary, 1860. Lorenz Hart, song writer and composer, New York City, 1895. Dr Benjamin Spock, child care specialist, New Haven, Connecticut, 1903. Bing Crosby, American popular singer and actor, Washington, 1904. Satyajit Ray, film director, *Pather Panchali,* Calcutta, 1921.

DIED: Leonardo da Vinci, poet, painter, writer and engineer, 1519. William Beckford, novelist, *Vathek,* 1844. Frederick Scott Archer, photographic inventor, 1857. Alfred de Musset, poet, novelist and dramatist, *Les Nuits,* Paris, 1857. Giacomo Meyerbeer, operatic composer, Paris, 1864. Senator Joseph McCarthy, prominent anti-communist and witch-hunter, Maryland, 1957. Lady Astor, the first woman to become a Member of Parliament, 1964. J. Edgar Hoover, founder and head of the Federal Bureau of Investigation, Washington D.C., 1972.

MAY 3

*The Feast of the Finding (or Invention) of the Holy Cross, celebrates
the discovery of the True Cross in Jerusalem, c. 326, by St Helen,
the Emperor Constantine's mother; first noted as a feast in a lectionary
of the 7th century. The Roman Floralia (see 28 April).
Dies Mala or 'Egyptian Day,' considered unlucky in the Middle Ages.
Constitution Memorial Day, Japan. Feasts of SS: Alexander,
Eventius and Theodulus, martyrs; Timothy and Maura, martyrs;
Juvenal, bishop; Philip of Zell.*

Columbus discovers Jamaica on his second expedition, 1494. ¶ Cabral the
Portuguese lands in Brazil, 1500. ¶ Pope Leo X's *Inter Sollicitudines* Bull is
promulgated, whereby *all* writings were to be examined by the Church prior to
their printing, 1515. ¶ Total eclipse, well-observed in England, 1715. ¶ US
create Navy Department to fight French in the West Indies, 1798. ¶ Louis XVIII
enters Paris, 1814. ¶ New Zealand proclaimed a British colony, 1841.
¶ Beginning of the war between the British, in India, and Afghanistan (ends
3 August), 1919. ¶ Hitler arrives in Rome to meet Benito Mussolini, 1938.

BORN: Nicolo Machiavelli, diplomat and writer, *The Prince*, Florence, 1469.
Emmanuel Sieyès, French Revolutionary leader, aided Napoleon in the Revolution of 18th Brumaire, Fréjus, France, 1748. François Coty, perfumier, Corsica,
1874. Mikhail Afanasyevich Bulgakov, dramatist and novelist, *The White Guard*,
Kiev, 1891. Golda Meir, Israeli Prime Minister, Kiev, 1898. William Inge,
dramatist, *Come back little Sheba*, Kansas, 1913. Pete Seeger, American folk-
singer, New York City, 1919.

DIED: Thomas Hood, poet and humorist, *The Song of the Shirt*, Finchley Road,
London, 1845. Henry Cornelius, film director, *Passport to Pimlico*, London, 1958.
Karl Freund, cinematographer, *Metropolis*, *Camille*, Santa Monica, California,
1969.

MAY 4

Rhode Island Independence Day, Rhode Island, USA.
The Feast of the Martyrs of England and Wales, generally observed
only in those two countries and at the church of the English College, Rome;
the collective feast celebrates some 200 beatified martyrs who died between
1535–1681. Feasts of SS: Monica, widow; Cyriacus, or Judas Quiriacus, bishop;
Pelagia of Tarsus, virgin and martyr; Florian, martyr; Venerius, bishop;
Godehard, or Gothard, bishop; Catherine of Parc-aux-Dames, virgin;
Gregory of Verucchio; Michael Gedroye.

Lancastrians defeated by the Yorkists at Tewkesbury, 1471. ¶ The Royal Charter of Incorporation for the Stationers' Company of London is issued, 1557. ¶ Natal is proclaimed a British Colony, 1843. ¶ Maori risings against the British in New Zealand, 1863. ¶ Inauguration of the (George) Washington Memorial Arch in New York, 1895. ¶ The *Daily Mail* first published, Britain's first halfpenny daily newspaper, 1896. ¶ The Geneva Conference on arms, poison gas, and related matters begins, 1925. ¶ The British General Strike begins (lasts until 12 May), 1926. ¶ Four students are shot dead by National Guardsmen at Kent State University in US during demonstrations against the Vietnam war, 1970. ¶ 'Waltzing Matilda' is officially adopted as Australia's national anthem, 1976.

BORN: Bartolommeo Cristofori, craftsman, developed the first pianofortes, Padua, Italy, 1655, Johann Herbart, philosopher and educationalist, Oldenburg, Germany, 1776. William Prescott, historian, *The History of the Conquest of Mexico*, *The History of the Conquest of Peru*, Salem, Massachusetts, 1796. Thomas Henry Huxley, biologist, Ealing, Middlesex, 1825. Alexandre Benois, painter and theatrical designer, St Petersburg, Russia, 1870. Sir Archibald McIndoe, plastic surgeon, New Zealand, 1900. Audrey Hepburn, actress, Brussels, 1929.

DIED: William Froude, naval architect, 1879. Carl von Ossietzky, pacifist and opponent of Hitler, Berlin, 1938. Georges Enesco, Rumanian composer and violinist, 1955. Sir Osbert Sitwell, poet and writer, *Laughter in the Next Room*, *Noble Essences*, near Florence, 1969.

MAY 5

Children's Day, Japan. Children's Day, Republic of Korea.
Coronation Day, Thailand. Feasts of SS: Pius V, pope. Hilary of Arles, bishop;
Mauruntius, abbot; Avertinus; Angelo, martyr; Jutta, widow.

Proserpine (Asteroid 26) discovered by R. Luther, 1853. ¶ Garibaldi sails for
Genoa, 1860. ¶ Panopoea (Asteroid 70) discovered by H. Goldschmidt, 1861.
¶ Spain renounces San Domingo after revolt, 1865. ¶ Addis Ababa is occupied
by the Italians, thus ends the war with Abyssinia, 1936. ¶ Major Yuri Gagarin of
USSR in orbiting the Earth becomes the first spaceman, 1961. ¶ The next
conjunction of the Sun, Moon, Mercury, Venus, Mars, Jupiter and Saturn, 2000.

BORN: Louis Hachette, bookseller, publisher and editor, Rethel, France, 1800.
Sören Kierkegaard, philosopher and theologian, *Either-Or*, Copenhagen,
Denmark, 1813. Eugène Labiche, dramatist, Paris, 1815. Karl Marx, philosopher
and economist, *The Communist Manifesto, Das Kapital*, Trier, Germany, 1818.
Henryk Sienkiewicz, novelist, *Quo Vadis?*, Poland, 1846. Sir Gordon Richards,
champion jockey, Shropshire, 1904.

DIED: Napoleon Bonaparte, French Emperor and military commander,
St Helena, 1821. August von Hofmann, chemist, dye technologist, Berlin, 1892.
Bret Harte, American writer, poet and editor, *Condensed Novels*, London, 1902.
Ludwig Erhard, German economist and statesman, 1977.

MAY 6

Feasts of SS: John before the Latin Gate; Evodius, bishop;
Edbert, bishop; Petronax, abbot; Prudence, virgin.

Frederick II of Prussia takes Prague (Seven Years War), 1757. ¶ The Canada Constitution Act divides Canada into two provinces: Lower (Quebec) and Upper (Ontario), 1791. ¶ Arkansas secedes from the Union (readmitted 22 June 1868), 1861. ¶ General Robert E. Lee of the Confederacy routes the Union Army under the command of Joseph E. Hooker at the battle of Chancellorsville in Virginia, 1863. ¶ Fenians murder Lord Frederick Cavendish and T. H. Burke at Phoenix Park, Dublin, 1882. ¶ Chinese immigrants are banned for ten years by US, 1882. ¶ Accession of George V to the throne upon the death of Edward VII, 1910. ¶ Josef Stalin is made leader of USSR government, 1941. ¶ Princess Margaret marries Antony Armstrong-Jones, a photographer, 1960. ¶ Ian Brady and Myra Hindley, the 'Moors Murderers', found guilty in Chester of murder on several counts, 1966.

BORN: Sigmund Freud, psychiatrist, founder of psychoanalysis, Moravia, 1856. Robert Edwin Peary, Arctic explorer, supposedly the first man to reach the North Pole, Cresson, Pennsylvania, 1856. Luis Drago, Argentinian statesman (Drago Doctrine), 1859. Nicholas II, Tsar of Russia, Tsarskoya Selo, Russia, 1868. Stanley Morison, typographer and type-designer, Wanstead, Essex, 1889. Rudolph Valentino, film actor, *The Sheik*, Castellaneta, Italy, 1895. Max Ophüls, film director, *Lola Montès*, Sarrebrück, Germany, 1902. Harry Martinson, poet and dramatist, Sweden, 1904. Orson Welles, actor, director, producer and writer in the cinema and theatre, *Citizen Kane*, *The Magnificent Ambersons*, Kenosha, Wisconsin, 1915.

DIED: Juan Luis Vives (Ludovicus Vives), Spanish humanist and philosopher, Bruges, Belgium, 1540. Cornelius Jansen, theologian and clergyman, 1638. Baron Alexander von Humboldt, explorer, naturalist and scientist, *Cosmos*, Berlin, 1859. Henry David Thoreau, writer and naturalist, *Walden, or Life in the Woods*, *A Week on the Concord and Merrimack Rivers*, Concord, Massachusetts, 1862. Edward VII of England, 1910. Maurice Maeterlinck, poet, dramatist and author, *The Blue Bird*, *The Life of the Bee*, Nice, 1949. Maria Montessori, educator and teacher, *The Montessori Method*, Holland, 1952.

MAY 7

Feasts of SS: Stanislaus, bishop and martyr; Domitian, bishop;
Liudhard, bishop; Serenicus and Serenus; John of Beverley, bishop.

Rising of Indians near Detroit under Pontiac, 1763. ¶ Sierra Leone, Gold Coast and Gambia become British West Africa after the Africa Company is dissolved, 1821. ¶ The *Lusitania* is sunk by the Germans off the coast of Ireland, nearly 2000 people perish, 1915. ¶ Suffrage for women reduced in Britain from the age of 30 to 21, 1926. ¶ General Eisenhower accepts the capitulation of Germany from General Jodl, 1945. ¶ The Communist Vietnamese capture Dien Bien Phu, 1954.

BORN: David Hume, philosopher and historian, *Treatise on Human Nature*, Edinburgh, 1711. Robert Browning, poet and writer, *The Ring and the Book*, London, 1812. Richard Norman Shaw, architect, Edinburgh, 1831. Johannes Brahms, composer, Hamburg, 1833. Sir Rabindranath Tagore, poet, novelist and essayist, Nobel Prize for Literature, *The Crescent Moon*, Calcutta, 1861. Archibald MacLeish, poet and playwright, *New Found Land*, Glencoe, Illinois, 1892. Marshal Tito, statesman, Prime Minister of Yugoslavia, Croatia, 1892. Gary Cooper, motion-picture actor, Montana, 1901. Edwin Herbert Land, inventor of the Polaroid camera, Connecticut, 1909.

DIED: Caspar David Friedrich, Romantic landscape painter, 1840. Thomas Barnes, editor of *The Times*, 1841. Henry, 1st Baron Brougham and Vaux, jurist and politician, 1868. James Nasmyth, engineer, invented the first steam hammer, London, 1890. George Lansbury, British Labour Party politician, London, 1940. Sir James Frazer, scholar and anthropologist, *The Golden Bough*, 1941.

MAY 8

Truman's Birthday, Missouri, USA (Harry S. Truman, 1884–1972,
US President). The Feast of the Appearing of St Michael the Archangel,
celebrating the manifestations of St Michael at Mount Garganus in Apulia,
AD492–6. Feasts of SS: Victor Maurus, martyr; Acacius, or Agathus, martyr;
Gibrian; Desideratus, bishop; Boniface IV, pope; Benedict II, pope; Wiro,
Plechelm and Otger; Peter of Tarentaise, archbishop.

Restoration of the British monarchy after the Commonwealth, 1660. ¶ The
French are defeated at Fuentes d'Onoro by Arthur Wellesley (Duke of Wellington), 1811. ¶ Mexicans defeated by US forces at Matamoros, 1846. ¶ Temple's
Comet observed at the Cape, 1894. ¶ Sweden abolishes capital punishment,
1921. ¶ 'V.E.' Day (Victory in Europe), 1945. ¶ China rejects a Soviet proposal
for a world conference of Communist parties to settle ideological disputes,
1964.

BORN: Miguel Hidalgo y Costilla, Mexican revolutionary leader and priest,
Mexico, 1753. Thomas Hancock, inventor, Wiltshire, 1786. Jean-Baptist,
Vianney, Catholic priest and preacher, Dardilly, France, 1786. Jean Henri
Dunant, founder of the International Red Cross, Geneva, 1828. Nevil Sidgwick,
chemist, Oxford, 1873. Harry S. Truman, US President, near Lamar, Missouri,
1884. Sir William Darling, soldier and civic dignitary, Lord Provost of Edin-
burgh, *A Book of Days*, Edinburgh, 1885. Edmund Wilson, novelist and critic,
Red Bank, New Jersey, 1895.

DIED: Antoine Laurent Lavoisier, chemist; guillotined, Paris, 1794. John Stuart
Mill, Utilitarian philosopher, economist, *Principles of Political Economy, On
Liberty, Autobiography*, Avignon, France, 1873. Truganini, the last Tasmanian
Aborigine, Tasmania, 1876. Gustave Flaubert, novelist, *Madame Bovary*, 1880.
Paul Gauguin, Post-Impressionist painter, 1903. Eadweard Muybridge, motion
photographer, Kingston-upon-Thames, Surrey, 1904. Oswald Spengler,
teacher and philosopher, *The Decline of the West*, Munich, 1936. Harry Gordon
Selfridge, American founder of the Oxford Street (London) Department Store,
London, 1947.

MAY 9

*The Roman Lemuralia, a festival propitiating the ghosts of the dead
(also 11 and 13 May). Liberation Day, Channel Islands (1945,
the ending of the German occupation of the Islands). Anniversary of the
Liberation, Czechoslovakia (from German occupation by Soviet and
US forces in 1945). Victory Day, USSR. Feasts of SS:
Gregory Nazianzen, bishop and doctor; Beatus; Pachomius, abbot;
Gerontius, bishop.*

Christopher Columbus sets sails on his fourth voyage, 1502. ¶ John Byron returns from around-the-world navigation, 1766. ¶ Motion by British Parliament for abolition of Slave Trade, 1788. ¶ Tram-ways from Brixton to Kennington, and from Whitechapel to Bow opened in London, 1870. ¶ The Victoria Embankment in London opened by the Duke of Edinburgh, 1874. ¶ The Imperial Customs Service taken over by the Chinese, 1906. ¶ Bix Beiderbecke records *River Boat Shuffle*, 1927. ¶ Abyssinia is annexed by Italy in a formal proclamation, 1936. ¶ Russian troops enter Prague, 1945. ¶ A beam of light was successfully bounced off the Moon by US scientists using a laser, 1962. ¶ Mines were dropped around all major North Vietnamese ports by US planes, 1972. ¶ Hearings into the possible impeachment of President Richard M. Nixon are begun by the Judiciary Committee of the House of Representatives, 1974.

BORN: John Brown, anti-slaver, agitator and campaigner, Connecticut, 1800. Sir James Barrie, dramatist and novelist, *Peter Pan*, Angus, Scotland, 1860. Howard Carter, Egyptologist, discovered the tomb of Tutankhamun, Norfolk, 1873. Dame Lilian Baylis, theatrical manager, founded the Old Vic and Sadler's Wells companies, London, 1874. José Ortega y Gasset, philosopher and statesman, *The Revolt of the Masses*, Madrid, 1883. Albert Finney, actor and director, Lancashire, 1936.

DIED: William Bradford, Puritan, Pilgrim Father, Governor of Plymouth, 1657. Count Zinzendorf, re-founder of the Moravian Brethren, Germany, 1760. Friedrich von Schiller, poet, dramatist and historian, *Wallenstein*, Weimar, Germany, 1805. Joseph Gay-Lussac, chemist, 1850. Anthony Wilding, New Zealand tennis champion, 1915. Albert Abraham Michelson, American physicist, Pasadena, California, 1931. Walter Philip Reuther, US labour leader, Michigan, 1970.

MAY 10

Confederate Memorial Day, North and South Carolina, USA.
Feasts of SS: Antoninus of Florence, archbishop; Galepodius, martyr;
Gordian and Epimachus, martyrs; Alphius and his Companions, martyrs;
Catald and Conleth, bishops; Solangia, virgin and martyr.

Rioting in St George's Fields over John Wilkes' imprisonment in the King's Bench, 1768. ¶ Accession of Louis XVI of France, 1774. ¶ Fort Ticonderoga in New York falls to the Americans in the War of Independence, 1775. ¶ Warren Hastings impeached by Edmund Burke, 1787. ¶ Napoleon defeats Austrians at Lodi, 1796. ¶ The Sepoy Revolt at Meerut begins the Indian Mutiny, 1857. ¶ The President of the Confederacy, Jefferson Davis, is taken prisoner by the Union at Irwinsville in Georgia, 1865. ¶ Transcontinental railway established in the US with the joining of the Central Pacific and Union Pacific lines at Promontory in Utah, 1869. ¶ Louis Armstrong records *Alligator Crawl* with his Hot Seven in Chicago, 1927. ¶ Local Defense Volunteers established in Britain (later known as the 'Home Guard'), 1940. ¶ German invasions of Holland, Belgium and Luxembourg, 1940.

BORN: Augustin-Jean Fresnel, physicist, France, 1788. John Wilkes Booth, actor, assassin of President Abraham Lincoln, Maryland, 1838. James Bryce, historian and diplomat, *The Holy Roman Empire*, Belfast, 1838. Benito Perez Galdos, novelist and dramatist, *Episodios nacionales* (a series of 46 novels), Las Palmas, Canary Islands, 1843. Gustav Stresemann, German statesman, Nobel Prize for Peace, Berlin, 1878. Karl Barth, theologian and writer, Switzerland, 1886. Fred Astaire, dancer and actor, Omaha, Nebraska, 1899. David O. Selznick, film producer, *Gone with the Wind*, Pittsburg, Pennsylvania, 1902.

DIED: Gaius Julius Verus Maximinus, Roman emperor; murdered at the siege of Aquileia by his own troops, 238. Leonhard Fuchs, physician and botanist, 1566. Louis XV of France, Versailles, 1774. George Vancouver, naval captain and explorer, Richmond, Surrey, 1798. Paul Revere, American patriot, Boston, Massachusetts, 1818. Thomas Young, physicist, London, 1829. Thomas Jonathan 'Stonewall' Jackson, Confederate general in the American Civil War, near Chancellorsville, Virginia, 1863. Sir Henry Stanley, explorer and journalist, London, 1904. John Wesley Hyatt, US inventor, discovered celluloid, 1920. Joan Crawford, actress, 1977.

MAY 11

*The Roman Lemuralia, a festival propitiating the ghosts of the dead (also
9 and 13 May). Feasts of SS: Mamertus, bishop; Comgall, abbot;
Asaph, bishop; Gengulf, or Gengoul; Majolus, or Mayeul, abbot;
Ansfrid, bishop; Walter of L'Esterp, abbot; The English Carthusian Martyrs;
Francis di Girolamo; Ignatius of Laconi.*

Assassination of the British Prime Minister Spencer Percival by Bellingham,
1812. ¶ British forces capture Rangoon, 1824. ¶ Parthenope (Asteroid 11)
discovered by de Gasparis, 1850. ¶ Minnesota made a US state (32nd), 1858.
¶ Thailand is adopted as the new name for Siam, 1949. ¶ The United Nations
admit Israel, 1949. ¶ During rioting in Augusta, Georgia, 6 blacks are killed,
1970.

BORN: Ottmar Mergenthaler, inventor of the Linotype composing machine,
Hachtel, Germany, 1854. Irving Berlin, American popular song writer, Russia,
1888. Martha Graham, dancer and choreographer, Pittsburgh, 1893. Salvador
Dali, Surrealist painter, Spain, 1904. Mikhail Aleksandrovich Sholokhov,
novelist, *And Quiet Flows the Don*, Veshenskaya, Russia, 1905. Mort Sahl,
satirist and actor, Montreal, Canada, 1927.

DIED: Matteo Ricci, Jesuit missionary in China, China, 1610. Otto von Guericke,
physicist, demonstrated the vacuum, Hamburg, Germany, 1686. Jean de La
Bruyère, writer and moralist, *Caractères*, 1696. Jules Hardouin Mansart, architect,
designed the Galerie de Glaces at Versailles, France, 1708. William Pitt ('the
Elder'), Earl of Chatham, statesman, Secretary of State, Hayes, Kent, 1778.
Spencer Percival, British Prime Minister; assassinated, London, 1812. Sir John
Herschel, astronomer, London, 1871. Juan Gris, Cubist painter, France, 1927.
Edward Herbert Thompson, South American explorer, excavated several
Mayan cities, Plainfield, New Jersey, 1935. Frederic William Goudy, American
printer and type designer, 1947.

Feasts of SS: Nereus, Achilleus and Domitilla, martyrs; Pancras, martyr;
Epiphanius of Salamis, bishop; Modoaldus, bishop; Rictrudis, widow;
Germanus of Constantinople, bishop; Dominic of the Causeway.

The French are defeated at Oporto by Arthur Wellesley, 1809. ¶ The 'Oxford Declaration', supposedly drawn up by Archdeacon Denison and Dr Pusey, is presented to the Archbishop of Canterbury bearing the signatures of over 3,000 clergy, 1864. ¶ Russian forces occupy Samarkand, 1868. ¶ Manitoba becomes a *province* of Canada, 1870. ¶ Hermione (Asteroid 121) discovered by J. C. Watson, 1872. ¶ Johann Most arrested in New York on charges arising from the 'eight hours' riots and outrages in Chicago and elsewhere, 1886. ¶ The British General Strike ends (began on 4 May), 1926. ¶ US Agricultural Adjustment Act, 1933. ¶ The *Mayaguez*, a US merchant ship, was seized by the Cambodian Navy, 1975.

BORN: Augustus II, Elector of Saxony and King of Poland, Dresden, 1670. Edward Lear, artist and poet, *The Book of Nonsense*, Highgate, London, 1812. Dante Gabriel Rossetti, poet and painter, a member of the Pre-Raphaelite Brotherhood, *The Blessed Damozel*, *The House of Life*, London, 1828. Jules Emile Massenet, composer, *Manon*, France, 1842. Gabriel Fauré, composer and organist, France, 1845. Lincoln Ellsworth, civil engineer and polar explorer, Chicago, 1880. Philip Wylie, novelist and critic, *Generation of Vipers*, Beverly, Massachusetts, 1902. Julius Rosenberg, convicted of spying for Soviet intelligence, New York City, 1918.

DIED: Waldemar the Great, King of Denmark, Denmark, 1182. Thomas Wentworth, Earl of Strafford, statesman and supporter of Charles I, Lord Deputy of Ireland; executed, London, 1641. August Wilhelm Schlegel, poet, critic and scholar, *Dramatic Art and Literature*, Bonn, 1845. Sir Charles Barry, architect, rebuilt the Houses of Parliament, 1860. Joris Karl Huysmans, novelist, *Là-Bas*, *The Oblate*, Paris, 1907. Amy Lowell, Imagist poet, Massachusetts, 1925. Józef Pilsudski, Polish soldier and revolutionary, Warsaw, 1935. Erich von Stroheim, actor and film director, *Greed*, *Queen Kelly*, 1957. John Masefield, Poet Laureate, *Salt Water Poems and Ballads*, *Reynard the Fox*, 1967.

MAY 13

*The Roman Lemuralia, a festival propitiating the ghosts of the dead
(also 9 and 11 May). Feasts of SS: Robert Bellarmine, archbishop and doctor;
Glyceria, virgin and martyr; Mucius, martyr; Servatius, or Servais, bishop;
John the Silent; Erconwald, bishop; Euthymius the Enlightener, abbot;
Peter Regalatus; Andrew Hubert Fournet.*

Mary of Scotland defeated at the battle of Langside, 1568. ¶ Formal declaration of war against Mexico by US, 1846. ¶ The Royal Flying Corps established in Britain, 1912. ¶ 'Black Friday' signals the total collapse of Germany's economic system, 1927. ¶ Violent demonstrations in Paris and throughout France by left-wing students and others (lasts for several days), 1968. ¶ A state of emergency is declared in Kuala Lumpur, Malaysia, after continued fighting between Malays and Chinese, 1969.

BORN: Maria Theresa, Queen of Hungary and Bohemia, Vienna, 1717. Sir Arthur Sullivan, composer, *The Mikado, Ruddigore*, London, 1842. Georges Braque, Cubist painter, France, 1882. Earl Birney, Canadian poet and writer, *Trial of a City*, 1904. Daphne Du Maurier, novelist, *Jamaica Inn*, London, 1907. Joe Louis, heavyweight boxer, Lexington, Alabama, 1914.

DIED: Baron Georges Cuvier, naturalist and taxonomist, 1832. John Nash, architect and planner, Isle of Wight, 1835. Joseph Henry, American physicist, 1878. Cyrus Hall McCormick, engineer, perfected the mechanical harvester, Chicago, 1884. Sholem Aleichem (Solomon J. Rabinowitz), Yiddish writer, New York City, 1916. Fridtjof Nansen, explorer, zoologist and statesman, Nobel Peace Prize, Lysaker, Norway, 1930. Frances Hodgkins, New Zealand painter, 1947. Gary Cooper, motion-picture actor, 1961.

MAY 14

Commonly accepted as the day of Christ's Ascension, AD33.
Mallard Day at All-Souls College, Oxford, an occasion for great 'merry-making';
supposedly originating in the discovery of a mallard, 'grown to a vast bigness',
when the College's foundations were being dug.
Anniversary of the Guinean Democratic Party, Republic of Guinea.
Kamazu Day, Malawi (birthday of Dr Hastings Kamuzu Banda, Life President).
National Flag Day, Paraguay. Feasts of SS: Pontius, martyr;
Boniface of Tarsus, martyr; Carthage, Carthach, or Mochuda, abbot;
Erembert, bishop; Michael Garicoits; Mary Mazzarello, virgin.

Victory of the English barons at the battle of Lewes, 1264. ¶ Assassination of Henry IV of France by Ravaillac, 1610. ¶ Accession of Louis XIV of France, aged 4 years (Anne of Austria was the regent), 1643. ¶ Tippoo of Mysore defeated at Seringapatam by Lord Cornwallis, 1791. ¶ Surrender of the Dutch army to Germany, 1940. ¶ Premier Khrushchev of the USSR and President Nasser of Egypt set off charges diverting the River Nile from the site of the Aswan High Dam, 1964. ¶ US launch *Skylab* space station from Cape Kennedy (first astronauts link-up with the station on 25 May), 1973.

BORN: Thomas Gainsborough, artist, portrait painter, 1727. Robert Owen, reformer and socialist, Montgomeryshire, Scotland, 1771. Otto Klemperer, conductor, Germany, 1885.

DIED: August Strindberg, dramatist, novelist and poet, *Miss Julie, The Red Room*, Stockholm, 1912. Henry John Heinz, US food manufacturer, 1919. Edmund, Viscount Allenby, military commander, 1936. Sir William Dobell, Australian painter, 1970.

Whitsunday, a fixed Scottish Quarter Day. Independence Day,
Paraguay (1811). Feasts of SS: John Baptist de la Salle; Torquatus and his
Companions, martyrs; Isidore of Chios, martyr; Peter of Lampsacus
and his Companions, martyrs; Hilary of Galeata, abbot; Dympna and
Gerebernus, martyrs; Bertha and Rupert; Hallvard, martyr;
Isaias of Rostov, bishop; Isidore the Husbandman.

Lancastrians defeated by the Yorkists at Hexham, 1464. ¶ The Anabaptists
defeated at the battle of Frankenhausen, 1525. ¶ Milan entered by Napoleon,
1796. ¶ Attempted assassination of George III by James Hatfield, 1800. ¶ The
world's first regular air mail service begins, between New York and Washington, operated for the US Post Office by the US Army, 1918. ¶ Beginning of the
Winnipeg General Strike, 1919. ¶ Upper Silesia ceded to Poland by Germany,
1922. ¶ In *Atlas* rocket US astronaut Gordon Cooper makes twenty-two orbits
of Earth, 1963. ¶ The first electricity flows from Benmore to North Island by
the Cook Strait cable, New Zealand, 1966. ¶ During rioting at Jackson State
College in Mississippi two black students are shot dead by the police, many more
injured, 1970. ¶ Attempted assassination of Governor George Wallace of
Alabama at Laurel, Maryland, 1972. ¶ Inauguration of General Spinola as
President of Portugal (after *coup* on 25 April), 1974.

BORN: Klemens Metternich, statesman and diplomat, Coldenz, Austria, 1773.
Clarence Dutton, geologist, Connecticut, 1841. Pierre Curie, French chemist,
physicist, Paris, 1859. Arthur Schnitzler, dramatist and author, *Reiger (La Ronde)*,
Anatol, Vienna, 1862. Edwin Muir, Scottish poet, translator and critic, *First*
Poems, *The Story and the Fable*, *Poor Tom*, Orkney, 1887. Katherine Anne Porter,
short-story writer and novelist, *Pale Horse, Pale Rider*, *Ship of Fools*, Indian Creek,
Texas, 1890. James Mason, actor, Huddersfield, Yorkshire, 1909. Max Frisch,
Swiss dramatist, *The Fire Raisers*, 1911.

DIED: Richard Wilson, landscape painter, near Caernarvon, Wales, 1782.
Edmund Kean, English actor, 1833. Emily Dickinson, American poetess, 1886.
Etienne-Jules Marey, pioneer of cinematography, Paris, 1904. Philip Snowden,
Labour Party politician, Tilford, Surrey, 1937. Herbert Wilcox, film producer,
Nurse Edith Cavell, 1977.

MAY 16

*Feasts of SS: Ubald of Gubbio, bishop; Peregrine of Auxerre,
bishop and martyr; Possidius, bishop; Germerius, bishop;
Brendan, abbot; Domnolus, bishop; Carantoc, or Carannog, abbot;
Honoratus of Amiens, bishop; Simon Stock; John Nepomucen, martyr.*

Elagabalus (Heliogabalus, originally Varius Avitus) is proclaimed Emperor of Rome at Raphaneae, 218. ¶ First meeting of Dr Johnson and James Boswell, 1763. ¶ The Dauphin of France marries Marie Antoinette, 1770. ¶ Establishment of the Batavian Republic in Holland, 1795. ¶ The Lombardic Republic is established, 1796. ¶ Napoleon is proclaimed Emperor by Senate and Tribune, 1804. ¶ Sylvia (Asteroid 87) discovered by Norman Pogson, 1866. ¶ British Columbia is admitted into the Dominion of Canada as a Province, 1871. ¶ The first Academy Awards were presented in Los Angeles, 1929. ¶ *Venus 5*, Russian spacecraft, touches down on Venus, 1969.

BORN: John Sell Cotman, watercolourist, Norwich, Norfolk, 1782. David Edward Hughes, inventor of the teleprinter and microphone, London, 1831. Philip Armour, food industrialist, founder of the Armour Company, New York, 1832. Henry Fonda, actor, Nebraska, 1905. Woody Herman, jazz clarinetist and band-leader, Milwaukee, Wisconsin, 1913. Liberace, pianist and entertainer, Wisconsin, 1919.

DIED: Pietro da Cortona, Florentine painter and architect, Rome, 1669. Charles Pérrault, writer and critic, collector and publisher of fairy tales, *Les Contes de Ma Mère L'Oye*, Paris, 1703. Jean Baptiste Fourier, mathematician and physicist, 1830. Felicia Hemans, poet, *The Landing of the Pilgrim Fathers, Casabianca*, Dublin, 1835. Mily Alexeyvich Balakirev, Russian composer, *Tamara*, 1910. William Pember Reeves, politician and poet. *The Long White Cloud*, New Zealand, 1932. Bronislaw Malinowski, anthropologist, New Haven, Connecticut, 1942.

MAY 17

*Independence Day, Norway (1814). Feasts of SS: Paschal Baylon;
Madron, or Madern; Bruno of Würzburg, bishop.*

The first regular comic is published, *Comic Cuts* by Alfred Harmsworth in London, 1890. ¶ Mafeking is relieved, 1900. ¶ The Daylight Saving Act is passed in Britain, 1916. ¶ Teddy Hill and his NBC Orchestra record *King Porter Stomp*, the first recording featuring Dizzy Gillespie, in New York City, 1937. ¶ The first American quiz show on radio. *Information Please*, 1938. ¶ US Senate Select Committee begins investigations into the 1972 presidential election ('Watergate' hearings), 1973.

BORN: Edward Jenner, physician, discovered vaccination, Berkeley, Gloucestershire, 1749. Robert Surtees, novelist and sports writer, *Jorrocks' Jaunts and Jollities, Mr Sponge's Sporting Tours*, Northumberland, 1803. Mikhail Bakunin, anarchist, Russia, 1814. Sir Norman Lockyer, astronomer, discovered helium, Rugby, 1836. Erik Satie, composer, *La Belle Eccentrique*, Calvados, France, 1866. Henri Barbusse, novelist, *Under Fire, Hell*, France, 1873. Dorothy Richardson, novelist, *Pilgrimage* (a sequence), Abingdon, Berkshire, 1873.

DIED: Sandro Botticelli, Florentine painter, *The Birth of Venus*, 1510. Leopold Auenbrugger, physician, 1809. Charles Maurice de Talleyrand-Périgord, statesman and politician, Paris, 1838. Paul Dukas, critic and composer, *The Sorcerer's Apprentice*, 1935.

MAY 18

Flag Day, Haiti. Anniversary of the Battle of Las Piedras, Uruguay.
Feasts of SS: Verantius, martyr; Theodotus, Thecusa and their
Companions, martyrs; Potamon, bishop and martyr; Eric of Sweden, martyr;
Felix of Cantalice.

Huntley defeats Crawford at Brechin in Scotland, 1452. ¶ Formal founding of Ville Marie (Montreal), Canada, 1642. ¶ Saint John in New Brunswick becomes the first Canadian city to be incorporated, 1785. ¶ Renewed conflict between Britain and France, 1803. ¶ The Tennessee Valley Authority is created in the US to develop the area's resources, 1933. ¶ Allies capture Monte Cassino in Italy, 1944.

BORN: Joseph Butler, theologian, *The Analogy of Religion*, Berkshire, 1692. Oliver Heaviside, physicist, London, 1850. Bertrand Russell, philosopher, mathematician and reformer, *An Introduction to Mathematical Philosophy*, *The Analysis of Mind*, Monmouthshire, Wales, 1872. Walter Gropius, architect, founder of the Bauhaus, Berlin, 1883. Richard Brooks, film director, *Key Largo*, *Elmer Gantry*, Philadelphia, Pennsylvania, 1912. Dame Margot Fonteyn, ballet dancer, Surrey, 1919.

DIED: Pierre de Beaumarchais, dramatist, *The Barber of Seville*, 1799. Isaac Albéniz, Spanish pianist and composer, 1909. George Meredith, novelist, poet and critic, *Ballads and Poems of Tragic Life*, *The Ordeal of Richard Feverel*, *The Egoist*, Boxhill, Surrey, 1909. Gustav Mahler, composer, *The Symphony of a Thousand*, Vienna, 1911.

MAY 19

*Youth and Sports Day, Turkey. Feasts of SS: Celestine V, pope;
Pudentiana and Pudens, martyrs; Calocerus and Parthenius, martyrs;
Dunstan, archbishop; Ivo of Kermartin.*

Anne Boleyn is beheaded, 1536. ¶ The Spanish Armada sets sail from Lisbon,
1588. ¶ Napoleon creates the Order of Legion of Honour, 1802. ¶ Attempted
assassination of Queen Victoria by William Hamilton, 1849. ¶ Irene (Asteroid
14) discovered by J. R. Hind, 1851. ¶ Tolosa (Asteroid 138) discovered by
M. Perrotin, 1874. ¶ Oscar Wilde is released from Pentonville Prison, 1895.
¶ The Tonga Islands are annexed by Britain, 1900. ¶ The US Emergency Quota
Immigration Act passed, 1921.

BORN: Jacob Jordaens, painter, Antwerp, Belgium, 1593. Johann Gottlieb
Fichte, philosopher of 'ethical idealism', Germany, 1762. Dame Nellie Melba,
operatic singer, Melbourne, Australia, 1861. Lady Astor, the first woman
Member of Parliament, Virginia, 1879. Ho Chi-Minh, revolutionary leader,
North Vietnam, 1890. Frank Capra, film director, *Mr Deeds goes to Town, It
Happened One Night*, Palermo, Italy, 1897. Malcolm X (Malcolm Little), US
Black Muslim leader, Omaha, Nebraska, 1925.

DIED: Alcuin, English theologian and scholar, 804. Anne Boleyn, wife of Henry
VIII; beheaded, 1536. Charles Montagu, 1st Earl of Halifax, politician and poet,
founder of the Bank of England, London, 1715. James Boswell, biographer and
lawyer, *The Life of Samuel Johnson, Journal of a Tour to the Hebrides*, 1795.
Nathaniel Hawthorne, novelist and short-story writer, *Twice-Told Tales, The
Scarlet Letter*, Plymouth, New Hampshire, 1865. José Marti, revolutionary and
poet, leader of the revolt against Spanish rule in Cuba, Dos Rios, Cuba, 1895.
William Ewart Gladstone, British Liberal leader, Prime Minister, 1898. Sir
William Throsby Bridges, Australian soldier; from wounds received at Gallipoli,
1915. Thomas Edward Lawrence, 'Lawrence of Arabia', soldier and writer, *The
Seven Pillars of Wisdom*; on his Brough Superior motor-bike, Dorset, 1935.
Charles Ives, US composer, 1954. Ogden Nash, writer of humorous verse, *The
Bad Parent's Garden of Verse, Everyone but Thee and Me*, Baltimore, Maryland,
1971.

National Holiday, Republic of Cameroun (commemorating the referendum that resulted in Independence, 1972). Lafayette's Day, Massachusetts, USA (the Marquis de Lafayette, 1757–1834, aided the colonists). Mecklenburg Independence Day, North Carolina, USA. M. P. R. Day, Zaire (commemorating the foundation of the Mouvement Populaire de la Révolution, Zaire's only political party). Feasts of SS: Bernardino of Siena; Thalelaeus, martyr; Basilla, or Basilissa, virgin and martyr; Baudelius, martyr; Austregislus, or Outril, bishop; Ethelbert, martyr.

Cola di Rienzi, tribune of the people, establishes a Republic in Rome, 1347. ¶ Vasco da Gama arrives in Calicut after discovering the Cape route to India, 1498. ¶ Ascension Island discovered by the Portuguese, 1501. ¶ Napoleon abandons the siege of Acre after two months, 1799. ¶ North Carolina secedes from the Union (readmitted 4 July 1868), 1861. ¶ The state of Kentucky declares its neutrality at the beginning of the American Civil War, 1861. ¶ Homestead Act is passed by US Congress, 1862. ¶ Income tax in US is declared unconstitutional, 1895. ¶ Regular commercial flights between US and Europe begun by Pan-American Airways, 1939. ¶ Crete invaded by German forces, 1941.

BORN: Sir Henry Percy, knight, supporter of Henry IV, known as Harry Hotspur, 1364. Pietro Bembo, cardinal and theologian (the typeface used in this book was originally cut for a work by Bembo, and the face bears his name), Venice, 1470. Hieronymus Fabricius, physician, Italy, 1537. William Thornton, architect, designed the Capitol building in Washington, British Virgin Islands, 1759. Honoré de Balzac, novelist, *Comédie Humaine*, Tours, France, 1799. John Stuart Mill, Utilitarian philosopher, economist, *Principles of Political Economy, On Liberty, Autobiography*, London, 1806. William George Fargo, co-founder of Wells-Fargo, New York, 1818. Wladyslaw Sikorski, Prime Minister of Poland, Poland, 1881. Margery Allingham, popular novelist, 1904. Moshe Dayan, military commander and politician, Israel, 1915.

DIED: Christopher Columbus, Genoese explorer, 1506. Marie Joseph, Marquis de Lafayette, statesman and soldier, Paris, 1834. John Clare, farm labourer and poet, *The Shepherd's Calendar, The Rural Muse*, Northampton, 1864. Sir Max Beerbohm, caricaturist and writer, *Seven Men*, 1956. Dame Barbara Hepworth, sculptress, St Ives, Cornwall, 1975.

MAY 21

Anniversary of the Battle of Iquique, Chile (a heroic naval action, 1879).
Feasts of SS: Godric; Andrew Bobola, martyr; Theophilus of Corte.

The cemetery of Père La Chaise opened in Paris, 1804. ¶ New Zealand is proclaimed a colony of Britain, 1840. ¶ The Manchester Ship Canal is opened, 1894. ¶ Charles A. Lindberg arrives in Paris after flying from New York in a little over 37 hours, 1927. ¶ Amiens and Arras taken by the Germans, 1940. ¶ Heavy bombing by the Allies of Duisberg and Hanover, 1944.

BORN: Albrecht Dürer, painter and engraver, Nürnberg, Germany, 1471. Philip II, King of Spain, Valladolid, Spain, 1527. Alexander Pope, poet and satirist, translator, *The Rape of the Lock, The Dunciad, An Essay on Man*, London, 1688. Joseph Fouché, revolutionary, head of secret police, France, 1758. Elizabeth Fry, social worker and prison reformer, Norwich, 1780. Mikhail Glinka, composer, *A Life for the Tsar*, Russia, 1804. Henri Rousseau (*Le Douanier*), French primitive painter, Laval, France, 1844. Willem Einthoven, physician, pioneer of electrocardiography, Java, 1860. Konstantin Paustovsky, short-story writer and journalist, *Story of a Life*, Moscow, 1892.

DIED: Henry VI, King of England; murdered, London, 1471. Hernando de Soto, Spanish explorer of southern North America, 1542. Hieronymus Fabricius, Italian physician, 1619. Pieter Hooft, historian and poet, Netherlands, 1647. James Graham, 1st Marquis of Montrose, Scottish Royalist, executed, Edinburgh, 1650. Karl Wilhelm Scheele, chemist, discovered oxygen and chlorine, Köping, Sweden, 1786. Christian Thomsen, archaeologist, responsible for the original divisioning of human prehistory (Stone, Bronze and Iron Ages), Copenhagen, 1865. Ronald Firbank, novelist, *Vainglory, Valmouth*, 1926. Hugo de Vries, geneticist, Amsterdam, 1935.

MAY 22

National Heroes Day, Socialist Republic of Sri Lanka (Republic Day prior to 1978). Feasts of SS: Castus and Aemilius, martyrs; Quiteria, virgin and martyr; Romanus; Julia, martyr; Aigulf, or Ayoul, bishop; Humility, widow; Rita of Cascia, widow.

Alexander the Great defeats Darius at Granicus, 334BC. ¶ Lancastrians defeated by the Yorkists at St Albans (23 May has also been accepted by some authorities as the date), 1455. ¶ Total eclipse observed in England, 1724. ¶ Mungo Park sets sail on his first voyage to Africa, 1795. ¶ Official opening of the Blackwall Tunnel under the Thames, by the Prince and Princess of Wales, 1897. ¶ The 'Pact of Steel' signed by Hitler and Mussolini, 1939. ¶ The Isle of Lundy is acquired by the British National Trust, 1969. ¶ Ceylon is declared a republic and changes its name to Sri Lanka, 1972.

BORN: Hubert Robert, landscape painter, Paris, 1733. William Sturgeon, physicist, built the first electromagnet, Whittington, Lancashire, 1783. Gérard de Nerval, poet and writer, *Les Chimères*, Paris, 1808. Richard Wagner, composer, *The Flying Dutchman, Lohengrin, The Ring of the Nibelung*, Leipzig, Germany, 1813. Sir Arthur Conan Doyle, writer, creator of Sherlock Holmes, Edinburgh, 1859. Phil May, humorous cartoonist, near Leeds, 1864. Daniel François Malan, architect of South Africa's apartheid policy, Cape Colony, South Africa, 1874. Sir Ernest Oppenheimer, South African mining industrialist and philanthropist, Friedberg, Germany, 1880. Giacomo Matteotti, anti-Fascist Italian politician, Italy, 1885. Lord Olivier, actor and director, Dorking, Surrey, 1907.

DIED: Constantine the Great, Roman Emperor and Christian, 337. Francesco Guicciardini, diplomat, statesman and historian, *History of Italy*, Arcetri, Italy, 1540. Maria Edgeworth, Irish novelist, *The Absentee*, 1849. Alessandro Francesco Manzoni, poet and novelist, *The Betrothed*, Milan, 1873. Victor Hugo, novelist and poet, *The Hunchback of Notre Dame, The Man Who Laughs*, Paris, 1885. Lady Augusta Gregory, dramatist and writer, 1932. Langston Hughes, American poet, *Weary Blues*, 1967. C. Day Lewis, writer, Poet Laureate, 1972.

MAY 23

Empire Air Day, on which many aerodromes were open to the public
throughout the British Empire, observed until the late 1930s.
Labour Day, Jamaica. Feasts of SS: Desiderius, or Didier, bishop and martyr;
Guilbert; Leontius of Rostov, bishop and martyr; Ivo of Chartres, bishop;
Euphrosyne of Polotsk, virgin; William of Rochester, martyr;
John Baptist Rossi.

Henry VIII divorced from Catherine, 1533. ¶ Captain William Kidd and three associates executed in London for piracy, 1701. ¶ Marlborough defeats the French at the battle of Ramillies, 1706. ¶ The state of South Carolina ratifies the Constitution of the United States of America, 1788. ¶ Isis (Asteroid 42) discovered by Norman Pogson, 1856. ¶ The North West Mounted Police are established in Canada (their name is changed to the Royal Canadian Mounted Police on 1 February 1920), 1873. ¶ War declared on Austria–Hungary by Italy, 1915. ¶ British Parliament approves a plan whereby an independent Palestine will be formed by 1949, 1939. ¶ Israelis announce the capture of the former German Gestapo chief Adolf Eichmann, 1960.

BORN: William Hunter, obstetrician and anatomist, East Kilbride, Scotland, 1718. Franz Mesmer, physician, hypnotist, Austria, 1734. Jules Sebastien Dumont d'Urville, explorer, France, 1790. Sir Charles Barry, architect, rebuilt the Houses of Parliament, London, 1795. Thomas Hood, poet and humorist, *The Song of the Shirt*, London, 1799. Otto Lilienthal, pioneer aviator, Germany, 1848. Douglas Fairbanks, film actor and producer, Colorado, 1883. Par Lagerkvist, novelist and poet, *The Hangman*, Sweden, 1891. Artie Shaw, clarinetist and bandleader, New York City, 1910. Rosemary Clooney, singer, Maysville, Kentucky, 1928.

DIED: Girolamo Savonarola, religious and political reformer, Florence, 1498. Luis de Góngora y Argote, poet and writer, Spain, 1627. Louis Le Nain, painter, France, 1648. Captain William Kidd, naval officer and pirate; hanged, London, 1701. John Wood, architect and planner of Bath, where he died, 1754. James Otis, lawyer, prominent in resisting the British government in Massachusetts, Andover, 1783. Kit Carson, American frontiersman, 1868. Leopold von Ranke, historian, *History of the Popes*, Berlin, 1881. Henrik Ibsen, poet and dramatist, *The Wild Duck, Hedda Gabbler*, Norway, 1906. John D. Rockefeller, founder of Standard Oil, philanthropist, Florida, 1937. Heinrich Himmler, Nazi Minister of the Interior; suicide, Germany, 1945. Georges Claude, engineer and inventor, devised a process for liquefying air, 1960. David Smith, sculptor, Albany, New York, 1965.

MAY 24

Empire Day (Queen Victoria's Birthday), celebrating the triumphs and
achievements of the British Empire, observed until the late 1930s.
Day of Slavonic Culture, Bulgaria. Anniversary of the Battle of Independence,
Ecuador. Commonwealth Day, Lesotho. Feasts of SS: Donatian and
Rogatian, martyrs; Vincent of Lérins; David I of Scotland;
Nicetas of Pereaslav, martyr.

Accession of Malcolm IV of Scotland (reigned until 9 December 1165), 1153.
¶ John Hancock of Massachusetts elected President of the Continental Congress,
1775. ¶ First message on US Telegraph Line transmitted by Samuel Morse
(Washington-Baltimore), 1844. ¶ Free-staters led by John Brown massacre
pro-slavers at Pottawatomie Creek, 1856. ¶ Vala (Asteroid 131) discovered by
C. H. F. Peters, 1873. ¶ The Brooklyn Bridge is opened, 1883. ¶ The Orange
Free State is annexed by Britain, 1900. ¶ Amy Johnson arrives in Australia after
flying solo from London (in a little over 19 days), 1930. ¶ The *Bismarck* sinks
HMS *Hood* off the Greenland coast, 1941. ¶ President Nasser of Egypt announces
the blockade of the Gulf of Aqaba, 1967.

BORN: Gabriel Daniel Fahrenheit, physicist, the first to use mercury in a
thermometer, Poland, 1686. Jean Paul Marat, revolutionary leader in the French
Revolution, Switzerland, 1743. William Whewell, philosopher and writer,
History of the Inductive Sciences, Elements of Morality, Lancaster, 1794. Victoria I,
Queen of the United Kingdom and Empress of India, Kensington Palace,
London, 1819. Sir Arthur Wing Pinero, playwright, *The Second Mrs Tanqueray*,
Trelawney of the 'Wells', London, 1855. Jan Christiaan Smuts, statesman and
soldier, founder of the South African United Party, Cape Colony (South Africa),
1870. Bob Dylan, folk-singer, Minnesota, 1941.

DIED: Nicolaus Copernicus, astronomer, proposed heliocentric theory of the
Solar System, 1543. George Brydges, 1st Baron Rodney, British admiral and
naval commander, London, 1792. William Lloyd Garrison, slave abolitionist,
1879. John Foster Dulles, American Secretary of State, 1959. Duke Ellington,
jazz composer and pianist, 1974.

MAY 25

*The Roman festival of Mercurius, god of trade and gain. Commonly
thought the first day of summer in Medieval times. Dies Mala or
'Egyptian Day', considered unlucky in the Middle Ages. National Holiday,
Argentina. Liberation of Africa Day, Republic of Chad. Independence
Day, Jordan. Africa Day, Republic of Mali. Africa's Liberation Day,
Mauritania. Revolution Day, Sudan. Africa Freedom Day, Zambia.
Feasts of SS: Gregory VII, pope; Urban I, pope and martyr;
Dionysius of Milan, bishop; Zenobius, bishop; Leo, or Lyé, abbot;
Aldhelm, bishop; Gennadius, bishop; Madeleine Sophie Barat, virgin.*

Captain James Cook sets sail on his first voyage of discovery, 1768. ¶ The
Philadelphia convention meets under George Washington to draw up a constitution, 1787. ¶ The Bank Holidays Act is passed in the House of Commons,
1871. ¶ The re-built Coventry Cathedral is consecrated, 1962. ¶ First link-up
with the orbiting space station *Skylab* by astronauts, 1973.

BORN: Ralph Waldo Emerson, philosopher and poet, Boston, 1803. Jacob
Burckhardt, historian, *The Civilization of the Renaissance in Italy*, Switzerland,
1818. Lord Beaverbrook, politician and newspaper proprietor, Ontario, 1879.
Igor Ivanovich Sikorsky, aeronautical engineer and inventor, Kiev, Russia, 1889.
Theodore Roethke, poet, *Open House, Words for the Wind*, Saginaw, Michigan,
1908. Miles Davis, modern jazz trumpeter and composer, Illinois, 1926.

DIED: Pedro Calderón de la Barca, Spanish dramatist, *The Mayor of Zalamea*,
1681. Marie, Comtesse de La Fayette, novelist, *La Princesse de Clèves*, France,
1693. Gustav Holst, composer, *The Planets, Egdon Heath*, 1934. Jacques Feyder,
film director, *Le Grand Jeu*, Switzerland, 1948. Robert Capa, war photographer,
1954.

MAY 26

*National Holiday, Turkey. Feasts of SS: Philip Neri; Quadratus, bishop;
Priscus, or Prix, and his Companions, martyrs; Lambert of Venice, bishop;
Mariana of Quito, virgin.*

Edward IV of England crowned (reign had begun 4 March 1461), 1465. ¶ In
Milan Cathedral Napoleon is crowned King of Italy, 1805. ¶ The Confederate
General Kirby Smith surrenders in Texas, end of the US Civil War, 1865.
¶ Execution of Michael Barrett, a Fenian, who was responsible for the Clerken-
well Outrage (13 deaths) in London. This was the last public execution in
England, 1868. ¶ Violent eruptions of Mount Etna in Sicily begin (last until
7 June), 1870. ¶ First US troops arrive in France, 1917. ¶ Bessie Smith's *Careless
Love Blues* is recorded in Chicago, 1925. ¶ The Riff war ends with surrender
to the French, 1926.

BORN: Philippe de Champaigne, painter, Belgium, 1602. John Churchill,
1st Duke of Marlborough, military commander, Ashe, Devon, 1650. Aleksandr
Sergeyevich Pushkin, novelist, dramatist and poet, *Eugene Onegin, Boris Godunov*,
Moscow, 1799. Edmond de Goncourt, novelist, author with his brother Jules
of the *Journal*, France, 1822. Al Jolson, American singer and entertainer, Russia,
1886. John Wayne, actor, Winterset, Iowa, 1907. Robert Morley, actor,
Wiltshire, 1908. János Kádár, Communist Premier of Hungary, 1912. Peggy
Lee, popular singer, North Dakota, 1920.

DIED: Augustine, first Archbishop of Canterbury, 604. Samuel Pepys, civil
servant and diarist, London, 1703. Vissarión Grigórievich Belinsky, Russian
literary critic, 1848. Charles Mayo, surgeon, Chicago, 1939. Lincoln Ellsworth,
civil engineer and polar explorer, 1951. Jacques Lipchitz, sculptor and poet,
Isle of Capri, 1973.

*Independence Day, Afghanistan. Army Day, Nicaragua. National
Holiday, Turkey. Feasts of SS: Bede the Venerable, doctor;
Restituta of Sora, virgin and martyr; Julius and his Companions, martyrs;
Eutropius of Orange, bishop; John I, pope and martyr;
Melangell, or Monacella, virgin.*

Accession of King John of England (reigns until 19 October 1216), 1199.
¶ The Habeas Corpus Act is passed in Britain, 1679. ¶ Czar Peter founds St
Petersburg as the new capital of Russia, 1703. ¶ Nysa (Asteroid 44) discovered
by H. Goldschmidt, 1857. ¶ Garibaldi takes Palermo, 1860. ¶ Complete destruction of the Russian Fleet at Tsushima Straits by Japanese forces, 1905. ¶ Auguste
Picard a Swiss physicist, becomes the first man to ascend into the stratosphere,
he rose to over 51,000 feet in a balloon, 1931.

BORN: Ibn Khaldun, Arab historian, Tunisia, 1332. Sir Henry Parkes, Australian
statesman and writer, Stoneleigh, Warwickshire, England, 1815. Amelia
Bloomer, campaigner for women's rights, popularized 'bloomers', New York,
1818. Jay Gould, financier and railway developer, New York, 1836. Wild Bill
(James Butler) Hickok, scout and US Marshal, Illinois, 1837. Arnold Bennett,
novelist and critic, *Anna of the Five Towns*, Staffordshire, 1867. Georges Rouault,
Expressionist painter, Paris, 1871. Isadora Duncan, choreographer, San Francisco,
1878. Sir John Douglas Cockcroft, physicist, split the atom with Ernest Walton,
Nobel Prize for Physics, Yorkshire, 1897. Hubert Horatio Humphrey, US
Senator and Vice-President (under Lyndon B. Johnson), South Dakota, 1911.
Herman Wouk, novelist, *The Caine Mutiny*, New York City, 1915. Henry
Kissinger, statesman, Germany, 1923.

DIED: Thomas Münzer, religious and political leader, Anabaptist; executed,
Germany, 1525. John Calvin, Protestant theologian, 1564. François Emile
Babeuf, French revolutionary socialist, 1797. Niccolo Paganini, violin virtuoso,
Nice, France, 1840. Robert Koch, bacteriologist, discovered the tuberculosis
bacillus, 1910. Sir Joseph Wilson Swan, chemist and physicist, Surrey, 1914.
Field-Marshall Sir Thomas Blamey, Australian soldier, 1951. Jawalharlal Nehru,
statesman, first Prime Minister of India after Independence (1947), New Delhi,
1964.

MAY 28

Feasts of SS: Augustine, or Austin, of Canterbury, archbishop;
Senator, bishop; Justus of Urgel, bishop; Germanus of Paris, bishop;
William of Gellone; Bernard of Montjoux; Ignatius of Rostov, bishop.

Dike (Asteroid 99) discovered by Alphonse Borelly, 1868. ¶ The defeat of the Paris Commune after 'Bloody Week', 1871. ¶ Nazis win the elections in Danzig, 1933. ¶ The Irish Senate is abolished, 1936. ¶ Capitulation of Belgium to Germany, 1940.

BORN: William Pitt ('The Younger'), Prime Minister, Hayes, Kent, 1759. Thomas Moore, poet and song writer, *Lalla Rookh, Loves of the Angels, The Harp That Once Through Tara's Halls*, Dublin, 1779. Jean Louis Agassiz, geologist and naturalist, Switzerland, 1807. Eduard Beneš, Czech statesman, Bohemia, 1884. Ian Fleming, popular novelist, creator of James Bond, London, 1908. Patrick White, Australian novelist, *The Tree of Man, Voss*, London, 1912. The Dionne quintuplets, Callendar, Ontario, Canada, 1934.

DIED: Luigi Boccherini, composer and cellist, 1805. Noah Webster, lexicographer and teacher, *English Grammar, American Dictionary of the English Language*, New Haven, Connecticut, 1843. John, Earl Russell, British Prime Minister, Richmond, Surrey, 1878. Sir George Grove, engineer and musicologist, *Grove's Dictionary of Music and Musicians*, London, 1900. Alfred Adler, Austrian psychologist, 1937.

*The Roman festival of Ambarvalia, an early celebration to secure the
growing crops against damage. Oak-Apple, Royal Oak or Restoration Day,
commemorating Charles II of Great Britain finding safety in the oak at Boscobel
(Staffordshire) and his subsequent Restoration. Feasts of SS:
Mary Magdalen dei Pazzi, virgin; Cyril of Caesarea, martyr;
Maximinus of Trier, bishop; Sisinnius, Martyrius and Alexander, martyrs;
Theodosia, virgin and martyr; William, Stephen, Raymund
and their Companions, martyrs.*

Charles II enters London upon the Restoration, 1660. ¶ Patrick Henry challenges
the proposed taxing of the American Colonies by the Stamp Act, in the
Virginian Assembly, 1765. ¶ The state of Rhode Island ratifies the Constitution
of the United States of America, 1790. ¶ Wisconsin is made a US state (30th),
1848. ¶ Feronia (Asteroid 71) discovered by Peters and Safford, 1861. ¶ Steam
cable tramway at Highgate in north London opened (the first in Europe), 1884.
¶ Einstein's Relativity Theory confirmed by observations of the total eclipse
of the sun, 1919. ¶ *Little Bits* recorded in Chicago by Jimmy Bertrand's
Washboard Wizards (with Johnny Dodds), 1926. ¶ Beginning of British
evacuation from Dunkirk (ends 4 June), 1940.

BORN: Charles II, King of Great Britain and Ireland, 1630. Phillipe Lebon,
inventor and chemist, developed gas illumination, France, 1767. Isaac Albéniz,
pianist and composer, Spain, 1860. Gilbert Keith Chesterton, writer and essayist,
The Napoleon of Notting Hill, The Man who was Thursday, Kensington, London,
1874. Oswald Spengler, teacher and philosopher, *The Decline of the West*,
Blankenburg, Germany, 1880. Josef von Sternberg, US film director, *The
Scarlett Empress*, Vienna, 1894. Beatrice Lillie, singer and entertainer, Toronto,
Canada, 1898. Bob Hope, comedian and actor, London, 1903. Gregg Toland,
cinematographer, *Citizen Kane*, Charleston, South Carolina, 1904. Terence
Hanbury White, novelist, *The Sword in the Stone*, Bombay, 1906. John Fitzgerald
Kennedy, US President, Massachusetts, 1917.

DIED: Sir Humphry Davy, chemist, inventor of a safety lamp for miners, 1829.
Julius von Sachs, botanist and naturalist, Würzburg, Germany, 1897. Sir
William Schwenck Gilbert, librettist, 1911. John Barrymore, actor, 1942.
Fanny Brice, actress, dancer and singer, 1951. Juan Ramón Jiménez, poet,
Silver and I, Nobel Prize for Literature, Puerto Rico, 1958.

Memorial or Decoration Day, USA (a legal holiday in most states,
first observed in 1868 by General John A. Logan who issued an order
that the graves of the dead [soldiers] should be decorated).
Memorial Day, Guam. Memorial Day, Puerto Rico. Memorial Day,
Virgin Islands. Feasts of SS: Felix I, pope; Eleutherius, pope;
Isaac of Constantinople, abbot; Exsuperantius, bishop; Madelgisilus,
or Mauguille; Walstan; Ferdinand of Castile; Joan of Arc, virgin.

Joan of Arc is burnt at the stake in Rouen, 1431. ¶ Christopher Columbus sails
on his third voyage, 1498. ¶ The House of Representatives is opened in Washington, 1808. ¶ Annexation of Tuscany by Napoleon, 1808. ¶ Attempted assassination of Queen Victoria by John Francis, 1842. ¶ The Japanese occupy Dairen in
Russia, 1904. ¶ RAF launches massive raid on Cologne, 1942. ¶ The world's
first flight by a Hovercraft, at Cowes on the Isle of Wight, 1959. ¶ *Mariner 9*
launched by the US at Cape Kennedy for Mars mission, 1971.

BORN: Peter the Great, Tsar of Russia, Moscow, 1672. Paul Verlaine, French
Symbolist poet, *Poèmes Saturniens, Sagesse*, Metz, 1844. Peter Carl Fabergé, artist
and designer, St Petersburg, 1846. Pierre Janet, psychologist, Paris, 1859. Ernest,
Lord Rutherford, physicist, founded contemporary atomic theory, Spring
Grove, New Zealand, 1871. Alexander Archipenko, sculptor, Russia, 1887.
Benny Goodman, clarinetist and bandleader, Illinois, 1909.

DIED: Joan of Arc, the Maid of Orleans; at the stake, Rouen, France, 1431.
Christopher Marlowe, dramatist, *The Jew of Malta, Edward II, Tragical History
of Dr Faustus*, London, 1593. Sir Peter Paul Rubens, Flemish painter, Antwerp,
1640. Alexander Pope, poet and satirist, translator, *The Rape of the Lock, The
Dunciad, An Essay on Man*, Twickenham, Middlesex, 1744. François Boucher,
artist and designer, Paris, 1770. Voltaire (François-Marie Arouet), philosopher,
historian, poet, dramatist and novelist, *Candide, Micromégas, Lettres Philosophiques*, Paris, 1778. Wilbur Wright, aviation pioneer, Dayton, Ohio, 1912.
Hermann Broch, poet and novelist, *The Death of Virgil*, 1951. Boris Pasternak,
novelist and poet, *Doctor Zhivago*, near Moscow, 1960.

MAY 31

Anniversary of the Royal Brunei Malay Regiment, State of Brunei.
Republic Day, Republic of South Africa. Feasts of SS: Angela Merici, virgin;
Petronilla, virgin and martyr; Cantius, Cantianus and Cantianella, martyrs;
Mechtildis of Edelstetten, virgin.

Universal suffrage in France is abolished, 1850. ¶ Beginning of the construction of the Siberian Railway, 1891. ¶ The Boer War ends with the Peace of Vereeniging, 1902. ¶ The Act of Union unites Natal and the Cape Colony, the beginning of the Union of South Africa, 1910. ¶ The Battle of Jutland, 1916. ¶ The USSR is recognized by China, 1924. ¶ Ending of the fighting for Crete, 1941. ¶ South Africa becomes a republic independent of British Commonwealth, 1961. ¶ Adolf Eichmann hanged in Jerusalem after an appeal is rejected, 1962. ¶ A great earthquake in the north of Peru destroys many towns and villages. The final death toll is in excess of 50,000 persons, 1970.

BORN: William Worrell Mayo, surgeon, a founder of the Mayo Clinic, Minnesota; Manchester, England, 1819. Walt Whitman, poet and essayist, *Leaves of Grass*, West Hills, Long Island, New York, 1819. Pope Pius XI, Desio, Italy, 1857. Walter Sickert, artist, Munich, Germany, 1860. Sir Francis Edward Younghusband, explorer and writer, *India and Tibet*, Murree, India, 1863. Judith Wright, Australian poet and critic, 1915.

DIED: Sallust (Giaus Sallustius Crispus), Roman historian, *Bellum Catilinae*, Rome (?), 34BC. Jacopo Robusti Tintoretto, Venetian painter, Venice, 1594. Franz Joseph Haydn, composer, *Creation, Seasons*, Vienna, 1809. Évariste Galois, mathematician; killed in a duel, 1832.

JUNE

THIRTY DAYS

June receives its name either from Juno, the Roman
goddess of womanhood, or from *Juniores*, the lower
branch of the early Roman Senate. This was
originally the fourth month of the Roman year.

JUNE 1

The Roman festival honouring Carna, the goddess who protected and cared for the physical well-being of humankind. Children's Day, Cape Verde Islands. Children's Day, People's Republic of Mongolia. Muslim Supreme Council Day, Uganda. Feasts of SS: Pamphilus and his Companions, martyrs; Wite, or Candida; Proculus, 'the Soldier', and St Proculus, bishop; Caprasius, or Caprais; Wistan; Simeon of Syracuse; Eneco, or Iñigo, abbot; Theobald of Alba; The Martyrs of Japan, II.

The Covenanters defeat Claverhouse at Drumclog in Scotland, 1679. ¶ Kentucky joins the Union (15th), 1792. ¶ French fleet defeated in the English Channel by Lord Howe, 1794. ¶ Tennessee joins the Union (16th), 1796. ¶ HMS *Shannon* captures the US frigate *Chesapeake*, 1813. ¶ Captain Jack of the Modoc Indians captured in Oregon by US troops (executed 3 October), 1873. ¶ The first Pullman carriages are used in England, by the Midland Railway Company, 1874. ¶ First attack on London by Zeppelins, 1915. ¶ The battle of Jutland ends, 1916. ¶ The British submarine HMS *Thetis* flounders and sinks off the coast near Liverpool, the crew of 99 perishes, 1939. ¶ The first premium bond prize winners are drawn by the computer ERNIE in Britain, 1957. ¶ Fishing limits extended to 12 miles by Iceland, 1958.

BORN: Nicolas Léonard Sadi Carnot, physicist, 1796. John Masefield, Poet Laureate, *Salt Water Poems and Ballads, Reynard the Fox*, Herefordshire, 1878. Sir Frank Whittle, aeronautical engineer and inventor, Coventry, Warwickshire, 1907. Marilyn Monroe, actress, *Some Like it Hot, The Misfits*, California, 1926.

DIED: Marcus Didius Salvius Julianus, Roman emperor, executed, 193. Honoré d'Urfé, author, *Astreé*, France, 1625. James Gillray, political caricaturist, London, 1815. Sir David Wilkie, Scottish artist, 1841. James Buchanan, fifteenth President of the US (1857–61), 1868. Camilo Castelo Branco, Portuguese novelist; suicide, 1890. Ion Antonescu, Rumanian dictator; executed for crimes committed during World War Two, 1946. John Dewey, American educationalist and philosopher, 1952. Helen Keller, writer and counselor (though blind, deaf and mute), *Out of the Dark*, 1968.

JUNE 2

Labour Day, Bahamas. Republic Day, Italy. Feasts of SS:
Marcellinus and Peter, martyrs; Erasmus, bishop and martyr;
Pothinus and his Companions, the Martyrs of Lyons and Vienne;
Eugenius I, pope; Stephen of Sweden, bishop and martyr;
Nicholas the Pilgrim.

Gordon's 'No Popery' riots in London began again on this day and last for over a week, 1780. ¶ Donati's Comet first observed by Dr Donati in Florence, 1858. ¶ First patent for broadcasting by means of electro-magnetic waves, by Guglielmo Marconi, 1896. ¶ Queen Elizabeth II crowned at Westminster Abbey, 1953. ¶ US *Surveyor 1* achieves successful soft-landing on the moon, 1966.

BORN: The Marquis de Sade, writer, philosopher and revolutionary, *Justine, Juliette, La Philosophie dans le boudoir*, Paris, 1740. Count Alessandro di Cagliostro, mountebank of international repute, Sicily, 1743. Thomas Hardy, poet and novelist, *Tess of the D'Urbervilles, The Mayor of Casterbridge*, Upper Bockhampton, Dorset, 1840. Sir Edward Elgar, composer, *The Enigma Variations*, Worcestershire, 1857. Lotte Reiniger, film animator (principally with silhouettes), Berlin, 1899.

DIED: Emile Littré, lexicographer and philosopher, *Auguste Comte and Positivist Philosophy*, Paris, 1881. Giuseppe Garibaldi, Italian patriot, 1882. Alexander Ostrovsky, dramatist, *The Bankrupt, The Diary of a Scoundrel, The Storm*, near Moscow, 1886. Alain, philosopher, *Les Propos d'Alain*, 1951. Victoria Sackville-West, novelist, poet and critic, *All Passion Spent, The Land*, Sissinghurst Castle, Kent, 1962.

JUNE 3

Martyrs Shrine Day, Uganda. Jefferson Davis's Birthday, some
southern states only of USA. Independence Holiday, Western Samoa.
Feasts of SS: Cecilius; Pergentinus and Laurentinus, martyrs;
Lucillian and his Companions, martyrs; Clotilda, widow;
Liphardus and Urbicius, abbots; Kevin, or Coemgen, abbot;
Genesius of Clermont, bishop; Isaac of Cordova, martyr; Morand.

The Duke of York defeats the Dutch fleet off the coast at Harwich, 1665. ¶ Vibilia (Asteroid 144) and Adeona (Asteroid 145) discovered by C. H. F. Peters, 1875. ¶ Surrender of Mesopotamia to Britain, 1915. ¶ US launches *Gemini 9* spacecraft with Lieutenant-Commander Eugene Cernan and Lieutenant-Colonel Thomas Stafford on board, 1966. ¶ Diplomatic missions are exchanged by Cuba and the US (the first since 1961), 1977.

BORN: James Hutton, geologist, *A Theory of the Earth*, Edinburgh, 1726. William Hone, writer, satirist, *The Every-day Book*, Bath, 1780. Richard Cobden, politician, a founder of the Anti-Corn Law League, Sussex, 1804. Johan Barthold Jongkind, artist, Netherlands, 1819. George V of Great Britain, 1865. Otto Loewi, physician and neuro-physiologist, Nobel Prize winner, Frankfurt, 1873. Raoul Dufy, Fauvist artist, France, 1877. Georg von Békésy, physicist, Nobel Prize for Medicine, Budapest, 1899. Paul Rotha, film director and critic, *The Face of Britain*, London, 1907. Alain Resnais, film director, *Hiroshima Mon Amour*, Vannes, France, 1922. Tony Curtis, actor, *The Boston Strangler*, New York City, 1925. Allen Ginsberg, poet, *Howl and Other Poems*, New Jersey, 1926.

DIED: William Harvey, physician, discovered the circulation of blood, near Saffron Walden, Essex, 1657. Georges Bizet, composer, *Carmen*, *The Pearl Fishers*, 1875. James Thomson, poet and writer, *The City of Dreadful Night*, London, 1882. Samuel Plimsoll, reformer, devised the Plimsoll line for ships, Folkestone, Kent, 1898. Franz Kafka, novelist, *The Castle*, *The Trial*, 1924. Pope John XXIII, Italy, 1963.

JUNE 4

Children's Day, Socialist Republic of Vietnam. Feasts of SS:
Francis Caracciolo; Quirinus, bishop and martyr; Metrophanes, bishop;
Optatus of Milevis, bishop; Petroc, abbot; Vincentia Gerosa, virgin.

The first woman to fly, Mme Thible, a French opera singer, in a hot-air balloon, 1784. ¶ Captain Vancouver lands on the site of the present city of Everett, Canada, and claims the territory for England, 1792. ¶ War begins between Mexico and the US, 1845. ¶ The French free Milan after defeating the Austrians at Magenta, 1859. ¶ Assassination of Abdul Aziz, Sultan of Turkey, 1876. ¶ *Jungle Blues* recorded by Jelly Roll Morton and his Red Hot Peppers in Chicago, 1927. ¶ Ministry formed in France by Pierre Laval, 1935. ¶ Completion of British evacuation from Dunkirk (began 29 May), 1940. ¶ Rome is entered by the Fifth Army, 1944. ¶ Beginning of Cuban expropriation of American-owned sugar plantations and mills, 1959. ¶ Independence of Tonga proclaimed, 1970.

BORN: King George III of Great Britain, London, 1738. John Scott, Earl of Eldon, Chancellor of England, Newcastle, 1751. Baron Carl Gustaf Emil von Mannerheim, military commander and statesman, secured the independence of Finland from Russia, France, 1867.

DIED: Giovanni Jacopo Casanova, adventurer, lover, romancer, 1798. William Rivers, anthropologist, *History of Melanesian Society*, Cambridge, 1922. William II, King of Prussia, Emperor of Germany, Doorn, Holland, 1941. Serge Koussevitsky, conductor and composer, Boston, Massachusetts, 1951. Dorothy Gish, actress, 1968. Hjalmar Schacht, Nazi Minister of Economics, Munich, 1970. György Lukács, critic and philosopher, *History and Class Consciousness*, Budapest, 1971.

JUNE 5

Constitution Day, Denmark (1953). Liberation Day, Seychelles.
Feasts of SS: Boniface, archbishop and martyr; Dorotheus of Tyre, martyr;
Sanctius, or Sancho, martyr.

Ascent and descent in a hot-air balloon by Joseph and Stephen Montgolfier, 1783. ¶ Louis Bonaparte becomes King of Holland, 1806. ¶ Republican insurrection in Paris, 1832. ¶ Redvers Buller takes Pretoria, 1900. ¶ Arrival of US marines in Cuba, 1912. ¶ Allied Control Commission takes authority over Germany, 1945. ¶ Ruling by US Supreme Court that the Communist Party is registered as a foreign-dominated organisation, 1961. ¶ Beginning of the 'Six Day War' in the Middle East, 1967. ¶ Senator Robert Kennedy shot by Sirhan Sirhan, a Jordanian Arab, in Los Angeles (Kennedy dies the following day), 1968. ¶ President Sadat of Egypt re-opened the Suez Canal, closed since the Middle East War, 1975. ¶ The Teton Dam, north of Idaho Falls in the US, collapses and floods a large area of the valley, over 100 persons are killed, 1976.

BORN: Adam Smith, economist, *The Wealth of Nations*, Kirkcaldy, Scotland, 1723. John Couch Adams, astronomer, co-discoverer of the planet Neptune, Cornwall, 1819. Pancho Villa, robber, revolutionary and dictator, San Juan del Rio, Mexico, 1878. Igor Stravinsky, composer, *The Firebird*, *The Rite of Spring*, Oranienbaum, Russia, 1882. John Maynard Keynes, economist, *The General Theory of Employment*, Cambridge, 1883. Dame Ivy Compton-Burnett, English novelist, Pinner, Middlesex, 1884. Ruth Benedict, sociologist and anthropologist, *Patterns of Culture*, New York, 1887. Frederico Garcia Lorca, dramatist and poet, *Poet in New York*, *Blood Wedding*, Spain, 1898. Tony Richardson, film and stage director, *Tom Jones*, Shipley, Yorkshire, 1928. Jacques Demy, film director, *Lola Umbrellas, of Cherbourg*, Pontchâteau, France, 1931. Margaret Drabble, novelist, Sheffield, 1939.

DIED: Orlando Gibbons, composer and organist, 1625. Carl von Weber, operatic composer, *Oberon*, London, 1826. Stephen Crane, poet and novelist, *The Red Badge of Courage*, 1900. O. Henry (William Sydney Porter), short-story writer, *The Four Million*, *Gift of the Magi*, New York City, 1910. Horatio Herbert, Lord Kitchener, soldier, 1916. Georges Feydeau, writer of theatrical farces, 1921.

JUNE 6

Memorial Day, Republic of Korea. Feasts of SS: Norbert, archbishop;
Philip the Deacon; Ceratius, or Cérase, bishop; Eustorgius II of
Milan, bishop; Jarlath, bishop; Gudwal, or Gurval;
Claud of Besançon, bishop.

In the Dyrrhacium campaign Gaius Julius Caesar defeats Pompey the Great at Pharsalus (9 August is considered by some authorities to be the true date), 48BC. ¶ The Papal Swiss defeat the French at Novara, 1513. ¶ The Treaty of Badajoz between Portugal and Spain, 1801. ¶ Memphis is evacuated by the Confederacy, 1862. ¶ The three-mile coastal limit for territorial waters is established by the Hague Convention, 1882. ¶ Beginning of the Arab Revolt in Hejaz, 1916. ¶ War declared on the USSR by Finland, 1919. ¶ Lidice in Bohemia is razed to the ground in reprisals by Nazis, 1942. ¶ Allied landings on the coast of Normandy, 'D-Day', including two American divisions on Omaha beach, 1944. ¶ Russians launch manned *Soyuz 11* space-craft (links up the the *Salyut* space station on 7 June), 1971. ¶ At the beginning of Silver Jubilee Week Queen Elizabeth II lights a bonfire in Windsor Great Park, the first of a chain throughout the country, 1977.

BORN: Diego Velasquez, painter, Seville, Spain, 1599. Robert Falcon Scott, Antarctic explorer, Devonport, Devon, 1868. Thomas Mann, novelist, *The Magic Mountain, Death in Venice*, Germany, 1875. Dame Ninette de Valois, ballerina, founded the British Royal Ballet, Blessington, County Wicklow, Ireland, 1898. Ahmed Sukarno, Nationalist leader and dictator of Indonesia, Java, 1901.

DIED: Henry Grattan, statesman and champion of Irish independence, 1820. Jeremy Bentham, Utilitarian philosopher, 1831. Sir John A. Macdonald, first Prime Minister of Canada, Ottawa, Ontario, 1891. Gerhart Hauptmann, dramatist, *The Weavers, The Sunken Bell*, 1946. Hiram Bingham, explorer and archaeologist in South America, 1956. Carl Gustav Jung, psychologist and philosopher, *Modern Man in Search of a Soul*, Switzerland, 1961. Jean Paul Getty, rich oil person, 1976.

Feasts of SS: Paul I of Constantinople, bishop; Meriadoc, bishop;
Colman of Dromore, bishop; Vulflagius, or Wulphy; Willibald, bishop;
Gottschalk, martyr; Robert of Newminster, abbot; Antony of Gianelli, bishop.

Accession of David II of Scotland (reigns until 22 February 1370), 1329. ¶ 'Field of the Cloth of Gold'—Henry VIII of England meets Francis I of France on a plain near Calais (continues until 25 June), 1520. ¶ Occupation of Mexico City by French forces, 1863. ¶ Abraham Lincoln is re-nominated for the presidency, by the Baltimore Convention, 1864. ¶ US refuses recognition of Mexican government, 1921. ¶ First sitting of Northern Ireland Parliament, 1921.

BORN: John Rennie, civil engineer, East Lothian, Scotland, 1761. Robert Banks Jenkinson, Second Earl of Liverpool, British Prime Minister (1812–27), London, 1770. Paul Gauguin, Post-Impressionist painter, Paris, 1848. Charles Rennie Mackintosh, Art Nouveau architect, Glasgow, 1868. Imre Nagy, Hungarian leader, Prime Minister at the time of the Russian invasion (1956), 1896. Elizabeth Bowen, novelist, *Death of the Heart*, Dublin, 1899. T. E. B. Clarke, film script-writer, *The Blue Lamp, Passport to Pimlico*, Watford, Hertfordshire, 1907.

DIED: Robert the Bruce, King of Scotland, Dunbartonshire, Scotland, 1329. Casimir IV, King of Poland, 1492. Joseph von Fraunhofer, physicist and optician, 1826. Johann Friedrich Holderlin, German poet, 1843. Richard Marshe Hoe, introduced the rotary printing press, New York, 1886. Charles Booth, social reformer, *Life and Labour of the People in London*, 1916. Cyrus Curtis, founder and publisher of the *Ladies' Home Journal*, 1933. Jean Harlow, actress, 1937. Dorothy Parker, short-story writer and critic, *Enough Rope, After Such Pleasures*; suicide, New York City, 1967. E. M. Forster, novelist and critic, *A Passage to India*, 1970.

JUNE 8

The Roman Vestalia, a festival honouring Vesta, the goddess of the hearth.
Public Holiday, Dominica, St Kitts, Grenada, West Indies.
Feasts of SS: Maximinus of Aix; Medard, bishop; Clodulf, or Cloud, bishop;
William of York, archbishop.

Tennessee secedes from the Union (readmitted 24 July 1866), 1861. ¶ General 'Stonewall' Jackson's Shenandoah Valley Campaign, 1862. ¶ Lucina (Asteroid 146) discovered by Alphonse Borelly, 1875. ¶ The first US to Australia flight, completed by Sir Charles Kingsford-Smith and Captain T. P. Ulm, both of Australia, from Oakland in California to Brisbane via Hawaii and Fiji (began 31 May), 1928. ¶ Oswald Mosley addresses rally of the British Union of Fascists held at Olympia in London, 1934. ¶ Admiral Luis Carrero Blanco is appointed as President of the Spanish Government by General Franco, 1973. ¶ The next transit of Venus across the face of the Sun, 2004.

BORN: Giovanni Cassini, astronomer, discovered the satellites of Saturn, Italy, 1625. Robert Schumann, composer, *Scenes from Childhood*, Zwickan, Saxony, 1810. Sir William White Baker, explorer, discovered Lake Albert, London, 1821. Frank Lloyd Wright, architect, Richland Center, Wisconsin, 1867. Ernest B. Schoesdack, film director and producer, *Grass*, *King Kong* (1933), 1893. George Antheil, composer, *Ballet mécanique*, Trenton, New Jersey, 1900. Roberto Rossellini, film director, *La Paura*, Rome, 1906. Francis Crick, geneticist, Nobel Prize in 1962, Northampton, 1916. Suharto, President of Indonesia, Java, 1921.

DIED: Hardecanute, King of Denmark and England, 1042. Edward, 'The Black Prince', led English campaigns against the French, 1376. Johann Joachim Winckelmann, German art historian and early archaeologist, *Geschichte der Kunst des Alterthums*, Trieste, Italy, 1768. Thomas Paine, writer, reformer and propagandist, *The Rights of Man*, *Common Sense*, New York City, 1809. Sarah Siddons, actress, London, 1831. Andrew Jackson, general and US President, 1845. Sir Joseph Paxton, designed the Crystal Palace at the Great Exhibition in London (1851), London, 1865. George Sand (Amantine Dupin), novelist, Nohant, France, 1876. Gerard Manley Hopkins, Jesuit priest and poet, *The Leaden Echo and the Golden Echo*, Dublin, 1889. Nikolai Rimsky-Korsakov, composer and teacher, *Scheherazade*, *Russian Easter*, Lyubensk, Russia, 1908. Bliss Carman, Canadian poet, 1929.

JUNE 9

Feasts of SS: Columba, or Colmcille, abbot; Primus and Felician, martyrs; Vincent of Agen, martyr; Pelagia of Antioch, virgin and martyr; Richard of Andria, bishop.

Crassus defeated by the Parthians at Carrhae, 53BC. ¶ General 'Stonewall' Jackson's Shenandoah Valley Campaign, 1862. ¶ The Rhodesian army commissions its first black officers, in Salisbury, 1977.

BORN: Andrew Ramsay, writer, *Les Voyages de Cyrus*, Ayr, Scotland, 1686. Georg Friedrich Grotefend, classical scholar, deciphered the cuneiform script, Munden, Hanover, Germany, 1775. George Stephenson, engineer and inventor, built the *Rocket* locomotive, Wylan, Northumberland, 1781. Elizabeth Garrett Anderson, doctor, Suffolk, 1836. Sir Henry Dale, neurophysiologist, London, 1875.

DIED: Charles Dickens, novelist, *David Copperfield*, near Rochester, Kent, 1870. Ugo Betti, dramatist, *The Joker*, 1953. Lord Beaverbrook, politician and newspaper proprietor, 1964. Dame Sybil Thorndike, actress, 1976.

JUNE 10

Dies Mala or 'Egyptian Day', considered unlucky in the Middle Ages.
Cameons' Day, Portugal and its territories (Luis de Cameons, national poet,
1524–80). Feasts of SS: Margaret of Scotland, matron; Getulius and
his Companions, martyrs; Ithamar, bishop; Landericus, or Landry, bishop;
Bogumilus, archbishop.

The revenue cutter *Gaspée* is burnt by a mob at Rhode Island, 1772. ¶ Great
Tarawera eruption in New Zealand, 101 lives are lost, 1886. ¶ Rioting by the
Sinn Fein in Dublin, 1917. ¶ Jelly Roll Morton and his Red Hot Peppers
record *The Pearls* (a Morton composition) in Chicago, 1927. ¶ War declared by
Italy on Britain and France, 1940. ¶ US Senate votes for closure on the Civil
Rights Bill after a 75-day filibuster by Southern states, 1964. ¶ Embargo on the
exporting of goods to China is lifted in the US by President Nixon, 1971.
¶ Great flooding throughout South Dakota after torrential rain in the Black
Hills, many hundreds of deaths, 1972.

BORN: John Morgan, physician, founded the medical faculty at the University
of Pennsylvania, Philadelphia, 1735. Gustave Courbet, painter and revolutionary,
France, 1819. Nicholaus Otto, invented and produced the first four-stroke
internal combustion engine, Holzhausen, Germany, 1832. André Derain,
Fauvist painter, France, 1880. Sir Terence Rattigan, dramatist, *French Without*
Tears, The Winslow Boy, London, 1911. Inia Te Wiata, operatic singer, Otaki,
New Zealand, 1915. Prince Philip, Duke of Edinburgh, married to Queen
Elizabeth II, Corfu, 1921. Judy Garland, actress and singer, *A Star is Born*,
Minnesota, 1922.

DIED: Frederick I, 'Barbarossa', Holy Roman Emperor, 1190. André-Marie
Ampère, French physicist, 1836. R. J. Seddon, Premier of New Zealand, 1906.
Pierre Loti, novelist, *Iceland Fisherman, Disenchanted*, 1923. Giacomo Matteotti,
anti-Fascist politician; murdered by supporters of Mussolini, Rome, 1924.
Antonio Gaudi, architect in the Art Nouveau style, 1926. Frederick Delius,
composer, 1934. Sir Robert Borden, Canadian Prime Minister, Ottawa,
Ontario, 1937.

JUNE 11

Feasts of SS: Barnabas, apostle; Felix and Fortunatus, martyrs; Parisio.

The *mad* parliament assembles in London, 1258. ¶ Accession of James IV of Scotland, 1488. ¶ Columbus returns to Spain after his second expedition, 1495. ¶ Admiral de Ruyter in a Dutch ship sails up the Thames and destroys several British ships, 1667. ¶ Accession of George II of Great Britain, 1727. ¶ *Kansas City Stomp* recorded by Jelly Roll Morton and his Red Hot Peppers in New York City, 1928.

BORN: Ben Jonson, dramatist and poet, *Volpone, The Alchemist*, Westminster, London, 1572. John Constable, landscape painter, Suffolk, 1776. Carl von Linde, chemist and engineer, Bavaria, 1842. Mrs Humphry Ward (Mary Augustus Arnold), novelist, *Robert Elsmere, The Marriage of Robert Elsmere*, Tasmania, 1851. Richard Strauss, composer, *Thus Spake Zarathustra, Salome*, Munich, Germany, 1864. Azorin, novelist, *The Villages*, Spain, 1874. Alfred Kroeber, anthropologist and archaeologist, New Jersey, 1876. Nikolai Alexandrovich Bulganin, Soviet statesman, Gorky, 1895. Kawabata Yasunari, novelist, *Snow Country*, Osaka, Japan, 1899. Jacques Cousteau, undersea explorer and writer, France, 1910.

DIED: Sir John Franklin, sought the 'North West Passage', 1847. Klemens Metternich, statesman and diplomat, Vienna, 1859. Franklin Giddings, sociologist, *Studies in the Theory of Human Society*, 1931. John Llewellyn Lewis, labour leader, founder of the AFL–CIO, Washington D.C., 1969. Alexander Kerensky, Premier of the Provisional Russian Government in 1917, New York City, 1970.

JUNE 12

Anniversary of the Peace with Bolivia, Paraguay. Independence Day, Philippines (1898). Feasts of SS: John of Sahagun; Basilides and his Companions, martyrs; Añtonina, martyr; Onuphrius; Ternan, bishop; Peter of Mount Athos; Leo III, pope; Odulf; Eskil, bishop and martyr.

The Act of Settlement was passed limiting succession to the British crown, 1701. ¶ Bill of Rights is proclaimed by Virginia, 1776. ¶ (Sir) William F. Cooke and (Sir) Charles Wheatstone patent 'the magnetic needle telegraph', 1837. ¶ The Reform Bill is introduced by W. E. Gladstone, 1866. ¶ First railway in Japan opened, 1872. ¶ Beginning of purges of generals and other army leaders in the USSR, 1937. ¶ The Prime Minister of India, Mrs Gandhi, is found guilty of electoral corruption in the 1971 Indian elections, 1975.

BORN: Harriet Martineau, novelist and historian, *Society in America*, Norwich, Norfolk, 1802. Charles Kingsley, novelist, *The Water Babies*, Devon, 1819. Anthony Eden, 1st Earl of Avon, British statesman, 1897. Brigid Brophy, novelist and critic, London, 1929. Anne Frank, author of *The Diary*, 1929.

DIED: William Collins, poet, 'To the Passions', 1759. Thomas Arnold, educationalist, head of Rugby School, 1842. John Nicholson Ireland, English composer, 1962. Sir Herbert Read, poet, literary and art critic, *Poetry and Anarchism, A Concise History of Modern Art*, Malton, Yorkshire, 1968.

JUNE 13

City Day, Lisbon, Portugal. Anniversary of the Reform Movement,
Yemen Arab Republic. Feasts of SS: Antony of Padua, doctor;
Felicula, martyr; Aquilina, martyr; Triphyllius, bishop.

Columbus discovers Evangelista (now the Isle of Pines) on his second expedition, 1494. ¶ First ride in a train by Queen Victoria, 1842. ¶ Aethra (Asteroid 132) discovered by J. C. Watson, 1873. ¶ Beginning of the Boxer Rising in China, 1900. ¶ The first German VI flying-bomb hits London, 1944. ¶ The last British troops leave the Suez Canal area, 1956.

BORN: Gnaeus Julius Agricola, Roman military commander, completed the invasion of Britain begun by Julius Caesar, 40. Fanny Burney, diarist and novelist, *Cecilia*, Norfolk, 1752. Thomas Young, physicist, Milverton, Somerset, 1773. Thomas Arnold, educationalist, head of Rugby School; Isle of Wight, 1795. Sir Charles Parsons, engineer, invented the steam turbine, London, 1854. William Butler Yeats, Irish poet and dramatist, *Easter 1916, The Countess Cathleen,* Sandymount, Dublin, 1865. Jules Bordet, bacteriologist, Nobel Prize for Medicine, Belgium, 1870. Carlos Chavez, composer, *Sinfonia India,* Mexico, 1899.

DIED: Alexander the Great, 323BC. Simon Tissot, physician, Switzerland, 1797. Richard Lovell Edgworth, educationalist and inventor, Ireland, 1817. Martin Buber, philosopher and theologian, *I and Thou,* 1965. Georg von Békésy, physicist, Nobel Prize for Medicine, 1972.

JUNE 14

*Flag Day, USA (celebrating the day when the Continental Congress
adopted the Stars and Stripes as the US flag, 1777; a legal holiday in
Pennsylvania only). Feasts of SS: Basil the Great, archbishop and doctor;
Valerius and Rufinus, martyrs; Dogmael; Methodius I
of Constantinople, bishop.*

Charles I completely defeated at Naseby, 1645. ¶ William III lands at Carrick-fergus in Ireland, 1690. ¶ The Austrians are defeated at the battle of Marengo by Napoleon, 1800. ¶ The first session of the first Parliament in Canada, at Kingston, 1841. ¶ Sir Thomas Lipton's *Shamrock I* and *Shamrock III* arrive in New York Harbour, 1903. ¶ Alcock and Brown land after flying the Atlantic in a little over 16 hours, 1919. ¶ Paris is entered by German forces, 1940. ¶ The Vatican announces that the Index of Prohibited Books is abolished, 1966. ¶ South England will be crossed by the centre of the path of totality of a solar eclipse, 2051.

BORN: Charles Augustin de Coulomb, physicist, France, 1736. Harriet Beecher Stowe, novelist and reformer, *Uncle Tom's Cabin*, Litchfield, Connecticut, 1811. Prince Aritomo Yamagata, military leader and minister, Prime Minister of Japan, Chóshú, Japan, 1838. Robert La Follette, Governor of Wisconsin and 'Progressive' US presidential candidate, Primrose, Wisconsin, 1855. Karl Landsteiner, pathologist, distinguished differing blood types, Vienna, 1868. John McCormack, Irish tenor, Athlone, 1884. Ernesto 'Che' Guevara, guerrilla leader and revolutionary, Argentina, 1928.

DIED: Colin Maclaurin, mathematician, Edinburgh, 1746. Benedict Arnold, US soldier and spy, 1801. Ciacomo Leopardi, poet and writer, *Centi*, 1837. Edward Fitzgerald, poet, translator of *Omar Khayyam*, Suffolk, 1883. Emmeline Pankhurst, suffragette, London, 1928. Gilbert Keith Chesterton, writer and essayist, *The Napoleon of Notting Hill, The Man who was Thursday*, 1936. Maksim Gorky, Russian novelist and dramatist, *The Lower Depths*, 1936. John Logie Baird, television pioneer, 1946.

Feasts of SS: Vitus, Modestus and Crescentia, martyrs; Hesychius, martyr;
Tatian Dulas, martyr; Orsiesius, abbot; Landelinus, abbot;
Edburga of Winchester, virgin; Bardo, archbishop; Aleydia, or Alice, virgin;
Germaine of Pibrac, virgin.

An eclipse recorded at Nineveh (according to computations by Sir Henry Rawlinson), 763BC. ¶ Magna Carta signed by King John at Runnymede, near Windsor, 1215. ¶ Wat Tyler's insurrection in England is suppressed, 1381. ¶ Mary of Scotland defeated at the battle of Carberry Hill, 1567. ¶ Commodore Anson arrives at Spithead in the *Centurion* having circumnavigated the globe, 1744. ¶ Arkansas made a US state (25th), 1836. ¶ The 49th Parallel is declared to be the boundary between Oregon and Canada by the Treaty of Washington, 1846. ¶ Stamp Duty on newspapers is abolished in Britain, 1855. ¶ Thisbe (Asteroid 88) discovered by C. H. F. Peters, 1866. ¶ The battle of Givenchy, 1915. ¶ US and Britain sign agreement on atomic energy, 1955. ¶ The first democratic general election is held in Spain for over forty years, 1977.

BORN: Edward, 'The Black Prince', led English campaigns against the French, 1330. Cesare Beccaria, jurist and economist, Milan, 1738. Edvard Grieg, composer, *Peer Gynt, Holberg Suite*, Norway, 1843. Harry Langdon, silent film comedian, Iowa, 1884. Thomas Weller, bacteriologist, Nobel Prize Winner, Ann Arbor, Michigan, 1915.

DIED: Wat Tyler, leader of the Peasants' Revolt in 1381; beheaded, London, 1381. Mihail Eminescu, Rumanian poet, 'The Evening Star', 1889. William Le Baron Jenney, American architect, 1907. Charles Francis Brush, devised the arc lamp, 1929. Wendell Stanley, biochemist, Nobel Prize winner, Spain, 1971.

JUNE 16

Dies Mala or 'Egyptian Day', considered unlucky in the Middle Ages.
All of the main narrative events in James Joyce's novel Ulysses *happen*
on this day in 1904. Feasts of SS: Ferreolus and Ferrutio, martyrs;
Cyricus and Julitta, martyrs; Tychon of Amathus, bishop;
Aurelian, bishop; Benno, bishop; Lutgardis, virgin; John Francis Regis.

Abdication of Christina of Sweden, 1654. ¶ The English and Dutch squadrons under Admiral Rooke are defeated by the French off St Vincent, 1693. ¶ George II defeats the French at Dettingen, 1743. ¶ War with Britain is declared by Spain, 1779. ¶ The Chartist Movement begins with the formation of the London Working Men's Association, 1836. ¶ First Congress of Soviets, 1917. ¶ Ban lifted in Germany on Nazi Storm Troopers, 1932. ¶ US National Industrial Recovery Act and Farm Credit Act, 1933. ¶ Valentina Tereshkova launched into orbit for three-day space-flight by USSR, 1963. ¶ The government of Tanzania announces that China has lent it £2-million interest free, 1966.

BORN: Sir John Cheke, writer and scholar, Cambridge, 1514. Henrietta Stuart, Duchess of Orleans, Exeter, Devon, 1644. Louis, Duc de Saint-Simon, writer and courtier, Paris, 1675. Arthur Meighen, Canadian Prime Minister, near Anderson, Ontario, 1874. Stan Laurel, film comedian (with Oliver Hardy), Lancashire, 1890. Lupino Lane, singer and music-hall entertainer, London, 1892.

DIED: John Churchill, 1st Duke of Marlborough, military commander, Windsor, 1722. Joseph Butler, theologian, *The Analogy of Religion,* 1752. Charles Sturt, British officer, explored the Australian interior, Cheltenham, Gloucestershire, 1869. Crawford Long, surgeon, pioneered the use of ether, New York, 1878. Elmer Sperry, inventor, principally known for his use of the gyroscope, Brooklyn, New York, 1930. Margaret Grace Bondfield, the first woman Cabinet member in Britain (1929), 1953. Imre Nagy, Hungarian leader, Prime Minister at the time of the Russian invasion (1956), Budapest, 1958. John Reith, the first Director-General of the British Broadcasting Corporation, Edinburgh, 1971.

JUNE 17

National Day, Federal Republic of Germany. Bunker Hill Day,
Massachusetts, USA (1775 battle). Feasts of SS: Nicander and
Marcian, martyrs; Bessarion; Hypatius, abbot; Avitus, abbot;
Nectan; Hervé, or Harvey, abbot; Botulf, or Botolph, abbot,
and Adulf; Moling, bishop; Rainerius of Pisa; Teresa and
Sanchia of Portugal; Emily de Vialar, virgin.

King Edward III renounces all claims of sovereignty over Scotland, 1328.
¶ The British Peace offer is rejected by US Congress, 1778. ¶ The Opera House
in London burns down, 1789. ¶ Maori uprisings in New Zealand against the
British, 1843. ¶ The last German air raid on Britain in the Great War, 1918.
¶ Beginning of the Russian occupation of the Baltic states, 1940. ¶ Revolts in
East Berlin against the Communist government, 1953. ¶ Seven men are arrested
attempting to burgle the headquarters of the Democratic Party National
Committee in the Watergate building in Washington D.C. (and thus begins the
'Watergate Affair'), 1972.

BORN: Edward I of England, 1239. Pedro Calderón de la Barca, Spanish
dramatist, *The Mayor of Zalamea*, Madrid, 1600. John Wesley, evangelist and
theologian, founder of Methodism, Epworth, Lincolnshire, 1703. William
Parsons, Earl of Rosse, astronomer and Member of Parliament, York, England,
1800. Charles-François Gounod, composer and conductor, Paris, 1818. Sir
William Crookes, physicist, discovered thallium, London, 1832. Henry Hertzberg Lawson, Australian writer, *Joe Wilson and his Mates*, 1867. John Hersey,
writer and journalist, *Hiroshima*, Tientsin, China, 1914.

DIED: Giacomo Torelli, theatrical designer, Italy, 1678. John III, King of
Poland, 1696. Joseph Addison, essayist and critic, 1719. Sir Edward Burne-Jones,
painter, 1898. Dorothy Richardson, novelist, *Pilgrimage* (a sequence), Becken-
ham, Kent, 1957. John Cowper Powys, novelist and writer, *A Glastonbury
Romance, Maiden Castle*, Blaenau, Wales, 1963.

JUNE 18

Feasts of SS: Ephraem, doctor; Mark and Marcellian, martyrs;
Amandus of Bordeaux, bishop; Elizabeth of Schönau, virgin.

The English are defeated by Joan of Arc at Patay, 1429. ¶ British troops are evacuated from Philadelphia by Henry Clinton, 1778. ¶ The Duke of Wellington with the aid of von Blücher defeats Napoleon at Waterloo, 1815. ¶ Waterloo Bridge in London is opened, 1817. ¶ Bilbao is taken by the Spanish rebels, 1937. ¶ A BEA Trident crashes at Staines shortly after take off from Heathrow Airport, all 118 people on board are killed, 1972. ¶ Prince Museid was publicly beheaded in Riyadh for the assassination of King Faisal of Saudi Arabia (on 25 March), 1975.

BORN: Viscount Castlereagh, Anglo-Irish statesman, Dublin, 1769. Cyrus Curtis, founder and publisher of the *Ladies' Home Journal*, Maine, 1850. Edward Scripps, journalist, founded the US newspaper chain, near Rushville, Illinois, 1854. Edouard Daladier, statesman, signatory of the Munich Agreement, France, 1884. Oscar Natzka, New Zealand opera singer, Waikato, 1912.

DIED: Rogier van der Weyden, Flemish painter, Brussels, 1464. William Cobbett, writer and politician, *Rural Rides*, 1835. Samuel Butler, novelist and satirist, *Erewhon*, *The Way of All Flesh*, 1902. Robert La Follette, Governor of Wisconsin and 'Progressive' US presidential candidate, 1925. Roald Amundsen, Norwegian polar explorer; in the North Sea after a flying accident, 1928. Arthur Edwin Kennelly, engineer and physicist, 1939. Ethel Barrymore, actress, 1959.

JUNE 19

National Holiday, Algeria. Artigas Day, Uruguay (José Artigas, revolutionary patriot, instrumental in gaining independence, 1825). Feasts of SS: Juliana Falconieri, virgin; Gervase and Protase, martyrs; Deodatus, or Dié, bishop; Bruno, or Boniface, of Querfurt, bishop and martyr.

Beginning of the General Council of Nicaea, which would settle rules for the computation of Easter, 325. ¶ Greek rebels are defeated at Dragashan by Turkish forces, 1821. ¶ Sir Robert Peel's Act for establishing the police force in London, 1829. ¶ German titles and names are renounced by the British royal family; the name of Windsor is adopted, 1917. ¶ Saipan taken by American troops, 1944. ¶ Execution of Julius and Ethel Rosenberg (convicted of atomic spying in US and sentenced in 1951), 1953. ¶ President John F. Kennedy addresses Congress on the subject of civil rights, 1963. ¶ The US Senate passes the Civil Rights Bill, 73–27, and returns it to the House of Representatives for concurrence, 1964.

BORN: James I, King of England and VI of Scotland, Edinburgh Castle, 1566. Thomas Fuller, clergyman and biographer, Northamptonshire, 1608. Blaise Pascal, philosopher and mathematician, *Les Pensées*, France, 1623. Jean Marie Collot d'Herbois, revolutionary, Paris, 1749. John Gibson, sculptor, member of the Royal Academy, Wales, 1790. Earl Haig, soldier, Edinburgh, 1861. The Duchess of Windsor (Bessie Wallis Warfield), Pennsylvania, 1896. Guy Lombardo, bandleader, London, Canada, 1902. Ernst Boris Chain, bacteriologist and biochemist, Nobel Prize winner, Berlin, 1906.

DIED: Maximilian, Archduke of Austria, Emperor of Mexico, Mexico, 1867. Mikhail Bakunin, Russian anarchist, 1876. Lord Acton, statesman and writer, 1902. Sir James Barrie, dramatist, and novelist, *Peter Pan*, 1937. Julius and Ethel Rosenberg, American spies for Soviet intelligence; executed, Ossining, New York, 1953.

JUNE 20

*The Roman festival honouring Summanus; originally an Etruscan deity,
he was later regarded in Rome as the god of the night sky.
The Translation of King Edward of the West Saxons, BCP, not
retained in the 1928 revision. Flag Day, Argentina. West Virginia Day,
West Virginia, USA. Feasts of SS: Silverius, pope and martyr;
Goban, or Gobain, martyr; Bagnus, or Bain, bishop; Adalbert of
Magdeburg, archbishop; John of Matera, abbot.*

Mobs invade Tuileries in Paris, 1792. ¶ Queen Victoria, on death of William IV, succeeds to the throne in Britain, 1837. ¶ Commencement of the second attempt at laying a trans-Atlantic telegraphic cable (called off because of violent storms on 21 June), 1858. ¶ West Virginia is made a US state (35th state), 1863. ¶ War declared on Austria by Italy, 1866. ¶ The Kiel Canal is formally opened, 1895. ¶ Invasion of Okinawa by US forces completed (began 1 April), 1945. ¶ Plans for 'hot line' between White House and Kremlin agreed by USSR and US, 1963.

BORN: Dr George Hickes, theologian, Yorkshire, 1642. Dr Adam Ferguson, historian, *History of the Roman Republic*, Perthshire, Scotland, 1723. Jacques Offenbach, composer of operettas, *Orpheus in the Underworld*, *Tales of Hoffman*, Cologne, 1819. Medardo Rosso, sculptor, Turin, Italy, 1858. Kurt Schwitters, painter and collagist, Hanover, Germany, 1887.

DIED: William Barents, Dutch explorer, the Barents Sea is named after him, 1597. Emmanuel Sieyès, French Revolutionary leader, aided Napoleon in the Revolution of 18th Brumaire, Paris, 1836. William IV, King of Great Britain, Windsor Castle, 1837. Jules de Goncourt, writer, author with his brother Edmond of the *Journal*, 1870. Pancho Villa, robber, revolutionary and dictator; murdered, Chihuahua, Mexico, 1923.

The foundation stone of the restored Capitoline Temple is laid in Rome, 70. ¶ The first stone of Christopher Wren's rebuilding of St Paul's Cathedral laid, 1675. ¶ The Black Hole of Calcutta, 1756. ¶ The US Constitution comes into force, 1788. ¶ The State of New Hampshire ratifies the Constitution of the United States of America, 1788. ¶ Irish rebels defeated at Vinegar Hill by Lord Lake, who then enters Wexford ending the Irish Rebellion, 1798. ¶ The French are overrun by the Duke of Wellington at Vittoria, 1813. ¶ The Golden Jubilee of Queen Victoria, 1887. ¶ Annexation of Zululand by the British, 1887. ¶ Scuttling of the German Fleet at Scapa Flow, 1919. ¶ Tobruk is taken by Afrika Corps under the command of Rommel, 1942.

BORN: Emile de Girardin, political journalist, Paris, 1806. Enrico Ceccetti, ballet teacher and director, Italy, 1850. Henry Major Tomlinson, maritime novelist and essayist, *The Sea and the Jungle, The Turn of the Tide*, London, 1873. Norman Bowen, geologist, Ontario, 1887. Pier Luigi Nervi, architect, designed the UNESCO building in Paris, Sondrio, Italy, 1891. Jean-Paul Sartre, Existentialist philosopher, novelist and dramatist, *L'Etre et le Néant, Les Chemins de la Liberté*, Paris, 1905.

DIED: Edward III of England, 1377. Nicolo Machiavelli, diplomat and writer, *The Prince*, Florence, 1527. Inigo Jones, architect and antiquary, Somerset House, London, 1652. Baron Paul d'Holbach, philosopher and encyclopedist, *The System of Nature*, Paris, 1789. Friedrich Froebel, educator, developed the idea of the *kindergarten*, 1852. Antonio Lopez de Santa-Anna, revolutionary, military commander and President of Mexico, Mexico City, 1876. Edouard Vuillard, painter, La Baule, France, 1940. Rex Ingram, actor and film director, *The Four Horsemen of the Apocalypse*, California, 1950. Ahmed Sukarno, Nationalist leader and dictator of Indonesia, Indonesia, 1970.

JUNE 22

Summer Solstice (or 21 June). National Thanksgiving Day, Haiti.
Anniversary of the Battle of Morat, Fribourg canton, Switzerland
(Charles the Bold of Burgundy defeated by the Swiss, 1476).
Feasts of SS: Alban, martyr; Nicetas of Remesiana, bishop;
Paulinus of Nola, bishop; Eberhard of Salzburg, archbishop.

Antiochus III, the Great, defeated at the battle of Raphia, near Gaza, by Ptolemy IV, King of Egypt, 217BC. ¶ Accession of Richard II of England, 1377. ¶ Charles the Bold defeated by the Swiss at Morat, 1476. ¶ Monmouth defeats the Covenanters at Bothwell Brigg in Scotland, 1679. ¶ Arkansas readmitted to the Union (seceded 6 May 1861), 1868. ¶ A bright comet with a fan-shaped tail was observed over London (and for several days after), 1881. ¶ The coronation of George V in England, 1911. ¶ *Dippermouth Blues* recorded by King Oliver and his Creole Jazzband with Louis Armstrong in Richmond, Virginia, 1923. ¶ Beginning of the German invasion of Russia, 1941.

BORN: George Vancouver, naval captain and explorer, King's Lynn, Norfolk, 1757. Karl von Humboldt, philologist, Potsdam, Germany, 1767. Giuseppe Mazzini, Italian patriot, Genoa, 1805. William MacDougal, psychologist, Lancashire, 1871. Erich Remarque, novelist, *All Quiet on the Western Front*, Osnabrück, Germany, 1898. Billy Wilder, film director and writer, *Sunset Boulevard, Some Like it Hot*, Vienna, 1906. Michael Todd, film producer, *Around the World in 80 Days*, Minneapolis, 1907. Katherine Dunham, choreographer, *Shango*, 1910.

DIED: John Logan Campbell, 'father' of Auckland, New Zealand, 1902. Felix Klein, German mathematician, 1925. C. J. Dennis, Australian poet, 1936. Moritz Schlick, philosopher, Vienna, 1936. Walter De La Mare, writer, anthologist, poet, 1956. Judy Garland, actress and singer, *A Star is Born*, 1969. Darius Milhaud, composer, France, 1974.

JUNE 23

Midsummer's Eve in England and many European countries.
National Holiday, Luxembourg. Feasts of SS: Agrippina, virgin
and martyr; Etheldreda, or Audrey, widow; Lietbertus, or Libert, bishop;
Joseph Cafasso.

Clive's victory at the battle of Plassey (Bengal) against the forces of Surajah Dowlah lays the foundations of the British empire in India, 1757. ¶ The Taft-Hartley Act is passed by US Congress (though vetoed by President Truman), 1947. ¶ A *subpoena* is served on President Richard M. Nixon by Archibald Cox and the Senate Select Committee demanding that he hand over tape recordings of conversations in the White House, 1973.

BORN: Giambattista Vico, philosopher and jurist, *The New Science*, Naples, 1668. Anna Akhmatova, Russian poet, 1889. Alfred Charles Kinsey, statistician and sexologist, New Jersey, 1894. The Duke of Windsor, London, 1894. Jean Anouilh, French dramatist, *Antigone*, 1910.

DIED: Pedro de Mendoza, Spanish explorer in South America, founded Buenos Aires; on a ship in mid-Atlantic, 1537. Mark Akenside, poet and physician, *Pleasures of the Imagination*, London, 1770. Sir James Hall, founder of experimental geology, Scotland, 1832. James Mill, writer and philosopher, *Elements of Political Economy*, Kensington, London, 1836. Lady Hester Lucy Stanhope, traveller and adventuress, Lebanon, 1839. Cecil James Sharp, folklorist, collected and published many volumes of folk-songs, London, 1924.

JUNE 24

St John's or Midsummer Day, an English Quarter Day. Countryman's
Day, Peru. City Day, Porto, Portugal. Anniversary of the Battle of Carabobo,
Venezuela (1822). New Constitution and Fishermen's Day, Zaire.
The Feast of the Birthday of St John the Baptist, an exception to the
rule that saints are only celebrated on the day of their death—St John
was sanctified within the womb of his mother. Feasts of SS:
Simplicius, bishop; Bartholomew of Farne; The Martyrs under Nero.

Bruce defeats the English at the battle of Bannockburn, 1314. ¶ John Cabot (Giovanni Cabotto) said to have discovered Labrador on the coast of North America, 1497. ¶ Henry VIII of England crowned, 1509. ¶ Napoleon enters Russia, 1812. ¶ Melpomene (Asteroid 18) discovered by J. R. Hind, 1852. ¶ Mutiny at Sebastopol by the Russian Black Sea fleet, 1917. ¶ All land traffic between Berlin and the West is stopped by USSR, airlift begins, 1948. ¶ Arrest of Ralph Abernathy and over 250 supporters of the Poor People's Campaign in Washington, D.C., 1968. ¶ 112 people were killed when an Eastern Airlines Boeing 727 crashed in an electric storm above Kennedy Airport, New York, 1975.

BORN: William Henry Smith, politician and founder of the English bookselling chain, London, 1825. Ambrose Bierce, writer and satirist, *The Devil's Dictionary*, Ohio, 1842. Horatio Herbert, Lord Kitchener, soldier, Kerry, Ireland, 1850. Oswald Veblen, mathematician, Decorah, Iowa, 1880. Jack Dempsey, champion boxer, Colorado, 1895. Juan Manuel Fangio, Argentinian racing driver, 1911. Claude Chabrol, film director, 1930.

DIED: Vespasian (Titus Flavius Sabinus Vespasianus), Roman Emperor, Rome, 79. Lucrezia Borgia, aristocrat and poisoner, Ferrara, Italy, 1519. Adam Lindsay Gordon, Azores-born Australian poet, *Sea-Spray and Smoke-drift*; suicide, near Melbourne, 1870. Grover Cleveland, US President, 1908. Walter Rathenau, German statesman and industrialist; murdered, Berlin, 1922. Stuart Davis, American modern painter, 1964.

JUNE 25

Independence and Frelimo's Foundation Day, People's Republic of Mozambique.
Feasts of SS: William of Vercelli, abbot; Febronia, virgin and martyr;
Gallicanus; Prosper of Aquitaine; Prosper of Reggio, bishop;
Maximus of Turin, bishop; Moloc, or Luan, bishop; Adalbert of Egmond;
Eurosis, virgin and martyr; Gohard, bishop, and his Companions, martyrs.

Horace Walpole begins his own private press at Strawberry Hill in Twickenham, Middlesex, 1757. ¶ The state of Virginia ratifies the Constitution of the United States of America, 1788. ¶ First patent for barbed wire taken out, by Lucien Smith of Ohio, 1867. ¶ Florida readmitted to the Union (seceded 10 January 1861), 1868. ¶ General George A. Custer leads US troops against the Sioux Indians on the Little Bighorn river in Montana, and is massacred, 1876. ¶ The Hague is made the permanent seat of the International Court of Justice, 1920. ¶ South Korea is invaded by North Korean forces, 1950.

BORN: Nicholas I, Tsar of Russia, Tsarskoya Selo, Russia, 1796. Antonio Gaudi, architect in the Art Nouveau style, Spain, 1852. Walter Hermann Nernst, chemist, Nobel Prize winner, Prussia, 1864. Robert Erskine Childers, Irish nationalist, writer, *The Riddle of the Sands*, London, 1870. William De Mille, film and theatre producer, writer, *Hollywood Saga*, Washington, D.C., 1878. Hermann Julius Oberth, German pioneer of rocket design, chiefly responsible for the V2 project, Hermannstadt, Transylvania, 1894. Louis Mountbatten, First Earl Mountbatten of Burma, Supreme Allied Commander in South-East Asia, last Viceroy of India, Frogmore House, Windsor, 1900. George Orwell (Eric Blair), novelist, critic and essayist, *Coming up for Air, Animal Farm*, Motihari, Bengal, India, 1903. Willard van Orman Quine, philosopher, *From a Logical Point of View*, Akron, Ohio, 1908.

DIED: John Marston, dramatist, *The Malcontent*, London, 1634. Roger Gale, writer and antiquary, Yorkshire, 1744. William Smellie, naturalist, editor of *The Scots Magazine, Natural History, General and Particular*, Edinburgh, 1795. Ernst Theodor Amadeus Hoffmann, author and composer, *The Devil's Elixirs*, Berlin, 1822. George Armstrong Custer, American soldier, 1876. Thomas Eakins, American realist painter, 1916.

JUNE 26

*Independence Day, Malagasy Republic. Independence Day, Somali
Democratic Republic. Feasts of SS: John and Paul, martyrs;
Vigilius, bishop and martyr; Maxentius, abbot; Salvius, or Sauve,
and Superius; John of the Goths, bishop; Pelagius, martyr; Anthelm, bishop.*

Accession of Richard III of England, 1483. ¶ Accession of William IV of Great
•Britain, 1830. ¶ Anglo–Chinese War ends with the Treaty of Tientsin, 1858.
¶ Queen Elizabeth II opens the St Lawrence Seaway in Canada, 1959.
¶ Proclamation of independence by the Malagasy Republic (Madagascar), 1960.
¶ Over 500 political opponents of Mrs Gandhi are arrested throughout India
and strict emergency regulations are brought into force, 1975.

BORN: Charles-Joseph Messier, astronomer, published the first list of nebulae,
France, 1730. Lord William Thomson Kelvin, physicist and inventor, Belfast,
Ireland, 1824. Sir Robert Borden, Canadian Prime Minister, Grand Pré, Nova
Scotia, 1854. Pearl Buck, novelist, *The Good Earth*, *A House Divided*, West
Virginia, 1892. Willi Messerschmitt, aircraft designer, Frankfurt, 1898. Laurie
Lee, poet and novelist, *Cider with Rosie*, Gloucestershire, 1914.

DIED: Francisco Pizarro, Spanish conqueror of the Inca Empire, Lima, Peru,
1541. Gilbert White, curate, naturalist and writer, *Natural History and Antiquities of Selborne*, Selborne, Hampshire, 1793. Joseph Michel Montgolfier,
balloonist and paper manufacturer, France, 1810. Samuel Crompton, inventor
of the spinning mule, 1827. George IV of Great Britain, 1830. Ford Maddox
Ford, novelist, *Parade's End*, 1939. Karl Landsteiner, Austrian pathologist, 1943.
R. B. Bennett, Canadian Prime Minister, England, 1947. Inia Te Wiata, New
Zealand operatic singer, 1971.

JUNE 27

Independence Day, Republic of Djibouti. Feasts of SS: Zoilus and his Companions, martyrs; Samson of Constantinople; John of Chinon; George Mtasmindeli, abbot; Ladislaus of Hungary.

Jack Cade defeats Stafford at Sevenoaks, 1450. ¶ Cairo falls to British forces, 1801. ¶ The French evacuate Egypt, 1801. ¶ British soldiers and others massacred at Cawnpore, India, 1857. ¶ Central London 'electric tube' railway opened between Bank and Shepherd's Bush, 1900. ¶ *West End Blues* is recorded by Louis Armstrong and his Hot Five in Chicago, 1928. ¶ Independence of the Republic of Djibouti proclaimed, 1977.

BORN: Louis XII of France, Blois, 1462. Charles IX of France, St Germain, 1550. Charles XII of Sweden, 1682. Charles Stewart Parnell, Member of Parliament and champion of Irish Home Rule, Avondale, County Wicklow, 1846. Ivan Vazov, national poet of Bulgaria, Sopot, Bulgaria, 1850. Sir John Monash, Australian engineer and soldier, 1865. Helen Keller, writer and counselor (though blind, deaf and mute), *Out of the Dark*, Alabama, 1880.

DIED: Giorgio Vasari, artist and writer, *Lives of the Painters*, Florence, 1574. Joseph Smith, founder of the Church of Jesus Christ of Latter-Day Saints (Mormons); shot by a mob, Carthage, Illinois, 1844. Christian Ehrenberg, founder of protozoology, 1876. Malcolm Lowry, novelist, *Under the Volcano*, Sussex, 1957. Sir Arthur David Waley, scholar and Oriental translator, *170 Chinese Poems*, *Monkey*, London, 1966.

JUNE 28

Feasts of SS: Irenaeus, bishop; Plutarch, Potamiaena and their Companions, martyrs; Paul I, pope; Heimrad; Sergius and Germanus, abbots.

British defeated at Monmouth, New Jersey, by George Washington, 1778. ¶ Queen Victoria of Great Britain crowned (reign had begun 20 June 1837), 1838. ¶ Eugenia (Asteroid 45) discovered by H. Goldschmidt, 1857. ¶ Naval mutiny on the Russian battleship *Potemkin*, 1905. ¶ The assassination of the Archduke Ferdinand of Austria and his wife at Sarajevo, 1914. ¶ Seoul is taken by North Korean forces, 1950.

BORN: Henry VIII, King of England, Greenwich, 1491. Sir Peter Paul Rubens, Flemish painter, Siegen, Westphalia, 1577. Jean-Jacques Rousseau, philosopher and author, *The Social Contract, Confessions*, Geneva, 1712. Joseph Joachim, composer and violinist, Presburg (Czechoslovakia), 1831. Luigi Pirandello, dramatist, *Six Characters in Search of an Author, Each in His Own Way*, Agrigento, Sicily, 1867. Pierre Laval, Prime Minister of France and Nazi collaborator, France, 1883. Eric Ambler, novelist, London, 1909.

DIED: George Hadley, meteorologist, 1768. Gerhard Johann von Scharnhorst, Prussian officer and soldier, reformed and remodelled the Prussian army, Prague, 1813. James Madison, fourth President of the US (1809–17), Virginia, 1836. Robert O'Hara Burke, explorer of Australia, 1861.

JUNE 29

Independence Day, Seychelles. Feasts of SS: Peter, apostle;
Paul, apostle; Cassius, bishop; Salome and Judith; Emma, widow.

Completion of US territory in the Far West when the Senate ratifies the Gadsden Purchase in respect of land in the south of New Mexico and Arizona, 1854. ¶ The *Daily Telegraph* is published in London for the first time, 1855. ¶ The 'Great Comet' is seen across France and England, 1861. ¶ Trade Unionism legalized in Britain by Act of Parliament, 1871. ¶ Act passed for the purchasing of Hampstead Heath for public use by the Metropolitan Board of Works, 1871. ¶ Tahiti is annexed by France, 1880. ¶ Landing of American troops in New Guinea, 1943. ¶ US forces withdraw from Cambodia, 1970.

BORN: Giacomo Leopardi, poet and writer, *Centi*, Recanti, 1798. William James Mayo, surgeon, a joint-founder of the Mayo Clinic, Minnesota, 1861. James Harvey Robinson, historian, *The New History*, Bloomington, Illinois, 1863. George Ellery Hale, astronomer, founded the Yerkes and Mount Palomar Observatories, Chicago, 1868. Nelson Eddy, popular singer, Rhode Island, 1901.

DIED: Elizabeth Barrett Browning, poet, wife of Robert Browning, 1861. Adolphe Monticelli, painter, Marseilles, 1886. Thomas Henry Huxley, biologist, Eastbourne, Sussex, 1895. Friedrich Brugmann, philologist, 1919. Paul Klee, artist, 1940. Ignacy Jan Paderewski, piano virtuoso, composer, first Prime Minister of Poland, New York City, 1941. Moise Tshombe, politician, premier of Katanga, Algiers, 1969.

JUNE 30

*Anniversary of the 1871 Revolution, Guatemala. Anniversary of
the Coronation of Pope Paul VI, Vatican City State (1963).
Independence Day, Zaire (1964). The Feast of the Commemoration
of St Paul. Feasts of SS: Martial, bishop; Bertrand of Le Mans, bishop;
Erentrude, virgin; Theobald, or Thibaud, of Provins.*

Victory of the Royalists at Atherton Moor, 1643. ¶ The English and the Dutch
are defeated off Beachy Head by the French under Tourville, 1690. ¶ The Nore
naval mutiny is suppressed, 1797. ¶ Niagara Falls is crossed on a tightrope by
Blondin, 1859. ¶ Alleged fall of a shower of frogs in Birmingham, England,
1892. ¶ The last Allied troops leave the Rhineland, 1930. ¶ Purge by the Nazis
in Germany results in execution of Ernst Roehm and others for alleged plot
against Hitler, 1934. ¶ Billie Holiday records *These Foolish Things* with Teddy
Wilson and His Orchestra in New York, 1936. ¶ The Fascist Party in France is
suppressed, 1936. ¶ US and West Germany sign military aid agreement, 1955.
¶ The last United Nations forces leave the Congo, 1964. ¶ The three crew
members of the *Soyuz* Soviet space craft are killed on re-entry path to Earth,
1971.

BORN: John Gay, dramatist, *The Beggar's Opera*, Devonshire, 1685. Vicomte
Paul François Barras, statesman and member of the Directory, France, 1755.
Sir Joseph Dalton Hooker, botanist and zoologist, Halesworth, Suffolk, 1817.
Sir Stanley Spencer, artist, Cookham, Buckinghamshire, 1891. Walter Ulbricht,
East German politician, Leipzig, 1893. Howard Hawks, film director, *Rio Bravo,
Red River*, New York, 1896. Anthony Mann, film director, *The Tin Star*,
San Diego, California, 1907. Susan Hayward, actress, Brooklyn, New York,
1919.

DIED: Montezuma II, Emperor of the Aztecs, Tenochtitlán (Mexico City),
1520. William Oughtred, mathematician and probable inventor of the slide rule,
Albury, Sussex, 1660. Abraham Werner, geologist, Professor of Minerology at
Freiburg, Dresden, Germany, 1817. Johann Strauss, composer, *The Blue Danube,
Tales from the Vienna Woods*, Vienna, 1899. Lord Rayleigh, physicist, Witham,
Essex, 1919. Lee De Forest, American radio and television inventor, 1961.
Margery Allingham, popular novelist, 1966.

JULY

THIRTY-ONE DAYS

Originally known as *Quintilis* as it was the *fifth*
month of the Roman year. In 44BC, the second
year of the Julian Calendar's implementation,
the name was changed by the Senate to *Julius*,
in honour of Julius Caesar.

JULY 1

Proclamation of Independence Day, Burundi. Dominion Day, Canada
(1867). Republic Day, Ghana (1965). Independence Day, Republic of Rwanda
(1962). Union Day, Somali Democratic Republic. Day of Freedom, Surinam.
The Feast of the Precious Blood of Our Lord Jesus Christ. Feasts of SS:
Shenute, abbot; Theodoric, or Thierry, abbot; Carilefus, or Calais, abbot;
Gall of Clermont, bishop; Eparchius, or Cybard; Simeon Salus;
Serf, or Servanus, bishop.

The Turks are defeated by the Crusaders at Dorylaeum, 1097. ¶ William III defeats James II at Boyne, 1690. ¶ The first volume of Diderot's *Encyclopédie*, is published in Paris, 1751. ¶ Hebe (Asteroid 6) discovered by K. C. Hencke, 1847. ¶ The Dominion of Canada is established by the British North America Act, 1867. ¶ The Albert Memorial in London is unveiled by Queen Victoria, 1872. ¶ Prince Edward Island is made part of the Dominion of Canada, 1873. ¶ The world's first air force is established with the founding of the Aeronautical Division of the US Army's Signal Office, 1907. ¶ British and French troops begin the offensive in the Somme (continues until 8 November), 1916. ¶ Beginning of the International Geophysical Year, 1957. ¶ Signing of the nuclear non-proliferation treaty in Washington, 1968. ¶ Investiture of the Prince of Wales at Caernarvon Castle, 1969.

BORN: Louis II, King of Hungary, 1506. Gottfried Leibniz, philosopher, Leipzig, Germany, 1646. George Sand (Amantine Dupin), novelist, Paris, 1804. Louis Blériot, aviator, the first man to fly the English Channel (1909), 1872. Isaak Babel, novelist, *Red Cavalry*, Odessa, 1894. Sir Bernard Heinze, Australian musician and conductor, Shepparton, Victoria, 1894. William Wyler, US film director and producer, *The Best Years of Our Lives*, 1902. Olivia de Havilland, actress, Tokyo, 1916. Hans Werner Henze, composer, *Elegy for Young Lovers*, Germany, 1926.

DIED: Martin Luther, theologian and reformer, Germany, 1546. James Oglethorpe, British colonist of the US state of Georgia, Essex, 1785. Charles Goodyear, inventor of vulcanized rubber, 1860. Allan Pinkerton, founder of the Pinkerton National Detective Agency, Chicago, 1884. Harriet Beecher Stowe, novelist and reformer, *Uncle Tom's Cabin*, Hartford, Connecticut, 1896. George Watts, painter, Compton, Surrey, 1904. Erik Satie, composer, *La Belle Eccentrique*, Paris, 1925. Alphonse Leon Daudet, French humorous writer, 1942. Carl Mayer, film director, *The Cabinet of Dr Caligari*, London, 1944. Juan Peron, Argentinian dictator, 1974.

JULY 2

The Feast of the Visitation of the Blessed Virgin Mary, when Mary
visited her cousin Elizabeth and blessed the child she, Elizabeth, had
miraculously conceived six months earlier (the child was St John the Baptist);
the feast was first observed by the Friars Minor, it was extended
throughout the Western church by Pope Urban VI in 1389.
Feasts of SS: Processus and Martinian, martyrs;
Monegundis, widow; Otto of Bamberg, bishop.

Prince Rupert defeated at Marston Moor, 1644. ¶ Covenanters defeated at Alford in Scotland by Montrose, 1645. ¶ The French commanded by Lally defeated by the British under Sir Eyre Coote near Wandewash in India, 1760. ¶ General Robert E. Lee succeeds in driving General George B. McClellan of the Union back from Richmond, Virginia, 1862. ¶ Assassination of President James Garfield of the US by Charles Jules Guiteau, at Washington railway station, 1881. ¶ The Sherman Anti-Trust law passed in the US, 1890. ¶ The first Zeppelin flight, by Count Ferdinand von Zeppelin from a field on the outskirts of Berlin, 1900. ¶ Beginning of heavy fighting in Dublin, 1922. ¶ The London Dock Strike begins (finishes 20/21 August), 1923.

BORN: Jacopo Tatti Sansovino, Florentine sculptor, Florence, 1486. Thomas Cranmer, archbishop and liturgist, Nottinghamshire, 1489. Christoph von Gluck, German operatic composer, *Alcestis*, 1714. Sir Charles Tupper, Canadian Prime Minister, Amherst, Nova Scotia, 1821. Sir William Henry Bragg, physicist, Nobel Prize winner, Cumberland, 1862. Herman Hesse, poet and novelist, *Steppenwolf*, Germany, 1877. Lord Home, politician, Prime Minister, London, 1903. Thurgood Marshall, jurist, the first black to be appointed to the US Supreme Court, Baltimore, Maryland, 1908.

DIED: Nostradamus (Michel de Nostre-Dame), astrologer and prophet, *Centuries*, Salon, France, 1566. Jean-Jacques Rousseau, philosopher and author, *The Social Contract, Confessions*, Ermenonville, France, 1778. Samuel Hahnemann, physician and doctor, the founder of homeopathic medicine, Paris, 1843. Sir Robert Peel, Prime Minister, London, 1850. Porfirio Diaz, military leader and Mexican dictator, 1915. Sir Herbert Beerbohm Tree, British theatrical actor-manager, London, 1917. Emile Coué, psychologist, *Suggestion and Auto-Suggestion*, 1926. Amelia Earhart, pioneer aviator; disappeared whilst flying, 1937. Ernest Hemingway, novelist and journalist, *For Whom the Bell Tolls*, suicide, 1961. Vladimir Nabokov, novelist and lepidopterist, *Pale Fire, Lolita*, 1977.

JULY 3

Beginning of the Dog Days in the Northern Hemisphere, they last until 15 August and are usually the hottest time of the year; the name is of Roman origin and is associated with the rising of the Dog Star, Sirius. Independence Day, Algeria (French claims relinquished in 1962). Family Day, Lesotho. Emancipation Day, Virgin Islands. Feasts of SS: Leo II, pope; Anatolius of Laodicea, bishop; Irenaeus and Mustiola, martyrs; Julius and Aaron, martyrs; Heliodorus, bishop; Anatolius of Constantinople, bishop; Rumold, or Rombaut, martyr; Bernardino Realino.

Licinius defeated at Adrianople by Constantine, 323. ¶ Quebec, Canada, founded by Samuel de Champlain, 1608. ¶ George Washington takes up command as Commander-in-Chief of American forces, at Cambridge, Massachusetts, 1775. ¶ General Meade's Union army defeats the Confederacy under the command of Robert E. Lee at Gettysburg, 1863. ¶ Austrians defeated at Sadowa by Prussians, 1866. ¶ A new comet is discovered by Temple in Milan (it now bears his name), 1873. ¶ Idaho made a US state (43rd), 1890. ¶ Naval victory by the US at Santiago, 1898. ¶ The world's first colour television transmission is accomplished by John Logie Baird in London, 1928. ¶ The London North-Eastern Region railway's *Mallard* achieves a speed of 126 mph, the world record for a steam locomotive, 1928. ¶ Israeli commandos raid the highjacked aeroplane at Entebbe Airport in Uganda, 1976.

BORN: Louis XI of France, 1423. Robert Adam, architect and designer, Fifeshire, 1728. Henry Grattan, statesman and champion of Irish Independence, Dublin, 1746. Leoš Janáček, composer, Czechoslovakia, 1854. R. B. Bennett, Canadian Prime Minister, Hopewell Hill, New Brunswick, 1870. William Henry Davies, poet and writer, *The Autobiography of a Super-Tramp*, Monmouth, Wales, 1871. Sir Apirana Ngata, Maori statesman, Kawakawa, New Zealand, 1874. Franz Kafka, novelist, *The Castle*, *The Trial*, Prague, 1838.

DIED: Marie de Medici, Louis XIII of France's consort, intriguer; destitute, in a hayloft, Cologne, 1642. Theodor Herzl, Zionist, *The Jewish State*, Vienna, 1904. Joel Chandler Harris, journalist and author, *Uncle Remus: His Songs and His Sayings*, Georgia, 1908.

JULY 4

*A Dog Day (see 3 July). Caricom Day, Barbados (the Caribbean
Community, established in 1973). Philippine-US Friendship Day,
Philippines (an agreement with America, 1946). Independence Day,
USA and its territories (celebrated since 1777 to commemorate the
signing of the Declaration of Independence in the previous year).
Independence Day, Virgin Islands. Fighters Day, Yugoslavia.
The Translation of St Martin, BCP, not retained in the 1928 revision.
Feasts of SS: Bertha, widow; Andrew of Crete, archbishop;
Odo of Canterbury, archbishop; Ulric of Augsburg, bishop.*

Saladin defeats the Crusaders at Tiberias, 1187. ¶ The 'Barebone's Parliament' meets for the first time in London, 1653. ¶ Congress carries the American Declaration of Independence, drafted by Jefferson with additions and revisions by Benjamin Franklin and John Adams, 1776. ¶ Union victory over the Confederacy at Vicksburg in Mississippi, 1863. ¶ North Carolina readmitted to the Union (seceded 20 May 1861), 1868. ¶ Hanna Reitsch pilots the first successful helicopter flight, at Bremen in Germany, 1937.

BORN: Murad III, Sultan of Turkey, Manisa, Turkey, 1546. Jean Pierre Blanchard, balloonist and early aeronaut, the first man to cross the English Channel by air, France, 1753. Nathaniel Hawthorne, novelist and short-story writer, *Twice-Told Tales, The Scarlet Letter*, Salem, Massachusetts, 1804. Giuseppe Garibaldi, Italian patriot, France, 1807. Stephen Collins Foster, popular song writer, *Swanee River*, Pennsylvania, 1826. Thomas Barnardo, doctor, founder of the orphan Homes that bear his name, Dublin, 1845. James Bailey, of Barnum and Bailey, Detroit, 1847. Hugo Winkler, archaeologist, Saxony, Germany, 1863. Calvin Coolidge, President of US, Vermont, 1872. Louis B. Mayer, pioneer film producer, a founder of Metro-Goldwyn-Mayer, Germany, 1885. Louis Armstrong, jazz trumpeter, New Orleans, 1900. Lionel Trilling, writer and critic, New York City, 1905. Ingmar Bergman, film director, *The Seventh Seal*, Uppsala, Sweden, 1918.

DIED: Ortelius (Abraham Oertel), cartographer and engraver, produced the first atlas, Antwerp, 1598. William Byrd, Elizabethan organist and composer, 1623. Samuel Richardson, novelist, *Pamela, or Virtue Rewarded, Clarissa Harlowe*, Parsons Green, Middlesex, 1761. John Adams, second President of the US (1797–1801), 1826. Thomas Jefferson, US President, Monticello, near Charlottsville, Virginia, 1826. James Monroe, fifth President of the US, New York City, 1831. François René de Chateaubriand, politician and writer, *Les Mémoires d'outre-tombe*, 1848. Marie Curie, French chemist, France, 1934. Wladyslaw Sikorski, Prime Minister of Poland, 1943. Sir Bernard Freyberg, Governor-General of New Zealand, 1963.

JULY 5

A Dog Day (see 3 July). Independence Day, Cape Verde Islands.
Tynwald Day, Isle of Man (honouring the foundation of the island's legislature,
the Tynwald). Peace Day, Republic of Rwanda (commemorating the bloodless
coup by General Habyaliman in 1973). Anniversary of Independence,
Venezuela (1811). Feasts of SS: Antony Zaccaria;
Athanasius the Athonite, abbot.

Abolition of the Star Chamber in London, 1641. ¶ Royalists defeat the Parliamentarians at Lansdown, 1643. ¶ The Turkish navy is defeated by Russians (under British officers) at Tchesme, 1770. ¶ British retreat after defeat by American forces, at Chippewa, 1814. ¶ The first sovereign coins are issued in Britain, 1817. ¶ The first excursion in England arranged by Thomas Cook, it runs from Leicester to Loughborough, 1841. ¶ The Salvation Army is founded, 1865. ¶ Billie Holiday records *Them There Eyes* in New York with her Orchestra, 1939.

BORN: Sarah Siddons, actress, Brecon, Wales, 1755. George Borrow, writer, *The Bible in Spain, Lavengro*, Norfolk, 1803. Phineas T. Barnum, of Barnum and Bailey, Connecticut, 1810. Cecil John Rhodes, colonialist, founder of Rhodesia, Premier of Cape Colony, Bishops Stortford, Hertfordshire, 1853. Dwight Davis, tennis enthusiast, founder of the Davis Cup, St Louis, Missouri, 1879. Jean Cocteau, poet, dramatist, novelist, film director, France, 1889. Georges Pompidou, President of France, France, 1911.

DIED: Sir Stamford Raffles, founded Singapore, London, 1826. Joseph Nicéphone Niepce, photographic pioneer and inventor, Châlons-sur-Marne, France, 1833. James Hall, pioneer of geology in the US, New York City, 1868. Sir Austen Henry Layard, archaeologist, excavated Nineveh, 1894. Georges Bernanos, novelist and writer, 1948. Wilhelm Backhaus, classical pianist, 1969. Walter Gropius, architect, founder of the Bauhaus, New York City, 1969. Thomas Joseph Mboya, Kenyan statesman; assassinated, Nairobi, 1969. Georgette Heyer, popular historical novelist, 1974.

JULY 6

A Dog Day (see 3 July). Old Midsummer Day in England (prior to the introduction of the Gregorian calendar in 1752). Republic Day, Malawi (1966). Feasts of SS: Romulus, bishop and martyr; Dominica, virgin and martyr; Sisoes; Goar; Sexburga, widow; Modwenna, virgin; Godeleva, martyr; Mary Goretti, virgin and martyr.

Richard III of England crowned (reign had begun 26 June), 1483. ¶ Sir Thomas More is beheaded in London, 1535. ¶ Accession of Queen Jane of England, 1553. ¶ Monmouth is defeated at the battle of Sedgemoor, 1685. ¶ Pope Pius VII is taken prisoner by the French after excommunicating Napoleon, 1809. ¶ Austrians defeated at Wagram by Napoleon, 1809. ¶ Formal establishment of the Republican Party in US, 1854. ¶ The first public showing of a 'talkie' film, *Lights of New York*, in New York, 1928. ¶ Dizzy Gillespie and his Orchestra record *Jumpin' with Symphony Sid* in New York City, 1949. ¶ The last tram in London runs, 1952. ¶ Alaska is made the 49th state of US, 1958. ¶ Independence of Malawi proclaimed, 1964. ¶ Malawi becomes a Republic, 1966.

BORN: John Paul Jones, American naval commander, Kircudbrightshire, Scotland, 1747. Alexander Wilson, astronomer, Paisley, Renfrewshire, 1766. Sir Stamford Raffles, founded Singapore; born at sea, off Jamaica, 1781. Sir William Jackson Hooker, botanist, first Director of the Royal Botanic Gardens at Kew; Norwich, Norfolk, 1785. Maximilian, Archduke of Austria, Emperor of Mexico, Vienna, 1832. Andrey Gromyko, Soviet Foreign Minister and politician, Russia, 1909.

DIED: Ludovico Ariosto, poet, *Orlando Furioso*, 1533. Sir Thomas More, humanist, statesman and writer, *Utopia, The History of Richard III*, executed, London, 1535. John Marshall, jurist, US Secretary of State, Philadelphia, 1835. Sir Edwin Chadwick, social reformer, 1890. Guy de Maupassant, short-story writer and novelist, *The Necklace, Pierre et Jean*, Paris, 1893. Odilon Redon, Symbolist painter and lithographer, Paris, 1916. Edward Goodrich Acheson, US industrial chemist, 1931. Kenneth Grahame, author, *The Wind in the Willows*, 1932. Aneurin Bevan, British Labour Party politician, 1960. William Faulkner, American novelist, *Sanctuary*, 1962. Louis Armstrong, jazz trumpeter, 1971. Otto Klemperer, German conductor, 1973.

JULY 7

A Dog Day (see 3 July). National Day, Equatorial Guinea. Farmers Day,
Tanzania (1977, formerly Saba Saba Day). Serbian Peoples
Uprising Day, Yugoslavia. Feasts of SS: Cyril and Methodius;
Pantaenus; Palladius, bishop; Felix of Nantes, bishop;
Ethelburga, Ercongota and Sethrida, virgins; Hedda, bishop.

Treaty of Tilsit between France and Russia, 1807. ¶ *Undina* (Asteroid 92) discovered by C. H. F. Peters, 1867. ¶ *Back Room Stomp* recorded in New York City by Rex Stewart and his 52nd Street Stompers (a Duke Ellington unit), 1937. ¶ *Between the Devil and the Deep Blue Sea* and *Bugle Call Rag* recorded in Paris by Dicky Wells and his Orchestra (with Django Reinhardt, Bill Coleman, etc.), 1937. ¶ Troops are sent to the Congo by Belgium, 1960.

BORN: Thomas Hooker, British Puritan clergyman, founded Hartford, Connecticut; Markfield, Leicester, 1586. Joseph Marie Jacquard, silk weaver, Lyons, France, 1752. Sir Morell Mackenzie, physician, Leytonstone, Essex, 1837. Gustav Mahler, composer, *The Symphony of a Thousand*, Bohemia, 1860. Marc Chagall, painter and designer, Russia, 1887. Vladimir Mayakovsky, Soviet dramatist and novelist, *The Bed Bug*, 1893. George Cukor, American film director, *The Philadelphia Story*, New York City, 1899. Vittorio De Sica, film director, *Umberto D*, Italy, 1901. James Cagney, actor, New York City, 1904. Gian-Carlo Menotti, operatic composer, *Amahl and the Night Visitors*, Italy, 1911.

DIED: Edward I of England, 1307. Sigismund II Augustus, King of Poland, Poland, 1572. Giacomo da Vignola, architect, Rome, 1573. Thomas Hooker, British Puritan clergyman, 1647. Richard Brinsley Sheridan, dramatist, *The School for Scandal*, *The Rivals*, London, 1816. George Ohm, physicist, chiefly remembered for his work on electricity, Munich, 1854. Sir Arthur Conan Doyle, writer, creator of Sherlock Holmes, 1930. Sir Allen Lane, publisher, founder of Penguin Books (1936), 1970.

JULY 8

*A Dog Day (see 3 July). Youth Day, Neuchâtel canton, Switzerland.
Feasts of SS: Elizabeth of Portugal, widow; Aquila and Prisca, or
Priscilla; Procopius, martyr; Kilian and his Companions, martyrs;
Withburga, virgin; Adrian III, pope; Grimbald; Sunniva and her
Companions; Raymund of Toulouse.*

Accession of Alexander III of Scotland, 1249. ¶ Accession of Edward II of England, 1307. ¶ Vasco da Gama leaves Lisbon for a voyage on which he discovers the Cape route to India, 1497. ¶ Probably the hottest day ever in London, temperatures were around 98.0°F, 36.6°C, 1808. ¶ Total eclipse, 1842. ¶ General Douglas MacArthur is made commander of the United Nations' forces in Korea, 1950.

BORN: Jean de La Fontaine, writer, *Fables*, Champagne, France, 1621. Graf Ferdinand von Zeppelin, airship pioneer, Constance, Baden, Germany, 1838. John D. Rockefeller, founder of Standard Oil, philanthropist, New York, 1839. Sir Arthur Evans, archaeologist, excavated Knossos, Hertfordshire, 1851. Alfred Binet, psychologist, France, 1857. Percy Grainger, composer and pianist, Melbourne, Australia, 1882. Richard Aldington, novelist, critic and biographer, *Death of a Hero*, Portsmouth, Hampshire, 1892. Billy Eckstine, jazz singer and composer, Pennsylvania, 1914.

DIED: Peter the Hermit, preacher of the First Crusade, 1108. Pope Gregory XV, 1623. Christiaan Huygens, physicist and mathematician, The Hague, Netherlands, 1695. Percy Bysshe Shelley, poet and writer, *The Necessity of Atheism, Prometheus Unbound, Ozymandias*; at sea, off Leghorn, Italy, 1822. Sir Edward Parry, naval officer and early Arctic explorer, 1855. Havelock Ellis, psychologist and writer, *Studies in the Psychology of Sex*, 1939.

JULY 9

A Dog Day (see 3 July). The King's Birthday Celebration, Morocco.
Feasts of SS: John Fisher, bishop and martyr; Thomas More, martyr;
Everild, virgin; Nicholas Pieck and his Companions, martyrs;
Veronica Giuliani, virgin; The Martyrs of Orange; The Martyrs of China, II.

Publius Aelius Hadrianus (Hadrian) arrives back in Rome after pacifying the Danube region, 118. ¶ Henry VIII divorces Anne of Cleves, 1540. ¶ Annexation of Holland by Napoleon, 1810. ¶ France and Britain aid Dom Pedro in taking Oporto, 1832. ¶ E. D. Young's expedition in search of Dr Livingstone leaves England, 1867. ¶ South Carolina readmitted to the Union (seceded 20 December 1860), 1868. ¶ Louisiana readmitted to the Union (seceded 26 January 1861), 1868. ¶ RAF's night-bombing of Germany begins, 1940. ¶ Independence of the Bahamas Islands proclaimed, 1973.

BORN: Ann Radcliffe, novelist, *The Mysteries of Udolpho*, London, 1764. Henry Hallam, historian, *Views of the State of Europe during the Middle Ages*, Windsor, 1777. Franz Boas, anthropologist, Germany, 1858. Ottorino Respighi, composer, *The Pines of Rome*, Bologna, Italy, 1879. Edward Richard George Heath, Conservative politician and Prime Minister, Broadstairs, Kent, 1916.

DIED: Sir William Berkeley, Governor of Virginia, 1677. Philip V, King of France, Madrid, 1746. Edmund Burke, politician and writer, *Reflections on the French Revolution*, 1797. Washington Allston, American landscape painter, 1843. Zachary Taylor, military general, fought in the Indian and Mexican wars, president of the US, Washington, D.C., 1850. King Camp Gillette, American inventor of the safety razor, 1932.

JULY 10

A Dog Day (see 3 July). Independence Day, Argentina (1816).
Rhodes Day, Rhodesia (Cecil Rhodes, statesman and founder, 1853–1902).
Feasts of SS: The Seven Brothers and St Felicity, martyrs;
Rufina and Secunda, virgins and martyrs; Amalburga, or Amelberga, widow;
Amalburga, virgin; Antony and Theodosius Pechersky, abbot.

The Yorkists defeat the Lancastrians and capture Henry VI at the battle of Northampton, 1460. ¶ Protogeneia (Asteroid 147) discovered by L. Schulhof, 1875. ¶ Wyoming made a US state (44th), 1890. ¶ Non-fascist political parties are dissolved in Italy, 1923. ¶ Landings in Sicily by the Allies, 1943. ¶ The Bell Telephone Company's *Telstar 1* is launched in the US, the world's first television telecommunications satellite, 1962.

BORN: John Calvin, Protestant theologian, Picardy, 1509. Sir William Blackstone, jurist, *Commentaries on the Laws of England*, London, 1723. Frederick Marryat, maritime novelist, *Mr Midshipman Easy*, London, 1792. Robert Chambers, publisher and author, *The Book of Days*, Peebles, Scotland, 1802. Camille Pissarro, Impressionist painter, St Thomas, Danish West Indies, 1830. Marcel Proust, novelist, *Remembrance of Things Past*, Anteuil, France, 1871. Carl Orff, composer, *Carmina Burana*, Munich, 1895. Saul Bellow, American novelist, *Henderson the Rain King*, 1915.

DIED: Hadrian (Publius Aelius Hadrianus), Roman Emperor, Baiae, Italy, 138. Rodrigo Diaz de Vivar (El Cid), military commander and adventurer, Valencia, Spain, 1099. William I, founder of the United Provinces (the Dutch Republic); murdered, Delft, Netherlands, 1584. George Stubbs, painter, London, 1806. Louis Jacques Mande Daguerre, French artist and photographic inventor, 1851. Karl Richard Lepsius, Egyptologist, *Monuments of Egypt and Ethiopia*, Berlin, 1884. Earl Warren, US Supreme Court Chief Justice, 1974.

[215]

JULY 11

A Dog Day (see 3 July). Regional Day, parts of north Belgium. National Day, People's Republic of Mongolia. Feasts of SS: Pius I, pope and martyr; Drostan, abbot; John of Bergamo, bishop; Hidulf, bishop; Olga, widow.

The Flemings defeat the Count of Artois at the battle of Courtray, 1302. ¶ The Duke of Marlborough is victorious at Oudenarde, 1708. ¶ Jubal A. Early's Confederate forces reach the outskirts of Washington, D.C., 1864. ¶ Hecate (Asteroid 100) discovered by J. C. Watson, 1868. ¶ Truce with Sinn Fein agreed by British, 1921. ¶ First satellite transatlantic television transmissions, via *Telstar I*, from Maine in the US to France, 1962.

BORN: Robert the Bruce, King of Scotland, 1274. Luis de Góngora y Argote, poet and writer, Cordoba, Spain, 1561. John Quincy Adams, sixth President of the US (1825–9), 1767. Edward Gough Whitlam, Australian Labour politician, Prime Minister, Australia, 1916. Theodore Harold Maiman, physicist, devised the first laser, Los Angeles, 1927.

DIED: Sir William Johnson, colonist, led the Iroquois Indians against the French at Lake George, 1774. William Ernest Henley, dramatist, poet and editor, *In Hospital, For England's Sake*, London, 1903. Simon Newcomb, Canadian astronomer, 1909. Alfred Dreyfus, French army officer, 1935. George Gershwin, composer, *Rhapsody in Blue*, 1937. Sir Arthur Evans, archaeologist, excavated Knossos, 1941.

JULY 12

A Dog Day (see 3 July). Orangeman's Day, Northern Ireland. Founders Day, Rhodesia. Feasts of SS: John Gualbert, abbot; Veronica; Jason; Hermagoras and Fortunatus, martyrs; Nabor and Felix, martyrs; John the Iberian, abbot.

William the Lion defeated at Alnwick, Scotland, 1174. ¶ Acre is taken by the Crusaders, 1191. ¶ Henry VIII marries Catherine Parr, 1543. ¶ Evacuation of the Crimea, 1856. ¶ Alfred Dreyfus is finally rehabilitated after lengthy imprisonment on Devil's Island, 1906.

BORN: Gaius Julius Caesar, Roman Emperor, writer and soldier, Rome, 100BC. Claude Bernard, physiologist, discovered vaso-motor nerves, 1813. Henry David Thoreau, writer and naturalist, *Walden, or Life in the Woods, A Week on the Concord and Merrimack Rivers*, Concord, Massachusetts, 1817. George Eastman, photographic pioneer, New York, 1854. Stefan George, poet, *The Year of the Soul*, Germany, 1868. F. E. Smith, Earl of Birkenhead, statesman and law reformer, Lord Chancellor, 1872. Amedeo Modigliani, painter and sculptor, Leghorn, Italy, 1884. Kirsten Flagstad, soprano, Norway, 1895. Oscar Hammerstein II, song writer and composer, New York City, 1895. Pablo Neruda, poet and critic, Nobel Prize for Literature, *Tercera residencia, Canto general*, Parral, Chile, 1904.

DIED: Desiderius Erasmus, scholar and writer, *In Praise of Folly*, 1536. Jean Picard, astronomer, the first to measure accurately a degree of longitude, Paris, 1682. Alexander Hamilton, US statesman and lawyer; after a duel with Aaron Burr, 1804. Charles Frederick Goldie, New Zealand artist, 1947. Mazo De La Roche, popular novelist, *Whiteoaks*, 1961.

JULY 13

A Dog Day (see 3 July). Dies Mala or 'Egyptian Day', considered unlucky in the Middle Ages. National Holiday, French West Indies. National Holiday, Tahiti. Nathan Bedford Forrest's Birthday, Tennessee, USA. Montenegrian Peoples Uprising Day, Yugoslavia. Feasts of SS: Silas; Maura and Brigid; Eugenius of Carthage, bishop; Mildred, virgin; Francis Solano.

The Spanish and English defeat the French in the naval battle at Gravelines, 1558. ¶ Loyalists defeat the Parliamentarians at Devizes (Roundway-down), Wiltshire, 1643. ¶ Marat murdered in his bath by Charlotte Corday, 1793. ¶ President Benito Juarez seizes church property throughout Mexico, 1859. ¶ Alabama readmitted to the Union (seceded 11 January 1861), 1868. ¶ Mayor Abraham Beame of New York declares a state of emergency in the city after a total black-out, 1977.

BORN: John Dee, scholar, mathematician and philosopher, London, 1527. John Clare, farm labourer and poet, *The Shepherd's Calendar, The Rural Muse*, Northampton, 1793. Patrice MacMahon, military commander and President of France, France, 1808. Eugen Huber, jurist and writer on civil law, Switzerland, 1849. Gavrilo Princip, the Bosnian revolutionary who, on 28 June, 1914, assassinated the Archduke Ferdinand at Sarajevo, Bosnia, 1894.

DIED: Titus Oates, Protestant paranoiac, London, 1705. James Bradley, astronomer, 1762. Jean Paul Marat, revolutionary leader in the French Revolution; assassinated by Charlotte Corday, Paris, 1793. John Charles Frémont, explorer, 1890. Alfred Marshall, economist, *Principles of Economics*, Cambridge, 1924. Arnold Schoenberg, composer, *Moses and Aaron*, Los Angeles, California, 1951.

JULY 14

A Dog Day (see 3 July). Bastille Day, France (commemorating the
storming of the castle in Paris, 1789). National Holiday, French
West Indies. National Day, Iraq (commemorating the declaration of the republic
in 1958). National Holiday, Nicaragua. National Holiday, Tahiti. Feasts of SS:
Bonaventure, bishop and doctor; Deusdedit, archbishop;
Marchelm; Ulric of Zell, abbot.

US, Japan and other forces take Tientsin in China, 1900. ¶ The first patent granted for a liquid-fuelled rocket, to Dr Robert Goddard in the US, 1914. ¶ All political parties other than the Nazis are suppressed in Germany, 1933. ¶ Severe race rioting in Newark in New Jersey (over 20 people are killed by 16 July), 1967. ¶ Jimmy Carter is nominated presidential candidate at the Democratic Convention in New York, 1976.

BORN: Jules Mazarin, cardinal and statesman, Italy, 1602. John Lockhart, essayist and critic, *Life of Scott* (Sir Walter), Lanarkshire, 1794. Johannes Müller, physiologist, Koblenz, Germany, 1801. James Abbott McNeill Whistler, painter, lithographer and wit, Lowell, Massachusetts, 1834. Emmeline Pankhurst, suffragette, Manchester, 1858. Gustav Klimt, Art Nouveau painter, Vienna, 1862. Paul Walden, German chemist, Latvia, 1863. Woody Guthrie, folk singer, Oklahoma, 1912.

DIED: Philip II, King of France, France, 1223. Madame de Staël (Anne Louise Germaine Necker), novelist and critic, *De l'Allemagne, Delphine*, Paris, 1817. Augustine-Jean Fresnel, physicist, 1827. Alfred Krupp, industrialist, Germany, 1887. Sir William Henry Perkin, chemist, discovered the first artificial dye, near Harrow, Middlesex, 1907. Sir Apirana Ngata, Maori statesman, New Zealand, 1950. Jacinto Benavente y Martinez, dramatist, poet and translator, Spain, 1954. Grock (Adrien Wettach), clown and entertainer, Switzerland, 1959. Adlai Ewing Stevenson, US Democratic statesman and politician, Ambassador at the UN, London, 1965. Konstantin Paustovsky, short-story writer and journalist, *Story of a Life*, Moscow, 1968.

JULY 15

*A Dog Day (see 3 July). St Swithin's Day: folk belief in England
and some European countries has it that the weather on this day will remain
the same for the following 40 days. National Holiday, Tahiti.
Feasts of SS: Henry the Emperor; James of Nisibis, bishop;
Barhadbesaba, martyr; Donald; Swithun, bishop; Athanasius of Naples;
Edith of Polesworth; Vladimir of Kiev; David of Munktorp, bishop;
Pompilio Pirrotti.*

Rome taken and pillaged by Genseric, 455. ¶ The Teutonic Knights are defeated by the Poles at Tannenberg, 1410. ¶ The second edition of John Milton's *Aeropagitica* is registered with the Stationers' Company in London, 1644. ¶ James, Duke of Monmouth, executed for treason at Tower Hill, London, 1685. ¶ Georgia's second readmission to the Union (seceded 19 January 1861), 1870. ¶ The National Health Insurance Act in Britain comes into force, 1912. ¶ The battle of Delville Wood, the fiercest action fought by South African troops in the European theatre during World War One, 1916. ¶ Beginning of the second battle of the Marne (ends 4 August), 1918. ¶ United Nations' forces arrive in the Belgium Congo, 1960. ¶ Close-up pictures of Mars transmitted by US *Mariner IV* satellite, 1965.

BORN: Inigo Jones, architect and antiquary, London, 1573. Rembrandt (Harmenszoon van Rijn), Dutch painter, Leiden, Netherlands, 1606. Vilfredo Pareto, economist and sociologist, Paris, 1848. Alfred Harmsworth, 1st Viscount Northcliffe, newspaper and magazine proprietor, Dublin, 1865. José Enrique Rodó, essayist, *Ariel, Los motivos de Proteo*, Montevideo, Uruguay, 1872.

DIED: Vladimir I, Prince of Kiev, responsible for the introduction of Christianity into Russia, Kiev, 1015. Rudolf I of Hapsburg, Holy Roman Emperor, Speyer, Germany, 1291. James Scott, Duke of Monmouth, illegitimate son of Charles II, executed, London, 1685. Jean Antoine Houdon, sculptor, France, 1828. Winthrop Mackworth Praed, poet and politician, London, 1839. Mikhail Yurevich Lermontov, Russian dramatist and poet; killed in a duel, 1841. Karl Czerny, Austrian composer and pianist, 1857. William Thomas Morton, dental surgeon, introduced ether as a general anaesthetic, New York City, 1868. Anton Chekhov, dramatist and writer, *The Seagull, The Three Sisters*, 1904. Hugo von Hofmannsthal, dramatist and poet, *Everyman, The Tower*, Austria, 1929. John Joseph Pershing, Commander-in-Chief of US troops in France during the First World War, Washington D.C., 1948. Paul Gallico, popular writer and journalist, 1976.

A Dog Day (see 3 July). National Holiday, Nepal. The Feast of the Commemoration of Our Lady of Mount Carmel, the Carmelite Order's patronal feast, extended to the Church as a whole by Pope Benedict XIII in 1726. Feasts of SS: Athenogenes, bishop and martyr; Eustathius of Antioch, bishop; Helier, martyr; Reineldis, virgin and martyr; Fulrad, abbot; Mary Magdalen Postel, virgin.

Brennus and the Gauls defeat the Romans at Allia, 390BC. ¶ The flight of Muhammad (the *Hegira*), 622. ¶ The Moors are defeated by the Spanish at Tolosa, 1212. ¶ Richard II of England crowned, 1377. ¶ First issue of *Punch* is published in London, 1842. ¶ The battle of Cawnpore in India, 1857. ¶ A new comet was discovered by Dr Barnard at Lick Observatory, 1884. ¶ Alleged murder of Tsar Nicholas II of Russia, his wife and family at Ipatiev House in Ekaterinburg, 1918. ¶ The first atomic bomb is exploded, by the US in New Mexico, 1945. ¶ The *Apollo XI* is launched from Cape Kennedy, 1969.

BORN: Andrea del Sarto, Florentine painter, 1486. Sir Joshua Reynolds, painter, Plympton, Devon, 1723. Jean Baptiste Corot, classical landscape painter, Paris, 1796. Mary Baker Eddy, founder of Christian Science, New Hampshire, 1821. Otto Jespersen, philologist and grammarian, *Growth and Structure of the English Language*, Denmark, 1860. Roald Amundsen, polar explorer, Oslo, 1872. Trygve Lie, the first Secretary-General of the United Nations, Norway, 1896. Barbara Stanwyck, actress, Brooklyn, New York, 1907. Ginger Rogers, dancer and actress, Missouri, 1911.

DIED: Anne of Cleves, wife of Henry VIII, 1557. Marquis de Louvois, statesman and minister of war, Versailles, 1691. Gottfried Keller, novelist and poet, *Green Henry*, Switzerland, 1890. Edmond de Goncourt, novelist, author with his brother Jules of the *Journal*, 1896. Nicholas II, Tsar of Russia; executed (?), Ekaterinburg, Russia, 1918. Hilaire Belloc, writer and propagandist, 1953.

JULY 17

A Dog Day (see 3 July). Anniversary of the July Revolution, Iraq (1958).
Constitution Day, Republic of Korea (1948).
Feasts of SS: Alexis; Speratus and his Companions, martyrs;
Marcellina, virgin; Ennodius, bishop; Kenelm; Leo IV, pope;
Clement of Okhrida and his Companions; Nerses Lampronatsi, archbishop.

Moors defeat the Spanish at Fraga, 1134. ¶ Martin Frobisher lands and explores Baffin Land, 1577. ¶ Swedish fleet destroyed by Russians, 1788. ¶ Cecil Rhodes is made the Premier of Cape Colony, 1890. ¶ Truman, Stalin, Churchill and Clement Attlee meet at the beginning of the Potsdam Conference, 1945. ¶ Donald Campbell achieves a speed of 429.3 mph in the *Bluebird* on the flats at Lake Eyre in South Australia, 1964. ¶ A US *Apollo* spacecraft and a Russian *Soyuz* craft successfully dock while in orbit, 1975.

BORN: John Jacob Astor, millionaire, Germany, 1763. Adam Smith, economist, *The Wealth of Nations*, Edinburgh, 1790. Paul Delaroche, painter, Paris, 1797. Maxim Litvinov, Soviet statesman, Poland, 1876. Erle Stanley Gardner, popular writer, creator of Perry Mason, Massachusetts, 1889. Christina Ellen Stead, Australian novelist, *The Man who loved Children*, 1907.

DIED: Charles, Earl Grey, Whig statesman and Prime Minister, Alnwick, Northumberland, 1845. James Abbott McNeill Whistler, painter, lithographer and wit, London, 1903. Giovanni Giolitti, statesman, Liberal reformer, 1928. Alvaro Obregon, revolutionary, reformer and President of Mexico; assassinated, Mexico City, 1928. George William Russell, Irish writer under the pen-name of 'AE', 1935. Draža Mihailović, Serbian nationalist and guerrilla; executed, 1946. Billie Holiday, jazz singer, 1959. John Coltrane, modern jazz tenor-saxophonist, 1967.

JULY 18

A Dog Day (see 3 July). National Holiday, Spain. Constitution Day,
Uruguay (1830). Feasts of SS: Camillus de Lellis; Symphorosa and
her Seven Sons, martyrs; Pambo; Philastrius, bishop; Arnulf, or Arnoul,
of Metz, bishop; Frederick of Utrecht, bishop and martyr;
Bruno of Segni, bishop.

The great fire begins in Rome and lasts for 9 days, 64. ¶ First solar eclipse ever to be photographed, by Warren de la Rue in London, 1861. ¶ Abortive attack on Fort Wagner, near Charleston, by Robert Gould Shaw's Negro troops, 1863. ¶ The British Ballot Act institutes private voting, 1872. ¶ Women granted equality in divorce cases by British Matrimonial Causes Act, 1923. ¶ The Spanish Civil War begins with an army revolt led by Francisco Franco and Emilio Mola, 1936. ¶ The President of Iraq, General Arif, deposed in military *coup*, 1968. ¶ The United Nations admit Vietnam as a member, 1977.

BORN: Robert Hooke, physicist, Freshwater, Isle of Wight, 1635. Gilbert White, curate, naturalist and writer, *Natural History and Antiquities of Selborne*, Selborne, Hampshire, 1720. Sir George Gilbert Scott, architect, designed St Pancras Station (London), Buckinghamshire, 1811. William Makepeace Thackeray, novelist and satirist, *Vanity Fair, The Book of Snobs*, Calcutta, 1811. W. G. Grace, English cricketer, Gloucestershire, 1848. Philip Snowden, Labour Party politician, Yorkshire, 1864. Vidkun Quisling, politician, collaborated with the Nazis in occupied Norway, Norway, 1887. John Glenn, American astronaut, Ohio, 1921.

DIED: Michelangelo Merisi da Caravaggio, Italian painter, 1610. Antonio Vieira, Portuguese Jesuit priest and missionary in Brazil, writer, Salvador, Brazil, 1697. Jean-Antoine Watteau, artist, Nogent-sur-Marne, France, 1721. John Paul Jones, American naval commander, Paris, 1792. Jane Austen, novelist, *Pride and Prejudice, Emma*, 1817. Benito Juarez, revolutionary, President of Mexico, 1872. Corneille Heymans, physician, Nobel Prize winner, Belgium, 1968.

JULY 19

A Dog Day (see 3 July). Feasts of SS: Vincent de Paul; Justa and Rufina, virgins and martyrs; Macrina the Younger, virgin; Arsenius the Great; Symmachus, pope; Ambrose Autpert.

Edward III defeats the Scots at Halidon Hill, 1333. ¶ Accession of Queen Mary of England, 1553. ¶ After being dispersed by a storm, the Spanish Armada recollects and enters the English Channel, 1588. ¶ William III defeated at Landen, 1693. ¶ George IV of Great Britain crowned (reign had begun 29 January 1820), 1821. ¶ War declared on Prussia by France, 1870. ¶ Heavy Zeppelin raids in Britain, 1917. ¶ *Gemini 10* is launched by US from Cape Kennedy, 1966. ¶ John Fairfax of Britain arrives at Fort Lauderdale on the Florida coast after having rowed across the Atlantic alone, the first man to do so, 1969.

BORN: Samuel Colt, American gunsmith and inventor, Connecticut, 1814. Edgar Degas, Impressionist painter, Paris, 1834. Edward Pickering, astronomer, Boston, Massachusetts, 1846. Charles Mayo, surgeon, a joint-founder of the Mayo Clinic, Rochester, Minnesota, 1865. A. J. Cronin, popular novelist, *The Stars Look Down*, Cardross, Scotland, 1896. Herbert Marcuse, political theorist and philosopher, *One Dimensional Man*, Berlin, 1900. George McGovern, Democratic politician, South Dakota, 1922.

DIED: Petrarch (Francesco Petrarca), poet and scholar, *During the Life, After the death of my Lady Laura*, near Padua, Italy, 1374. Dr John Caius, physician, founder of the Cambridge college that bears his name, Cambridge, 1573. William Somerville, writer, *The Chase*, Warwickshire, 1742. Matthew Flinders, early explorer of Australia, 1814. Professor John Playfair, scholar, *Outlines of Natural Philosophy*, Edinburgh, 1819. Syngman Rhee, the founder of South Korea, Honolulu, 1965.

JULY 20

*A Dog Day (see 3 July). National Holiday, Colombia. Feasts of SS:
Jerome Emiliani; Wilgefortis, or Liberata; Margaret, or Marina,
virgin and martyr; Joseph Barsabas; Aurelius of Carthage, bishop;
Flavian and Elias, bishops; Vulmar, abbot; Ansegisus, abbot.*

Charles XII defeats the Poles at Clissau, 1702. ¶ Abortive assassination attempt on Hitler by the German staff officer, Count Claus Schenk von Stauffenberg, 1944. ¶ Assassination of Abdullah of Jordan in Jerusalem, 1951. ¶ The Lunar Module *Eagle* touches down on the Moon's surface (*Apollo XI* mission), 1969. ¶ Turkish invasion of Cyprus begins, 1974.

BORN: Petrarch (Francesco Petrarca), poet and scholar, *During the Life, After the death of my Lady Laura*, Arezzo, Italy, 1304. Sir Richard Owen, biologist and palaeontologist, *History of British Fossil Reptiles*, Newtown, Montgomeryshire, Wales, 1771. Eric Axel Karlfeldt, poet, refused the Nobel Prize for Literature, Sweden, 1864. John Reith, first Director-General of the British Broadcasting Corporation, Stonehaven, Scotland, 1889. Theda Bara, silent-film actress, Ohio, 1890. Sir Edmund Hillary, mountaineer, the first man to climb Mount Everest (with Sherpa Tenzing), New Zealand, 1919.

DIED: Hugh O'Neill, 2nd Earl of Tyrone, led the opposition to the English in northern Ireland, Rome, 1616. Guglielmo Marconi, inventor, pioneer of the wireless, Rome, 1937. Count Claus Schenk von Stauffenberg, officer, attempted to assassinate Hitler in 1944; executed, Berlin, 1944. Paul Valéry, poet and critic, *La Jeune Parque, Le Cimetière Marin*, Paris, 1945.

JULY 21

*A Dog Day (see 3 July). National Day, Belgium. Feast of
Schoelcher's Birthday, French West Indies (Victor Schoelcher, 1804–93,
politician and slavery abolitionist). Liberation Day, Guam.
Feasts of SS: Praxedes, virgin; Victor of Marseilles, martyr;
Arbogast, bishop.*

Gibraltar is attacked by the British under Sir George Rooke, 1704. ¶ The
Jesuit order is dissolved by Pope Clement XIV, 1773. ¶ Confederate victory at
the first battle of Bull Run in the American Civil War, 1861. ¶ Georgia's first
readmission to the Union (seceded 19 January 1861), 1868. ¶ First atomic-
powered passenger ship launched, by the US, *Savannah*, 1959. ¶ Commander
Neil Armstrong of the US is the first man to set foot on the Moon's surface
(*Apollo XI*), 1969.

BORN: Jean Picard, astronomer, the first to measure accurately a degree of
longitude, France, 1620. Paul Julius von Reuter, founder of the news agency,
Kassel, Germany, 1816. Jacques Feyder, film director, *Le Grand Jeu*, Belgium,
1888. Eugene Schuftan, cinematographer, *The Hustler*, Breslau, Poland, 1893.
Hart Crane, poet, *The Bridge*, Ohio, 1899. Ernest Hemingway, novelist and
journalist, *For Whom the Bell Tolls*, Illinois, 1899.

DIED: Sir Henry Percy, knight, supporter of Henry IV, known as Harry
Hotspur; near Shrewsbury, Shropshire, 1403. Robert Burns, poet, 1796. Dame
Ellen Terry, actress, Hythe, Kent, 1928. Louis Hubert Lyautey, soldier and
colonial governor, 1934. Albert John Luthuli, Zulu chieftain and African
nationalist leader, South Africa, 1967.

A Dog Day (see 3 July). Dies Mala or 'Egyptian Day', considered unlucky in the Middle Ages. National Liberation Day, Poland. Organic Act Day, Virgin Islands (commemorating the act giving the US Ministry of the Interior full jurisdiction over the island, 1954). Slovenian People's Uprising Day, Yugoslavia. Feasts of SS: Mary Magdalen; Joseph of Palestine; Wandregisilus, or Wandrille, abbot.

The English defeat Wallace at the battle of Falkirk, 1298. ¶ Alexander Mackenzie reaches the Pacific Ocean after crossing Canada overland, 1793. ¶ Urania (Asteroid 30) discovered by J. R. Hind, 1854. ¶ Allied forces cross the River Marne, 1918. ¶ Wiley Post completes the first around the world solo aeroplane flight, the 15,596 miles were flown in 7 days, 18 hours and 49 minutes, 1933. ¶ A chemical processing plant at Seveso, near Milan, explodes and a cloud of poisonous gas contaminates a large surrounding area.

BORN: Friedrich Bessel, astronomer and mathematician, Germany, 1784. Gregor Mendel, Augustine monk, pioneered the study of heredity, Heinzendorf, Austria, 1822. Frederick William Rolfe (Baron Corvo), novelist, *Hadrian the Seventh*, London, 1860. Lev Borisovich Kamenev, Russian revolutionary, Moscow, 1883. Selman Waksman, US microbiologist, Nobel Prize winner, Prilukii, Russia, 1888. Artur von Seyss-Inquart, Austrian minister, German High Commissioner of the Occupied Netherlands, Bohemia, 1892. Stephen Vincent Benet, poet, *John Brown's Body*, Pennsylvania, 1898. Alexander Calder, sculptor, Pennsylvania, 1898. James Whale, film director, *Frankenstein* (with Boris Karloff), 1898.

DIED: Charles VII of France, Meun, France, 1461. Henry III of France; assassinated, Paris, 1589. Pope Clement X, 1676. Marie François Bichat, pathologist and anatomist, 1802. Joseph Piazzi, astronomer, Palermo, Italy, 1826. Florenz Ziegfeld, theatrical producer and impresario, Hollywood, California, 1932. Mackenzie King, Canadian Prime Minister, Kingsmere, Quebec, 1950. Carl Sandburg, poet and biographer, *Smoke and Steel, Abraham Lincoln*, Flat Rock, North Carolina, 1967.

JULY 23

A Dog Day (see 3 July). National Day, Arab Republic of Egypt.
Arab Egyptian Revolution Day, Arab Republic of Syria. The Feast of
the Three Wise Men, that is the Magi, called Balthazar, Melchior
and Caspar, observed as a feast since about the 8th century; the bones in
Cologne Cathedral are said to be their remains. Feasts of SS:
Apollinaris of Ravenna, bishop and martyr; Liborius, bishop;
John Cassian, abbot; Romula and her Companions, virgins; Anne, or
Susanna, virgin; Laurence of Brindisi.

Defeat of Percies and supporters at Shrewsbury, 1403. ¶ Parliamentary Act for Union of Upper and Lower Canada, 1840. ¶ Dr Livingstone returns to England, 1864. ¶ Cassandra (Asteroid 114) discovered by C. H. F. Peters, 1871. ¶ The Matrimonial Causes Act eases divorce procedure in England and Wales, 1937. ¶ Doctor Stephen Ward found guilty of living on immoral earnings at the Central Criminal Court (the 'Profumo Affair'), 1963. ¶ The Sultan of Muscat and Oman is deposed by his son, 1970. ¶ Two cannisters of CS gas (used by the British Government in Northern Ireland) are thrown into the House of Commons, 1970.

BORN: Francesco Sforza, *condottiere* (soldier of fortune), fought against and for Venice, Milan and the Pope, San Miniato, Italy, 1401. Coventry Kersey Dighton Patmore, poet and critic, *The Betrothal, Faithful Forever*, Woodford, Essex, 1823. Sir Arthur Whitten Brown, aviator, Glasgow, 1886. Raymond Chandler, detective novelist, *The Big Sleep*, 1888. Haile Selassie, Emperor of Ethiopia, Abyssinia, 1891.

DIED: Domenico Scarlatti, virtuoso harpsichordist and composer, Madrid, 1757. Isaac Singer, US inventor of the modern sewing machine, Torquay, Devon, 1875. Ulysses Simpson Grant, Commander of the Union Army, American President, 1885. Sir John Simon, physician, London, 1904. Sir William Ramsay, chemist, discovered 'inert' gases, High Wycombe, Buckinghamshire, 1916. David Wark Griffith, film director and producer, *The Birth of a Nation*, Hollywood, California, 1948. Robert Flaherty, film maker, *Nanook of the North*, 1951. Henri Philippe Pétain, puppet governor of France for the Germans in the Second World War; in prison, Ile d'Yeu, 1951. Sir Henry Dale, neurophysiologist, 1968. Eddie Rickenbacker, US fighter pilot of the First World War, Zurich, 1973.

JULY 24

A Dog Day (see 3 July). Bolívar's Day, Ecuador (Simón Bolívar's birthday, 1783, liberator). Pioneer Day, Utah, USA. Bolívar's Birthday, Venezuela. Feasts of SS: Christina, virgin and martyr; Lewina, virgin and martyr; Declan, bishop; Boris and Gleb, martyrs; Christina the Astonishing, virgin.

Jacques Cartier lands at Gaspé in Canada and claims the territory for France, 1534. ¶ Accession of James VI of Scotland (became James I of England on 24 March 1603), 1567. ¶ William III defeated at Enghein, 1692. ¶ Gibraltar is taken by the British under Sir George Rooke, 1704. ¶ The Turks are defeated at Aboukir by Napoleon, 1799. ¶ The iron tram-road (a precursor of the railway) was opened in South London between Croydon and Wandsworth, 1801. ¶ British Window Tax is abolished, 1851. ¶ Tennessee readmitted to the Union (seceded 8 June 1861), 1866. ¶ The first life peerages are established in Britain, 1958.

BORN: Simón Bolívar, revolutionary leader in South America, Caracas, 1783. Alexandre Dumas, novelist and dramatist, *The Three Musketeers*, France, 1802. Frank Wedekind, dramatist and actor, *Spring's Awakening, Pandora's Box*, Hanover, Germany, 1864. Lord Dunsany, short-story writer, London, 1878. Ernst Bloch, American composer, *Sacred Service*, Switzerland, 1880. Amelia Earhart, pioneer aviator, Kansas, 1898.

DIED: George Vertue, engraver and antiquary, London, 1756. John Dyer, poet, *The Fleece*, Lincolnshire, 1758. John Sell Cotman, watercolourist, 1842. Martin van Buren, lawyer and senator, US President, Kinderhook, New York, 1862. Sacha Guitry, actor, playwright and film director, *The Story of a Cheat*, France, 1957.

*A Dog Day (see 3 July). St James's Day, in England popularly known
as Grotto Day because of the grotto-like shrine erected over the saint's tomb.
Grand Fête des Escaldes, Andorra (the carnival at Escaldes).
Constitution Day, Puerto Rico (1952). Feasts of SS: James the Greater,
apostle; Christopher, martyr; Thea, Valentina and Paul, martyrs;
Magnericus, bishop.*

Portuguese defeat the Moors at Ourique, 1139. ¶ Marriage of Queen Mary of England with Philip, King of Spain, 1554. ¶ Henry IV of France becomes a Roman Catholic, 1593. ¶ James I of England crowned, 1603. ¶ Invasion of Puerto Rico by the US, 1898. ¶ The first cross-Channel flight, by the Frenchman Louis Blériot (36 minutes), 1909. ¶ End of bread rationing in Britain, 1945. ¶ The Channel is first crossed by a British hovercraft, in a little over 2 hours, 1959. ¶ Sharon Adams of the US puts in at San Diego after sailing the Pacific alone, the first woman to do so, 1969.

BORN: William Burkitt, theologian and writer, Northamptonshire, 1650. Elizabeth Hamilton, writer, *The Cottagers of Glenburrie*, Belfast, 1758. Thomas Eakins, American realist painter, 1844. Arthur James Balfour, statesman, East Lothian, Scotland, 1848.

DIED: Flavius Valerius Constantius, Roman Emperor and military commander, father of Constantine the Great, Eburacum (York) in England, 306. Ferdinand I, Austrian Holy Roman Emperor, 1564. André Marie de Chénier, poet, executed, 1794. Charles Dibdin, actor and dramatist, 1814. Samuel Taylor Coleridge, critic and poet, *Kubla Khan*, 1834. Charles Macintosh, chemist, pioneer of the water-proofing of fabrics, near Glasgow, 1843. Henry Mayhew, journalist and writer, co-founder of *Punch, London Labour and the London Poor*, London, 1887. Engelbert Dollfuss, Austrian politician; murdered by the Nazis, 1934. Louis St Laurent, Canadian Prime Minister, Quebec City, 1973.

JULY 26

*A Dog Day (see 3 July). Grand Fête des Escaldes, Andorra (the
carnival at Escaldes). National Rebellion Day, Cuba (the
beginning of Fidel Castro's struggle against Batista, 1953).
Independence Day, Liberia (1847). Feasts of SS: Anne, matron;
Simeon the Armenian; Bartholomea Capitanio, virgin.*

Roderic defeated at the battle of Xeres by the Saracens, 711. ¶ Defeat of the
Yorkists by the Lancastrians at Edgecote (or Banbury), 1469. ¶ Louisbourg, the
great French citadel on Cape Breton, Nova Scotia, surrenders to British forces,
1758. ¶ The State of New York ratifies the Constitution of the United States of
America, 1788. ¶ Earthquake in Naples results in over 6,000 people losing their
lives, 1805. ¶ Violent rioting in Chicago by communists and anarchists, the
military are sent in, 15 deaths and over 100 injured, 1877. ¶ Rising by the Irish in
Dublin, 1914. ¶ President Nasser of Egypt takes the Suez Canal, 1956. ¶ Final
presentation of débutantes at the Royal court in Britain, 1958. ¶ Prince Charles,
eldest son of Queen Elizabeth II, becomes the Prince of Wales, 1958. ¶ The
President of the International Brotherhood of Teamsters, Jimmy Hoffa, is
convicted in a Federal trial at Chicago of wire and mail fraud, 1964.

BORN: John Field, composer and pianist, Dublin, 1782. Winthrop Mackworth
Praed, poet and politician, London, 1802. George Bernard Shaw, dramatist,
critic and reformer, *Man and Superman, Pygmalion, The Black Girl in Search of
God*, Dublin, 1856. Serge Koussevitsky, conductor and composer, Russia, 1874.
Carl Gustav Jung, psychologist and philosopher, *Modern Man in Search of a Soul*,
Switzerland, 1875. André Maurois, novelist and biographer, *Ariel, Don Juan,
Bernard Quesnay*, France, 1885. Aldous Huxley, novelist, essayist and critic,
Antic Hay, Brave New World, Godalming, Surrey, 1894. Robert Graves, poet
and novelist, *Goodbye to All That*, London, 1895. Paul Gallico, popular writer
and novelist, New York City, 1897. Salvador Allende, Chilean statesman, 1908.
Stanley Kubrick, film director, *Dr Strangelove, 2001: A Space Odyssey*, New
York City, 1928.

DIED: John Wilmot, 2nd Earl of Rochester, poet and courtier, *A Satire Against
Mankind*, Woodstock, Oxfordshire, 1680. Samuel Houston, soldier, first
President of the Republic of Texas, Texas, 1863. George Borrow, writer, *The
Bible in Spain, Lavengro*, 1881. Sir James Murray, philologist, editor of the
Oxford *New English Dictionary*, Oxford, 1915. Benjamin Whorf, linguist and
anthropologist, *Language, Thought and Reality*, Wethersfield, Connecticut, 1941.

A Dog Day (see 3 July). Grand Fête des Escaldes, Andorra (the carnival at Escaldes). Anniversary of Barbosa's Birthday, Puerto Rico (Ruy Barbosa, 1848–1923, slavery abolitionist and republican). People's Uprising Day, parts of Yugoslavia. Feasts of SS: Pantaleon, or Panteleimon, martyr; The Seven Sleepers of Ephesus; Aurelia, Natalia and their Companions, martyrs; Theobald of Marly, abbot.

Cromwell wins the battle of Gainsborough, 1643. ¶ The Highlanders defeat Mackay at Killiecrankie, 1689. ¶ The Bank of England is incorporated, 1694. ¶ Diplomatic relations with England and France broken off by Mexico, 1861. ¶ General George B. McClellan assumes command of the Union forces in Washington and surrounding areas, 1861. ¶ The *Great Eastern* arrives at Heart's Content in Newfoundland having successfully laid the trans-Atlantic telegraph cable, 1866. ¶ Dr Livingstone's first letter from Africa printed in *The Times*, 1872. ¶ Ukraine is entered by German troops, 1941. ¶ The House of Representatives Judiciary Committee adopts the first article of a bill urging that President Nixon be impeached as a result of his part in the Watergate Affair, 1974. ¶ China launches her third orbiting satellite, 1975.

BORN: Johann Bernoulli, mathematician, Switzerland, 1667. Sir George Biddell Airy, Astronomer Royal, 1801. Giosuè Carducci, poet, Nobel Prize for Literature, Italy, 1835. Enrique Granados, composer and pianist, Spain, 1867. Hilaire Belloc, writer and propagandist, 1870. The Lawson quintuplets, New Zealand, 1965.

DIED: James I, King of Aragon, Spain, 1276. Vicomte de Turenne, Marshal-General of France, Sasbach, Germany, 1675. Pierre de Maupertius, astronomer and mathematician, Basel, Switzerland, 1759. John Dalton, English chemist and physicist, 1844. Ferrucio Busoni, pianist and composer, 1924. Gertrude Stein, poet, novelist and critic, *The Making of Americans*, Paris, 1946. Richard Aldington, novelist, critic and biographer, *Death of a Hero*, Maison Sallé, France, 1962. Antonio de Oliveira Salazar, Prime Minister of Portugal, Lisbon, 1970.

JULY 28

A Dog Day (see 3 July). Independence Day, Peru (1821). Feasts of SS:
Nazarius and Celsus, martyrs; Victor I, pope and martyr;
Innocent I, pope; Samson, bishop; Botvid.

The Spanish Armada in the English Channel is dispersed by fire-ships sent into its midst, 1588. ¶ Arthur Wellesley defeats the French at Talavera, 1809. ¶ Independence of Peru proclaimed, 1821. ¶ The Russian Minister of the Interior, Plehve, is assassinated, 1904. ¶ War declared on Serbia by Austria-Hungary, 1914. ¶ Alliance of USA and Panama to protect the Panama Canal in wartime, 1926. ¶ The British Trade Union Acts make some strikes and lock-outs illegal, 1927. ¶ *Royal Garden Blues* recorded in New York by John Kirby and his Sextette, 1939. ¶ Great earthquake in the Tangsham Province of China, estimated number of deaths is in excess of 1,000,000, 1976.

BORN: Jacopo Sannazaro, Neapolitan poet, *Arcadia*, Naples, 1456. Ludwig Feuerbach, philosopher and economist, Germany, 1804. Gerard Manley Hopkins, Jesuit priest and poet, *The Leaden Echo and the Golden Echo*, Stratford, near London, 1844. Beatrix Potter, children's writer, created Peter Rabbit, South Kensington, London, 1866. Marcel Duchamp, Surrealist artist, France, 1887. Leonide Massine, ballet dancer and choreographer, with Diaghilev, Moscow, 1896. Rudy Vallee, singer and actor, Vermont, 1901. Sir Karl Popper, philosopher, *The Open Society and its Enemies*, Vienna, 1902. Malcolm Lowry, novelist, *Under the Volcano*, Birkenhead, Cheshire, 1909.

DIED: Thomas Cromwell, statesman, secretary to Henry VIII, 1540. Cyrano de Bergerac, dramatist, model for a play by Rostand, 1655. Antonio Vivaldi, composer and violinist, *The Four Seasons, Concerto for flute, oboe and bassoon*, Vienna, 1741. Johann Sebastian Bach, 'Genesis: 1, 1' (H. L. Mencken's description of Bach's musical importance), 1750. Maximilien de Robespierre, lawyer, a leader of the French Revolution; guillotined, Paris, 1794. Gaspard Monge, mathematician, Paris, 1818. William James Mayo, surgeon, Rochester, Minnesota, 1939. Otto Hahn, German chemist and physicist, discovered nuclear fission, 1968.

JULY 29

A Dog Day (see 3 July). Feasts of SS: Martha, virgin; Simplicius, Faustinus and Beatrice, martyrs; Felix 'II'; Lupus of Troyes, bishop; Olaf of Norway, martyr; William Pinchon, bishop.

Final routing of the Spanish Armada, 1588. ¶ Eunomia (Asteroid 15) discovered by de Gasparis, 1851. ¶ King Humbert I of Italy is assassinated, 1900. ¶ Beginning of Lieutenant-General Robert Baden-Powell's camp on Brownsea Island at Poole in Dorset (the camp lasted until 9 August, and from it grew the Boy Scout Movement), 1907. ¶ The Pope announces that the Catholic ban on artificial contraception will continue, 1968. ¶ General Gowon of Nigeria is deposed in a military *coup*, 1975.

BORN: Jan Kollár, Slavonic scholar and poet, 1793. Alexis Charles de Tocqueville, historian, *Democracy in America, The Old Regime and the Revolution*, Paris, 1805. Benito Mussolini, dictator, 'Il Duce', Predappio, Italy, 1883. William Cameron Menzies, film director and designer, *Things to Come*, New Haven, Connecticut, 1896. Dag Hjalmar Hammarskjöld, Secretary-General of the United Nations, Sweden, 1905.

DIED: William Wilberforce, philanthropist, anti-slavery campaigner, London, 1833. Robert Schumann, composer, *Scenes from Childhood*; in an asylum, near Bonn, Germany, 1856. Vincent Van Gogh, painter; suicide after prolonged insanity, 1890. Gordon Craig, stage designer and director, 1966. Erich Kastner, German writer, *Emil and the Detectives*, 1974.

JULY 30

A Dog Day (see 3 July). Feasts of SS: Abdon and Sennen, martyrs; Julitta, widow and martyr.

The Jacobites are defeated at Newtown-butler, 1689. ¶ York (Toronto) in Canada is founded by General John Simcoe, 1793. ¶ Great fire in central New York causes over $1 million damage, 1890. ¶ Tipperary is captured by Nationalist forces, 1922. ¶ All Commonwealth citizens are given the status of British subjects by the British Citizenship Act, 1948. ¶ Kim Philby is granted political asylum in USSR, 1963. ¶ President Johnson signs Medical Care for the Aged Bill, 1965. ¶ The US *Mariner 6* spacecraft begins transmission of Mars pictures, 1969.

BORN: Giorgio Vasari, artist and writer, *Lives of the Painters*, Arezzo, Italy, 1511. Samuel Rogers, poet, *The Pleasures of Memory*, Stoke Newington, Middlesex, 1763. Emily Brontë, novelist, *Wuthering Heights*, Yorkshire, 1818. Richard Burdon, Lord Haldane, philosopher and politician, founded the Territorial Army, *Philosophy of Humanism*, Edinburgh, 1856. Henry Ford, industrialist and car manufacturer, Michigan, 1863.

DIED: Philip I, King of France, 1108. William Penn, English Quaker who founded the US state of Pennsylvania, Buckinghamshire, 1718. Thomas Gray, poet and scholar, 'Elegy Written in a Country Churchyard', *Pindaric Odes*, London, 1771. Denis Diderot, philosopher and *encyclopédiste*, 1784. Prince Otto von Bismarck, German militarist and statesman, 1898.

A Dog Day (see 3 July). Feasts of SS: Ignatius of Loyola; Neot; Helen of Skövde, widow.

Columbus discovers Trinidad on his third voyage, 1498. ¶ First storm-warnings in Britain are published by the Meteorological Department of the Board of Trade, 1861. ¶ Gerda (Asteroid 122) and Brunhilda (Asteroid 123) discovered by C. H. F. Peters, 1872. ¶ Under the command of Haig the third battle of Ypres (Passchendaele) begins, 1917. ¶ The Weimar Constitution is adopted by Germany, 1919. ¶ The British Unemployment Insurance Act is passed, 1925. ¶ *What a Night! What a Moon!* recorded by Teddy Wilson, 1935. ¶ The US Lunar Roving Vehicle is operated on the Moon's surface by Commander David R. Scott of *Apollo 15,* 1971.

BORN: John Canton, experimented with electricity, a fellow of the Royal Society, Stroud, Gloucestershire, 1718. Friedrich Wöhler, chemist, near Frankfurt, Germany, 1800. John Ericsson, inventor of the screw propeller, Sweden, 1803. Theobold Smith, pathologist, Albany, New York, 1859. Henri Decae, cinematographer, *Les Quatre Cents Coups,* Saint-Denis, France, 1915.

DIED: Saint Ignatius Loyola, founder of the Society of Jesus, Rome, 1556. Miguel Hidalgo y Costilla, Mexican revolutionary leader and priest; shot by the Spanish, Mexico, 1811. Louis Hachette, bookseller, publisher and editor, Paris, 1864. Benoît Fourneyron, engineer, devised the water turbine, 1867. Andrew Johnson, US President, Washington D.C., 1875. Franz Liszt, composer and pianist, Bayreuth, 1886. Jean Jaurès, socialist writer and orator; assassinated, France, 1914. Sir Francis Edward Younghusband, explorer and writer, Lytchett Minster, Dorset, 1942.

AUGUST

THIRTY-ONE DAYS

This was the *sixth* month of the old Roman year and
was known as *Sextilis*. But in 8BC the Emperor
Augustus Caesar persuaded the Senate to change it
to *Augustus* in his honour.

A Dog Day (see 3 July). Dies Mala or 'Egyptian Day', considered unlucky
in the Middle Ages. Lammas Day, BCP, known also as the Feast of the Wheat
Harvest, or the Gule of August, originating as a harvest festival; Lammas is derived
from the Sexon hlafmaesse, meaning 'loaf mass'; a Quarter Day in Scotland.
National Day, observed by most cantons in Switzerland.
Colorado Day, Colorado, USA (a legal holiday). Parents' Day, Zaire. The
Feast of St Peter ad Vincula, commemorating the dedication of the church of SS
Peter and Paul in Rome, 'St Peter's where the Fetters are.' Feast of the
Holy Machabees, martyrs. Feasts of SS: Faith, Hope, Charity and
their Mother, Wisdom, martyrs; Aled, Eiluned, or Almedha,
virgin and martyr; Ethelwold of Winchester, bishop.

Christopher Columbus lands on Terra Firma (America) and names it Isla Santa, 1498. ¶ Jacques Cartier sights the north shore of the Gulf of St Lawrence in Canada, 1534. ¶ Accession of George I of Great Britain, 1714. ¶ Foundation stones laid of the Bank of England's building in Threadneedle Street, London, 1732. ¶ The English, Hessians and Hanoverians under Prince Ferdinand of Brunswick defeat the French under Marshal De Contades at the battle of Minden, 1759. ¶ Oxygen discovered by (Sir) Joseph Priestley, 1774. ¶ The French fleet destroyed off Aboukir by Horatio Nelson, 1798. ¶ British forces sent to Portugal, 1808. ¶ The new London Bridge is opened, 1831. ¶ Slavery is abolished in the British Empire, 1834. ¶ Colorado made a US state (38th), 1876. ¶ War declared on Russia by Germany, mobilization of France, 1914. ¶ Begining of the Warsaw Rising, 1944. ¶ First close-up pictures of Mars sent back by US *Mariner 6* spacecraft, 1969.

BORN: Sigismund II Augustus, King of Poland, Cracow, Poland, 1520. Richard Wilson, landscape painter, Penegoes, Wales, 1714. Jean Baptiste de Lamarck, naturalist, originated the terms *vertebrate* and *invertebrate*, Bazentin, France, 1744. William Clark, explored north-west US with Meriwether Lewis, Virginia, 1770. Richard Henry Dana, novelist, *Two Years Before the Mast*, Massachusetts, 1815. Herman Melville, novelist and poet, *Moby Dick*, *Billy Budd*, New York City, 1819.

DIED: Louis VI of France, 1137. Queen Anne of Great Britain, 1714. Theodore Roethke, poet, *Open House, Words for the Wind*, Bainbridge Island, Washington, 1963. Walter Ulbricht, East German politician, East Berlin, 1973.

AUGUST 2

A Dog Day (see 3 July). National Holiday, Macedonia, Yugoslavia.
Feasts of SS: Alphonsus de Liguori, bishop and doctor; Stephen I,
pope; Theodots, martyr; 'St' Thomas of Dover.

Hannibal victorious at Cannae, 216BC. ¶ The Duke of Marlborough is victorious at the battle of Blenheim, 1704. ¶ Napoleon Bonaparte becomes the First Consul for life, 1802. ¶ Abdication of King Charles X of France, 1830. ¶ The powers of the East India Company are made over to the British Crown, 1858. ¶ Invasion of East Prussia by Russian forces, 1914.

BORN: Henry Olcott, co-founder, with Helena Blavatsky, of the Theosophical Society, Orange, New Jersey, 1832. Sir Arthur Bliss, composer, *Morning Heroes*, 1891. James Baldwin, writer and novelist, *The Fire Next Time*, New York, 1924. Peter O'Toole, actor, *Lawrence of Arabia*, Connemara, Ireland, 1933.

DIED: Thomas Gainsborough, artist, portrait painter, 1788. Jacques Etienne Montgolfier, balloonist and paper manufacturer, near Annonay, France, 1799. Wild Bill (James Butler) Hickok, scout and US Marshal; murdered, South Dakota, 1876. Enrico Caruso, operatic tenor, 1921. Alexander Graham Bell, inventor of the telephone, 1922. Warren Gamaliel Harding, US President, Washington D.C., 1923. Paul von Hindenburg, soldier and statesman, President of the Weimar Republic, Germany, 1934. Louis Blériot, aviator, the first man to fly the English Channel in an aeroplane (1909), 1936. Wallace Stevens, poet, *Ideas of Order, Notes Towards a Supreme Fiction*, Hartford, Connecticut, 1955. Fritz Lang, film director, *Metropolis, M, The Ministry of Fear*, 1976.

AUGUST 3

A Dog Day (see 3 July). Ernie Pyle Day, New Mexico, USA. The Feast of the Finding of St Stephen, commemorating Lucian's discovery of the saint's relics in Palestine, AD415. Feasts of SS: Germanus of Auxerre, bishop; Waltheof, or Walthen, abbot.

Marcus Aurelius leaves Rome to settle the unrest of the tribes on the Danube, 178. ¶ Accession of James III of Scotland, 1460. ¶ Christopher Columbus sets sail from Palos in Andalusia on his first expedition, 1492. ¶ The 'Moray Floods' in Scotland with the Spey and Findhorn rising over 50 feet, many lives lost (also on 4 and 27 August), 1829. ¶ War declared on France by Germany, 1914. ¶ Roger Casement is executed in London after a treason trial, 1916. ¶ End of the war between the British, in India, and Afghanistan, 1919. ¶ Inauguration of Calvin Coolidge as US President, 1923.

BORN: James Wyatt, architect, built and designed Fonthill Abbey; Burton Constable, Staffordshire, 1746. Sir Joseph Paxton, designed the Crystal Palace, near Woburn, Bedfordshire, 1801. Elisha Graves Otis, inventor of the modern safety lift, Halifax, Vermont, 1811. Stanley Baldwin, British statesman and Prime Minister, Worcester, 1876. Rupert Brooke, poet, Rugby, 1887.

DIED: Grinling Gibbons, sculptor, 1721. Étienne de Condillac, philosopher and writer, 1780. Sir Richard Arkwright, inventor, 1792. William George Fargo, co-founder of Wells-Fargo, 1881. Jean Louis Charles Garnier, architect in France, 1898. Sir Roger Casement, Irish nationalist and diplomat; hanged in London, 1916. Joseph Conrad, novelist, *Lord Jim*, 1924. Richard Willstätter, chemist, Locarno, Switzerland, 1942. Colette, novelist, *Gigi, La Chatte*, 1954. Archbishop Makarios III, Cypriot politician and religious leader, 1977.

AUGUST 4

A Dog Day (see 3 July). Feasts of SS: Dominic;
Is and her Companions, martyrs; Molua, or Lughaidh, abbot.

The Barons are defeated and Simon de Montfort killed at the battle of Evesham, 1265. ¶ The 'Moray Floods' in Scotland with the Spey and Findhorn overflowing, many lives lost (also on 3 and 27 August), 1829. ¶ Britain declares war on Germany, 1914. ¶ US declares neutrality, 1914. ¶ The second battle of the Marne ends (began 15 July), 1918. ¶ Badajoz falls to forces led by Franco in the Spanish Civil War, 1936.

BORN: John Tradescant, gardener and naturalist, Meopham, Kent, 1608. Edward Irving, clergyman, the Catholic Apostolic Church grew from his teachings, Dumfries, Scotland, 1792. Percy Bysshe Shelley, poet and writer, *The Necessity of Atheism, Prometheus Unbound,* near Horsham, Sussex, 1792. William Henry Hudson, English nature writer, *Green Mansions, Far Away and Long Ago,* near Buenos Aires, Argentina, 1841. Knut Hamsun, novelist and poet, *The Growth of the Soil,* Norway, 1859. Sir Harry Lauder, Scottish entertainer, Edinburgh, 1870. Queen Elizabeth, the Queen Mother, 1900.

DIED: Simon de Montfort, Earl of Leicester, led the rebellion against Henry III; killed at the Battle of Evesham, Worcestershire, 1265. William Cecil, Lord Burghley, Elizabethan statesman and minister, 1598. John Burgoyne, British military leader, defeated at Saratoga, and dramatist, *The Heiress,* 1792. Jean-Baptist Vianney, Catholic priest and preacher, Ars-en-Dombes, France, 1859. Hans Christian Anderson, writer, *Fairy Tales,* 1875. Baron Carl Auer von Welsbach, chemist and physicist, invented the gas mantle for illumination, Treibach, Austria, 1929. James Cruze, film director, *The Covered Wagon,* Hollywood, California, 1942.

AUGUST 5

The Feast of the Dedication of the Basilica of St Mary Major;
this was the third patriarchal basilica in Rome and was originally
founded in the 4th century. A Dog Day (see 3 July). Constitution Day, Iran.
Feasts of SS: Addai and Mari, bishops; Afra, martyr; Nonna, matron.

Accession of Henry I of England (reigns until 1 December 1135), 1100. ¶ Marl-borough forces the French lines at Arleux, 1711. ¶ The first trans-Atlantic telegraph line was formally opened when Queen Victoria sent a message to President Pierce of the US, 1858. ¶ The cornerstone of 'The Statue of Liberty' is laid on Bedloe's Island (later re-named Liberty Island. The statue was unveiled on 28 October 1886), 1884. ¶ Warsaw entered by German forces, 1915. ¶ US, USSR, and Britain sign Nuclear Test Ban Treaty, 1963.

BORN: Count Johann von Struensee, physician and politician, Halle, Germany, 1737. Niels Henrik Abel, Norwegian mathematician, 1802. Alexander William Kinglake, historian, *History of the War in the Crimea*, near Taunton, Somerset, 1809. Edward John Eyre, explorer, Governor of Australia, Yorkshire, 1815. Guy de Maupassant, short-story writer and novelist, *The Necklace, Pierre et Jean*, near Dieppe, 1850. Conrad Aiken, novelist and poet, *Blue Voyage*, Savannah, 1889. John Huston, film director, *The Treasure of Sierra Madre, Moby Dick*, Nevada, 1906. Harold Holt, Liberal politician, Prime Minister of Australia, 1908. Neil Armstrong, astronaut, Ohio, 1930.

DIED: Thomas Newcomen, engineer, built the 'first self-acting steam engine', London, 1729. James Gibbs, Scottish architect, 1754. Frederick North, 2nd Earl of Guildford (Lord North), British Prime Minister, London, 1792. Ferdinand von Hebra, physician, researched skin diseases, Austria, 1880. Friedrich Engels, political writer, co-author with Karl Marx of *The Communist Manifesto*, 1895. Phil May, humorous cartoonist, 1903. Arthur Meighen, Canadian Prime Minister, Toronto, 1960. Marilyn Monroe, actress, *Some Like it Hot, The Misfits;* suicide, Los Angeles, 1962.

The Feast of the Transfiguration of our Lord Jesus Christ,
celebrating Christ's demonstration of his holiness to SS Peter, James
and John on Mount Tabor near Galilee; the feast originated in the
Byzantine church and was not made a general observance in the West
until 1456. A Dog Day (see 3 July). Hiroshima Day, observed in Japan
and also by peace groups throughout the world. Feasts of SS: Sixtus II,
Felicissimus and Agapitus, with their Companions, martyrs; Justus
and Pastor, martyrs; Hormisdas, pope.

Moors defeated by the Spaniards at Simancas, 939. ¶ Execution of Eugene Aram at York, for murder, 1759. ¶ The Holy Roman Empire is formally ended, 1806. ¶ Spanish forces defeated at Junin in Peru by Simon Bolivar, 1824. ¶ Bolivia establishes independence from Peru, 1825. ¶ Abortive rising by Louis Napoleon at Boulogne, 1840. ¶ The French war with Morocco begins, 1844. ¶ Julia (Asteroid 89) discovered by M. Stephan, 1866. ¶ Thyra (Asteroid 115) discovered by J. C. Watson, 1871. ¶ William Kemmler was the first criminal in the US to be electrocuted, in Auburn Prison, Auburn, New York, 1890. ¶ Opening of the Corinth Canal, 1893. ¶ An atomic bomb is dropped on Hiroshima by US, 1945.

BORN: Nicolas Malebranche, philosopher, Paris, 1638. François de Salignac de la Mothe Fénelon, theologian and writer, France, 1651. Rolf Boldrewood (pseudonym of T. A. Browne), popular writer, *Robbery Under Arms*, London, 1826. Paul Claudel, dramatist and poet, France, 1868. Sir Alexander Fleming, bacteriologist, Ayrshire, 1881. Charles Crichton, film director, *Hue and Cry*, *The Lavender Hill Mob*, Wallasey, Cheshire, 1910. Robert Mitchum, actor, Bridgeport, Connecticut, 1917.

DIED: Anne Hathaway, wife of William Shakespeare, 1623. Ben Jonson, dramatist and poet, *Volpone*, *The Alchemist*, London, 1637. Diego Velasquez, painter, Madrid, 1660. Joseph Achille Le Bel, French chemist, 1930. Preston Sturges, film director, *Lady Eve*, New York City, 1959. Fulgencio Batista y Zaldivar, Cuban dictator, 1973.

AUGUST 7

A Dog Day (see 3 July). National Holiday, Colombia. The Feast of the
Name of Jesus, BCP (2 January in the Catholic Church).
Feasts of SS: Cajetan; Claudia, matron; Donatus of Arezzo, bishop;
Dometius the Persian, martyr; Victricius, bishop; Albert of Trapani.

Ship money is declared illegal by Britain, 1641. ¶ The *New England Courant* first published in Boston, by James Franklin, Benjamin's half-brother, 1721. ¶ The Irish Reform Act is finally passed, 1832. ¶ Ottawa is made the capital of the Dominion of Canada, 1858. ¶ Gallia (Asteroid 148) discovered by Prosper Henry, 1875. ¶ The British Trans-Atlantic air mail service begins, 1939. ¶ Billie Holiday records *I Cover the Waterfront* with Teddy Wilson and his Orchestra in New York City, 1941. ¶ US landings at Guadalcanal, 1942.

BORN: Mata Hari, courtesan and spy, Netherlands, 1876. Louis Leakey, palae-ontologist and anthropologist, excavated at the Olduvai Gorge; Kenya, 1903. Ralph Johnson Bunche, diplomat, Nobel Prize for Peace, Detroit, 1904. Nicholas Ray, film director, *Rebel without a Cause*, La Crosse, Kansas, 1911.

DIED: Robert Blake, naval commander and Admiral, 1657. Joseph Marie Jacquard, silk weaver, invented the Jacquard Loom, France, 1834. Aleksandr Aleksandrovich Blok, Russian Symbolist poet, *Verses about Russia*, 1921. Curbastro Gregorio Ricci, mathematician, Bologna, Italy, 1925. Bix Beider-becke, early jazz cornetist and composer, *In a mist*, 1931. Konstantin Sergeyevich Stanislavsky, actor and drama teacher, Moscow, 1938. Sir Rabindranath Tagore, poet, novelist and essayist, Nobel Prize for Literature, *The Crescent Moon*, Calcutta, 1941.

AUGUST 8

A Dog Day (see 3 July). Feasts of SS: Cyriacus, Largus and Smaragdus, martyrs; The Fourteen Holy Helpers; Hormisdas, martyr; Altman, bishop.

The Coronation stone is sent to London, 1296. ¶ Great eruptions by Mount Vesuvius, 1767 ¶ The English Poor Law Act is passed, 1834. ¶ First British troops land in France, 1914. ¶ Delhi is made the capital of India and Karachi of Pakistan, 1947. ¶ Robbery of £2½ million from Glasgow–London mail train at Cheddington, 1963. ¶ Resignation of Richard M. Nixon as a result of the Watergate Affair, 1974.

BORN: Jacques Bosnage de Beauval, theologian, Rouen, France, 1653. Francis Hutcheson, philosopher, *Essay on the Passions*, Armagh, Ireland, 1694. William Bateson, biologist, originated the term 'genetics', Yorkshire, 1861. Ernest Orlando Lawrence, physicist, invented the cyclotron, South Dakota, 1901. P. A. M. Dirac, physicist, Nobel Prize winner, Bristol, 1902.

DIED: Thomas à Kempis (Thomas Hammerken von Kempen), monk and writer, *The Imitation of Christ*, near Zwolle, Netherlands, 1471. Girolamo Fracastoro, Italian physician and poet, 1553. Antoine Arnauld, Jansenist theologian, 1694. George Canning, politician and Prime Minister, 1827. Madame Vestris, actress, London, 1856. Jacob Burckhardt, historian, *The Civilization of the Renaissance in Italy*, 1897. Viktor Meyer, chemist, Heidelberg, 1897.

AUGUST 9

A Dog Day (see 3 July). National Holiday, Singapore. Feasts of SS:
John Vianney; Romanus, martyr; Emygdius, martyr; Nathy and Felim, bishops;
Oswald of Northumbria, martyr.

Leonidas is finally defeated by the Persians at the battle of Thermopylae, 480BC. ¶ In the Dyrrhacium campaign Gaius Julius Caesar defeats Pompey the Great at Pharsalus (6 June is considered by some authorities to be the true date), 48BC. ¶ Gauls defeat Valens at Adrianople, 378. ¶ Commune established in Paris by revolutionaries, 1792. ¶ The frontier betweeen Canada and US defined by Webster–Ashburton treaty, signed by US and Britain, 1842. ¶ The Married Woman's Property Act greatly improves position of wives in Britain, 1870. ¶ An atomic bomb is dropped on Nagasaki by US, 1945. ¶ Gerald Ford is sworn-in as President of the US, 1974.

BORN: Thomas Telford, road, bridge and canal builder, built the Menai suspension bridge; near Dumfries, Scotland, 1757. Fabian Gottlieb Bellingshausen, polar explorer and naval commander, Russia, 1778. William Thomas Morton, dental surgeon, introduced ether as a general anaesthetic, Charlestown, Massachusetts, 1819. Leonid Andreyev, dramatist, *He Who Gets Slapped*, Russia, 1871. Jean Piaget, child psychologist, *The Child's Conception of the World*, Neuchâtel, Switzerland, 1896. Robert Aldrich, film director, *Kiss me Deadly*, *The Big Knife*, Cranston, Rhode Island, 1918. Philip Larkin, poet and novelist, *A Girl in Winter*, Coventry, 1922.

DIED: Trajan (Marcus Ulpius Traianus), Roman emperor, Selinus, Cilicia, 117. Maarten Harpertszoon Tromp, Dutch admiral and naval commander; off the Dutch coast in an engagement with Admiral George Monck, 1653. Frederick Marryat, maritime novelist, *Mr Midshipman Easy*, Langham, Norfolk, 1848. Sir Edward Frankland, chemist, proposed the theory of valence, 1899. Ernst Haeckel, biologist, Jena, Germany, 1919. Herman Hesse, poet and novelist, *Steppenwolf*, Switzerland, 1962. Dmitry Shostakovich, composer, 1975.

AUGUST 10

A Dog Day (see 3 July). Independence Day, Ecuador. Feasts of SS:
Laurence, martyr; Philomena, or Philumena.

Victory of the Scots at Otterburn, 1388. ¶ The Spanish and English defeat the French at St Quentin, 1557. ¶ Arras is taken by the French, 1640. ¶ Tuileries invaded by mob, Swiss Guard massacred, 1792. ¶ Missouri made a US state (24th), 1821. ¶ The Mines Act promoted by Lord Ashley prohibits women and young children from working underground, 1842. ¶ Heavy losses are inflicted on the Russian fleet off Port Arthur by the Japanese, 1904. ¶ War with Austria declared by France, 1914. ¶ Formal establishment of the US Defense Department, 1949. ¶ Membership of EEC applied for by Britain, 1961. ¶ Violent encounters between workers and Red Guards in Canton, China, 1967.

BORN: Bernard Nieuwentyt, mathematician, Netherlands, 1654. Armand Gensonné, Girondist, Bordeaux, France, 1758. Sir Charles James Napier, soldier, conqueror of Sind, London, 1782. Hugo Eckener, aeronautical engineer and pilot, Prussia, 1868. Laurence Binyon, poet and dramatist, Keeper of Prints and Drawings at the British Museum, Lancaster, 1869. Herbert Hoover, Republican US President, West Branch, Iowa, 1874.

DIED: John and Cornelius de Witt, Dutch statesmen; murdered by rioters at The Hague, 1672. Ferdinand VI of Spain, Madrid, 1759. John Wilson Croker, Tory politician and writer, London, 1857. Otto Lilienthal, pioneer aviator, Germany, 1896. Robert Hutchings Goddard, pioneer of rocketry, 1945. Oswald Veblen, mathematician, Maine, 1960.

AUGUST 11

A Dog Day (see 3 July). Independence Day, Republic of Chad
(granted by France in 1960). Feasts of SS: Tiburtius and Susanna, martyrs;
Alexander the Charcoal-Burner, bishop and martyr; Equitius, abbot;
Blaan, or Blane, bishop; Attracta, or Araght, virgin; Lelia, virgin;
Gaugericus, or Géry, bishop; Gerard of Gallinaro and his Companions.

The Rajah of Kedah cedes Penang to the British, 1786. ¶ Severe earthquakes throughout the Azores, the village of St Michael 'sunk, and a lake of boiling water appeared in its place', 1810. ¶ Professor Asaph Hall discovers Phobos and Deimos, satellites of Mars, at Washington, 1877. ¶ Canton is entered by Chiang Kai-shek and his supporters, 1936. ¶ The Atlantic Charter is signed by Churchill and Roosevelt, 1941. ¶ Race riots in Watts, Los Angeles, 1965. ¶ Malaysia and Indonesia sign a peace treaty at Jakarta, 1966.

BORN: Christian Eijkman, physician, Nobel Prize for Medicine, Netherlands, 1858. Hugh MacDiarmid, Scottish poet, Dumfrieshire, 1892. Angus Wilson, novelist and critic, *Anglo-Saxon Attitudes*, *The Old Men at the Zoo*, Boxhill, Surrey, 1913.

DIED: Hans Memling, painter, Bruges, 1494. Johann Tetzel, Dominican, sold indulgences to finance the building of St Peter's in Rome that were eventually to provoke Luther's theses, Leipzig, 1519. Marshall Hall, physician and physiologist, *Respiration and Irritability*, Bristol, 1831. Andrew Carnegie, industrialist and philanthropist, 1919. Jackson Pollock, Abstract Expressionist painter, East Hampton, New York, 1956.

AUGUST 12

*A Dog Day (see 3 July). Anniversary of the Accession of
HM King Hussein of Jordan, Jordan. Feasts of SS: Clare, virgin;
Euplus, martyr; Murtagh, or Muredach, bishop;
Porcarius and his Companions, martyrs.*

Victory of the Crusaders at the battle of Ascalon, 1099. ¶ The Duke of Wellington enters Madrid, 1812. ¶ War declared against Napoleon by Austria, 1813. ¶ War with Austria–Hungary declared by Britain, 1914. ¶ Averell Harriman, Churchill and Stalin meet for discussions in Moscow, 1942. ¶ A radio-reflector space satellite is launched by US, 1960. ¶ The next total eclipse of the sun will be observed on this day (in England), 1999.

BORN: Thomas Bewick, engraver, Newcastle, 1753. George IV of Great Britain, 1762. Robert Southey, poet and writer, *The Curse of Kehama, Thalaba, Life of Nelson*, Bristol, Gloucestershire, 1774. Cecil B. de Mille, Hollywood film producer, Massachusetts, 1881. Erwin Schrödinger, physicist, Nobel Prize winner, Vienna, 1887.

DIED: Philippe de Champaigne, painter, 1674. Viscount Castlereagh, Anglo-Irish statesman; suicide, London, 1822. William Blake, writer and artist, *Songs of Innocence, The Marriage of Heaven and Hell*, 1827. George Stephenson, engineer and inventor, built the *Rocket* locomotive, Tapton, near Chesterfield, 1848. Sir William Jackson Hooker, botanist, London, 1865. James Lowell, poet and diplomat, *Biglow Papers*, Cambridge, Massachusetts, 1891. Nils Eric Nordenskjöld, Arctic explorer, discovered the North East passage, Sweden, 1901. John Philip Holland, pioneered the modern submarine, 1914. Leoš Janáček, Czech composer, 1928. Thomas Mann, novelist, *The Magic Mountain, Death in Venice*, Zurich, 1955. Ian Fleming, popular novelist, creator of James Bond, 1964.

AUGUST 13

*The Roman Vortumnalia, a festival honouring Vertumnus, a deity
associated with growth and change; this festival also marked the
change from high summer to the cooler fruit-gathering season.
Woman's Day, Tunisia. Feasts of SS: Hippolytus, martyr;
Cassian of Imola, martyr; Simplician, bishop; Radegund, matron;
Maximus the Confessor, abbot; Wigbert, abbot; Nerses Klaietsi, bishop.*

Triple triumph of Octavian in Rome after his successes in Egypt (until 15 August), 29BC. ¶ A panic is created throughout London by Titus Oates's 'Popish plot', 1678. ¶ The East India Company is placed under a government Board of Control, 1784. ¶ The French royal family is imprisoned, 1792. ¶ The Cape of Good Hope is made a British Colony, 1814. ¶ Iris (Asteroid 7) discovered by J. R. Hind, 1847. ¶ Niobe (Asteroid 72) discovered by R. Luther, 1861. ¶ Franz Josef Land discovered by Weyprecht and Payer, 1873. ¶ Manila taken by US forces, 1898. ¶ The Angora Assembly elects Mustapha Kemal as President of Turkey, 1923. ¶ Adolf Hitler rejects Hindenburg's request to serve as Vice-Chancellor under von Papen, 1932. ¶ Border between East and West Berlin sealed off by East Germany with closure of the Brandenburg Gate, 1961.

BORN: Erasmus Bartholin, physicist, Denmark, 1625. James Gillray, political caricaturist, Chelsea, London, 1756. Sir George Grove, engineer and musicologist, *Grove's Dictionary of Music and Musicians*, London, 1820. John Nicholson Ireland, composer, Cheshire, 1879. John Logie Baird, television pioneer, Scotland, 1888. Alfred Hitchcock, film director, *North by Northwest, Psycho*, London, 1899. Felix Wankel, engineer and inventor, Lahr, Germany, 1902. Ben Hogan, champion golfer, Texas, 1912. Archbishop Makarios III, Cypriot politician and religious leader, Cyprus, 1913. Fidel Castro, revolutionary, deposed Batista, Cuba, 1926.

DIED: René Laënnec, army doctor and physician, invented the stethoscope, France, 1826. Eugène Delacroix, Romantic artist, 1863. Florence Nightingale, the founder of modern nursing, hospital reformer, London, 1910. Jules Emile Massenet, composer, *Manon*, Paris, 1912. Herbert George Wells, novelist, social critic and educator, *The Time Machine, Kipps, A Short History of the World*, London, 1946. Henry Williamson, novelist, *Tarka the Otter*, 1977.

AUGUST 14

*Independence Day, Pakistan (1947). Feasts of SS: Eusebius of Rome;
Marcellus of Apamea, bishop and martyr; Eachanan, bishop;
Athanasia, matron.*

Portuguese defeat the Spanish at Aljubarrota, 1385. ¶ Independence declared by
Paraguay, 1811. ¶ Até (Asteroid 111) discovered by C. H. F. Peters, 1870.
¶ The legations in Peking are relieved by international forces, 1900. ¶ War
declared on Germany and Austria by China, 1917. ¶ President Roosevelt signs
the Social Security Act, 1935. ¶ The Battle of Britain is at its height, 1940.
¶ Surrender of the Japanese to the Allies ends the Second World War, 1945.
¶ US *Orbiter 1* begins orbiting of the Moon, 1966.

BORN: Fra Paolo Sarpi, philosopher and scholar, excommunicated by Pope
Paul V, Venice, 1552. Pope Pius VI, Cesna, Italy, 1717. Dr Charles Hutton,
mathematician and physicist, *Recreations in Mathematics*, Newcastle, 1737.
John Galsworthy, novelist, *The Forsyte Saga*, Surrey, 1867.

DIED: Johann Herbart, philosopher and educationalist, Gottingen, Germany,
1841. Richard Jefferies, essayist and novelist, *The Gamekeeper at Home*, *Bevis*,
Goring, Sussex, 1887. Alfred Harmsworth, 1st Viscount Northcliffe, newspaper
and magazine proprietor, founded the *Daily Mail*, London, 1922. William
Randolph Hearst, newspaper publisher, California, 1951. Bertolt Brecht,
dramatist and theatrical director, *The Caucasian Chalk Circle*, *Mother Courage*,
1956. Henri Breuil, archaeologist and priest, 1961. Jules Romains (Louis
Farigoule), novelist, dramatist and poet, *The Boys in the Back Room*, *Men of Good
Will*, Paris, 1972.

The Feast of the Assumption of the Blessed Virgin Mary, 'the happy departure of the Virgin and her translation into the Kingdom of her son', her death that is; a feast firmly established in the Western church by the 6th century. End of the Dog Days (see 3 July). Independence Day, India (1947). Liberation Day, Republic of Korea (liberated from Japanese forces, 1945). Day of the Foundation of Panama City, Panama. Feasts of SS: Tarsicius, martyr; Arnulf, or Arnoul, of Soissons, bishop.

The Duke of Bedford takes or destroys nearly 500 French ships off Harfleur, 1416. ¶ Montrose defeats the Covenanters at Kilsyth, 1645. ¶ Cardinal de Rohan is arrested in the 'Diamond Necklace Affair', 1785. ¶ Helena (Asteroid 101) discovered by J. C. Watson, 1868. ¶ The Panama Canal is formally opened for shipping, 1914. ¶ Diplomatic relations between US and Russia are cut off, 1918. ¶ Éamon de Valéra is arrested by Irish Free State forces, 1923. ¶ Assassination of Sheik Mujibur Rahman at Dacca in Bangladesh during *coup* by Army officers, 1975.

BORN: Luigi Pulci, Florentine poet, *Morgante Maggiore*, Florence, 1432. Napoleon Bonaparte, French Emperor, Ajaccio, Corsica, 1769. Sir Walter Scott, novelist and poet, *The Heart of Midlothian, Quentin Durward*, Edinburgh, 1771. Sir Henry Maine, jurist and historian, *Ancient Law*, Roxburgh, 1822. Baron Richard von Krafft-Ebing, neuro-psychiatrist, *Psychopathia Sexualis*, Mannheim, Germany, 1840. James Keir Hardie, Labour politician, Lanark, Scotland, 1856. Samuel Coleridge-Taylor, composer, London, 1875. Ethel Barrymore, actress, 1879. Sir Peter Buck, Maori politician, Urenui, New Zealand, 1880. Edna Ferber, novelist, *Giant*, Michigan, 1887. Thomas Edward Lawrence, 'Lawrence of Arabia', soldier and writer, *The Seven Pillars of Wisdom*, Tremadoc, Wales, 1888. Prince Louis de Broglie, physicist, France, 1892. Gerty Cori, American biochemist, wife of Charles Cori, Prague, 1896. Thomas Joseph Mboya, Kenyan statesman, near Nairobi, 1903. Robert Bolt, dramatist, *A Man for All Seasons*, Manchester, 1924. HRH Princess Anne (Mrs Mark Phillips), 1950.

DIED: Macbeth, King of Scotland, chiefly remembered through Shakespeare's play, Aberdeen, 1057. Joseph Joachim, Hungarian composer and violinist, 1907. Paul Signac, Neo-Impressionist painter, France, 1935. René Magritte, Belgian Surrealist painter, Brussels, 1967.

AUGUST 16

Anniversary of the Restoration of the Republic, Dominican Republic (in 1924 after occupation by US Marines). Bennington Battle Day, Vermont, USA (1777). Feasts of SS: Joachim; Arsacius; Armel, abbot; Rock.

Prince Eugène defeats the Turks at Belgrade, 1717. ¶ Expulsion of the Jesuits from Rome, 1773. ¶ British force defeated at Bennington by the American army, 1777. ¶ American army under Horatio Gates defeated at Camden by Cornwallis, 1780. ¶ Detroit, under General Hull, surrenders to the British, and the US invasion of Canada is postponed, 1812. ¶ Peterloo Massacre in Manchester when militia open fire on a crowd gathered to hear discussion of reform, 1819. ¶ Hestia (Asteroid 46) discovered by Norman Pogson, 1857. ¶ Cyrene (Asteroid 133) discovered by J. C. Watson, 1873. ¶ The Tate Gallery in London is opened, 1897. ¶ Messina is taken by American forces, 1943.

BORN: Alfred, Lord Tennyson, poet, made Poet Laureate in 1850, 'In Memoriam,' *Idylls of the King*, Somersby, Lincolnshire, 1809. Arthur Cayley, mathematician, 1821. Jules Laforgue, poet, *Les Complaintes*, Montevideo, 1860. Dame Mary Gilmore, Australian poet and writer, 1865. Wendell Stanley, biochemist, Nobel Prize winner, Ridgeville, Indiana, 1904. Ted Hughes, poet, *The Hawk in the Rain*, Yorkshire, 1930.

DIED: Thomas Fuller, clergyman and biographer, 1661. Ramakrishna, Hindu teacher and writer, Calcutta, 1886. Robert Bunsen, chemist, inventor of the burner named after him, 1899. José Maria de Eça de Queirós, Portuguese novelist, *The Relic*, 1900. Umberto Boccioni, Futurist sculptor, 1916. Sir Norman Lockyer, astronomer, discovered helium, Devon, 1920. 'Babe' Ruth, champion baseball player, New York City, 1948. Louis Jouvet, theatrical actor and director, France, 1951. Irving Langmuir, US physicist, 1957. Wanda Landowska, Polish virtuoso harpsichordist and pianist, 1959. Selman Waksman, microbiologist, Nobel Prize winner, Hyannis, Massachusetts, 1973. Elvis Presley, popular rock-and-roll singer, 1977.

AUGUST 17

*The Roman festival of Portunus, an early god of doors and gates who
came to be identified with harbours. Anniversary of General San Martin's
Death, Argentina (José de San Martin, 1778–1850). Independence Day,
Gabon Republic (1960, formerly one of the four territories of French
Equatorial Africa). Independence Day, Indonesia (1945). Feasts of SS:
Hyacinth; Mamas, martyr; Eusebius, pope; Liberatus and his Companions,
martyrs; Clare of Montefalco, virgin.*

The English defeat the French and Scots at Verneuil, 1424. ¶ Cromwell victorious at the battle of Preston, 1648. ¶ Legislation enacted in Britain for registration of births, deaths and marriages, 1836. ¶ The French Panama Canal Company established under the control of Ferndinand de Lesseps, 1879. ¶ George Carmack and two Indian companions discover the first gold in the Klondyke, Canada, 1896. ¶ Construction of the Berlin Wall begins, 1961. ¶ Jimmy Hoffa, President of the International Brotherhood of Teamsters, is sentenced to 5 years' imprisonment for wire and mail fraud, 1964. ¶ Philip Blaiberg dies in Cape Town, 19 months after receiving a heart transplant from Dr Christian Barnard, 1969. ¶ Earthquakes and tidal waves in the Philippines result in the deaths of over 6,000 people, 1976.

BORN: Pierre de Fermat, mathematician, France, 1601. John III, King of Poland, 1629. Davy Crockett, frontiersman and politician, Tennessee, 1786. Oliver St John Gogarty, writer and politician, Dublin, 1878. Mae West, film actress, *She Done Him Wrong. I'm no Angel*, Brooklyn, New York, 1893.

DIED: Frederick (II) the Great, King of Prussia, Potsdam, Germany, 1786. José de Sán Martin, Argentinian revolutionary, Boulogne, France, 1850. Fernand Léger, French Cubist painter, 1955. Sir John Hubert Marshall, archaeologist, discovered the Indus Valley Civilization, 1958. Ludwig Mies van der Rohe, architect, Chicago, 1969. Conrad Aiken, novelist and poet, *Blue Voyage*, 1973.

AUGUST 18

Feasts of SS: Agapitus, martyr; Florus and Laurus, martyrs;
Helen, widow; Alipius, bishop.

Defeat of the French under De la Clue off Cape Lagos by Admiral Boscawen, 1759. ¶ Napoleon defeats the Russians at Smolensk, 1812. ¶ Santa Fé is captured by US forces, 1846. ¶ Abortive Sioux revolt in Minnesota begins, 1862. ¶ Prussia victorious over the French at Gravelotte, 1870. ¶ Second day of a great hurricane along the coast of Mississippi, over 400 people lose their lives, 1969.

BORN: Meriwether Lewis, explorer of the north-western US, Virginia, 1774. Earl Russell, British Prime Minister, London, 1792. Francis Joseph I, Emperor of Austria, Vienna, 1830. Marshall Field, founder of the modern department store, Massachusetts, 1834. Viljaya Pandit, diplomat, the first woman President of the United Nations Assembly, Allahabad, India, 1900. Marcel Carné, film director, *Les Enfants du Paradis*, Paris, 1909. Henry Cornelius, film director, *Passport to Pimlico*, South Africa, 1913. Alain Robbe-Grillet, novelist, *Le Voyeur*, *L'Immortelle* (screenplay), Brest, France, 1922.

DIED: Genghis Khan, Mongol emperor, 1227. Guido Reni, painter, Bologna, Italy, 1642. André Jacques Garnerin, balloonist, 1823. Honoré de Balzac, French novelist, *Comédie Humaine*, 1850. William Henry Hudson, English nature writer, *Green Mansions, Far Away and Long Ago*, 1922.

AUGUST 19

*Feasts of SS: John Eudes; Andrew the Tribune, martyr; Timothy,
Agapius and Thecla, martyrs; Sixtus, or Xystus, III, pope;
Mochta, abbot; Bertulf, abbot; Sebald; Louis of Anjou, bishop.*

Edward I of England crowned, 1274. ¶ Mary, Queen of Scots, lands at Leith,
1561. ¶ France and Spain form alliance against Britain, 1796. ¶ Beginning of
the trial of Queen Caroline, 1820. ¶ British forces are driven out of Somaliland,
1940. ¶ The raid on Dieppe by Canadian troops supported by British, US and
French forces, 1942. ¶ Florence is taken by the Eighth Army, 1944. ¶ A Day of
Thanksgiving in Britain, 1945. ¶ Severe earthquakes in the eastern regions of
Turkey, over 2,500 people are believed to have lost their lives, 1966.

BORN: John Dryden, poet, translator, dramatist, Northampton, 1631. John
Flamsteed, the first Astronomer Royal, Denby, 1646. Comtesse du Barry,
mistress of Louis XV of France, 1743. James Hall, pioneer of geology in the US,
Pennsylvania, 1793. James Nasmyth, engineer, invented the first steam hammer,
Edinburgh, 1808. Charles Doughty, writer, *Travels in Arabia Deserta*, Suffolk,
1843. Auguste Marie Louis Lumière, cinema pioneer, France, 1862. Orville
Wright, aviation pioneer, Dayton, Ohio, 1871. Georges Enesco, composer and
violinist, Rumania, 1881. Coco Chanel, fashion designer, France, 1883. Sir
Arthur David Waley, scholar and oriental translator, *170 Chinese Poems*,
Monkey, London, 1889. Ogden Nash, writer of humorous verse, *The Bad
Parent's Garden of Verse*, Rye, New York, 1902.

DIED: Octavian/Augustus (Gaius Julius Caesar Octavianus), Roman Emperor,
at Nola, 14. Blaise Pascal, philosopher and mathematician, *Les Pensées*, Paris,
1662. George Smith, Assyriologist, deciphered many cunieform scripts,
Assyrian Discoveries, Aleppo, Syria, 1876. Richard Burdon, Lord Haldane,
philosopher and politician, founded the Territorial Army, *Philosophy of
Humanism*, London, 1928. Sergei Diaghilev, ballet and theatre impresario, 1929.
Sir Henry Wood, conductor and composer, Hitchin, Hertfordshire, 1944.
Subhas Chandra Bose, Indian nationalist, 1945. Groucho Marx, comedian and
actor, *Duck Soup*, Santa Monica, California, 1977.

Feasts of SS: Bernard, abbot and doctor; Amadour; Oswin, martyr;
Philibert, abbot.

The Austrians defeat the French at Saragossa, 1710. ¶ Ascent of the River Niger begun by the British steamships *Albert*, *Wilberforce*, and *Soudan*, 1841. ¶German forces occupy Brussels after invasion of Belgium, 1914. ¶ Beginning of the Allied offensive in Mesopotamia, 1916. ¶ Beginning of major British offensive on the Western Front, 1918. ¶ The American Army reaches Versailles, 1944. ¶ Russian troops invade Czechoslovakia, violent fighting in Prague, 1968.

BORN: Jons Jacob Berzelius, chemist and physicist, Sweden, 1779. Benjamin Harrison, US President, North Bend, Ohio, 1833. Raymond Poincaré, statesman, President of France during the First World War, Bar-le-Duc, France, 1860. Shaul Tchernichowski, Hebrew poet, Crimea, 1875. Howard Phillips Lovecraft, writer of ghost and horror stories, Providence, Rhode Island, 1890.

DIED: Jules Laforgue, Symbolist poet, *Les Complaintes*, 1887. William Booth, founder of the Salvation Army, 1912. Paul Ehrlich, German bacteriologist, 1915. Vilfredo Pareto, economist and sociologist, Geneva, 1923. Federico Garcia Lorca, dramatist and poet, *Poet in New York, Blood Wedding;* murdered, Granada, 1936. Lev Trotsky, revolutionary, a leader of the Bolshevik revolution, writer, *History of the Russian Revolution*; murdered by order of Stalin, Mexico City, 1940.

AUGUST 21

The Roman festival of Consus, originally a corn god but later associated with good counsel (also on 15 December). Feasts of SS: Jane Frances de Chantal, widow; Luxorius, Cisellus and Camerinus, martyrs; Bonosus and Maximian, martyrs; Sidonius Apollinaris, bishop; Abraham of Smolensk, abbot.

Arthur Wellesley defeats the French at Vimiero, 1808. ¶ The battle of Bapaume, 1918. ¶ Civil Defence officially formed in Britain, 1939. ¶ Hawaii made a US state (50th), 1959. ¶ Martial law is declared in South Vietnam, 1963. ¶ Continued invasion of Czechoslovakia by Russian troops, Mr Dubcek is arrested, 1968.

BORN: Philip II, King of France, Paris, 1165. Jean Baptiste Greuze, artist, near Mâcon, France, 1725. William Murdock, steam and gas engineer and inventor, Auchinleck, Ayrshire, 1754. William IV, King of Great Britain and Ireland, Buckingham Palace, London, 1765. August Bournonville, writer, *La Sylphide*, Copenhagen, 1805. Charles Gerhardt, chemist, France, 1816. Aubrey Beardsley, artist and illustrator, Brighton, 1872. Count Basie, jazz pianist and bandleader, Red Bank, New Jersey, 1906. Robert Krasker, cinematographer, *Caesar and Cleopatra*, Australia, 1913. Princess Margaret Rose, 1930.

DIED: Richard Crashaw, Baroque poet, *Steps to the Temple*, 1649. Sir Benjamin Thompson Rumford, physicist and inventor, Auteuil, France, 1814. Conrad Martens, Australian painter, 1878. Marcus Andrew Hislop Clarke, Australian writer, *For the Term of his Natural Life*, 1881. Sir Jacob Epstein, British sculptor, 1959. Palmiro Togliatti, leader of the Italian Communist Party, Yalta, Ukraine, 1964.

*The Feast of the Immaculate Heart of Mary, celebrating the Virgin's
love and virtues; accepted as a general feast by Pope Pius VII in 1805.
Feasts of SS: Timothy, Hippolytus and Symphorian, martyrs; Sigfrid, abbot;
Andrew of Fiesole.*

The Scots defeated at Northallerton (the Battle of the Standard), 1138.
¶ Richard III defeated at the battle of Bosworth, 1485. ¶ Accession of Henry VII
of England (reigned until 21 April 1509), 1485. ¶ British settlement in Sierra
Leone founded as slave asylum, 1788. ¶ Black revolt in French San Domingo,
1791. ¶ Landing of French forces in Ireland, 1798. ¶ Napoleon leaves Egypt,
1799. ¶ Annexation of New Mexico by US, 1846. ¶ Fortuna (Asteroid 19) discovered by J. R. Hind, 1852. ¶ Garibaldi crosses the Straits with British assistance,
1860. ¶ Miriam (Asteroid 102) discovered by C. H. F. Peters, 1868. ¶ Korea
annexed by Japan, 1910. ¶ First public television transmissions in Britain, 1932.
¶ *Oop-pop-a-da, Two bass hit* and *Ow!* recorded in New York City by Dizzy
Gillespie and his Orchestra, 1947. ¶ The Pope arrives in Colombia, the first
papal visit to South America, 1968.

BORN: Denis Papin, physicist and mathematician, Blois, France, 1647. Count
Jean François de La Pérouse, explorer in the Pacific, near Albi, France, 1741.
Gustaf Fröding, poet, *Guitar and Concertina*, Sweden, 1860. Claude Debussy,
Impressionist composer, France, 1862. Jacques Lipchitz, sculptor and poet,
Latvia, 1891. Dorothy Parker, short-story writer and critic, *Enough Rope, After
Such Pleasures*, New Jersey, 1893. Leni Riefenstahl, photographer, *Triumph of
the Will*, Berlin, 1902. Henri Cartier-Bresson, photographer, France, 1908.
Karlheinz Stockhausen, experimental composer, near Cologne, 1928.

DIED: Philip VI, King of France, near Paris, 1350. Richard III, King of England,
Bosworth, Leicestershire, 1485. Jan Kochanowski, poet, *Laments*, Poland, 1584.
Jean Honoré Fragonard, painter, 1806. Warren Hastings, first Governor-
General of India, Worcestershire, 1818. Franz Gall, neurophysiologist, 1828.
Ivan Turgenev, novelist, *A Nest of Gentlefolk, Fathers and Children*, near Paris,
1883. Lord Robert Cecil, Marquess of Salisbury, statesman and Prime Minister,
Hatfield House, Hertfordshire, 1903. Michael Collins, a founder of the I.R.A.;
assassinated, near Bandon, Ireland, 1922. Michel Fokine, dancer and choreo-
grapher, 1942. Roger Martin du Gard, dramatist, novelist, France, 1958. Lord
Nuffield, industrialist and philanthropist, founder of the Morris Motor Company,
near Henley-on-Thames, Oxfordshire, 1963.

AUGUST 23

National Holiday, Socialist Republic of Romania. Feasts of SS:
Philip Benizi; Claudius, Asterius and other Martyrs; Eugene, or Eoghan, bishop.

Rome is taken by the Visigoths, 410. ¶ George Villiers, Duke of Buckingham, assassinated by John Felton, 1628. ¶ Mexico declared independent by the Treaty of Aquala, 1821. ¶ The British take Hong Kong from the Chinese, 1839. ¶ Alceste (Asteroid 124) discovered by C. H. F. Peters, 1872. ¶ German–USSR non-aggression pact, 1939. ¶ John Cobb reaches the speed of 368.85mph at the Bonneville Salt Flats in Utah, 1939. ¶ The 'Blitz' begins with an all-night raid by German planes on London, 1940.

BORN: Louis XVI of France, Versailles, 1754. Baron Georges Cuvier, naturalist and taxonomist, France, 1769. William Ernest Henley, dramatist, poet and editor, *In Hospital, For England's Sake*, Gloucester, 1849. Eleutherios Venizelos, statesman and Prime Minister of Greece, Crete, 1864. Edgar Lee Masters, poet and novelist, *Spoon River Anthology*, *Mirage*, Kentucky, 1869. Gene Kelly, dancer and actor, Pennsylvania, 1912.

DIED: Gnaeus Julius Agricola, Roman military commander, completed the invasion of Britain begun by Julius Caesar, 93. Sir William Wallace, Scottish patriot and leader; beheaded and quartered, London, 1305. Sir Thomas Littleton, jurist and writer on law, 1481. Luis de Leon, scholar and poet, translated many of the books of *The Bible* into Spanish, *Christ's Names*, 1591. Charles Augustin de Coulomb, French physicist, 1806. Alexander Wilson, astronomer, identified and explained sunspots, Philadelphia, 1813. Rudolph Valentino, film actor, *The Sheik*, New York City, 1926. Adolf Loos, architect, Vienna, 1933. Oscar Hammerstein II, song writer and composer, New York City, 1960.

AUGUST 24

Flag Day, Liberia. National Holiday, Socialist Republic of Romania.
Feasts of SS: Bartholomew, apostle; The Martyrs of Utica;
Audoenus, or Ouen, bishop.

The eruption of Mount Vesuvius results in the total destruction of Pompeii and Herculaneum, 79. ¶ Rome is taken by Alaric, 410. ¶ Massacre of Protestants throughout France known as the 'Massacre of St Bartholomew', 1572. ¶ New York confirmed to the British by the peace of Breda, 1667. ¶ Monterey is taken from Mexican forces by US troops, 1846. ¶ Minerva (Asteroid 93) discovered by J. C. Watson, 1867. ¶ Beginning of the Allied retreat from Mons (ends 7 September), 1914. ¶ Lend-Lease ended by President Truman, 1945.

BORN: George Stubbs, painter, Liverpool, 1724. William Wilberforce, philanthropist, anti-slavery campaigner, Hull, Yorkshire, 1759. James Weddell, navigator and Antarctic explorer, Ostend, Netherlands, 1787. Sir Max Beerbohm, caricaturist and writer, *Seven Men*, London, 1872. Jorge Luis Borges, poet and short-story writer, *Labyrinths*, Buenos Aires, 1899. Graham Sutherland, painter, London, 1903.

DIED: Pliny the Elder, naturalist and Roman writer, *Historia Naturalis*; at Pompeii during the eruption of Vesuvius, 79. Il Parmigianino (Francesco Mazzola), painter, Cremona, 1540. Cardinal de Retz, politician and memoirist, Paris, 1679. Nicolas Léonard Sadi Carnot, physicist, 1832. Getulio Dornelles Vargas, dictator and President of Brazil; suicide, Rio de Janeiro, 1954.

AUGUST 25

Constitution Day, Paraguay. Independence Day, Uruguay (1825).
Feasts of SS: Louis of France; Genesius the Comedian (or Actor), martyr;
Genesius of Arles, martyr; Patricia, virgin; Mennas, bishop;
Ebba, virgin; Gregory of Utrecht, abbot; Joan Antide-Thouret, virgin;
Mary Michaela Desmaisières, virgin.

Ending of the General Council of Nicaea, which settled the rules for the computation of Easter, 325. ¶ Incorporation of the Honourable Artillery Company by Henry VIII of England, 1537. ¶ Uruguay establishes independence from Brazil, 1825. ¶ Clio (Asteroid 84) discovered by R. Luther, 1865. ¶ Tientsin taken by Anglo-French troops in China, 1860. ¶ National Government formed in Britain by Ramsay McDonald, 1931. ¶ A sniper assassinates George Lincoln Rockwell of the American Nazi Party at Arlington in Virginia, 1967.

BORN: Ivan IV (Ivan the Terrible), Tsar of Russia, Moscow, 1530. Johann Herder, critic, theologian and poet, *Outlines of a Philosophy of the History of Man,* Mohrungen, Germany, 1744. Allan Pinkerton, founder of the Pinkerton National Detective Agency, Glasgow, Scotland, 1819. Bret Harte, writer, poet and editor, *Condensed Novels,* Albany, New York, 1836. Leonard Bernstein, composer and conductor, *West Side Story,* Massachusetts, 1918. George Corley Wallace, Governor of Alabama, Alabama, 1919.

DIED: Louis IX of France; from the plague, Tunis, 1270. Sir Henry Morgan, buccaneer, Lieutenant-Governor of Jamaica, Jamaica, 1688. David Hume, philosopher and historian, *Treatise on Human Nature,* Edinburgh, 1776. Jean Portalis, jurist, principally responsible for drafting the *Code Napoleon,* Paris, 1807. James Watt, engineer, inventor and industrialist, perfected the steam engine, Heathfield, near Birmingham, 1819. Sir William Herschel, astronomer, organist, discovered the planet Uranus, 1822. Michael Faraday, physicist, discoverer of electro-magnetic induction, 1867. Friedrich Nietzsche, philosopher and writer, *Thus Spake Zarathustra, The Will to Power,* Weimar, Germany, 1900. Henri Fantin-Latour, artist, 1904. Gregori Zinoviev, revolutionary and politician, executed, Moscow, 1936. Alfred Charles Kinsey, American statistician and writer, 1956.

AUGUST 26

Feasts of SS: Zephyrinus, pope and martyr; Elizabeth Bichier des Ages, virgin.

Julius Caesar lands on the coast of Britain, 55BC. ¶ Edward III defeats the French at the battle of Crécy, 1346. ¶ Frederick II of Prussia defeats the Russians at Zorndorff (Seven Years War), 1758. ¶ Algiers bombarded, 1826. ¶ Britain and China conclude a Peace Treaty, 1842. ¶ 19th Amendment (Article XIX) to the Constitution of the US becomes effective, women are enfranchised, 1920. ¶ Anglo-Egyptian peace treaty is signed in London, 1936.

BORN: Sir Robert Walpole, Whig statesman and British 'prime minister', Houghton, Norfolk, 1676. Johann Heinrich Lambert, mathematician, France, 1728. Joseph Michel Montgolfier, balloonist and paper manufacturer, Annonay, France, 1740. Antoine Laurent Lavoisier, chemist, Paris, 1743. Albert, Prince Consort, husband of Queen Victoria of England, Bavaria, 1819. Lee De Forest, American radio and television inventor, 1873. John Buchan (Lord Tweedsmuir), novelist, *The 39 Steps*, *Prester John*, Perthshire, 1875. Guillaume Apollinaire, poet, *Alcools*, 1880. Jules Romains (Louis Farigoule), novelist, dramatist and poet, *The Boys in the Back Room*, *Men of Good Will*, Saint Julien, Chapteuil, France, 1885. Christopher Isherwood, poet and novelist, *Mr Norris Changes Trains*, *Goodbye to Berlin*, High Lane, Cheshire, 1904.

DIED: Ottokar II, King of Bohemia, 1278. Anton van Leeuwenhoek, microscopist, *Opera*, Netherlands, 1723. Count Alessandro di Cagliostro, mountebank of international repute, 1795. William James, psychologist and philosopher, *Principles of Psychology*, *The Varieties of Religious Experience*, 1910. Lon Chaney, film actor, 1930. Frank Harris, Irish writer, journalist and editor, 1931. Ralph Vaughan Williams, composer, *Fantasia on a Theme of Thomas Tallis*, *Antarctica Symphony*, London, 1958. Sir Francis Chichester, sailor, circumnavigated the world alone in 1966–7, 1972.

AUGUST 27

Feasts of SS: Joseph Calasanctius; Marcellus and his Companions, martyrs;
Poemen, abbot; Caesarius of Arles, bishop; Syagrius, bishop;
Little St Hugh of Lincoln; Margaret the Barefooted, widow.

The first hydrogen-filled balloon, flown to a height of over 3,000 feet by Jacques Charles in Paris, 1783. ¶ The Declaration of the Rights of Man is adopted by the French Assembly, 1789. ¶ The 'Moray Floods' in Scotland with the Spey and Findhorn bursting their banks, many lives lost (also on 3 and 4 August), 1829. ¶ The eruption of Krakatoa in Indonesia results in upwards of 35,000 people perishing, 1883. ¶ Inauguration of the telegraphic cable between Lisbon and the Azores, 1893. ¶ The first aeroplane with turbo-jet engines was tested, in Germany, 1939.

BORN: Alexander Farnese, Duke of Parma, Spanish soldier, Rome, 1545. Georg Wilhelm Friedrich Hegel, philosopher, *The Phenomenology of the Spirit*, Stuttgart, Germany, 1770. Karl Haushofer, German officer and geographer, Munich, 1869. Theodore Dreiser, novelist, *Sister Carrie*, Indiana, 1871. Karl Bosch, pioneered the industrial production of nitrogenous fertilizers, Nobel Prize for Chemistry, Cologne, 1874. Samuel Goldwyn, American film producer, Warsaw, Poland, 1884. C. S. Forester, popular novelist, *Hornblower* series, Cairo, 1899. Sir Donald Bradman, cricketer, Australia, 1908. Lyndon B. Johnson, US President, Texas, 1908.

DIED: Titian (Tiziano Vecelli), Venetian painter, Venice, 1576. Lope de Vega, dramatist and poet, *Fuenteovejuna, Las almenas de Toro*, Madrid, 1635. James Thomson, poet, *The Seasons, The Castle of Indolence*, wrote *Rule, Britannia*, Richmond, Surrey, 1748. Eugène Fromentin, novelist and painter, 1876. Louis Botha, soldier, Premier of the Union of South Africa, 1919. Dame Ivy Compton-Burnett, English novelist, 1969. Haile Selassie, Emperor of Ethiopia, 1975.

AUGUST 28

Feasts of SS: Augustine, bishop and doctor; Hermes, martyr;
Julian of Brioude, martyr; Alexander, John III and Paul IV, bishops;
Moses the Black; The London Martyrs of 1588.

Venice is taken by the Austrians after a siege, 1849. ¶ Cetywayo taken by the British in the Zulu War, 1879. ¶ Raid on the Bight of Heligoland by the Royal Navy, 1914. ¶ War on Germany declared by Italy, 1916. ¶ US forces under General Marshall land in Japan and Allied occupation begins, 1945. ¶ 200,000 blacks in peaceful civil rights demonstration in Washington, 1963. ¶ Severe earthquakes in Mexico, over 500 people killed, 1973.

BORN: Johann Wolfgang von Goethe, poet, novelist, dramatist, Germany, 1749. Antoine Cournot, mathematician and economist, France, 1801. Joseph Sheridan Le Fanu, novelist, *Uncle Silas*, *In a Glass Darkly*, Dublin, 1814. Count Leo Tolstoy, novelist and philosopher, *War and Peace*, *Anna Karenina*, Yasnaya Polyana, Tula, Russia, 1828. Sir Edward Burne-Jones, painter, Birmingham, England, 1833. George Whipple, physician, Nobel Prize winner, New Hampshire, 1878. C. Wright Mills, Marxist sociologist, *The Power Elite*, Waco, Texas, 1916.

DIED: St Augustine of Hippo, theologian, 430. Louis II the German, King of the East Franks, Frankfurt, 876. Hugo Grotius, jurist and lawyer, *On the Law of War and Peace*, Rostock, Germany, 1645. Leigh Hunt, essayist and poet, *A Jar of Honey from Mount Hybla*, Putney, Surrey, 1859.

AUGUST 29

The Feast of the Beheading of St John the Baptist.
Feasts of SS: Sabina, martyr; Medericus, or Merry, abbot.

Edward III defeats the Spanish fleet of 40 large ships off the British coast at Winchelsea, 1350. ¶ The Hungarians are defeated by the Turks at Mohaez, 1526. ¶ The British Factory Act is passed regulating the employment of children, 1833. ¶ British forces defeat Boers at Boomplatz, 1848. ¶ Galatea (Asteroid 74) discovered by M. Tempel, 1862. ¶ Garibaldi is captured by Royalist troops after planning to take Rome, 1862. ¶ Germany declares a state of emergency as a result of economic crisis, 1921. ¶ Hydrogen bomb exploded by USSR, 1953. ¶ Assassination of the premier of Jordan, Hazza El-Majali, 1960.

BORN: Jean Baptiste Colbert, statesman, founded the French navy, 1619. John Locke, philosopher, *Essay Concerning Human Understanding*, Somerset, 1632. Jean Ingres, artist, Montauban, France, 1780. Oliver Wendell Holmes, physician and writer, *The Autocrat of the Breakfast Table*, Cambridge, Massachusetts, 1809. John Leech, artist and illustrator, London, 1817. Maurice Maeterlinck, poet, dramatist and author, *The Blue Bird*, *The Life of the Bee*, Ghent, 1862. Ingrid Bergman, actress, Stockholm, 1915.

DIED: Louis II, King of Hungary, Mohács, Hungary, 1526. John Lilburne, leader of the Levellers, Eltham, Kent, 1657. Edmond Hoyle, card player and popularizer of whist, *Short Treatise on Whist*, London, 1769. Christian Schonbein, chemist, invented gun-cotton, near Baden-Baden, Austria, 1868. Cesare Pavese, novelist and translator, *La Bella Estate*, *Notte di Festa*, Torino, 1950. Éamon De Valera, Irish statesman, Ireland, 1975.

AUGUST 30

Dies Mala or 'Egyptian Day', considered unlucky in the Middle Ages.
Liberation Day, Hong Kong (liberated from Japanese occupation in 1945).
Victory Day, Turkey. Huey P. Long Day, Louisiana, USA
(State Governor born 1893). Feasts of SS: Rose of Lima, virgin;
Felix and Adauctus, martyrs; Pammachius; Rumon, or Ruan; Fantinus, abbot.

The French defeat Frederick II of Prussia's forces at Johannisberg, 1762. ¶ John C. Frémont, Union commander of the West declares martial law and frees slaves throughout the state of Missouri, 1861. ¶ The Union is defeated at the second battle of Bull Run, by Thomas 'Stonewall' Jackson of the Confederacy, 1862. ¶ Miskolcz in Hungary is completely destroyed by a waterspout, many hundreds of persons are killed, 1878. ¶ German forces take Amiens, 1914. ¶ Beginning of the siege of Leningrad by German forces, 1941.

BORN: Jacques David, French Neo-classical artist, Paris, 1748. Mary Wollstonecraft Shelley, novelist, wife of Percy Bysshe Shelley, *Frankenstein, The Last Man*, London, 1797. Friedrich Ratzel, geographer, *Anthropogeographie*, Germany, 1844. Huey Long, Governor of Louisiana, 1893. John Gunther, journalist and writer, *Inside*-series, Chicago, Illinois, 1901.

DIED: Theodoric the Great, founder of the Ostrogoth line, ruler of Italy, Ravenna, Italy, 526. Louis XI of France, 1483. Feargus O'Connor, Chartist leader, London, 1855. Georges Sorel, syndicalist and philosopher, *Reflections on Violence*, Boulogne-sur-Seine, France, 1922. Henri Barbusse, novelist, *Under Fire, Hell*, 1935. Sir Joseph John Thomson, physicist, discovered the electron, Nobel Prize for Physics, Cambridge, 1940.

AUGUST 31

Independence Day, Trinidad and Tobago (1962). Feasts of SS:
Raymund Nonnatus; Paulinus of Trier, bishop; Aidan of Lindisfarne, bishop.

Gaius arrives back in Rome after expedition to the English Channel and neighbouring regions, 40. ¶ Siege of San Sebastian begins, 1813. ¶ The Trocadero is stormed by the French and they enter Cadiz, 1823. ¶ Earthquakes in America, particularly in South Carolina, Georgia and Alabama. The city of Charleston is almost completely destroyed, 1886. ¶ Murder of Mary Ann Nichols, first victim of Jack the Ripper, 1888. ¶ Beginning of evacuation of women and children from London begins, 1939.

BORN: Jahangir, Mogul Emperor of India, 1569. Theophile Gautier, poet and author, France, 1811. Hermann von Helmholtz, scientist, invented the opthalmoscope, Potsdam, Germany, 1821. Maria Montessori, educator and teacher, *The Montessori Method*, Chiaravelle, Italy, 1870. Fredric March, actor, Racine, Wisconsin, 1897. Sir Bernard Lovell, astronomer, Gloucestershire, 1913.

DIED: Henry V, King of England (1413–22), Vincennes, France, 1422. John Bunyan, preacher and writer, *Pilgrim's Progress*, 1688. Arthur Phillip, founded the penal colony at Sydney in Australia, first Governor of New South Wales, Bath, Somerset, 1814. Charles Baudelaire, poet, *Les Fleurs du Mal*, 1867. Georges Braque, Cubist painter, 1963. John Ford, film director, *Stagecoach*, *The Informer*, 1973.

SEPTEMBER

THIRTY DAYS

When the old Roman year began in March this was the
seventh (*septem*) month, thus September.

SEPTEMBER 1

New Year's Day in the Greek or Byzantine (Constantinople)
Indication, used by the Popes until 1087. Libyan Revolution
Anniversary, Arab Republic of Egypt. Independence Day, Qatar (1971).
Feasts of SS: Giles, abbot; The Twelve Brothers, martyrs;
Verena, virgin; Lupus, or Leu, of Sens, bishop; Fiacre; Sebbe; Drithelm.

Accession of Henry VI of England (deposed 4 March 1461, restored 9 October 1470, deposed 14 April 1471), 1422. ¶ Montrose defeats the Covenanters at Tippermuir in Scotland, 1644. ¶ The British ship *Coronation*, with 90 guns, founders off Ramhead and sinks, the crew is saved, 1691. ¶ Hyderabad Treaty between Britain and the Nizam, 1798. ¶ Juno (Asteroid 3) discovered by Harding, 1804. ¶ Euphrosyne (Asteroid 31) discovered by James Ferguson, 1854. ¶ The Confederacy abandons Atlanta, Georgia, 1864. ¶ Prussia wins the battle at Sedan with the French, 1870. ¶ Peace treaty signed with the Zulus by Britain, 1879. ¶ The Provinces of Alberta and Saskatchewan are established in Canada, 1905. ¶ Germany invades Poland, 1939. ¶ Foundation of Communist North China People's Republic, 1948.

BORN: Giacomo Torelli, theatrical designer, Italy, 1608. Baron Carl Auer von Welsbach, chemist and physicist, invented the gas mantle for illumination, Vienna, 1858. Adolph Appia, theatrical designer, Geneva, 1862. Sir Roger Casement, Irish nationalist and diplomat, Dublin, 1864. James Corbett (Gentleman Jim), pugilist and prize fighter, San Francisco, 1866. Edgar Rice Burroughs, popular writer, creator of Tarzan, Chicago, 1875. Walter Philip Reuther, US labour leader, Wheeling, West Virginia, 1907.

DIED: Pope Adrian (or Hadrian) IV, the only English-born pope, 1159. Marin Mersenne, mathematician, Paris, 1648. Louis XIV of France, Versailles, 1715. Sir Richard Steele, essayist and dramatist, Carmarthen, Wales, 1729. William Clark, explored north-west US, 1838. Samuel Coleridge-Taylor, composer, 1912. Ilya Grigoryevich Ehrenburg, novelist and poet, 1967. Siegfried Sassoon, poet and writer, *Counter-Attack*, *Memoirs of a Fox-Hunting Man*, Wiltshire, 1967. François Mauriac, novelist, poet and biographer, *The Desert of Love*, *The Dark Angels*, Paris, 1970.

SEPTEMBER 2

Day of Revelation of Koran, Malaysia. Independence Day,
Socialist Republic of Vietnam, Feasts of SS: Stephens of Hungary;
Antoninus, martyr; Castor, bishop; Agricolus, bishop;
William of Roskilde, bishop; Brocard.

Cicero's first *Philippic* proclaimed in Rome, 44BC. ¶ Defeat of Antony at Actium by Octavius, 31BC. ¶ The Great Fire of London begins at Farriner's bakehouse, 1666. ¶ British begin bombardment of Copenhagen, 1807. ¶Union forces under General Sherman enter Atlanta, Georgia, 1864. ¶ National Service Bill in Britain conscripting men between the ages of 19 and 41 comes into force, 1939. ¶ Ho Chi Minh is made President of the newly-formed Vietnam Republic, 1945. ¶ Dr Henry Verwoerd becomes Prime Minister of South Africa, 1958.

BORN: John Howard, prison reformer and philanthropist, London, 1726. Giovanni Verga, novelist and dramatist, *The Vanquished, Mastro Don Gesualdo,* Catania, Sicily, 1840. Frederick Soddy, chemist and physicist, Eastbourne, Sussex, 1877. Sir Robert Bruce Lockhart, diplomat and writer, Scotland, 1887.

DIED: Jusepe de Ribera, painter, Naples, 1652. Thomas Telford, road, bridge and canal builder, London, 1834. Henri Rousseau (*Le Douanier*), French primitive painter, Paris, 1910. Henry Hertzberg Lawson, Australian writer, *Joe Wilson and his Mates,* 1922. John Ronald Reuel Tolkien, philologist and writer, *The Lord of the Rings,* Bournemouth, England, 1973.

SEPTEMBER 3

*Dies Mala or 'Egyptian Day', considered unlucky in the Middle Ages.
Day of the Liberation of Monaco, Monaco. National Holiday of
Commemoration, Tunisia. Feasts of SS: Pius X, pope; Phoebe;
Macanisius, bishop; Simeon Stylites the Younger; Remaclus, bishop;
Aigulf, martyr; Hildelitha, virgin; Cuthburga, widow.*

The limit of British legal memory is dated back to this day in 1189. ¶ Accession of Richard I of England, 1189. ¶ Cromwell defeats the Scots at Dunbar, 1650. ¶ Cromwell defeats Charles II at Worcester, 1651. ¶ Oliver Cromwell succeeded by his son, Richard, as protector, 1658. ¶ What should have been this day in England in 1752 became, instead, the 14 September when the Julian calendar was replaced with the Gregorian reckoning, 1752. ¶ The Peace of Versailles between USA, Britain, France, and Spain. The independence of USA is recognized by Britain, 1783. ¶ The British legation at Kabul is massacred by Afghans, 1879. ¶ The French government moves to Bordeaux, 1914. ¶ German forces cross the River Marne, 1914. ¶ The Mexican Government is recognized by the US, 1923. ¶ Two French pilots, Diedonné Coste and Maurice Bellonte, arrive in New York after completing the first Paris–New York non-stop flight, 1930. ¶ War is declared on Germany by Britain and France, 1939. ¶ The *Athenia* is sunk off the coast of Ireland by Germany, 1939. ¶ *Special Delivery Stomp, Summit Ridge Drive* and other tracks recorded by Artie Shaw and his Gramercy Five, Hollywood, 1940. ¶ Allied invasion of Italy begins, 1943. ¶ The US *Viking II* touches down on the planet Mars, 1976.

BORN: James Sylvester, mathematician, London, 1814. Louis Henri Sullivan, architect of the 'Chicago school', Boston, Massachusetts, 1856. Jean Jaurès, socialist writer and orator, Castres, France, 1859. Sir Frank Macfarlane Burnet, immunologist, Nobel Prize winner, Australia, 1899. Carl David Anderson, nuclear physicist, New York, 1905.

DIED: Seleucus IV, Philopator, King of Syria, assassinated, 175 BC. Gian Galeazzo Visconti, Duke of Milan, Melegnano, Italy, 1402. Sir Edward Coke, jurist and statesman, 1634. Oliver Cromwell, Lord Protector of England, 1658. Louis Adolphe Thiers, President of France, near Paris, 1877. Sir Arthur Streeton, Australian painter, 1943. Eduard Beneš, Czech statesman, 1948. E. E. Cummings, American poet, 1962. Louis MacNeice, poet and broadcaster, London, 1963. Ho Chi Minh, Vietnamese revolutionary leader, 1969.

SEPTEMBER 4

Feasts of SS: Marcellus and Valerian, martyrs; Marinus; Boniface I, pope;
Ultan, bishop; Ida of Herzfeld, widow; Rosalia, virgin;
Rose of Viterbo, virgin.

Mahomet II repulsed at Belgrade, 1456. ¶ States of Holland sign commerce treaty with America, 1778. ¶ Annexation of Avignon by France, 1791. ¶ First disclosure of the corruption in the municipal government of New York (the 'Tammany frauds'), 1871. ¶ Rheims is occupied by German forces, 1916. ¶ Dar-es-Salaam taken by British forces, 1916. ¶ De-segregation of schools in Birmingham, Alabama, results in riots, 1963. ¶ The US swimmer Mark Spitz becomes the first man to win seven Olympic gold medals, 1972.

BORN: Robert Raikes, founded and promoted Sunday schools, Gloucester, 1736. François René de Chateaubriand, politician and writer, *Les Mémoires d'outre-tombe*, France, 1768. Anton Bruckner, composer, Austria, 1824. Darius Milhaud, composer, *La Creation du Monde*, Aix-en-Provence, France, 1892. Antonin Artaud, stage director and dramatist, France, 1896. Edward Dmytryk, film director, *Crossfire*, *Obsession*, Grand Forks, North Dakota, 1908. Richard Wright, novelist and essayist, *Native Son*, *Black Boy*, near Natchez, Mississippi, 1908.

DIED: James Wyatt, architect, built and designed Fonthill Abbey, near Marl-borough, Berkshire, 1813. Edvard Grieg, composer, *Peer Gynt*, *Holberg Suite*, Bergen, Norway, 1907. Albert Schweitzer, philosopher, musician and mission-ary, *The Quest of the Historical Jesus*, *On the Edge of the Primeval Forest*, Lambarene, Gabon Republic, 1965.

SEPTEMBER 5

Settlers Day, Republic of South Africa. Feasts of SS:
Laurence Giustiniani, bishop; Bertinus, abbot.

First meeting of the Continental Congress, in Philadelphia, 1774. ¶ Malta captured by the British, 1800. ¶ First train passes through the Severn Tunnel at Bristol, 1885. ¶ William McKinley, President of the United States, fatally wounded by Leon Czolgosz at Buffalo, New York (McKinley dies nine days later on 14 September), 1901. ¶ Beginning of the first Marne battle (ends 12 September), 1914. ¶ Arab terrorists, members of the Black September group, kill eleven Israelis at the Olympic Games in Germany, 1972.

BORN: Louis XIV of France, 1638. Johann Christian Bach, composer, a son of J. S. Bach, Leipzig, 1735. Mikhail Kutuzov, Prince of Smolensk, Russian military commander, St Petersburg, 1745. Caspar David Friedrich, Romantic landscape painter, Germany, 1774. Giacomo Meyerbeer, operatic composer, near Berlin, 1791. Victorien Sardou, dramatist, *A Scrap of Paper, Fedora*, Paris, 1831. Jesse James, outlaw and robber, Missouri, 1847. Arthur Koestler, novelist and writer, *Darkness at Noon*, Hungary, 1905.

DIED: Edmund Bonner, Bishop of London, Marshalsea Prison, 1569. Jean François Regnard, poet and dramatist, *Le Divorce*, near Paris, 1709. John Home, cleric and writer, *Douglas*, Edinburgh, 1808. Dr William Mcgillivray, naturalist and writer, *Lives of Eminent Zoologists, from Aristotle to Linnaeus*, Aberdeen, 1852. Charles Péguy, poet and sociologist, near Valleroy, France, 1914.

SEPTEMBER 6

Defence of Pakistan Day, Pakistan (1965, attacked by India).
Independence Day, Swaziland. Feasts of SS: Donatian, Laetus and others,
bishops and martyrs; Eleutherius, abbot; Chainoaldus, or
Cagnoald, bishop; Bega, or Bee, virgin.

Richard I defeats the Saracens at Arsouf, 1191. ¶ The Cape of Good Hope is occupied by British forces under James Craig, 1795. ¶ Aurora (Asteroid 94) discovered by J. C. Watson, 1867. ¶ First British telephone exchange opens, at Lombard Street in the City of London, 1879. ¶ *Jersey Lightning* and other titles recorded in New York City by Luis Russell and his Orchestra (with Albert Nicholas, Henry Allen, etc.), 1929. ¶ South Africa declares war on Germany, Hertzog resigns in protest and General Smuts takes over as Premier, 1939. ¶ The first Canadian television broadcasts, from Montreal, 1952. ¶ The Prime Minister of South Africa, Dr Verwoerd, is assassinated in Parliament at Cape Town, 1966. ¶ Independence in Swaziland proclaimed, 1968.

BORN: Sebastiano Serlio, architect, Bologna, Italy, 1475. Marie Joseph, Marquis de Lafayette, statesman and soldier, Auvergne, France, 1757. John Dalton, chemist and physicist, Cumberland, 1766. J. J. R. Macleod, joint-discoverer of the insulin treatment for diabetes, Perthshire, 1876. Joseph P. Kennedy, diplomat and financier, Massachusetts, 1888. Sir Edward Appleton, physicist, Yorkshire, 1892.

DIED: Suleiman the Magnificent, Sultan of Turkey, Hungary, 1566. Jean Baptiste Colbert, statesman, founded the French navy, 1685. Edmund Gibson, Bishop of Lincoln and of London, jurist, Bath, 1748. George Alexander Stevens, comic writer, 1784. Hendrik Freusch Verwoerd, Prime Minister of the Republic of South Africa, assassinated, Cape Town, 1966.

SEPTEMBER 7

Independence Day, Brazil (proclaimed by Dom Pedro in 1822).
Feasts of SS: Regina, or Reine, virgin and martyr; Sozon, martyr;
Grimonia, virgin and martyr; John of Nicomedia, martyr; Anastasius
the Fuller, martyr; Clodoald, or Cloud; Alcmund and Tilbert, bishops.

French defeated by Prince Eugène at Turin, 1706. ¶ The Danes surrender to the British at Copenhagen, 1807. ¶ Moscow abandoned after the Russian defeat at Borodino, 1812. ¶ Serfdom is abolished in Austria, 1848. ¶ Garibaldi enters Naples, 1860. ¶ Hera (Asteroid 103) discovered by J. C. Watson, 1868. ¶ The Boxer Rising in China ends with the Peace of Peking, 1901. ¶ End of the Allied retreat from Mons (began 24 August), 1914.

BORN: Thomas Erastus, theologian, Switzerland, 1524. Elizabeth I of England, 1533. Stephen Hales, clergyman, inventor and chemist, *Vegetable Staticks*, Bekesbourne, Kent, 1677. Comte George Louis Buffon, naturalist, France, 1707. William Butterfield, architect of the Gothic Revival in England, London, 1814. Ferdinand von Hebra, physician, researched skin diseases, Czechoslovakia, 1816. Henry Campbell-Bannerman, Liberal, British Prime Minister, Glasgow, 1836. C. J. Dennis, Australian poet, 1876. Dame Edith Sitwell, poet and writer, *Clowns' Houses, The English Eccentrics*, Scarborough, Yorkshire, 1887.

DIED: Frederick IV of Germany, 1493. Catharine Parr, wife of Henry VIII, 1548. Hannah More, writer and social reformer, *The Religion of the Fashionable World*, Clifton, Bristol, 1833. John Greenleaf Whittier, Quaker poet and essayist, *At Sundown, Legends of New England in Prose and Verse*, Massachusetts, 1892. William Holman Hunt, painter, a member of the Pre-Raphaelite Brotherhood, London, 1910.

SEPTEMBER 8

*The Feast of the Birthday of the Blessed Virgin Mary: it originated in
the Eastern church and has been observed in the West since about the
year 600. National Day, Andorra. The Commemoration of the Two Sieges,
Malta (Malta's National Day, besieged by the Turks in 1565 for
three months without success, June to September, and by the Germans
in 1942). Feasts of SS: Adrian and Natalia, martyrs; Eusebius,
Nestabus, Zeno and Nestor, martyrs; Disibod; Sergius I, pope;
Corbinian, bishop.*

Greene defeated at Eutaw Springs, North Carolina, by Cornwallis, 1781.
¶ William IV of Great Britain crowned, 1831. ¶ Sirona (Asteroid 116) discovered by C. H. F. Peters, 1871. ¶ Proclamation of the Witwatersrand goldfields in South Africa, 1886. ¶ A great hurricane and tidal wave at Galveston in Texas results in over 4,500 deaths, 1900. ¶ General Smuts becomes Prime Minister of the Union of South Africa, 1919. ¶ Senator Huey P. Long of Louisiana shot by Dr Carl A. Weiss at Baton Rouge (Long dies 10 September), 1935. ¶ First landing in Britain of a German V-2 rocket, 1944. ¶ President Gerald Ford pardons former President Richard M. Nixon for all offences he may have committed in the Watergate Affair, 1974.

BORN: Richard I, King of England, Oxford, 1157. Ludovico Ariosto, poet, *Orlando Furioso*, Italy, 1474. Prince de Condé, Louis II de Bourbon, military commander, Paris, 1621. August Wilhelm Schlegel, poet, critic and scholar, *Dramatic Art and Literature*, Hanover, 1767. Frédéric Mistral, Provençal poet, *Lou Pouème dou Rose, Lis Isclo d'Or*, Nobel Prize for Literature, France, 1830. Antonin Dvořák, composer, *Slavonic Dances*, Bohemia, 1841. Viktor Meyer, chemist, Berlin, 1848. Alfred Jarry, dramatist and poet, founder of pataphysics, *Ubu Roi*, France, 1873. Siegfried Sassoon, poet and writer, *Counter-Attack, Memoirs of a Fox-Hunting Man*, Kent, 1886. Hendrik Freusch Verwoerd, Prime Minister of the Republic of South Africa, Amsterdam, Holland, 1901.

DIED: Francisco Gómez de Quevado y Villegas, satirist and poet, *El Buscón, Sueños*, Spain, 1645. Ann Lee, religious teacher, founded a colony of Shakers in the US, 1784. Joseph Lioville, mathematician, Paris, 1882. Hermann von Helmholtz, scientist, invented the opthalmoscope, Charlottenburg, Germany, 1894. Richard Strauss, composer, *Thus Spake Zarathustra, Salome*, Garmisch-Parten-kirchen, West Germany, 1949. André Derain, Fauvist painter, 1954.

National Holiday, Bulgaria. Feasts of SS: Gorgonius, martyr;
Issac, or Sahak, the Great, bishop; Kieran, or Ciaran, abbot;
Audomarus, or Omer, bishop; Bettelin; Peter Claver.

The English defeat the Scots at Flodden, 1513. ¶ Accession of James V of Scotland, 1513. ¶ San Sebastian capitulates to the Duke of Wellington, 1813. ¶ The British Municipal Corporations Act establishes modern local government in Britain, 1835. ¶ California made a US state (31st), 1850. ¶ Meletè (Asteroid 47) discovered by H. Goldschmidt, 1857. ¶ Danae (Asteroid 59) discovered by H. Goldschmidt, 1860. ¶ Fifth satellite of Jupiter discovered, (V) Amalthea, by Dr Barnard at Lick Observatory, 1892. ¶ International Conference in London on non-intervention in the Spanish Civil War, 1936. ¶ Prince Sihanouk returned to Phnom Penh in Cambodia after five years' exile in Peking, 1975.

BORN: Duc de Richelieu, cardinal and statesman in the reign of Louis XIII, Richelieu, France, 1585. Luigi Galvani, anatomist, Italy, 1737. William Bligh, captain of the *Bounty*, Cornwall, 1754. Max Reinhardt, stage and film director and producer, Baden, Austria, 1873. Cesare Pavese, novelist and translator, *La Bella Estate, Notte di Festa*, Italy, 1908. John Grey Gorton, Australian Prime Minister, Australia, 1911.

DIED: William (I) the Conqueror, King of England, Rouen, France, 1087. Tobias Smollett, novelist, *Roderick Random, Peregrine Pickle*, near Leghorn, Italy, 1771. Shaka, King of the Zulus; assassinated, Natal, 1828. Stéphane Mallarmé, Symbolist poet, *L'Après-midi d'un faune*, Fontainebleau, 1898. Henri de Toulouse-Lautrec, painter, lithographer and graphic designer, Malrome, France, 1901. Mao Tse-Tung, Chairman of the Central Committee of the Chinese Communist Party, China, 1976.

SEPTEMBER 10

National Day, Belize (sometimes 11 September). National Holiday, Bulgaria.
Feasts of SS: Nicholas of Tolentino; Nemesian and many Companions,
martyrs; Menodora, Metrodora and Nymphodora, virgins and martyrs;
Pulcheria, virgin; Finnian of Moville, bishop; Salvius of Albi, bishop;
Theodard, bishop; Aubert, bishop.

Wallace defeats the English at Cambuskenneth, Scotland, 1297. ¶ The English defeat the Scots at Pinkey, 1547. ¶ Bolivar becomes dictator of Peru, 1823. ¶ The Treaty of Tangier ends French war with Morocco, 1844. ¶ Alexandra (Asteroid 55) discovered by H. Goldschmidt and Pandora (Asteroid 56), by Searle, 1858. ¶ British government's economic measures result in riots in London and Glasgow, 1931. ¶ Canada declares war on Germany, 1939. ¶ The 'puppet' premier of Norway Vidkun Quisling is sentenced to death for collaboration, 1945.

BORN: John Needham, scientist and cleric, London, 1713. Sir John Soane, architect, Goring, Oxfordshire, 1753. Mungo Park, African explorer, near Selkirk, Scotland, 1771. Jacques Boucher de Crêvecoeur de Perthes, Palaeolithic archaeologist, France, 1788. Charles Peirce, philosopher and scientist, Cambridge, Massachusetts, 1839. Robert Koldewey, archaeologist, excavated Babylon, Germany, 1855. Arthur Holly Compton, American physicist, Ohio, 1892. Cyril Connolly, critic and essayist, Coventry, 1903. Robert Wise, film director and producer, *West Side Story*, Winchester, Connecticut, 1914. Arnold Palmer, golfer, Youngstown, Pennsylvania, 1929.

DIED: Dr Edward Pococke, orientalist and scholar, Professor of Arabic at Oxford, 1691. Dr Thomas Sheridan, scholar and translator, friend of Dean Swift, 1738. Mary Wollstonecraft, writer, wife of William Godwin, *Vindication of the Rights of Woman*, London, 1797. Ugo Foscolo, Italian novelist and poet, 1827. Captain William Hobson, first Governor of New Zealand, 1842. Huey Long, Governor of Louisiana, 1935.

SEPTEMBER 11

*National Day, Belize (sometimes 10 September). New Year's Day[1]
and Anniversary of the Reunion of Eritrea with Ethiopia, Ethiopia
(Eritrea was handed over by the UN in 1952). Anniversary of the Death
of the Leader (Quaid-i-Azam), Pakistan (Muhammad ali Jinnah,
statesman, 1876–1948). Feasts of SS: Protus and Hyacinth, martyrs;
Theodora of Alexandria; Paphnutius, bishop; Patiens of Lyons, bishop;
Deiniol, bishop; Peter of Chavanon.*

The Duke of Marlborough is victorious at the battle of Malplaquet, 1709.
¶ Americans defeated at Brandywine, Pennsylvania, by General Howe, 1777.
¶ US captures British flotilla on Lake Champlain, 1814. ¶ Mehemet Ali
bombarded in Beirut by British forces, 1840. ¶ Sebastopol is taken by the Allies
after capitulation by the Russians, 1855. ¶ Liberatrix (Asteroid 125) discovered
by Prosper Henry, 1872. ¶ Cholera panic on Long Island, New York; an
armed mob prevents foreigners landing on Fire Island, 1892. ¶ Britain declares
mandate in Palestine, 1922. ¶ A French nuclear bomb was exploded in the
South Pacific, over Mururao, 1966. ¶ Indian and Chinese troops engaged in
heavy fighting on the border of Sikkim, 1967. ¶ Assassination (?) of President
Allende of Chile during a military *coup*, 1973.

BORN: Pierre de Ronsard, poet, *Odes, Amours de Cassandre*, Vendôme, France,
1524. Vicomte de Turenne, Marshal-General of France, Sedan, France, 1611.
James Thomson, poet, *The Seasons, The Castle of Indolence*, wrote *Rule, Britannia*,
Roxburgh, Scotland, 1700. O. Henry (William Sydney Porter), short-story
writer, *The Four Million, Gift of the Magi*, Greensboro, North Carolina, 1862.
Sir James Jeans, mathematician, cosmologist and astronomer, *The Mysterious
Universe, The Stars in their Courses*, London, 1877. David Herbert Lawrence,
novelist and critic, *Sons and Lovers, The Rainbow*, near Nottingham, 1885.
Acharya Vinoba Bhave, philosopher and reformer, disciple of Gandhi, India,
1895.

DIED: Thomas Graham, chemist, 1869. Antero Tarquínio de Quental, Portu-
guese poet, *Sonetos Completos, Raios de Extinta Luz*, Porta Delgada, Azores, 1891.
Muhammad ali Jinnah, Governor-General of Pakistan, 1948. Jan Christiaan
Smuts, statesman and soldier, founder of the South African United Party, Irene,
South Africa, 1950. Robert Service, Canadian poet, *Trail of '98*, Lancieux,
France, 1958. Nikita Khrushchev, Soviet statesman and Premier, near Moscow,
1971. Salvador Allende, Chilean statesman; died in a *coup*, 1973.

[1] The Diocletian Era, dated from AD284 when the Roman Emperor Diocletian persecuted
the Christians. Known as the Era of the Martyrs.

SEPTEMBER 12

Nationality Day, Cape Verde Islands. Revolution Day, Ethiopia.
Pioneers Day, Rhodesia. Defenders Day, Maryland, USA. The Feast
of the Holy Name of Mary, of 14th century origin, Pope Innocent XI
extended it to the whole Church in 1683. Feasts of SS: Ailbhe, bishop;
Eanswida, virgin; Guy of Anderlecht.

Albigenses defeated at Muret, 1213. ¶ Drogheda is taken by Cromwell, 1649. ¶ The Turks are defeated by Sobieski at Vienna, 1683. ¶ Olympia (Asteroid 60) discovered by Chacornac, 1860. ¶ Lomia (Asteroid 117) discovered by Alphonse Borelly, 1871. ¶ 'Cleopatra's Needle' erected on the Thames embankment near Charing Cross, 1878. ¶ End of the first Marne battle (began 5 September), 1914. ¶ Italian 'militia' led by Gabriele D'Annunzio (the 'Warrior-Poet') marches on Fiume, 1919. ¶ Little Rock High School in Arkansas is ordered by the US Supreme Court to admit blacks, 1958. ¶ Heavy bombing in Vietnam resumed by order of President Nixon, 1969. ¶ Emperor Hailé Selassié of Ethiopia is deposed by a military *coup*, 1974. ¶ The black student leader Steve Biko dies whilst in the custody of the South African security services, 1977.

BORN: Francis I of France, France, 1494. Richard Marsh Hoe, introduced the rotary printing press, New York City, 1812. Richard Gatling, inventor of the Gatling gun, North Carolina, 1818. Herbert Henry Asquith, Liberal politician and Prime Minister, Yorkshire, 1852. Henry Louis Mencken, journalist, editor, critic and scholar, *The American Language, A Treatise on the Gods*, Baltimore, Maryland, 1880. Maurice Chevalier, singer and entertainer, Paris, 1888. Giuseppe Saragat, socialist President of Italy, Turin, 1898. Dmitri Shostakovich, composer, *The Lady Macbeth of Mtzensk*, St Petersburg, Russia, 1906. Louis MacNeice, poet and broadcaster, Belfast, 1907. Jesse Owens, athlete, Gold Medal winner at the 1936 Olympic Games in Berlin, Danville, Alabama, 1913.

DIED: François Couperin, composer and harpsichordist, 1733. Jean Philippe Rameau, organist and composer, *Castor et Pollux*, Dardanus, Paris, 1764. Gebhard von Blücher, Prussian military commander, 1819. Leonid Andreyev, dramatist, *He Who Gets Slapped*, 1919. Robert Lowell, American poet, 1977.

*Feasts of SS: Maurilius of Angers, bishop; Eulogius of Alexandria, bishop;
Amatus, or Amé, abbot; Amatus, or Amé, bishop.*

Covenanters defeat Montrose at Philiphaugh in Scotland, 1645. ¶ New York becomes the federal capital of US, 1788. ¶ Victoria (Asteroid 12) discovered by J. R. Hind, 1850. ¶ Clymene (Asteroid 104) discovered by J. C. Watson, 1868. ¶ The *Volta*, an electric launch constructed in London, crosses the Channel and back in four hours, powered only by its batteries, 1886. ¶ Beginning of the revolution in San Domingo, 1912. ¶ Major German offensive on Stalingrad begins, 1942. ¶ Mr Vorster is sworn in as Prime Minister of South Africa, 1966. ¶ Violent rioting in Attica State Prison, New York, results in troops being called in, 1971.

BORN: William Cecil, Lord Burghley, Elizabethan statesman, Lincolnshire, 1520. Oliver Evans, American inventor, 1755. Walter Reed, US army surgeon, Belroi, Virginia, 1851. John Joseph Pershing, Commander-in-Chief of US troops in France during the First World War, Missouri, 1860. Arthur Henderson, Labour Party politician and statesman, Nobel Prize for Peace, Glasgow, Scotland, 1863. Arnold Schoenberg, composer, *Moses and Aaron*, Vienna, 1874. Sherwood Anderson, novelist, *Winesburg, Ohio*, Ohio, 1876. J. B. Priestley, author and playwright, *The Good Companions*, *Time and the Conways*, Bradford, Yorkshire, 1894.

DIED: Titus Flavius Sabinus Vespanianus, Roman emperor, Rome (?), 81. Andrea Mantegna, painter, Mantua, 1506. Philip II, King of Spain, El Escorial, near Madrid, 1598. James Wolfe, military commander, conqueror of Quebec; Quebec, Canada, 1759. Charles James Fox, liberal statesman, 1806. Ludwig Feuerbach, philosopher and economist, 1872. Alexandre Herculano, poet, historian and politician, Portugal, 1877. Alexis Emmanuel Chabrier, composer, 1894. August Krogh, Danish physiologist, Nobel Prize winner, 1949. Leopold Stokowski, conductor, 1977.

SEPTEMBER 14

The Feast of the Exaltation of the Holy Cross, celebrating the
veneration of the relics of the True Cross in Jerusalem after their
recovery from the Persians by Heraclius (AD629); observed in the
Western church since the 7th century, possibly earlier; known also as
Holy Cross or Holyrood Day. Anniversary of Cochabama, a
department of Bolivia. Feasts of SS: Maternus, bishop; Notburga, virgin.

The English defeat the Scots at Homildon-hill, 1402. ¶ This day in England in
1752 had been preceded not by 13 September, but by the 2 September. 11 days
were thus 'lost' when the Gregorian calendar replaced the Julian reckoning, 1752.
¶ Napoleon enters Moscow, 1812. ¶ Francis Scott Key composes a poem, 'The
Star-Spangled Banner', 1814. ¶ Mexico City is taken by US forces, 1847. ¶
British and Allied forces land without incident in the Crimea, 1854. ¶ Erato
(Asteroid 61) discovered by Förster and Lessing, 1860. ¶ Eurynome (Asteroid 79)
discovered by James C. Watson, 1863. ¶ Theodore Roosevelt becomes President
of the US, 1901. ¶ Miguel Primo de Rivera begins dictatorship in Spain, 1923.
¶ The US finally joins the International Court of Justice (at The Hague), 1929.
¶ The first landing on the Moon of an Earth-launched space vehicle, the Soviet
probe *Lunik II*, 1959. ¶ Pope Paul VI formally opens the third session of the
Ecumenical Council, Vatican II, 1964. ¶ First canonization of an American
citizen, Mother Elizabeth Seton (1775–1822), 1975.

BORN: Cornelius Agrippa, scholar and astrologer, *The Three Books on Occult*
Philosophy, Cologne, 1486. Luigi Cherubini, operatic composer, Italy, 1760.
Baron Alexander von Humboldt, explorer, naturalist and scientist, *Cosmos*,
Berlin, 1769. Theodor Storm, German poet and novelist, *Immensee, Sunken in*
the Water, Schleswig, 1817. Ivan Pavlov, physiologist and psychologist, Ryazan,
Russia, 1849. Jan Masaryk, Czech Foreign Secretary, Prague, 1886.

DIED: Dante Alighieri, Italian poet, *The Divine Comedy*, 1321. Giovanni Cassini,
astronomer, 1712. Marquis de Montcalm de Saint-Véran, commander of
French forces in Canada; Quebec, 1759. James Fenimore Cooper, novelist,
The Last of the Mohicans, 1851. Augustus Welby Pugin, Victorian Gothic
architect, Ramsgate, Kent, 1852. Arthur Wellesley, Duke of Wellington,
military commander and statesman, Walmer Castle, Kent, 1852. Georges
Leclanché, inventor and engineer, 1882. William McKinley, US President;
assassinated, New York, 1901. Josiah Royce, philosopher and teacher, *The*
Religious Aspect of Philosophy, Cambridge, Massachusetts, 1916. Isadora Duncan,
choreographer, 1927. Thomáš Masaryk, Czech statesman and philosopher,
Lány, 1937.

SEPTEMBER 15

*Battle of Britain Day, recalling the RAF's battle with the Luftwaffe in
1940. Independence Day, El Salvador (1841). Independence Day, Guatemala
(1821). Independence Day, Honduras (1821). Respect for the Aged Day,
Japan. Birthday of the Sultan, Perak state, Malaysia. Independence Day,
Nicaragua (1838). The Feast of the Seven Sorrows of the Blessed Virgin
Mary, known also as the Compassion of Our Lady, first included as a
feast in the Church's calendar in 1727.[1] Feasts of SS: Nicomedes, martyr;
Nicetas the Goth, martyr; Aichardus, or Achard, abbot; Mirin;
Catherine of Genoa, widow.*

The French defeat the Swiss at Marignano, 1515. ¶ New York is taken by
General Howe, 1776. ¶ Guatemala proclaimed independent, 1821. ¶ William
Huskisson, ex-President of the Board of Trade, is the first man to be fatally
injured by a train, George Stephenson's *Rocket*, at the opening of the Liverpool
and Manchester Railway, 1830. ¶ For the week ending on this day, 3,183 people
had died in London of Asiatic cholera, 1849. ¶ Aglaia (Asteroid 48) discovered
by R. Luther, 1857. ¶ Echo (Asteroid 62), originally named Titania, discovered
by James Ferguson, 1860. ¶ German evacuation of France, 1873. ¶ Violent
eruptions of Mount Vesuvius result in seven new craters being formed, 1898.
¶ The first tanks were used in battle, at Flers in the Somme Offensive, by the
British Machine Gun Corps, 1916. ¶ The Russian Republic is proclaimed, with
Alexander Kerensky as Premier, 1917. ¶ China ends war with Germany, 1919.
¶ The bank rate in Germany exceeds 90%, 1923. ¶ The Nuremberg Laws
outlaw Jews and recognize the Swastika as the official flag of Germany, 1935.
¶ Neville Chamberlain visits Adolf Hitler at Berchtesgaden, 1938.

BORN: Trajan (Marcus Ulpius Traianus), Roman emperor, Italica, Spain, 53.
François, Duc de La Rochefoucauld, courtier and writer, *Maximes*, Paris, 1613.
Titus Oates, Protestant paranoiac, Oakham, Rutland, 1649. James Fenimore
Cooper, novelist, *The Last of the Mohicans*, New Jersey, 1789. Porfirio Diaz,
military leader and dictator, Mexico, 1830. Jean Renoir, French film director,
La Regle du Jeu, La Grande Illusion, Paris, 1894. Jean Batten, aviator, New
Zealand, 1909.

DIED: Isambard Kingdom Brunel, engineer, 1859. William Seward Burroughs,
inventor of the first popular adding machine, 1898. Thomas Wolfe, novelist,
Look Homeward, Angel, You Can't Go Home Again, Baltimore, Maryland, 1938.
Anton von Webern, composer, near Salzburg, Austria, 1945.

[1] The Seven Sorrows: Holy Simeon's prophecy, the flight into Egypt, Christ's disappearance
for three days as a child, the journey to Calvary, the crucifixion, the taking down from the
cross, the entombment.

Independence Day, Papua New Guinea. Cherokee Strip Day, Oklahoma, USA.
Feasts of SS: Cornelius, pope and martyr; Cyprian, bishop and martyr;
Abundius, Abundantius and their Companions, martyrs; Ninian, bishop;
Ludmila, martyr; Edith of Wilton, virgin.

Revolt against Spanish authority and rule, in Mexico, 1810. ¶ Artemis (Asteroid 105) discovered by J. C. Watson, 1868. ¶ Cherokee Strip, an Indian reserve in Arkansas, is opened to non-Indian settlers, 1893. ¶ US introduces Selective Training and Service Act, 1940.

BORN: Henry V, King of England, Monmouth, Wales, 1387. Thomás Barnes, editor of *The Times*, London, 1785. Francis Parkman, historian, *The Oregon Trail, The Jesuits in North America*, Boston, Massachusetts, 1823. Ellsworth Huntingdon, geographer, *Civilization and Climate*, Illinois, 1876. Sir Alexander Korda, film producer, *The Private Life of Henry VIII, Four Feathers*, Hungary, 1893.

DIED: Tomás de Torquemada, Dominican monk, largely responsible for the Spanish Inquisition, Avila, Spain, 1498. John Colet, theologian and scholar, London, 1519. Gabriel Daniel Fahrenheit, physicist, the first to use mercury in a thermometer, 1736. Louis XVIII of France, Paris, 1824. Edward Whymper, artist and mountaineer, the first man to climb the Matterhorn (Switzerland), *Scrambles Amongst the Alps*, Chamonix, France, 1911. Sir Lander Brunton, pharmacologist and physician, *The Action of Medicines*, 1916. John McCormack, Irish tenor, near Dublin, 1945. Sir James Jeans, mathematician, cosmologist and astronomer, *The Mysterious Universe, The Stars in their Courses*, 1946. Sir Ernest Davis, New Zealand business man and philanthropist, 1962. Maria Callas, opera singer, 1977.

SEPTEMBER 17

The Feast of the Impression of the Stigmata Upon St Francis,
commemorating the stigmata that appeared on the hands and feet of
St Francis of Assisi at La Verna in the Appenines, 1224.
Feasts of SS: Socrates and Stephen, martyrs; Satyrus; Lambert
of Maestricht, bishop and martyr; Columba, virgin and martyr;
Hildegard, virgin; Peter Arbues, martyr.

The US Constitution is signed, 1787. ¶ George Washington delivers his farewell address, 1796. ¶ The US national cemetery at Antietam dedicated, 1867. ¶ A new comet was discovered by Dr Max Wolf at Heidelberg, 1884. ¶ Formal proclamation of the Commonwealth of Australia, 1900. ¶ Lieutenant Thomas E. Selfridge of the US Army Signal Corps became the first man to die in a flying accident, 1908. ¶ Landing by air of British forces at Arnhem and Eindhoven, 1944. ¶ Beginning of Civil War in Lebanon, 1970.

BORN: Francisco Gómez de Quevado y Villegas, satirist and poet, *El Buscón, Sueños*, Madrid, 1580. Jean, Marquis de Condorcet, philosopher and writer, Picardy, 1743. William Carlos Williams, physician and poet, *Journey to Love, Paterson*, Rutherford, New Jersey, 1883. Sir Francis Chichester, sailor, circumnavigated the world alone in 1966–7, Devon, 1901. Sir Frederick Ashton, choreographer, Ecuador, 1906.

DIED: Pedro Menendez de Aviles, soldier and navigator, settled Florida as a Spanish colony, Santander, Spain, 1574. Alfred de Vigny, poet, novelist and playwright, *Les Destinées, Chatterton*, Paris, 1863. Walter Savage Landor, poet and writer, *Imaginary Conversations*, Florence, 1864. William Henry Fox Talbot, photographic pioneer, author, *The Pencil of Nature*, Lacock Abbey, Wiltshire, 1877. Eugène-Emmanuel Viollet-Le-Duc, architect, Lausanne, Switzerland, 1879. Henry Louis Le Châtelier, chemist, France, 1936. Ruth Benedict, sociologist and anthropologist, *Patterns of Culture*, 1948.

SEPTEMBER 18

*Victory of 'Uprona', Burundi (Unité et Progrès National Party won the
1961 election, resulting in independence the following year).
Independence Day, Chile (Spanish rule overthrown in 1810). Feasts of SS:
Joseph of Cupertino; Ferreolus, martyr; Methodius of Olympus,
bishop and martyr; Richardis, widow.*

Constantine the Great's victory over Licinius Licinianus at the battle of Chryso-
polis, 324. ¶ The great Sanhedrim convened by Napoleon Bonaparte, 1806.
¶ Richard Cobden establishes Anti-Corn Law League in Manchester, 1838.
¶ The *New York Times* first appears, 1851. ¶ Massacre of approximately 136
emigrants at Mountain Meadows in Utah by members of the Mormon Church,
1857. ¶ Encke's Comet observed in Washington, 1881. ¶ The first troops from
the Union of South Africa land in German South West Africa, 1914. ¶ The
USSR is admitted to the League of Nations, 1934. ¶ Dag Hammarskjöld is
killed in an air crash in the Congo, 1961.

BORN: Gilbert Burnet, Bishop of Salisbury, writer, *History of the Reformation*,
Edinburgh, 1643. Samuel Johnson, essayist, lexicographer and critic, Lichfield,
Staffordshire, 1709. William Collins, landscape painter, London, 1788. Leon
Foucault, physicist, Paris, 1819. John Diefenbaker, Canadian Prime Minister,
Grey County, Ontario, 1895. Greta Garbo, film actress, *Camille*, 1905. Edwin
McMillan, physicist, discoverer of plutonium, Redondo Beach, California, 1907.
Kwame Nkrumah, Ghanaian politician, Gold Coast, 1909. Peter Sellers, actor
and comic, *Dr Strangelove*, London, 1925. Nicholas Frewin, dedicatee, Dover,
1971.

DIED: Domitian (Titus Flavius Domitianus), Roman Emperor, Rome, 96.
Louis VII of France, 1180. Hugo van der Goes, Flemish painter, 1684. Matthew
Prior, poet, ambassador, Cambridgeshire, 1721. Olaf Swartz, Swedish botanist,
1818. William Hazlitt, essayist and critic, *Lectures on the Dramatic Literature of
the Age of Elizabeth*, London, 1830. Joseph Locke, engineer, London, 1860.
Armand-Hippolyte Louis Fizeau, physicist, measured the speed of light, 1896.
Francis Herbert Bradley, philosopher, *Appearance and Reality*, 1924. Dag
Hjalmar Hammarskjöld, Secretary-General of the United Nations; in an
aeroplane crash, Zambia, 1961. Sean O'Casey, dramatist and writer, *Juno and
the Paycock, The Plough and the Stars*, Torquay, Devon, 1964. Sir John Douglas
Cockcroft, physicist, split the atom with Ernest Walton, Nobel Prize for
Physics, 1967.

SEPTEMBER 19

Feasts of SS: Januarius, bishop, and his Companions, martyrs;
Peleus and his Companions, martyrs; Sequanus, or Seine, abbot;
Goericus, or Abbo, bishop; Theodore of Canterbury, archbishop;
Mary of Cerevellon, virgin; Theodore, David and Constantine;
Emily de Rodat, virgin.

The French are defeated at the battle of Poitiers by Edward III, 1356. ¶ Massilia (Asteroid 20) discovered by de Gasparis, 1852. ¶ Doris and Pales (Asteroids 49 and 50) discovered by H. Goldschmidt, 1857. ¶ Io (Asteroid 85) discovered by C. H. F. Peters, 1865. ¶ The *Great Eastern* arrives in Liverpool after successfully laying a trans-Atlantic telegraph cable, 1886. ¶ Iphigenia (Asteroid 112) discovered by C. H. F. Peters, 1870. ¶ Beginning of the Siege of Paris by the Prussians, 1870. ¶ General Chester A. Arthur is sworn in as President of the US, 1881. ¶ Kiev is taken by the Germans, 1941. ¶ Resignation of Juan Pérón of Argentina who then goes into exile, 1955.

BORN: Antonius Pius, Roman emperor, near Rome, 86. Henry III of France, 1551. Robert Sanderson, Bishop of Lincoln, writer, probably wrote the Second Preface to *The Book of Common Prayer*, Sheffield (?), 1587. Rev. William Kirby, rector and entomologist, *Habits and Instincts of Animals*, Suffolk, 1759. Henry, 1st Baron Brougham and Vaux, jurist and politician, Edinburgh, 1778. Lajos Kossuth, Hungarian revolutionary and leader, near Zemplin, Hungary, 1802. George Cadbury, businessman and philanthropist, Birmingham, 1839. Arthur Rackham, illustrator and artist, 1867. Herbert Wilcox, film producer, *Nurse Edith Cavell*, Ireland, 1891. William Golding, novelist, *Lord of the Flies*, Cornwall, 1911.

DIED: Meyer Amschel Rothschild, banker and founder of a dynasty, Frankfurt, Germany, 1812. James Abraham Garfield, US President, 1881. Masaoka Shiki, poet, revived the traditional Japanese *haiku* and *tanka* verse forms, Tokyo, 1902. Thomas Barnardo, doctor, founder of the orphan Homes that bear his name, 1905. Miles Franklin, Australian novelist, 1954. Sir David Low, political cartoonist, London, 1963. Chester Carlson, inventor of the Xerox copying process, 1968.

SEPTEMBER 20

Feasts of SS: Eustace and his Companions, martyrs;
Vincent Madelgarius, abbot.

English defeated by the Norwegians at Fulford, 1066. ¶ Richard I defeats the French at Gisors, 1198. ¶ First meeting of the American Association for the Advancement of Science, at Philadelphia, 1848. ¶ Britain and France defeat Russian forces at Alma, 1854. ¶ Delhi falls to the British after lengthy siege, 1857. ¶ Italian troops enter Rome, 1870. ¶ Queen Elizabeth II launches *Queen Elizabeth II*, a new Cunard liner, at Clydebank, 1966.

BORN: Prince Arthur, eldest son of Henry VII, Winchester, 1486. Sir James Dewar, physicist, inventor of the vacuum flask, Scotland, 1842. Upton Sinclair, novelist and reformer, *The Jungle*, *King Coal*, Baltimore, Maryland, 1878. Sophia Loren, actress, Rome, 1934.

DIED: Jacob Grimm, philologist, historian and folklore collector, *Fairy Tales*, Berlin, 1863. Fiorello Henry La Guardia, Mayor of New York, 1947. Jean Sibelius, composer, *Finlandia*, *Tapiola*, Finland, 1957. George Seferis, poet and critic, Athens, 1971.

SEPTEMBER 21

Dies Mala or 'Egyptian Day', considered unlucky in the Middle Ages.
Independence Day, Malta (1964). Feasts of SS: Matthew, apostle and
evangelist; Maura of Troyes, virgin; Michael of Chernigov and
St Theodore, martyrs.

Scottish rebels defeat Cope at Gladsmuir near Preston Pans, 1745. ¶ The Chinese are defeated at Pali-chi-ao by British and French troops, 1860. ¶ Medusa (Asteroid 149) discovered by M. Perrotin, 1875. ¶ Total eclipse over the South Pole, 1903. ¶ *Sidewalk Blues* is recorded in Chicago by Jelly Roll Morton and his Red Hot Peppers, 1926. ¶ The Gold Standard is abandoned by British government after dramatic fall of the £, 1931. ¶ Malta is granted independence by Britain, 1964.

BORN: Girolamo Savonarola, religious and political reformer, Ferrara, Italy, 1452. John McAdam, inventor and engineer, Ayr, Scotland, 1756. Herbert George Wells, novelist, social critic and educator, *The Time Machine, Kipps, A Short History of the World*, Bromley, Kent, 1866. Gustav Holst, composer, *The Planets, Egdon Heath*, Cheltenham, Gloucestershire, 1874. Sir Allen Lane, publisher, founder of Penguin Books (1936), Bristol, 1902.

DIED: Virgil (Publius Vergilius Maro), Roman poet, *Georgics, Aeneid, Ecologues*, Brundusium, Italy, 19BC. Sir Walter Scott, novelist and poet, *The Heart of Midlothian, Quentin Durward*, Abbotsford, Roxburgh, Scotland, 1832. Arthur Schopenhauer, philosopher, *The World as Will and Idea*, Frankfurt, Germany, 1860. Chief Joseph, Nez Percé warrior and leader, 1904. Henry de Montherlant, novelist and dramatist, *Chaos and Night, Port-Royal*, Paris, 1972.

Autumn Equinox (or 23 or 24 September). National Holiday,
Republic of Mali (commemorating independence in 1960, formerly
French Sudan). Feasts of SS: Thomas of Villanova, archbishop; Phocas
the Gardener, martyr; Maurice and his Companions, martyrs of the
Theban Legion; Felix III (IV), pope; Salaberga, matron, and
St Bodo, bishop; Emmeramus, bishop.

Persians defeated by the Greeks at Mycale, 479BC. ¶ The Dutch and English defeat the Spanish at Zutphen, 1586. ¶ King George III of Great Britain crowned, 1761. ¶ The French Republic is proclaimed, 1792. ¶ Mnemosyne (Asteroid 57) discovered by R. Luther, 1859. ¶ Eurydice (Asteroid 75) discovered by C. H. F. Peters, 1862. ¶ Otto von Bismarck is made the Prussian premier, 1862. ¶ President Lincoln proclaims all slaves to be free as from 1 January 1863, 1862. ¶ At the Electrical Congress in Paris the following terms were adopted for international use: ohm, volt, ampère, coulomb, and farad, 1881. ¶ Sierra Leone abolishes slavery, 1927. ¶ General Idi Amin gives Uganda's 8,000 Asians 48 hours in which to leave the country, 1972.

BORN: Anne of Cleves, wife of Henry III, 1515. Jean-Etienne Guettard, naturalist and geologist, France, 1715. Michael Faraday, physicist, discoverer of electro-magnetic induction, London, 1791. Shigeru Yoshida, Prime Minister of Japan, Tokyo, 1878. Erich von Stroheim, actor and film director, *Greed*, *Queen Kelly*, Vienna, 1885. Paul Muni, actor, Austria, 1895. John Houseman, actor and producer, Rumania, 1902.

DIED: Sturluson Snorri, poet and historian, *Edda*, *Heimskringla*, Iceland, 1179. Selim I, Sultan of Turkey, Corlu, Turkey, 1520. Johann Agricola, theologian and reformer, 1566. Ivan Vazov, Bulgarian national poet, Sofia, 1921. Frederick Soddy, chemist and physicist, Brighton, Sussex, 1956. Oliver St John Gogarty, Irish writer and politician, 1957.

SEPTEMBER 23

Autumn Equinox (or 22 or 24 September). Feasts of SS: Linus, pope and martyr;
Thecla of Iconium, virgin and martyr; Adamnan, or Eunan, abbot.

The Yorkists defeat the Lancastrians at Bloreheath, 1459. ¶ Prince Rupert wins
the battle of Worcester, 1642. ¶ A captured British agent, John André, reveals
Benedict Arnold's intention to surrender West Point, 1780. ¶ The planet
Neptune is discovered by Dr Galie at Berlin, 1846. ¶ The George Cross is
initiated, 1940. ¶ Juan Perón is elected President of Argentina and Mrs Perón
Vice-President, 1973.

BORN: Octavian/Augustus, Roman Emperor, Rome, 63BC. Armand-Hippolyte
Louis Fizeau, physicist, measured the speed of light, Paris, 1819. Walter Lippman,
journalist and writer, co-founder of the *New Republic*, New York, 1889.
Paul Delraux, Surrealist painter, Belgium, 1897. Mickey Rooney, actor,
Brooklyn, New York, 1922. John Coltrane, modern jazz tenor-saxophonist,
North Carolina, 1926.

DIED: Hermann Boerhaave, physician and teacher, Netherlands, 1738. Richard
P. Bonnington, watercolourist, 1828. Prosper Mérimée, novelist and man-of-
letters, *Carmen*, Cannes, 1870. Urbain Le Verrier, astronomer, co-discoverer of
Neptune, Paris, 1877. Wilkie Collins, novelist, *The Woman in White*, London,
1889. Sigmund Freud, psychiatrist, founder of psychoanalysis, 1939. Pablo
Neruda, poet and critic, Nobel Prize for Literature, *Tercera residencia*, *Canto
general*, Santiago, Chile, 1973.

SEPTEMBER 24

Autumn Equinox (or 22 or 23 September). The Feast of Ingathering or
Harvest Home, a harvest custom in England until the 19th century.
The Feast of Our Lady of Ransom (or Pity), the Virgin Mary, that is.
Feasts of SS: Geremarus, or Germer, abbot; Gerard of Csanad, bishop
and martyr; Pacifico of San Severino.

The first dirigible is flown by Henri Giffard, a French mechanic, from Paris to Trappe; the balloon is 150 feet long and 39 feet in diameter, it flys at a speed of just over 6mph, 1852. ¶ Annexation of New Caledonia by France, 1853. ¶ The first contingent of Canadian troops sets sail for England in World War One, 1914. ¶ James H. Doolittle achieves the first aeroplane 'blind flight', that is taking-off and landing relying entirely on automatic instruments, in US, 1929.

BORN: Geronimo Cardano, physician and mathematician, *The Book of the Game of Chance*, Italy, 1501. Albrecht von Wallenstein, Austrian general and military commander, Jaromef, Bohemia, 1583. Horace Walpole, novelist and historian, *The Castle of Otranto, Anecdotes of Painting in England*, London, 1717. John Marshall, US Secretary of State, jurist, Germantown, Virginia, 1755. Georges Claude, engineer and inventor, devised a process for liquefying air, Paris, 1870. André Cournand, physician, Nobel Prize for Medicine, 1895. F. Scott Fitzgerald, novelist, *The Great Gatsby*, Minnesota, 1896.

DIED: Michael III, Emperor of Greece; assassinated, 867. Pope Innocent II, 1143. Paracelsus, alchemist and physician, Salzburg, Austria, 1541. Niels Finsen, Danish physician, Nobel Prize winner, 1904. Carl Laemmle, film producer, founder of Universal Pictures, California, 1939. Melanie Klein, Austrian child psychologist, 1960.

*Mozambican Popular Liberation Forces and Revolution Day, People's
Republic of Mozambique. Kamarampaka Day, Republic of Rwanda.
Republic Day, Trinidad and Tobago. Feasts of SS: Firminus, bishop and martyr;
Cadoc, abbot; Aunacharius, or Aunaire, bishop; Finbar, bishop;
Ceolfrid, abbot; Albert of Jerusalem, bishop; Sergius of Radonezh, abbot;
Vincent Strambi, bishop.*

King Harold defeats Tostig at Stamford Bridge, 1066. ¶ Christopher Columbus
sets sail on his second expedition, 1493. ¶ *Publick Occurrences, Both Foreign and
Domestic* is published in Boston, it is the first newspaper to be issued in the US,
1690. ¶ First successful demonstration of 'quadruplex telegraphy' (four messages
simultaneously along one line), between London and Liverpool, 1877.
¶ Beginning of the battle of the Loos (ends 8 October), 1915. ¶ International
convention on slavery, 1926. ¶ Catalonia in Spain becomes autonomous with
its own Parliament, flag and language, 1932. ¶ The trans-Atlantic telephone
service begins, 1956. ¶ Assassination of the Ceylonese premier Bandaranaike,
1959. ¶ Second party of US astronauts returns to earth after lengthy stay aboard
orbiting space station *Skylab* (59 days aboard, from 28 July), 1973.

BORN: Jacques-Bénigne Bossuet, theologian, tutor of the Dauphin, Burgundy,
1627. Ch'ien Lung, Chinese Emperor, 1711. Abraham Werner, German
geologist, Professor of Minerology at Freiburg, Wehrau, Silesia, 1750. Felicia
Hemans, poet, *The Landing of the Pilgrim Fathers, Casabianca*, Liverpool, 1793.
Thomas Morgan, genetic biologist, Nobel Prize for Medicine, Lexington,
Kentucky, 1866. Sir C. B. Cochran, theatrical producer and impresario, Sussex,
1872. John Howard Lawson, scriptwriter and playwright, *Film in the Battle of
Ideas*, New York City, 1886. William Faulkner, novelist, *Sanctuary*, Mississippi,
1897. Mark Rothko, American painter, Dvinsk, Russia, 1903. Robert Bresson,
film director, *Le Procès de Jeanne d'Arc*, France, 1907.

DIED: Philip I of Spain, Burgos, 1506. Samuel Butler, poet and writer, *Hudibras*,
1680. Johann Heinrich Lambert, mathematician, Berlin, 1777. John Watson,
behaviourist psychologist, New York City, 1958. Erich Remarque, novelist,
All Quiet on the Western Front, Locarno, Switzerland, 1970.

SEPTEMBER 26

National Day, Republic of Yemen (1962). National Day, Yemen Arab Republic (1962). The Feast of the Martyrs of North America, commemorating eight missionary martyrs slain by Indians in 1642–9. Feasts of SS: Cyprian and Justina, martyrs; Colman of Lann Elo, abbot; Nilus of Rossano, abbot; John of Meda.

Accession of William II (Rufus) of England, 1087. ¶ Surrender of the Spanish expedition sent against Mexico, 1829. ¶ Foundation of the British Association for the Advancement of Science, 1831. ¶ New Zealand is constituted as a Dominion, 1907. ¶ Prince Ito of Japan is assassinated by a Korean revolutionary, 1909. ¶ First reported dive-bomb attack on Allied warships, 1939. ¶ The British Eighth Army is formed, 1941. ¶ Seoul in South Korea is taken by United Nations' Forces, 1950.

BORN: Théodore Géricault, painter, *Raft of the Medusa*, France, 1791. Charles Bradlaugh, politician and free-thinker, London, 1833. T. S. Eliot, poet and critic, *The Waste Land*, St Louis, Missouri, 1888. Martin Heidegger, Existentialist philosopher, *Being and Time*, Germany, 1889. Giovanni Battista Montini, Pope Paul VI, Concesio, Italy, 1897. George Gershwin, composer, *Rhapsody in Blue*, New York City, 1898.

DIED: Daniel Boone, American frontiersman and colonizer, 1820. August Ferdinand Möbius, astronomer and mathematician, Leipzig, 1868. Hermann Grassmann, German mathematician, 1877. James Keir Hardie, Labour politician, founded the Independent Labour Party, 1915. George Simnel, philosopher and sociologist, Strasbourg, Germany, 1918. William Henry Davies, poet and writer, *The Autobiography of a Super-Tramp*, 1940. Béla Bartok, composer, *Bluebeard's Castle*, 1945. Solomon Bandaranaike, Ceylonese Prime Minister, assassinated (from wounds received on 25 September), 1959.

SEPTEMBER 27

Regional Day, parts of south Belgium. The Feast of the Finding of the True
Cross, Ethiopia. Feasts of SS: Cosmas and Damian, martyrs; Elzear.

Theodoric defeats Odoacer at Verona, 489. ¶ Assassination of Edward II, 1327. ¶ First appearance of *The Rhode Island Gazette*, Rhode Island, printed and published by James Franklin, Benjamin's half-brother, 1727. ¶ Philadelphia is occupied by William Howe, 1777. ¶ Sophrosyne (Asteroid 138) discovered by R. Luther, 1873. ¶ The Carpathian Mountains are crossed by Russian forces and Hungary invaded, 1914. ¶ Abdication of King Constantine I of Greece, 1922. ¶ Launching of the SS *Queen Elizabeth*, 1938. ¶ Mobilization of the Royal Navy, 1938. ¶ The Royal Navy sinks the *Bismarck* off the Brest coast, 1941. ¶ A general strike in the Basque region of Spain by workers demanding the release of political prisoners, 1976.

BORN: Samuel Adams, US revolutionary and politician, 1722. George Cruikshank, caricaturist and illustrator, London, 1792. Alfred Mahan, naval commander and historian, *The Influence of Sea Power Upon History, 1660–1783*, West Point, New York, 1840. Louis Botha, soldier, Premier of the Union of South Africa, 1862. Nikolai Ivanovich Bukharin, Soviet journalist and politician, Moscow, 1888. William Empson, poet and critic, *The Seven Types of Ambiguity*, Yorkshire, 1906.

DIED: William of Wykeham, Lord Chancellor, Bishop of Winchester, founded New College, Oxford; Bishop's Waltham, Hampshire, 1404. Rémy de Gourmont, writer, *A Night in the Luxembourg*, 1915. Edgar Degas, Impressionist painter, 1917. Aristide Maillol, sculptor, France, 1944. Clara Bow, silent-film actress, 1965.

*Referendum Anniversary Day, Republic of Guinea (the result of the
referendum was in favour of leaving the French community, 1958).
Birthday of Confucius, Taiwan. Feasts of SS: Wenceslaus of Bohemia, martyr;
Exsuperius, bishop; Eustochium, virgin; Faustus of Riez, bishop;
Annemund, bishop; Lioba, virgin.*

Greeks defeat the Persians at the battle of Marathon, 490BC. ¶ Triumph of
Pompey the Great in Rome, after making Syria a Roman province and capturing
Jerusalem, 61BC. ¶ The Dutch Admiral Van Tromp is defeated in the Straits of
Dover by Admiral Blake, 1652. ¶ Britain, Russia and Austria form Alliance of
St Petersburg against France, 1794. ¶ Turkish forces defeated at Kut-al-Amara
in Mesopotamia by British, 1915. ¶ German forces reach Warsaw, 1939.

BORN: Pompey the Great, Roman statesman and military commander, Rome,
106BC. Michelangelo Merisi da Caravaggio, painter, Italy, 1573. Pierre de
Maupertius, astronomer and mathematician, Saint-Malo, France, 1698. Richard
Bright, physician, Bright's Disease is named after him, Bristol, 1789. Prosper
Mérimée, novelist and man-of-letters, *Carmen*, Paris, 1803. Georges Clemenceau,
statesman, French Prime Minister during the First World War, 1841. Edward
Herbert Thompson, South American explorer, excavated several Mayan cities,
Worcester, Massachusetts, 1856. Pietro Badoglio, statesman and soldier, led
the Italian Army in Ethiopia, 1871. Al Capp, cartoonist, creator of *Li'l Abner*,
Connecticut, 1909. Ethel Rosenberg, convicted with her husband as an American
spy for Soviet intelligence, New York City, 1915.

DIED: Wenceslaus, King of Bohemia, the patron saint of Czechoslovakia,
Stará Boleslav, Czechoslovakia, 929. Andrea del Sarto, Florentine painter, 1530.
Herman Melville, novelist and poet, *Moby Dick, Billy Budd*, New York City,
1891. Louis Pasteur, chemist and bacteriologist, Saint-Cloud, near Paris, 1895.
Emile Zola, novelist and critic, *Nana, Germinal*, Paris, 1902. Gregg Toland,
cinematographer, *Citizen Kane*, California, 1948. Edwin Powell Hubble,
astronomer, 1953. André Breton, founder of the Surrealist movement, art
critic, poet, *Nadja*, 1966. Gamal Abdul Nasser, politician, President of Egypt,
1970. John Don Passos, American novelist, *USA* trilogy, 1970.

SEPTEMBER 29

The Feast of the Dedication of the Basilica of St Michael the Archangel,
commemorating the consecration of the church situated to the north of Rome;
the feast has been observed by the Western church since the 6th century;
BCP as St Michael and All Angels; known also as Michaelmas, and
in England it is a Quarter Day. Constitution Day, State of Brunei (1959).
Battle of Boqueron Day, Paraguay (1932). Feasts of SS: Rhipsime,
Gaiana, and their Companions, virgins and martyrs; Theodota, martyr.

Parliament of one day (King Richard II is deposed), 1399. ¶ The London Police, remodelled by (Sir) Robert Peel, begin duty, 1829.

BORN: Miguel de Cervantes Saavedra, dramatist and novelist, *Don Quixote*, *Exemplary Novels*, Spain, 1547. François Boucher, artist and designer, Paris, 1703. Robert Clive, statesman and soldier, Shropshire, 1725. Horatio Nelson, British naval commander, defeated the Franco-Spanish forces at Trafalgar, Burnham Thorpe, Norfolk, 1758. Mrs Elizabeth Gaskell, novelist, *Cranford*, Chelsea, London, 1810. Henry Hobson Richardson, architect, Louisiana, 1838. Miguel de Unamuno, philosopher, essayist and poet, *The Tragic Sense of Life*, *Mist*, Bilbao, Spain, 1864. Walter Rathenau, German statesman and industrialist, Berlin, 1867. Enrico Fermi, physicist, developed the atomic bomb, Rome, 1901. Michelangelo Antonioni, film director, *L'Avventura*, *La Notte*, Ferrara, Italy, 1912. Stanley Kramer, film director and producer, *Judgement at Nuremberg*, New York City, 1913.

DIED: Pompey the Great, Roman statesman and military commander, Egypt, 48BC. Winslow Homer, painter, Maine, 1910. Rudolf Diesel, German inventor and engineer, 1913. Willem Einthoven, physician, pioneer of electrocardiography, 1927. Carson McCullers, novelist, *The Heart is a Lonely Hunter*, *Member of the Wedding*, New York, 1967. W. H. Auden, poet and writer, 1973.

SEPTEMBER 30

Botswana Day, Botswana (commemorating independence in 1966).
National Day, Nigeria. Feasts of SS: Jerome, doctor; Gregory the
Enlightener, bishop; Honorius of Canterbury, archbishop; Simon of Crépy.

Accession of Henry IV of England, 1399. ¶ Siege of Yorktown in Virginia begins, 1781. ¶ Terpsichore (Asteroid 81) discovered by M. Tempel, 1864. ¶ Tempel Swift's Comet observed in London (also on 1 October), 1891. ¶ USSR-German amity treaty settles Poland's partition, 1939. ¶ The Nuremberg Tribunal's verdicts are delivered, 1946. ¶ End of the Berlin Airlift (began 24 June 1948), 1949. ¶ Botswana in Africa is declared a Republic, 1966.

BORN: Étienne de Condillac, French philosopher and writer, France, 1715. Hermann Sudermann, German dramatist and novelist, *Sodom's End*, *The Narrow Path*, Matzicken, East Prussia, 1857. Lewis Milestone, film director, *All Quiet on the Western Front*, Russia, 1895. Michael Powell, film director and producer, *The Red Shoes*, Canterbury, Kent, 1905. David Oistrakh, violin virtuoso, Odessa, 1908. Truman Capote, novelist and essayist, *In Cold Blood*, New Orleans, 1924.

DIED: Nurhachi, Emperor of China, founder of the Ching (or Manchu) dynasty, Mukden (?), 1626. James Brindley, early British canal engineer, 1772. Georges Boulanger, soldier and politician; suicide, 1891. F. E. Smith, Earl of Birkenhead, statesman and law reformer, Lord Chancellor, 1930. Sir Robert Hadfield, metallurgist, near Sheffield, 1940. Lewis Fry Richardson, mathematician, notably concerned with weather forecasting, Argyll, Scotland, 1953. James Dean, film actor, *Rebel Without a Cause*; a car crash, California, 1955.

OCTOBER

THIRTY-ONE DAYS

October means the 'eighth month', and this it
was in the pre-Julian Roman calendar that began
the year in March.

OCTOBER 1

*Sacrifices offered in Rome to Fides Publica, the goddess embodying the honour
of the people, by the three flamines majores (members of the priestly college).
Armed Forces Day, Republic of Korea. Feasts of SS: Remigius, or
Remi, bishop; Romanus the Melodist; Melorus, Melar or Mylor, martyr;
Bavo; The Canterbury Martyrs of 1588.*

Alexander the Great defeats Darius at Arbela, 331BC. ¶ Spain sells Louisiana to France by secret treaty, 1800. ¶ Antiope (Asteroid 90) discovered by R. Luther, 1866. ¶ St Pancras, the London terminus of the Midland Railway, is formally opened, 1868. ¶ The first postcards were printed and put on sale, by the Austrian Government, 1869. ¶ Railway service, via Dover and Ostend, between London, Berlin and St Petersburg begins, 1903. ¶ Damascus is occupied by British and Arab forces, 1918. ¶ General Franco is appointed Chief of State by Spanish rebels, 1936. ¶ Nuclear Test Ban Treaty signed by Britain, US, and USSR, comes into force, 1963. ¶ The US Senate rejects President Johnson's nomination of Abe Fortas as next Chief Justice, 1968.

BORN: Giacomo da Vignola, architect, Vignola, Italy, 1507. William Beckford, novelist, *Vathek*, Wiltshire, 1760. Paul Dukas, critic and composer, *The Sorcerer's Apprentice*, Paris, 1865. Louis Untermeyer, writer and critic, New York City, 1885. James Earl Carter, US President, Plains, Georgia, 1924. Laurence Harvey, actor, *Room at the Top*, Lithuania, 1928.

DIED: Marsilio Ficino, classical scholar and philosopher, 1499. John of Austria, defeated the Turks at Lepanto; Namur, Belgium, 1578. Sir Edwin Henry Landseer, painter, London, 1873. Lord Shaftesbury (Anthony Ashley Cooper), social reformer and Member of Parliament, Folkestone, Kent, 1885. Wilhelm Dilthey, philosopher, 1911. Louis Leakey, palaeontologist and anthropologist, excavated at the Olduvai Gorge, 1972.

National Day, People's Republic of China. Anniversary of Guinean Independence, Republic of Guinea (1958). Anniversary of Mahatma Gandhi's Birthday, India (Gandhi, 1869–1948). The Feast of the Guardian Angels, an obligatory observance entered into the Church's calendar in 1670 by Pope Clement X. Feasts of SS: Eleutherius, martyr; Leodegarius, or Leger, bishop and martyr.

Rome and its provinces are formally made part of Italy, and Rome is declared the Italian capital, 1870. ¶ Abyssinia is invaded by Italian forces, 1935. ¶ *Flying Home* recorded by Benny Goodman in New York City, 1939. ¶ The *Empress of Britain* on her way to Canada with evacuated children is sunk by enemy action, 1940. ¶ Legal Aid comes into operation in Britain, 1950.

BORN: Richard III, King of England, Fotheringhay Castle, Northamptonshire, 1452. Julius von Sachs, botanist and naturalist, Breslau, Poland, 1832. Sir Edward Burnett Tylor, anthropologist, *Researches into the Early History of Mankind*, Camberwell, London, 1832. Paul von Hindenburg, soldier and statesman, President of the Weimar Republic, 1847. Ferdinand Foch, military commander, Marshal of France, France, 1851. Sir William Ramsay, chemist, discovered 'inert' gases, Glasgow, 1852. Mahatma Gandhi, architect of India's Independence, India, 1869. Wallace Stevens, poet, *Ideas of Order, Notes towards a Supreme Fiction*, Reading, Pennsylvania, 1879. Groucho Marx, actor and comedian, *Duck Soup*, New York City, 1895. Roy Campbell, poet, South Africa, 1901. Graham Greene, novelist and critic, *The Third Man, Brighton Rock*, Berkhampstead, Hertfordshire, 1904. Shri Lal Bahadur Shastri, statesman, Indian Prime Minister, Mughalsarai, India, 1904.

DIED: Aristotle, Greek philosopher; of indigestion, Chalcis, 322BC. Major John André, British officer, hanged as a spy by George Washington, Tappantown, 1780. Samuel Adams, US revolutionary and politician, 1803. Dr William Ellery Channing, writer and divine, Bennington, Vermont, 1842. José Maria Heredia, Cuban poet and revolutionary, *Niagara*, Mexico, 1905. Svante August Arrhenius, Swedish chemist, Nobel Prize winner, 1927. Marcel Duchamp, French Surrealist artist, 1968.

OCTOBER 3

Dies Mala or 'Egyptian Day', considered unlucky in the Middle Ages.
National Day, People's Republic of China. Anniversary of the Birth
of Francisco Morazan, Honduras (Morazan, a founder and liberator,
1789–1821). National Foundation Day, Republic of Korea (2333BC [sic]).
Feasts of SS: Teresa of Lisieux, virgin; Hesychius; The Two Ewalds, martyrs;
Gerard of Brogne, abbot; Foilan and Attilanus, bishops;
Thomas Cantelupe of Hereford, bishop.

Scots defeat the Northmen at the battle of Largs, 1263. ¶ A national flag-day was held for the Belgian Relief Fund, in England (probably the world's first flag-day), 1914. ¶ The Serbo–Croat–Slovene Kingdom now becomes known as Yugoslavia, 1929. ¶ Relations with the USSR resumed by Britain, 1929. ¶ First British atomic bomb test, on islands off the North-West coast of Australia, 1952. ¶ Independence of the African Kingdom of Lesotho (formerly Basutoland), 1966.

BORN: George Bancroft, diplomat, historian, *History of the United States*, Massachusetts, 1800. Mikhail Hurevich Lermontov, dramatist and poet, Moscow, 1814. Eleanora Duse, actress, Italy, 1858. Sergey Yesenin, poet, *Black Man*, Konstantinovka, 1865. Pierre Bonnard, French painter, 1867. Louis Aragon, Surrealist writer and poet, Paris, 1897. Leo McCarey, film director, *Duck Soup*, *Going My Way*, Los Angeles, 1898. Thomas Wolfe, novelist, *Look Homeward*, *Angel, You Can't Go Home Again*, Asheville, North Carolina, 1900. Gore Vidal, novelist and essayist, *Burr*, West Point, New York, 1925.

DIED: St Francis of Assisi, founder of the Franciscan order, 1226. Admiral Viscount Keppel, naval commander, First Lord of the Admiralty, 1786. William Morris, painter, poet, printer and designer, *News From Nowhere*, Hammersmith, Middlesex, 1896. Gustav Stresemann, German statesman, secured his country's admission to the League of Nations, Nobel Prize for Peace, Berlin, 1929. Woody Guthrie, American folk singer, 1967. Katharine Susannah Prichard, Australian novelist, *Black Opal*, 1969.

OCTOBER 4

Independence Day, Lesotho (1966, formerly Basutoland).
Feasts of SS: Francis of Assisi: Ammon; Petronius, bishop.

The printing in London of Miles Coverdale's version of *The Bible* is completed, 1535. ¶ Defeat of George Washington at Germantown, Pennsylvania, 1777. ¶ The Mexican Federal Republic is declared, 1823. ¶ Virginia (Asteroid 51) discovered by James Ferguson, 1857. ¶ Denning's Comet observed throughout Europe, 1881. ¶ Orville Wright pilots his aeroplane through the air for a little over 33 minutes, 1905. ¶ Adolf Hitler and Mussolini meet at the Brenner Pass, 1940. ¶ *Sputnik I* space satellite launched by the Russians, 1957. ¶ First close-up photographs of the moon, by the Russian-launched *Lunik III*, 1959. ¶ Disclosure of Prince Bernhard's involvement in the Lockheed bribes scandal, 1976. ¶ First scheduled run of British Rail's high-speed 125mph diesel service between London and the South Wales region, 1976.

BORN: François Pierre Guizot, statesman and historian, Nîmes, France, 1787. Rutherford B. Hayes, US President, Delaware, Ohio, 1822. Engelbert Dollfuss, politician, Austria, 1892. Buster Keaton, film comedian, *The Navigator*, *The General*, Kansas, 1895. Richard Sorge, German spy for the Soviet Union, Baku, Russia, 1895.

DIED: St Teresa of Avila (Teresa de Cepeda y Ahumada), Carmelite nun and mystic, *El castillo interior* (*The Interior Castle*), *Life*, Alba-de-Tormes, Spain, 1582. Rembrandt (Harmenszoon van Rijn), Dutch painter, Amsterdam, 1669. John Rennie, civil engineer, London, 1821. Max Ludwig Planck, physicist, Nobel Prize winner, Gottingen, Germany, 1947. Sir Arthur Whitten Brown, aviator, 1948. Janis Joplin, American rock singer, 1970.

OCTOBER 5

Republic Day, Portugal and its possessions (1910). Feasts of SS:
Placid, martyr; Apollinaris of Valence, bishop; Galla, widow;
Magenulf, or Meinulf; Flora of Beaulieu, virgin.

Bruce defeated at the battle of Dundalk, in Scotland, 1318. ¶ This day in Italy and Spain became 15 October when the Gregorian calendar was introduced in 1582. ¶ France abolishes Christianity, 1793. ¶ 'A whiff of grapeshot' (Napoleon) quells insurrection on Day of the Sections, 1795. ¶ Spain declares war on Britain, 1796. ¶ Fides (Asteroid 37) discovered by R. Luther, 1855. ¶ The Toll is removed from Waterloo Bridge, London, 1878. ¶ Allied landings at Salonika, 1915. ¶ Beginning of the Locarno Conference on matters of European security etc., 1925.

BORN: Jonathon Edwards, Calvinist divine, Connecticut, 1703. Denis Diderot, philosopher and *encyclopédiste*, France, 1713. Dr William Wilkie, writer, *The Epigoniad*, Dalmeny, Scotland, 1721. Chester Arthur, US President (after Garfield's assassination), Vermont, 1831. Robert Hutchings Goddard, pioneer of rocketry, Massachusetts, 1882. Joshua Logan, film and stage director, *Picnic*, *Bus Stop*, Texakarna, Texas, 1908.

DIED: Joachim Patenier, Dutch painter, Antwerp, 1524. Lodovico Ferrari, mathematician, 1565. Charles, Marquess Cornwallis, military commander, 1805. Jacques Offenbach, composer of operettas, *Orpheus in the Underworld*, *Tales of Hoffman*, Paris, 1880. Jean Vigo, film director, *Zéro de Conduite*, Paris, 1934. Alfred Kroeber, anthropologist and archaeologist, 1960.

OCTOBER 6

*Military Day, Arab Republic of Egypt. Feasts of SS: Bruno; Faith,
virgin and martyr; Nicetas of Constantinople; Mary Frances of Naples, virgin.*

Parliamentum Indoctum at Coventry, 1404. ¶ William Tyndale strangled in Antwerp on the orders of King Henry VIII, 1536. ¶ Pilgrimage of over 20,000 persons to Lourdes in France (where, on 11 February 1858, two young girls claimed the Virgin Mary had appeared to them), 1872. ¶ Chiang Kai-shek becomes President of China, 1928. ¶ The Mutual Defense Assistance Act is signed by President Truman giving military assistance to NATO countries, 1949. ¶ Combined Egyptian and Syrian offensives against Israel, 1973.

BORN: Matteo Ricci, Jesuit missionary in China, responsible for many cultural and technical exchanges, Macerata, Italy, 1552. Thomas Attwood, Chartist leader, 1783. Julius Dedekind, mathematician, Germany, 1831. George Westinghouse, inventor, mechanic and industrialist, patented the Westinghouse railway brake, Central Bridge, New York, 1846. Earnest Walton, physicist, split the atom with Sir John Cockcroft, Dungarvan, Ireland, 1903. Thor Heyerdahl, ethnologist and archaeologist, writer, *Kon-Tiki*, Norway, 1914.

DIED: Wang Mang, Chinese emperor; assassinated, 23. William Tyndale, English clergyman, Antwerp, Belgium, 1536. Charles Stewart Parnell, Member of Parliament and champion of Irish Home Rule, Brighton, 1891. William Henry Smith, politician and founder of the English book-selling chain, London, 1891. Alfred, Lord Tennyson, poet, made Poet Laureate in 1850. *Locksley Hall, In Memoriam, Idylls of the King*, Aldworth, Surrey, 1892. George Du Maurier, artist and novelist, *Trilby*, 1896.

OCTOBER 7

October Revolution Day, Bulgaria. Day of the Foundation of the
German Democratic Republic, GDR (1949). Evacuation Day, Arab
Republic of Libya (celebrating the withdrawal of Italian troops in 1942).
The Feast of Our Lady's Rosary, first observed in 1572 by order of Pope St Pius V.
Feasts of SS: Sergius and Bacchus, martyrs; Marcellus and Apuleius, martyrs;
Justina, virgin and martyr; Mark, pope; Osyth, virgin and martyr;
Artaldus, or Arthaud, bishop.

King Edward III of England assumes the title of King of France, 1337. ¶ Don John defeats the Turks in the naval engagement at Lepanto, 1571. ¶ General Burgoyne loses for the second time at Bemis Heights, New York, 1777. ¶ British defeat at battle of King's Mountain in South Carolina, 1780. ¶ Earl Macartney and his embassy in Peking are ordered to leave by the emperor, 1793. ¶ Great fire of Chicago begins, it lasts for 4 days. Over 250 people are killed and over 95,000 rendered homeless and destitute, 1871. ¶ Union with Greece proclaimed by Crete, 1908. ¶ The R101 airship crashes near Beauvais, 1930. ¶ General Juan Torres declared President of Bolivia after many days of rioting and unrest, 1970.

BORN: William Laud, Archbishop of Canterbury, Reading, 1573. Niels Bohr, atomic physicist, Nobel Prize winner, Copenhagen, 1885. Heinrich Himmler, Nazi Minister of the Interior, Munich, Germany, 1900.

DIED: Giovanni Battista Guarini, poet and playwright, *The Faithful Shepherd*, Italy, 1612. Edgar Allan Poe, short story writer, poet and critic, *Murders in the Rue Morgue, The Raven*, Baltimore, Maryland, 1849. Oliver Wendell Holmes, physician and writer, *The Autocrat of the Breakfast Table*, Boston, Massachusetts, 1894. Harvey Cushing, pioneer neuro-surgeon in America, 1939. Willis Haviland Carrier, air-conditioning engineer, 1950. Clarence Birdseye, industrialist, inventor of a process for deep-freezing foodstuffs, 1956.

OCTOBER 8

Feasts of SS: Bridget, widow; Holy Simeon; Pelagia the Penitent;
Thais; Reparata, virgin and martyr; Demetrius, martyr; Keyne, virgin.

Charles the Bald defeated at the battle of Andernach, 876. ¶ The Duke of Wellington enters France, 1813. ¶ Abdication of King William I of Holland, 1840. ¶ The *Arrow*, a ship flying the British flag, is boarded by Chinese who arrest the crew, thus beginning the Second Chinese War, 1855. ¶ Great typhoon in China, an estimated 300,000 people die, 1881. ¶ End of the battle of the Loos, 1915. ¶ The US Senate and House of Representatives pass the Volstead Prohibition Enforcement Bill, 1919.

BORN: Heinrich Schutz, composer, *Daphne* (the first German opera, now lost), Kostritz, Germany, 1585. Henri Louis Le Châtelier, chemist, Paris, 1850. John Cowper Powys, novelist and writer, *A Glastonbury Romance, Maiden Castle*, Shirley, Derbyshire, 1872. Ejnar Hertzsprung, astronomer, Copenhagen, 1873. Ernst Kretschmer, psychologist, Germany, 1888. Eddie Rickenbacker, US fighter pilot of the First World War, Columbus, Ohio, 1890. Juan Perón, Argentinian dictator, Buenos Aires Province, Argentina, 1895. Rouben Mamoulian, film director, *City Streets, Dr Jekyll and Mr Hyde* (1934, with Fredric March), Tiflis, 1898.

DIED: Cola di Rienzi, populist revolutionary, Rome, 1354. Henry Fielding, magistrate and novelist, *Tom Jones*, 1754. Pierre Fournier, engraver and typefounder, 1768. Franklin Pierce, fourteenth President of the US, Concord, New Hampshire, 1869. Sir John Monash, Australian engineer and soldier, 1931. Wendell Louis Wilkie, Republican politician, New York City, 1944. Kathleen Ferrier, contralto singer, 1953. Clement Attlee, British Labour Prime Minister, 1967.

OCTOBER 9

Independence of Guayaquil, Ecuador. Korean Alphabet Day, Republic of Korea (the Hangul character promulgated in AD1446). Day of National Dignity, Peru. Independence Day, Uganda (1962). Columbus Day and Puerto Rico Friendship Day, Virgin Islands. Feasts of SS: John Leonardi; Dionysius the Areopagite; Demetrius of Alexandria, bishop; Dionysius, or Denis, Rusticus and Eleutherius, martyrs; Publia, widow; Andronicus and Athanasia; Savin; Gislenus, or Ghislain, abbot; Louis Bertrand.

Dedication of the Temple of Apollo on the Palatine Hill in Rome, 28BC. ¶ Henry VI of England restored to the throne (reign had begun 1 September 1422. Deposed 4 March 1461), 1470. ¶ Canada's first institute of higher education is founded, the Quebec Seminary by Bishop Laval, 1668. ¶ Captain Cook first steps foot on New Zealand, 1769. ¶ Napoleon lands at Fréjus, 1799. ¶ Turkey recovers possession of Egypt after treaty with France, 1801. ¶ Hobart in Tasmania is founded, 1804. ¶ Felicitas (Asteroid 109) discovered by C. H. F. Peters, 1869. ¶ First motor omnibus goes into service in London, 1899. ¶ The breathalyser test came into force in Britain to help the police assess the alcohol in a driver's blood, 1967. ¶ Ernesto 'Ché' Guevara shot in Bolivia, 1967. ¶ Cambodia proclaims its statehood as a republic and changes its name to Khmer, 1970.

BORN: Bishop George Tomline, writer and divine, 1753. Charles Camille Saint-Saëns, composer, *Carnival of Animals*, Paris, 1835. Emil Fischer, organic chemist, Germany, 1852. Max Theodor Felix von Laue, physicist, Germany, 1879. Jacques Tati, actor and film director, *Monsieur Hulot's Holiday*, Le Pecq, France, 1908.

DIED: Gabriel Fallopius, Italian anatomist, 1562. Jonathan Swift, satirist and writer, Dean of St Patrick's Cathedral in Dublin, *Gulliver's Travels*, *The Tale of A Tub*, Dublin, 1745. Joseph Farwell Glidden, farmer, devised a machine for making barbed wire, 1906. Pope Pius XII, Castel Gandolfo, Italy, 1958. Ernesto 'Ché' Guevara, guerrilla leader and revolutionary; murdered, Bolivia, 1967. André Maurois, novelist and biographer, *Ariel*, *Don Juan*, Paris, 1967.

*Anniversary of the beginning of the Wars of Independence, Cuba.
Fiji Day, Fiji. Discoverer's Day, Hawaii. Physical Education Day, Japan.
Kruger Day, Republic of South Africa (S. J. P. Kruger, a founder and
statesman, 1825–1904). National Day, Taiwan. National Holiday,
Western Samoa (commemorating the resolution passed by the UN in 1961
ending trusteeship). Feasts of SS: Francis Borgia; Gereon and his
Companions, martyrs; Eulampius and Eulampia, martyrs;
Maharsapor, martyr; Cerbonius, bishop; Paulinus of York, bishop;
Daniel and his Companions, martyrs.*

Saracens defeated at Tours by Charles Martel, 732. ¶ Nottingham Castle burnt by rioters, 1831. ¶ Dione (Asteroid 106) discovered by J. C. Watson, 1868. ¶ Juewa (Asteroid 139) discovered by J. C. Watson, 1874. ¶ German occupation of Sudetenland complete, 1938. ¶ Massive volcanic eruptions in Tristan de Cunha, 1961. ¶ Talks between the British Prime Minister, Harold Wilson, and Ian Smith of Rhodesia aboard HMS *Fearless* anchored off Gibraltar, 1968. ¶ The Canadian Minister of Labour, Pierre Laporte, is kidnapped by terrorists, 1970. ¶ Proclamation of the Independence of the Fiji Islands, 1970. ¶ Spiro T. Agnew resigns as Vice-President of the US, 1973.

BORN: Jacobus Arminius, theologian, Netherlands, 1560. Jean-Antoine Watteau, artist, Valenciennes, France, 1684. Henry Cavendish, physicist, 1731. Benjamin West, painter, President of the Royal Academy, near Springfield, Pennsylvania, 1738. Giuseppe Verdi, composer, *Rigoletto, La Traviata*, Roncole, Parma, Italy, 1813. Fridtjof Nansen, explorer, zoologist and statesman, Nobel Peace Prize, Norway, 1861. Ivan Alexeyvich Bunin, Russian writer, *The Village*, 1870. Lord Nuffield, industrialist and philanthropist, founder of the Morris Motors Company, Worcestershire, 1877. Helen Hayes, actress, Washington D.C., 1900. Alberto Giacometti, sculptor, Switzerland, 1901. Thelonius Monk, jazz pianist and composer, New York City, 1920. Harold Pinter, dramatist and actor, *The Birthday Party, The Caretaker*, London, 1930.

DIED: Fra Filippo Lippi, Florentine painter, Italy, 1469. Sir Mackenzie Bowell, Canadian Prime Minister, Belleville, Ontario, 1917. Edouard Daladier, French statesman, signatory of the Munich Agreement, 1970. Adam Rapacki, Polish politician, Warsaw, 1970. Sir Cyril Burt, psychologist, 1971.

OCTOBER 11

*Anniversary of the Revolution, Panama (1968). Pulaski Memorial
Day, USA (some states only). Macedonian People's Uprising Day, Yugoslavia.
The Feast of the Motherhood of Our Lady, promoted by Pope Pius XI
in 1931. Feasts of SS: Tarachus, Probus and Andronicus, martyrs;
Nectarius, archbishop; Canice, or Kenneth, abbot; Agilbert, bishop;
Gummarus, or Gommaire; Bruno the Great; archbishop,
Alexander Sauli, bishop.*

Pope Leo X confers the title Defender of the Faith (*Fidei Defensor*) upon Henry
VIII of England, 1521. ¶ George II of England crowned, 1727. ¶ Great storm in
India, over 30,000 people are estimated to have perished, 1737. ¶ The Dutch are
defeated off Camperdown by Adam Duncan, 1797. ¶ Beginning of the Red
River Rebellion in Canada, 1869. ¶ Beginnings of revolution in Central China,
1911. ¶ Nurse Edith Cavell is executed in Brussels, 1915. ¶ The German mark
drops to exchange rate of 10,000 million to the £, 1923. ¶ Hitler forms alliance
with the industrialist Hugenberg to support the National Socialist Party, 1931.
¶ Coleman Hawkins records *Body and Soul* in New York, 1939. ¶ The *Apollo 7*
spacecraft, with 3 men aboard, is successfully launched from Cape Kennedy by
US, 1968. ¶ Chairman Mao Tse-tung's widow, Chiang Ching, and three of her
associates (the 'Gang of Four') are arrested in Peking, 1976.

BORN: Arthur Phillip, founded the penal colony at Sydney in Australia, first
Governor of New South Wales, London, 1738. Heinrich Olbers, astronomer,
discovered several comets and asteroids, Germany, 1758. Joseph Gillot, perfected
the steel writing pen, Sheffield, 1799. Henry John Heinz, food manufacturer,
Pittsburgh, Pennsylvania, 1844. Lewis Fry Richardson, mathematician,
Newcastle-upon-Tyne, 1881. Friedrich Bergius, inventor of a process for
extracting petrol from coal, Germany, 1884. François Mauriac, novelist, poet,
and biographer, *The Desert of Love, The Dark Angels*, Bordeaux, 1885. Richard
Burton, actor, Wales, 1925.

DIED: Sir Thomas Wyatt, courtier and poet, Sherborne, Dorset, 1542. Meri-
wether Lewis, explorer of the north-western US, near Nashville, 1809. James
Prescott Joule, physicist, the measure of a unit of energy bears his name, 1889.
Anton Bruckner, composer, Austria, 1896. Jean Henry Fabre, entomologist
and naturalist, 1915. Maurice Vlaminck, Fauvist painter, France, 1958. Jean
Cocteau, poet, dramatist, novelist, film director, 1963.

OCTOBER 12

Discovery Day, Bahamas. Columbus Day, Ecuador. Columbus Day,
El Salvador. Independence Day, Equatorial Guinea (1968, formerly a
Spanish colony). Columbus Day, Nicaragua. Hispanic Day, Spain.
Republic Day, Sudan. Feasts of SS: Maximilian of Lorch, bishop and martyr;
Felix and Cyprian, and many other martyrs; Edwin, martyr;
Ethelburga, virgin; Wilfrid of York, bishop.

Columbus lands on the island of Guanahani, 1492. ¶ Admiral Sir George Rooke defeats the French fleet off Vigo, 1702. ¶ Independence of Brazil proclaimed, 1822. ¶ Beginning of the Anglo-Boer War, 1899. ¶ Oswald Mosley and the British Union of Fascists stage an anti-Jewish march through the East End of London, 1936.

BORN: Pedro I, Emperor of Brazil, 1798. Elmer Sperry, inventor, principally known for his use of the gyroscope, Cortland, New York, 1860. James Ramsay MacDonald, statesman, the first Labour Party Prime Minister of Britain, Moray, 1866. Ralph Vaughan Williams, composer, *Fantasia on a Theme of Thomas Tallis*, *Antarctica Symphony*, Ampney, Gloucestershire, 1872. James McAuley, Australian poet, 1917.

DIED: Piero della Francesca, painter, Italy, 1492. Matsuo Bashoh, poet, master of the *haiku* form, Osaka, Japan, 1694. Elizabeth Fry, social worker and prison reformer, 1845. Robert Stephenson, railway and civil engineer, London, 1859. Roger Brooke Taney, politician and jurist, Chief Justice of the US Supreme Court, Washington D.C., 1864. General Robert E. Lee, Confederate Commander-in-Chief, Lexington, Virginia, 1870. François Pierre Guizot, statesman and historian, Val Richer, Normandy, 1874. Edith Cavell, nurse, executed by the Germans, 1915. Anatole France, novelist and critic, *Penguin Island*, 1924. Princess Te Puea Herangi, Maori nationalist, New Zealand, 1952. Paul Müller, chemist, formulated dichlorodiphenyltichloroethane (DDT), Basel, 1965. Dean Gooderham Acheson, American lawyer and statesman, 1971.

Feasts of SS: Edward the Confessor; Faustus, Januarius and Martial, martyrs; Comgan, abbot; Gerald of Aurillac; Coloman, martyr; Maurice of Carnoët, abbot.

Henry IV of England crowned, 1399. ¶ Final defeat of Benedict Arnold at Lake Champlain, 1776. ¶ British forces defeat the US at Queenston Heights, 1812. ¶ Murat is shot after attempted repossession of Naples, 1815. ¶ Siwa (Asteroid 140) discovered by J. Palisa, 1874. ¶ The Public Bank in Detroit is declared insolvent, 1966. ¶ After the resignation of Vice-President Spiro T. Agnew, President Nixon nominates Gerald Ford to replace him, 1973.

BORN: Sophia, Electress of Hanover, mother of George I, Mayence, 1630. Ferdinand VII, King of Spain, 1784. Rudolph Virchow, German politician, pathologist and archaeologist, *Freedom of Science*, Pomerania, 1821. Lillie Langtry, actress and entertainer, Jersey, 1853. Sir Geoffrey Vickers, V.C., army officer and civil servant, Nottingham, 1894.

DIED: Pope Gregory XII, 1417. Nicolas Malebranche, philosopher, Paris, 1715. Dr John Gill, Baptist divine, Southwark, London, 1771. Antonio Canova, sculptor, *Cupid and Psyche*, 1822. Sir Henry Irving, theatrical actor and manager, London, 1905. Shaul Tchernichowski, Hebrew poet, Jerusalem, 1943.

OCTOBER 14

Anniversary of the South Yemen Revolution, Yemen Arab Republic.
Day of the Anniversary of President Mobutu, Zaire. Feasts of SS:
Callistus, or Calixtus, pope and martyr; Justus of Lyons, bishop;
Manechildis, virgin; Angadrisma, virgin; Burchard, bishop;
Dominic Loricatus.

William I defeats Harold at the battle of Hastings, 1066. ¶ Accession of William I of England (reigned until 9 September 1087), 1066. ¶ Prussians defeated at Jena by Napoleon, 1806. ¶ Riots over the price of bread, in Hyde Park, London, 1855. ¶ Encke's Comet observed in Britain, 1871. ¶ Landing of the first Canadian troops in Britain, 1914. ¶ HMS *Royal Oak* is sunk by Germany in the Scapa Flow, 1939. ¶ The world's first supersonic aeroplane flight, over Southern California, 1947. ¶ The Rev. Martin Luther King is awarded the Nobel Peace Prize for advocating a policy of non-violence, 1964. ¶ The first 50p decimal coin is issued in Britain, 1970. ¶ Major Egyptian offensive against Israel at Sinai, 1973.

BORN: William Penn, English Quaker who founded the state of Pennsylvania, London, 1644. Adolphe Monticelli, painter, Marseilles, 1824. Masaoka Shiki, poet, revived the traditional *haiku* and *tanka* verse forms, Matsuyama, Japan, 1867. Miles Franklin, Australian novelist, 1879. Éamon De Valera, Irish statesman, New York City, 1882. Katherine Mansfield, writer, *Bliss, The Garden Party*, Wellington, New Zealand, 1888. Dwight David Eisenhower, statesman and soldier, Texas, 1890. E. E. Cummings, American poet, Massachusetts, 1894. Lilian Gish, film actress, Ohio, 1896.

DIED: Hugh Capet, King of France, Paris, 996. Hassan ibn-ali Nizam-al-Mulik, Persian statesman, near Nehbandan, Iran, 1092. James, Marshall Keith, Scottish military commander, Hochkirchen, Germany, 1758. Samuel Phillips, novelist, *Caleb Stukely*, Brighton, Sussex, 1854. Dame Edith Evans, actress, 1976. Bing Crosby, American popular singer and actor, 1977.

OCTOBER 15

Cayenne Holiday, French Guiana. Evacuation Day, Tunisia.
Feasts of SS: Teresa of Avila, virgin; Leonard of Vandoeuvre, abbot;
Thecla of Kitzingen, virgin; Euthymius the Younger, abbot.

The Gregorian calendar is introduced in Italy and Spain, 1582. ¶ The first human flight in a balloon is achieved by Jean de Rozier, near Paris, 1783. ¶ A great comet is observed throughout Europe, 1812. ¶ Alfred Dreyfus is arrested on a charge of treason, 1894. ¶ Clayton Anti-Trust Act enacted in US, 1914. ¶ Nikita S. Khrushchev is replaced as leader of the USSR by Leonid I. Brezhnev, 1964.

BORN: Virgil (Publius Vergilius Maro), Roman poet, *Georgics, Aeneid, Ecologues*, Andes, near Mantua, Cisalpine Gaul (now Italy), 70BC. Akbar (I) the Great, Mogul Emperor, 1542. Evangelista Torricelli, mathematician and scientist, devised the barometer, Faenza, Italy, 1608. Florence Nightingale, hospital reformer, Florence, Italy, 1820. Friedrich Nietzsche, philosopher and writer, *Thus Spake Zarathustra, The Will to Power*, Röcken, Germany, 1844. John L. Sullivan, champion heavy-weight boxer, Roxbury, Massachusetts, 1858. Pelham Grenville Wodehouse, writer and humorist, Guildford, Surrey, 1881. Mervyn Le Roy, film director, *Little Caesar, Quo Vadis?* (1951), San Francisco, 1900.

DIED: Antoine de la Mothe Cadillac, soldier, founded the city of Detroit, Governor of Louisiana, 1730. John Morgan, physician, Philadelphia, 1789. Tadeusz Kosciuszko, Polish patriot and fighter, 1817. Mata Hari, courtesan and spy, Vincennes, 1917. Raymond Poincaré, President of France, Paris, 1934. Pierre Laval, Prime Minister of France and Nazi collaborator; executed, 1945. Hermann Goering, Nazi leader, creator of the Luftwaffe; suicide, 1946. James McAuley, Australian poet, 1976.

Feasts of SS: Hedwig, widow; Martinian and other martyrs, and Maxima Gall; Mommolinus, bishop; Bercharius, abbot; Lull, bishop; Anastasius of Cluny; Bertrand of Comminges, bishop; Gerard Majella.

The Houses of Parliament in London burn down, 1834. ¶ Massacre of Christians at Aleppo, 1850. ¶ The first aeroplane flight in England, by Samuel Cody (a US citizen) in a bi-plane at Farnborough, 1908. ¶ Assassination of Ali Khan of Pakistan, 1951. ¶ China explodes its first atomic bomb, 1964. ¶ Harold Wilson of the Labour Party becomes the British Prime Minister, 1964.

BORN: Albrecht von Haller, botanist, anatomist and poet, Bern, Switzerland, 1708. Noah Webster, lexicographer and teacher, *English Grammar, American Dictionary of the English Language*, West Hartford, Connecticut, 1758. Robert Stephenson, railway and civil engineer, Willington Quay, Northumberland, 1803. Arnold Böcklin, painter, *The Isle of the Dead*, Sweden, 1827. Oscar Wills Wilde, dramatist, poet, novelist and critic, *The Picture of Dorian Gray, The Importance of Being Earnest*, Dublin, 1854. David Ben Gurion, Israeli Prime Minister, Poland, 1886. Eugene O'Neill, dramatist, *Mourning becomes Electra, Desire under the Elms*, New York City, 1888. Michael Collins, a founder of the I. R. A., County Cork, Ireland, 1890. Enver Hoxha, Albanian Premier, 1908. Günter Grass, German novelist, *The Tin Drum*, Poland, 1927.

DIED: Luca Signorelli, painter, Cortona, Italy, 1523. Hugh Latimer, Protestant reformer and martyr, Oxford, 1555. Nicholas Ridley, Protestant reformer and martyr, burnt at the stake, Oxford, 1555. Marie Antoinette, Queen of France; executed, Paris, 1793. Joachim von Ribbentrop, Hitler's Foreign Minister, hanged, Nuremberg, 1946. Artur von Seyss-Inquart, Austrian minister, German High Commissioner of the Occupied Netherlands; hanged, Nuremberg, 1946. George Catlett Marshall, directed American war efforts in the Second World War, formulated the Marshall Aid Plan, Washington D.C., 1959.

*Feast of St Etheldreda, BCP, observed by the Catholic Church on 23 June.
Anniversary of Dessalines's Death, Haiti (Jean-Jacques Dessalines, Emperor of
Haiti, born 1758, assassinated in 1806). Mothers Day, Malawi.
Feasts of SS: Margaret Mary, virgin; John the Dwarf; Anstrudis, or
Austrude, virgin; Nothelm, archbishop; Seraphino; The Ursuline
Martyrs of Valenciennes.*

Horatio Gates obtains surrender of General Burgoyne at Saratoga, New York, 1777. ¶ The siege of Sebastopol is begun by British and French forces, 1854. ¶ General Ulysses S. Grant is appointed overall Union Commander of the West, 1863. ¶ The Boers are defeated at Glencoe by British troops, 1899. ¶ Yugoslavian Republic comes into being, 1819. ¶ The nuclear power station Calder Hall is opened in Britain, 1956.

BORN: John Wilkes, parliamentarian and political reformer, published *The North Briton*, Clerkenwell, London, 1727. Claude, Comte de Saint-Simon, philosopher and socialist, Paris, 1760. Georg Büchner, dramatist, *Danton's Death*, Germany, 1913. Nathanael West (Nathan Wallenstein Weinstein), novelist, *Miss Lonelyhearts, The Day of the Locust*, New York City, 1903. Arthur Miller, dramatist, *Death of a Salesman, A View from the Bridge*, New York City, 1915. Sumner Locke Elliott, Australian novelist, *Edens Lost*, 1917. Rita Hayworth, actress, New York City, 1918.

DIED: René Reamur, inventor, naturalist and writer, France, 1757. Edward, Lord Hawke, naval commander, Shepperton, Middlesex, 1781. Frédéric François Chopin, composer, 1849. Gustav Robert Kirchoff, German physicist, made the first spectroscope, 1887. Patrice MacMahon, military commander and President of France, France, 1893. Karl Kautsky, anti-Bolshevik Marxist, philosopher, Vienna, 1938. Ellsworth Huntingdon, geographer, pioneered the study of climatic influences on culture, *Civilization and Climate*, 1947.

OCTOBER 18

Alaska Day, Alaska, USA. Feasts of SS: Luke, evangelist; Justus of Beauvais, martyr.

The Battle of Leipzig, 1813. ¶ The last lottery to be held in England, 1826. ¶ Flora (Asteroid 8) discovered by J. R. Hind, 1847. ¶ The raid on Harper's Ferry led by John Brown ends abortively, 1859. ¶ Nuwa (Asteroid 150) discovered by J. C. Watson, 1875. ¶ The Burma Road is reopened by the British, 1940.

BORN: Gianbattista Marino, poet, Naples, 1569. Luca Giordano, painter, Naples, 1632. Eugene of Savoy, Austrian soldier and statesman, Paris, 1663. Antonio Canaletto, artist, Venice, 1697. Pierre Choderlos de Laclos, artillery officer and writer, *Les Liaisons dangereuses*, France, 1741. Christian Schonbein, chemist, invented gun-cotton, Metzingen, Swabia, 1799. Henri Bergson, philosopher and writer, *Creative Evolution*, Paris, 1859. Thomas Love Peacock, novelist and poet, *Headlong Hall, Nightmare Abbey, Crotchet Castle*, Weymouth, Dorset, 1885. Pierre Trudeau, Canadian Prime Minister, Montreal, Quebec, 1919. Lee Harvey Oswald, a conspirator in the assassination of President John F. Kennedy, New Orleans, 1939.

DIED: Philippe de Commynes, French chronicler and historian, 1511. Jacob Jordaens, Dutch painter, 1678. Henry John Temple, 3rd Viscount Palmerston, British Prime Minister, Brocket Hall, Welwyn, Hertfordshire, 1865. Charles Babbage, inventor of calculating machines, 1871. Charles-François Gounod, composer and conductor, 1893. Alfred Binet, psychologist, devised a test for measuring intelligence, 1911. Thomas Alva Edison, inventor, 1931. José Ortega y Gasset, philosopher and statesman, *The Revolt of the Masses*, Madrid, 1955.

Feasts of SS: Peter of Alcantara; Ptolemaeus, Lucius and another, martyrs;
Varus, martyr, and St Cleopatra, widow; Ethbin; Aquilinus, bishop;
Frideswide, virgin.

A declaration of rights and liberties is drawn up by delegates at the Stamp Act Congress in New York, 1765. ¶ Capitulation of Cornwallis at Yorktown with over 7000 men, 1781. ¶ Napoleon's retreat from Moscow begins, 1812. ¶ Fall of the Coalition formed by David Lloyd George, 1922. ¶ The League of Nations imposes sanctions against Italy after the invasion of Abyssinia, 1935. ¶ The People's Republic of China is formally proclaimed, 1949.

BORN: Marsilio Ficino, classical scholar and philosopher, Italy, 1433. Sir Thomas Browne, physician and writer, *Religio Medici, Pseudoxica Epidemica, Urn Burial,* London, 1605. Leigh Hunt, essayist and poet. *A Jar of Honey from Mount Hybla,* Southgate, Middlesex, 1784. Adam Lindsay Gordon, Australian poet, *Sea-spray and Smoke-drift,* Azores, 1833. Alfred Dreyfus, army officer (the Dreyfus affair), France, 1859. Lewis Mumford, historian and philosopher, *The Culture of Cities, The City in History,* Flushing, Long Island, 1895. Yakubu Gowon, military commander, Nigeria, 1934.

DIED: John Lackland, King of England, Newark, 1216. Jacobus Arminius, theologian, 1609. Sir Thomas Browne, physician and writer, *Religio Medici, Pseudoxica Epidemica,* 1682. Sir Charles Wheatstone, inventor and physicist, Paris, 1875. George Mortimer Pullman, industrialist, Chicago, 1897. Cesare Lombroso, criminologist, Turin, 1909. Ernest, Lord Rutherford, physicist, Cambridge, 1937. Edna St Vincent Millay, poet, *A Few Figs from Thistles, The Harp-Weaver and Other Poems,* Austerlitz, New York, 1950.

OCTOBER 20

_Anniversary of the 1944 Revolution, Guatemala. Kenyatta Day,
Kenya (President Jomo Kenyatta's birthday). Feasts of SS:
John of Kanti; Caprasius, martyr; Artemius, martyr; Acca, bishop;
Andrew of Crete, martyr._

Naval battle at Salamis, the Persians are defeated by the Greeks, 480BC. ¶ George
I of Great Britain crowned, 1714. ¶ Austrians are defeated at Ulm by the French,
1805. ¶ US and Britain establish boundary between Canada and US as 49th
Parallel, 1818. ¶ Allied vessels defeat Turkish and Egyptian fleets at Navarino,
1826. ¶ Lieutenant (later Major-General) Harold Harris is the first man to have
his life saved by a parachute, 1922. ¶ Mau-Mau disorders result in a state of
emergency being declared in Kenya, 1952. ¶ Aristotle Onassis marries Jacqueline
Kennedy, 1968. ¶ Archibald Cox, the Watergate Special Prosecutor, is dis-
missed by President Nixon, 1973. ¶ The Sydney Opera House is opened by
Queen Elizabeth II, 1973.

BORN: Sir Christopher Wren, astronomer and architect, East Knoyle, Wiltshire,
1632. Henry John Temple, 3rd Viscount Palmerston, British Prime Minister,
Hampshire, 1784. Odilon Redon, Sympolist painter and lithographer, Bordeaux,
France, 1840. Arthur Rimbaud, poet, _Le Bâteau Ivre, Une Saison en Enfer_,
Charleville, France, 1854. John Dewey, educationalist and philosopher, Vermont,
1859. Charles Ives, composer, Connecticut, 1874. Sir James Chadwick, physicist,
discovered the neutron, Manchester, 1891.

DIED: Jacopo della Quercia, sculptor, Bologna, 1438. Sir Richard Burton,
explorer and writer, discovered Lake Tanganyika, 1890. Arthur Henderson,
Labour Party politician and statesman, Nobel Prize for Peace, 1935. Herbert
Hoover, Republican US President, 1964. Shigeru Yoshida, Prime Minister of
Japan, Oishi, Japan, 1967.

Trafalgar Day, honouring Admiral Nelson's defeat of the French fleet in 1805.
Armed Forces Day, Honduras. Anniversary of the Revolution Day,
Somali Democratic Republic. Feasts of SS: Hilarion, abbot; Ursula and her
Maidens, martyrs; Malchus; Fintan, or Munnu, of Taghmon, abbot;
Condedus; John of Bridlington.

The Franco-Spanish fleet is defeated at Trafalgar by Nelson, 1805. ¶ Riots in Hyde Park, London, over the cost of bread, 1855. ¶ Freia (Asteroid 76) discovered by M. d'Arrest, 1862. ¶ Occupation of Tibet by Chinese troops, 1950. ¶ A colliery slag tip at Aberfan in Wales slips and engulfs a school, rows of houses, and a farm. Over 140 people lose their lives, 1966.

BORN: Georg Ernst Stahl, chemist, Ansbach, Germany, 1660. Samuel Taylor Coleridge, critic and poet, 'Kubla Khan', Devon, 1772. Alphonse de Lamartine, poet and statesman, *Jocelyn*, Mâcon, France, 1790. Alfred Nobel, industrialist, inventor of dynamite and cordite, instituted the Nobel Prizes, Stockholm, Sweden, 1833. Dizzy Gillespie, modern jazz trumpeter, South Carolina, 1917.

DIED: Pietro Aretino, satirist, 1556. Edmund Waller, poet, *Go, Lovely Rose*, Beaconsfield, Buckinghamshire, 1687. Viscount Horatio Nelson, British naval commander; off Cape Trafalgar, Spain, 1758. Arthur Schnitzler, dramatist and author, *Reiger (La Ronde)*, *Anatol*, Vienna, 1931. Ejnar Hertzsprung, astronomer, Denmark, 1967. Jack Kerouac, writer, On the Road, Satori in Paris, Lowell, Massachusetts, 1969.

OCTOBER 22

Dies Mala or 'Egyptian Day', considered unlucky in the Middle Ages.
Feasts of SS: Abercius, bishop; Philip of Heracles, bishop,
and his Companions, martyrs; Mallonus, or Mellon, bishop;
Nunilo and Alodia, virgins and martyrs; Donatus of Fiesole, bishop.

The first parachute descent, by André-Jacques Garnerin, jumping from a balloon at a height of over 6,000 feet, in Paris, 1797. ¶ War declared on the Moors in Morocco by Spain, 1859. ¶ Army revolt in Athens forces King Otto I to resign, 1862. ¶ *Farewell Blues* recorded by Joe Venuti and Eddie Lang in Chicago, 1931. ¶ President John F. Kennedy announces that USSR missile bases have been established in Cuba, 1962. ¶ The *Eilat*, an Israeli destroyer, is sunk off the coast of Sinai by Egyptian missiles, over 40 deaths, 1967.

BORN: Nadir Shah, Shah of Persia, restored the Persian Empire, Iran, 1688. Franz Liszt, composer and pianist, Hungary, 1811. Charles Marie Leconte de Lisle, Parnassian poet, *Poèmes barbares*, Isle de Réunion (Indian Ocean), 1818. Giovanni Giolitti, statesman, Liberal reformer, Italy, 1842. Sarah Bernhardt, actress, Paris, 1844. Robert Rauschenberg, Pop artist, Port Arthur, Texas, 1925.

DIED: Charles Martel, 'Charles the Hammer', Frankish emperor, Quierzy-sur-Oise, France, 741. Mathurin Régnier, satirical poet, Rouen, France, 1613. Sir Roderick Murchison, geologist, London, 1871. William Edward Hartpole Lecky, historian, *History of the Rise and Influence of the Spirit of Rationalism in Europe*, 1903. Paul Cézanne, Impressionist painter, 1906. Edward Carson, Anglo-Irish politician, 1935. Pablo Casals, cellist, 1973. Arnold Toynbee, historian and philosopher, 1975.

OCTOBER 23

Feasts of SS: Theodoret, martyr; Severinus, or Seurin, bishop;
Severinus Boethius, martyr; Romanus of Rouen, bishop;
Ignatius of Constantinople, bishop; Allucio.

The world was created on this day, a Sunday, at 9 o'clock in the morning – according to the seventeenth-century divine James Ussher, Archbishop of Armagh, and Dr John Lightfoot of Cambridge – in 4004BC. ¶ English civil war battle at Edgehill, 1642. ¶ Elizabeth Gaunt burnt at Tyburn for concealing a number of Clarendon's rebels, 1685. ¶ First Parliament of Great Britain meets, 1707. ¶ Hector Munro defeats the Nabob of Oudh in Bengal, 1764. ¶ The defeat of Sterling Price of the Confederacy at Westport, Missouri, brings to a conclusion fighting west of the Mississippi, 1864. ¶ The United Nations General Assembly meets in New York for the first time, 1946 ¶ The foundation of the Federation of Rhodesia and Nyasaland, 1953. ¶ Gary Gabelich in the rocket-powered *Blue Flame* achieves a speed of just over 650mph on the Bonneville Salt Flats in Utah, 1970. ¶ Severe earthquakes in Nicaragua, over 10,000 people are killed, 1972.

BORN: Adalbert Stifter, novelist, *Indian Summer*, Austria, 1805. Pierre Larousse, editor and lexicographer, Yonne, France, 1817. Robert Bridges, poet, Poet Laureate, 'A Testament of Beauty', Walmer, Kent, 1844. Louis Riel, Canadian insurgent, led the Red River rebellion, St Boniface, Manitoba, 1844. Pele, Brazilian footballer, Brazil, 1940.

DIED: Thomas Pride, colonel in the Parliamentary Army during the English Civil War, Surrey, 1658. Théophile Gautier, poet and author, 1872. W. G. Grace, English cricketer, 1915. John Boyd Dunlop, Scottish inventor of the pneumatic tyre, 1921. Zane Grey, writer of cowboy and western stories, Ohio, 1939. Al Jolson, American singer and entertainer, California, 1950.

OCTOBER 24

United Nations Day, observed since 1946 when the UN Charter came into operation.
Republic Day, Rhodesia. King Chulalongkorn Memorial Day, Thailand.
Independence Day, Zambia (1964, formerly Northern Rhodesia).
Feasts of SS: Raphael the Archangel; Felix of Thibiuca, bishop and martyr;
Proclus, archbishop; Aretas and the Martyrs of Najran, and St Elesbaan;
Senoch, abbot; Martin, or Mark; Maglorius, or Maelor, bishop;
Martin of Vertou, abbot; Evergislus, bishop; Antony Claret, archbishop.

Benefit of Clergy no longer allowed to murderers in Britain, 1513. ¶ The title of 'King of Great Britain' is adopted, 1604. ¶ The end of the Thirty Years' War with the signing of the Treaty of Westphalia, 1648. ¶ First publication of the Zinoviev Letter, 1924. ¶ Beginning of the German siege of Sebastopol, 1941. ¶ The United Nations formally comes into being, 1945. ¶ Blockade of Cuba by US begins, 1962. ¶ Severe flooding in Tunisia, over 300 people dead and 150,000 made homeless, 1969.

BORN: Aurangzeb, last Mogul emperor of India, 1618. Anton van Leeuwenhoek, microscopist, *Opera*, Delft, Netherlands, 1632. Eugène Fromentin, novelist and painter, France, 1820. Dame Sybil Thorndike, actress, Gainsborough, Lincolnshire, 1882. Merian C. Cooper, film director and producer, *Grass, King Kong* (1933), Jacksonville, Alabama, 1893.

DIED: Tycho Brahe, astronomer and mathematician, Denmark, 1601. Pierre Gassendi, scientist and philosopher, 1655. Alessandro Scarlatti, Baroque composer, Naples, 1725. Peter Ilyich Tchaikovsky, composer, *Romeo and Juliet, Swan Lake*, St Petersburg, Russia, 1893. Pierre Puvis de Chavannes, mural painter, Paris, 1898. Vidkun Quisling, politician, executed, Akershus Fortress, Oslo, 1945. Franz Lehár, Hungarian composer, *The Merry Widow*, 1948. George Edward Moore, philosopher, editor of *Mind* 1921–47, *Principia Ethica, Philosophical Studies*, Cambridge, 1958.

OCTOBER 25

St Crispin's Day, remembering the patron saint of shoemakers;
his remains and those of his brother Crispinian were said to have been
washed ashore in Kent after martyrdom in France. Taiwan
Restoration Day, Taiwan (1945). Feasts of SS: Chrysanthus and Daria,
martyrs; Crispin and Crispinian, martyrs; Fronto and George, bishops;
Gaudentius, bishop.

The English defeat the French at Agincourt, 1415. ¶ Accession of George III of Great Britain, 1760. ¶ Allied victory at the battle of Balaclava in the Crimea, 1854. ¶ Annexation of the Fiji Islands by Britain, 1874. ¶ Annexation of Transvaal by Britain, 1900. ¶ The British Foreign Office publishes the Zinoviev Letter, 1924. ¶ Vatican Council approves immovable Easter *in principle*, 1963. ¶ Port Suez in Egypt shelled by the Israelis and an oil refinery, supplying most of Egypt's own needs, is destroyed, 1967. ¶ Independence of the Republic of the Transkei proclaimed in Africa, 1976.

BORN: Thomas Macaulay, statesman and historian, *History of England*, Leicestershire, 1800. Richard P. Bonnington, watercolourist, Nottinghamshire, 1801. Johann Strauss, composer, *The Blue Danube, Tales from the Vienna Woods*, Vienna, 1825. Georges Bizet, composer, *Carmen, The Pearl Fishers*, Paris, 1838. Pablo Picasso, painter, sculptor and lithographer, Malaga, Spain, 1881. Richard Byrd, aviator and polar explorer, Virginia, 1888. Abel Gance, film director and producer, *Napoléon*, Paris, 1889. Levi Eshkol, Israeli statesman, Kiev, Russia, 1895.

DIED: Geoffrey Chaucer, poet and writer, *The Canterbury Tales*, 1400. Evangelista Torricelli, mathematician and scientist, devised the barometer, Florence, 1647. Sir Charles Hallé, pianist and conductor, Manchester, 1895. Frank Norris, novelist, *McTeague, The Octopus*, San Francisco, 1902. Frederick William Rolfe (Baron Corvo), novelist, *Hadrian the Seventh*, Venice, 1913. Lord Dunsany, writer, 1957.

OCTOBER 26

National Holiday, Austria. Benin Armed Forces Day, Popular Republic of Benin.
The Birthday of Shahanshah Aryamehr, Iran (the Shah of Iran).
Armed Forces Day, Republic of Rwanda. Feasts of SS:
Evaristus, pope and martyr; Lucian and Marcian, martyrs;
Rusticus of Narbonne, bishop; Cedd, bishop; Eata, bishop; Bean, bishop.

First appearance of the Asiatic cholera in England, at Sunderland, 1831. ¶ Pomona (Asteroid 32) discovered by H. Goldschmidt, 1854. ¶ Victor Emmanuel proclaimed King of Italy by Garibaldi, 1860. ¶ First Russian Soviet formed, by workers and others in St Petersburg, 1905. ¶ Bolsheviks led by Lenin overthrow Kerensky's government in Petrograd; the 'October Revolution' (New Style date – 7 November), 1917. ¶ The USSR Minister of Defence, Marshall Zhukov, is relieved of his post, 1957. ¶ The first New York – Paris transatlantic jet passenger service, inaugurated by Pan Am, 1958. ¶ The first New York – London transatlantic jet passenger service, inaugurated by BOAC, 1958. ¶ Bomb outrages by extremist Puerto Ricans in New York City, several at Rockfeller Centre, 1974.

BORN: Domenico Scarlatti, virtuoso harpsichordist and composer, Naples, 1685. Georges-Jacques Danton, revolutionary and orator, France, 1759. Lev Trotsky, revolutionary, a leader of the Bolshevik Revolution, writer, *History of the Russian Revolution*, near Kirovo, Russia, 1879. Andrei Bely, poet and novelist, Moscow, 1880. Mahalia Jackson, jazz and gospel singer, New Orleans, 1911. John Arden, playwright, *Sergeant Musgrave's Dance*, Yorkshire, 1930.

DIED: William Hogarth, artist and engraver, *A Rake's Progress*, London, 1764. Sir Aurel Stein, archaeologist, Kabul, Afghanistan, 1943. Gerty Cori, American biochemist, wife of Charles Cori, 1957. Igor Ivanovich Sikorsky, aeronautical engineer and inventor, pioneered the modern helicopter, Easton, Connecticut, 1972.

Feasts of SS: Frumentius, bishop; Otteran, or Odhuran, abbot.

Battle of Newbury in the English Civil War, 1644. ¶ The Stamp Act Congress in New York, 1765. ¶ Treaty of San Lorenzo between Spain and US settles boundary with Florida, and gives US Mississippi navigation rights, 1795. ¶ Final failure of French invasion of Ireland, 1798. ¶ Berlin occupied by Napoleon, 1806. ¶ Garibaldi begins the march on Rome, 1867. ¶ Surrender of the French at Metz, 1870. ¶ The League of Nations' headquarters are settled in Geneva, 1920. ¶ A great earthquake in central Yugoslavia destroyed the town of Banja Luka, many deaths, 1969.

BORN: Desiderius Erasmus, scholar and writer, *In Praise of Folly*, 1466. Captain James Cook, explorer, Yorkshire, 1728. James Macpherson, poet, *The Ossian Poems*, Inverness, 1736. Niccolo Paganini, violin virtuoso, Genoa, 1782. Isaac Singer, inventor of the sewing machine, Pittstown, New York, 1811. Pierre Berthelot, organic chemist, Paris, 1827. Theodore Roosevelt, President of the US, New York City, 1858. Dylan Thomas, poet, *Deaths and Entrances*, *Under Milk Wood*, Swansea, Wales, 1914. Roy Lichtenstein, Pop artist, New York, 1923.

DIED: Marcus Brutus, assassin of Julius Caesar, Rome, 42BC. Pope Eugenius II, 827. Ivan III (Ivan the Great), 1505. George Morland, rural painter; of 'brain fever', London, 1806. Lascelles Abercrombie, writer and critic, 1938. Lise Meitner, physicist, co-discovered nuclear fission with Otto Hahn, Cambridge, 1968.

Old day for election of the Lord Mayor of London. National Day, Greece.
Feasts of SS: Simon and Jude, or Thaddeus, apostles;
Anastasia and Cyril, martyrs; Fidelis of Como, martyr;
Salvius, or Saire; Faro, bishop.

Constantine the Great victorious over Marcus Aurelius Valerius Maxentius at the Mulvian Bridge, 312. ¶ Accession of Henry III of England, 1216. ¶ Christopher Columbus discovers Cuba (first expedition), 1492. ¶ Polyhymnia (Asteroid 33) discovered by Chacornac, 1854. ¶ Formation of the Aerated Bread Company in London, 1862. ¶ Strasbourg falls to the Prussians, 1870. ¶ The Statue of Liberty is publicly unveiled in New York Harbour, 1886. ¶ 'The Plague of the Spanish Lady', an influenza epidemic, reaches its height in Britain, 1918. ¶ Benito Mussolini marches upon Rome, 1922. ¶ The US Stock Exchange collapses and world-wide economic crises follow, 1929. ¶ The Spanish Government is moved to Barcelona, 1937.

BORN: Cornelius Jansen, theologian and clergyman, near Leerdam, Netherlands, 1585. Ivan Turgenev, novelist, *A Nest of Gentlefolk, Fathers and Children*, Orel, Russia, 1818. Evelyn Waugh, novelist, *Decline and Fall, Brideshead Revisited*, London, 1903. Albert Maltz, film writer and director, *Destination Tokyo, Tell them Willy-boy is here*, New York City, 1908.

DIED: Jahangir, Mogul Emperor of India, 1627. John Wallis, mathematician, Professor of Geometry at Oxford, Oxford, 1703. John Locke, philosopher, *Essay Concerning Human Understanding*, Essex, 1704. Ottmar Mergenthaler, inventor of the Linotype composing machine, Baltimore, Maryland, 1899. David Jones, writer and artist, *In Parenthesis*, Harrow, 1974.

Old Day for the swearing-in of the Lord Mayor of London.
Suez National Day, Arab Republic of Egypt (commemorating the
Constantinople Convention of 1888 that opened the canal to all vessels).
Republic Day, Turkey (1923). Public Holiday, St Vincent, West Indies.
Feasts of SS: Narcissus of Jerusalem, bishop; Theuderius, or Chef, abbot;
Colman of Kilmacduagh, bishop; Abraham of Rostov, abbot; The Martyrs of Douay.

Frederick II of Prussia's forces defeat the Austrians at Freiberg, 1762. ¶ Reform Riots at Bristol, 1831. ¶ Leon Czolgosz electrocuted for the assassination of President McKinley, 1901. ¶ End of the battle for Warsaw when Austrian and German forces are driven back by the Russians (battle began on 15 October), 1914. ¶ President Batistá formally suspends the constitution of Cuba, 1957.

BORN: The Duke of Alba, Spanish military commander, 1507. James Boswell, biographer and lawyer, *The Life of Samuel Johnson, Journal of a Tour to the Hebrides*, Scotland, 1746. Jean Charles Louis Blanc, socialist and writer, Madrid, 1811. Jean Giraudoux, dramatist, *Siegfried*, France, 1882. Fanny Brice, actress, dancer and singer, 1891. Joseph Goebbels, Nazi leader and propagandist, Germany, 1897.

DIED: Sir Walter Raleigh, explorer, writer and courtier, *The Nymph's Reply to the Shepherd, History of the World*, London, 1618. James Shirley, dramatist, *The Witty Fair One*, London, 1666. Jean le Rond d'Alembert, philosopher, *encyclopédist*, 1783. John Leech, artist and illustrator, Kensington, London, 1864. Joseph Pulitzer, journalist and newspaper owner, endowed Columbia University with a School of Journalism (hence the Pulitzer Prize), Charleston, South Carolina, 1911.

OCTOBER 30

Feasts of SS: Serapion of Antioch, bishop;
Marcellus the Centurion, martyr; Asterius, bishop;
Germanus of Capua, bishop; Ethelnoth, archbishop; Alphonsus Rodriguez.

Publius Aelius Hadrianus (Hadrian) founds Antinopölis in Middle Egypt, 130.
¶ Henry VII of England crowned, 1485. ¶ Bolivar establishes independent
government of Venezuela, 1817. ¶ The Caledonian Canal is completed, 1822.
¶ Beginning of the first battle of Ypres (ends 21 November), 1914. ¶ Formation
of Fascist Government in Rome by Benito Mussolini, 1922. ¶ Release of Cardinal
Mindszenty, 1956.

BORN: John Adams, second President of the US (1797–1801), 1735. André Marie
de Chénier, poet, 1762. Fyodor Dostoyevsky, novelist, *Crime and Punishment,*
The Brothers Karamazov, Moscow, 1821. Alfred Sisley, Impressionist painter,
Paris, 1839. Paul Valéry, poet and critic, *La Jeune Parque, Le Cimetière Marin,*
Sète, France, 1871. Francisco Idalecio Madero, politician, Mexico, 1873. Ezra
Pound, poet, translator and critic, *Hugh Selwyn Mauberley, The Cantos,* Hailey,
Idaho, 1885. Gerhard Domagk, German biochemist, Nobel Prize winner, Poland,
1895. Louis Malle, film director, *Les Amants, Zazie dans le Metro,* Thumeries,
France, 1932.

DIED: Edmund Cartwright, inventor of the power-driven loom, 1823. Charles
Robert Maturin, curate, dramatist and novelist, *Melmoth the Wanderer,* Dublin,
1824. Sir John Abbott, Canadian Prime Minister, Montreal, Quebec, 1893.
Jean Henri Dunant, founder of the International Red Cross, 1910. Sir Charles
Tupper, Canadian Prime Minister, Bexley Heath, England, 1915. Pio Baroja,
Spanish novelist, *Struggle for Life,* 1956.

OCTOBER 31

*All Hallow's Eve, Halloween, Hallowmass or Allhallow Even, the night when
spirits, witches and other supernatural agencies are abroad;
a popular belief having its origin in pre-Christian times (cf. Walpurgisnacht,
30 April); Samian Eve in the Celtic calendar, the last day of the year and a
time when supernatural beings abound.
Birthday of President Chiang, Taiwan (Chiang Kai-Shek).
National Magic Day (commemorating the death of Houdini in 1926),
celebrated by magicians and others, mainly in USA.
Nevada Day, Nevada, USA (a legal holiday). Feasts of SS:
Quintus, or Quentin, martyr; Foillan, abbot; Wolfgang, bishop.*

Martin Luther's proclamation nailed to the door of the church at Wittenberg in
Germany, 1517. ¶ First stone laid of Blackfriars Bridge in London, 1760.
¶ Girondins guillotined in Place de la Concorde, Paris, 1793. ¶ Nevada made a
US state (36th), 1864. ¶ The Free and United Presbyterian Churches of Scotland
united under the title of the United Free Church of Scotland, 1900. ¶ A bomb
explodes at the top of the Post Office Tower in London, 1971.

BORN: John Evelyn, diarist and writer, *Sylvana*, Surrey, 1620. Jan Vermeer,
Dutch painter, Delft, Netherlands, 1632. John Keats, poet, 'On First Looking
into Chapman's Homer', 'Ode to a Nightingale', London, 1795. Benîot
Fourneyron, engineer, devised the water turbine, France, 1802. Sir Joseph Wilson
Swan, chemist and physicist, Sunderland, 1828. Aleksandr Borodin, chemist and
composer, *Prince Igor*, Russia, 1833. Chiang Kai-Shek, Chinese Nationalist, 1887.

DIED: William Augustus, Duke of Cumberland, military commander, 1765.
William Parsons, Earl of Rosse, astronomer and Member of Parliament, a
pioneer of the reflecting telescope, Monkstown, County Cork, 1867. Harry
Houdini, escapologist and magician, 1926. Otto Rank, Austrian psychologist,
The Myth of the Birth of the Hero, New York City, 1939. Max Reinhardt, stage
and film director and producer, New York City, 1943. Augustus John, artist,
Fordingbridge, Hampshire, 1961.

NOVEMBER

THIRTY DAYS

The ninth month in the old Roman calendar that began
the year in March, from *novem* meaning nine.

The Feast of All Saints, celebrating not only all saints but also all
of the departed who have passed to Heaven;
fixed on this day since the 8th century, but originating probably in the 4th;
BCP as All Saints Day; popularly known as All Hallows. Samian,
the Celtic New Year's celebrations. Revolution Day, Algeria
(guerrilla warfare against the French by the National Liberation Front
began, 1951). Liberty Day, St Croix, Virgin Islands.
Statehood Day, Antigua, West Indies. Feasts of SS: Caesarius and
Julian, martyrs; Benignus of Dijon, martyr; Austremonius, bishop;
Mary, virgin and martyr; Maturinus, or Mathurin; Marcellus of Paris, bishop;
Vigor, bishop; Cadfan, abbot.

The Bank of Scotland founded, 1695. ¶ The great earthquake at Lisbon, over 50,000 people perish. 1755. ¶ W. H. Smith and Son's first railway bookstall is opened, at Euston Station in London, 1848. ¶ General George B. McClellan is appointed General-in-Chief of the Union Armies, 1861. ¶ Fort Garry in Winnipeg is seized by Louis Riel during the Red River Rebellion, 1869. ¶ Abundantia (Asteroid 151) discovered by J. Palisa, 1875. ¶ Ladysmith in Natal surrenders to Boers under the command of Piet Joubert, 1899. ¶ Turkish Republic proclaimed by Kemal Pasha, 1922. ¶ Mussolini announces the Rome–Berlin axis after Count Ciano's visit to Germany, 1936. ¶ American troops land in the Solomon Islands, 1943. ¶ First part of the M.1. London–Birmingham motorway is opened for traffic, 1959.

BORN: Benvenuto Cellini, sculptor and autobiographer, Florence, 1500. Pietro da Cortona, painter and architect, Cortona, Italy, 1596. Antonio Canova, sculptor, *Cupid and Psyche*, Italy, 1757. Spencer Perceval, British Prime Minister, London, 1762. Stefan Zeromski, mathematician, Poland, 1864. Stephen Crane, poet and novelist, *The Red Badge of Courage*, New Jersey, 1871. L. S. Lowry, painter, Rusholme, Manchester, 1887. Edmund Blunden, poet and literary critic, *Undertones of War*, Kent, 1896.

DIED: Charles II, King of Spain, 1700. Dr John Radcliffe, founder of the Radcliffe Library at Oxford, where he died, 1714. Alexander Cruden, of *Concordance* repute, Islington, London, 1770. Lord George Gordon, Protestant extremist, Newgate Prison, London, 1793. Theodor Mommsen, historian and classical scholar, *Corpus Inscriptionum Latinarum*, Germany, 1903. Alfred Jarry, dramatist and poet, founder of pataphysics, *Ubu Roi*, Paris, 1907. Pietro Badoglio, statesman and soldier, led the Italian Army in Ethiopia, 1956. Ezra Pound, poet, translator and critic, *Hugh Selwyn Mauberley*, *The Cantos*, Venice, 1972.

NOVEMBER 2

The Feast of the Commemoration of All the Faithful Departed, when
God's mercy is sought for those in Purgatory; of 9th century origin;
commonly called All Souls Day; not in the 1662 BCP but proposed by
the 1928 revision as the Commemoration of All Souls.
Memorial Day, Brazil. Memorial Day, Nicaragua. Feasts of SS:
Victorinus of Pettau, bishop and martyr; Marcian.

First Committees of Correspondence are formed in Massachusetts under Samuel Adams, 1772. ¶ The property of the Church in France is taken over by the state, 1789. ¶ Second Afghan War begins, 1841. ¶ Egeria (Asteroid 13) discovered by de Gasparis, 1850. ¶ Atala (Asteroid 152) discovered by Paul Henry and Hilda (Asteroid 153) by J. Palisa, 1875. ¶ North Dakota is made a US state (39th), 1889. ¶ South Dakota is made a US state (40th), 1889. ¶ In London the *Daily Mirror* is first published, 1903. ¶ Russia declares war with Turkey, 1914. ¶ First radio broadcast in US at Pittsburgh, 1920. ¶ The world's first high-definition public television transmissions (405 lines) begin from Alexandra Palace in north London, 1936. ¶ Madagascar capitulates to South African forces, 1942. ¶ President John F. Kennedy announces that Cuban missile bases are being dismantled by USSR, 1962.

BORN: Jean Baptiste Chardin, painter, Paris, 1699. Daniel Boone, frontiersman and colonizer, Pennsylvania, 1734. Marie Antoinette, Queen of France, Vienna, 1755. Georges Sorel, syndicalist and philosopher, *Reflections on Violence*, Cherbourg, France, 1847. Warren Harding, US President, Ohio, 1865. Harlow Shapley, astronomer, *Of Stars and Men, View from a Distant Star*, Nashville, Missouri, 1885. Luchino Visconti, film director, *Death in Venice*, Milan, 1906.

DIED: Sir Samuel Romilly, lawyer and reformer; suicide, London, 1818. Erwin Rommel, Commander of the Afrika Korps, Herringen, Germany, 1944. George Bernard Shaw, dramatist, critic and reformer, *Man and Superman, Pygmalion, The Black Girl in Search of God*, Ayot St Lawrence, Hertfordshire, 1950. James Thurber, humorous writer and artist, *The Secret Life of Walter Mitty*, New York City, 1961.

NOVEMBER 3

Independence of Cuenca, Ecuador. Culture Day, Japan.
Anniversary of the Separation from Colombia, Panama (1903).
National Day, Dominica, West Indies (and 4 November).
Feasts of SS: Winifred, or Gwenfrewi, virgin and martyr; Rumwald;
Hubert, bishop; Pirminus, bishop; Amicus; Malachy of Armagh, archbishop.

Christopher Columbus discovers the Caribbee Isles (Dominica) on his second expedition, 1493. ¶ First assembly of the Long Parliament, 1640. ¶ Great panics throughout Britain and Europe owing to the close approach of a comet (visible until 9 March 1680), 1679. ¶ The Directory in France, 1795. ¶ British capture Acre and Ibrahim, son of Mohammed Ali, is forced to abandon Syria, 1840. ¶ At Mentana Garibaldi is defeated by French and Papal troops, 1867. ¶ Mutiny of the German fleet at Kiel, 1918. ¶ The Latin alphabet is adopted in Turkey, 1928. ¶ Left-wing groups in France form the Socialist and Republican Union, 1935. ¶ Re-election of President Roosevelt in US, 1936. ¶ *Sputnik II* is launched by the Russians, 1957.

BORN: Bernardino Ramazzini, physician, recognized the importance of environmental influences on diseases, Carpi, Italy, 1633. John Logan Campbell, 'father' of Auckland, New Zealand, 1817. Leopold III, King of the Belgians, Brussels, 1901. André Malraux, novelist and politician, *Man's Fate, The Voices of Silence*, Paris, 1901.

DIED: James II, King of Aragon, Barcelona, 1327. Robert Lowth, writer, Bishop of London, professor of Poetry at Oxford; Fulham, London, 1787. Dr Felix Bartholdy, composer, Leipzig, Germany, 1847. Henri Matisse, painter, Nice, 1954.

NOVEMBER 4

Day of National Unity, Italy. Flag Day, Panama. National Day,
Dominica, West Indies (and 3 November). Feasts of SS: Charles Borromeo,
archbishop; Vitalis and Agricola, martyrs; Pierius;
John Zedazneli and his Companions; Clarus, martyr; Joannicius.

Columbus discovers Guadaloupe on his second expedition, 1493. ¶ Discovery of
the Gunpowder Plot for blowing up the Houses of Parliament, 1605. ¶ Aegina
(Asteroid 91) discovered by Alphonse Borelly, 1866. ¶ Bertha (Asteroid 154)
discovered by Prosper Henry, 1875. ¶ President Roosevelt signs bill permitting
Britain and France to purchase arms on 'cash and carry' system, 1939. ¶ The
United Nations Educational, Scientific and Cultural Organization (UNESCO)
established, 1946. ¶ Russian troops attack Budapest in Hungary, 1956.

BORN: Guido Reni, painter, Bologna, Italy, 1575. William III, Prince of Orange,
King of England, The Hague, Holland, 1650. Augustus Toplady, Calvinist poet
and divine, wrote the hymn *Rock of Ages*, Farnham, Surrey, 1740. James
Montgomery, poet, Ayr, Scotland, 1771. Eden Phillpotts, poet and novelist,
India, 1862. George Edward Moore, philosopher, editor of *Mind*, 1921–47,
Principia Ethica, Philosophical Studies, London, 1873.

DIED: Erasmus Bartholin, physicist, 1698. Felix Mendelssohn, Romantic composer, *Midsummer Night's Dream*, Leipzig, 1847. Paul Delaroche, French painter,
1859. Wilfred Owen, poet, killed in action, France, 1918. Gabriel Fauré, composer and organist, 1924. Manuel Azaña, President of the Spanish Republic at the
time of the Civil War, 1940.

Dies Mala or 'Egyptian Day', considered unlucky in the Middle Ages.
Guy Fawkes Day or Bonfire Night, celebrating the discovery of the
Gunpowder Plot in 1605, an attempt by several Catholic extremists
at blowing up the Houses of Parliament in London. Anniversary of
the First Cry of Independence, Ecuador. Feasts of SS:
Zachary and Elizabeth; Galation and Episteme; Bertilla, virgin.

Frederick II of Prussia defeats the French at Rosbach (Seven Years War), 1757. ¶ Afghanistan surrenders to Britain, 1840. ¶ Russians defeated by the British and French at Inkerman in the Crimea, 1854. ¶ Velleda (Asteroid 126) discovered by Paul Henry and Johanna (Asteroid 127) discovered by Prosper Henry, 1872. ¶ Annexation of Cyprus by Britain, 1914. ¶ War declared on Turkey by France and Britain, 1914. ¶ General Pershing leads US troops in first American action against German forces, 1917.

BORN: Washington Allston, American landscape painter, 1779. Léon Philippe Teisserenc de Bort, meteorologist, experimented with balloons and discovered the stratosphere, Paris, 1855. James Elroy Flecker, dramatist and poet, London, 1884. John Burdon Haldane, Marxist biochemist and geneticist, Oxford, 1892. Vivien Leigh, actress, Darjeeling, India, 1913.

DIED: Casimir III, King of Poland, founded Cracow University, 1370. Bernardino Ramazzini, physician, Padua, Italy, 1714. Pierre Choderlos de Laclos, artillery officer and writer, *Les Liaisons dangereuses*, 1803. Karel Hynek Mácham, Czech poet, *May*, Bohemia, 1836. James Clerk Maxwell, physicist, Cambridge, 1879. August Weismann, biologist and geneticist, Freiburg, Saxony, Germany, 1914. Christian Eijkman, physician, Nobel Prize for Medicine, 1930. George M. Cohan, popular songwriter and showman, 1942. Oscar Natzka, New Zealand opera singer, 1951. Maurice Utrillo, painter, France, 1955. Mack Sennett, film comedian and producer, Richmond, Canada, 1960.

The Feast of All Saints of Ireland, observed only in Ireland.
Feasts of SS: Leonard of Noblac; Melaine, bishop; Illtud, or Illtyd, abbot;
Winnoc, abbot; Demetrian, bishop; Barlaam of Khutyn, abbot.

Henry VI of England crowned, 1429. ¶ Independence declared by Mexico, 1813. ¶ Abraham Lincoln is elected President of the United States of America, 1860. ¶ Jefferson Davis, President of the Confederacy, is elected to a six-year term of office, 1861. ¶ The first diamonds are discovered that will eventually lead to the Kimberley Diamond Rush (1871), South Africa, 1869. ¶ Passchendaele Ridge is taken by British and Canadian troops, 1917. ¶ Proclamation of the Polish Republic in Cracow, 1918. ¶ The Spanish government moves to Valencia after rebels lay siege to Madrid, 1936. ¶ First hydrogen bomb exploded by the US, at Eniwetok Atoll in the Pacific, 1952.

BORN: Colley Cibber, dramatist and stage manager, *The Careless Husband*, London, 1671. Alois Senefelder, inventor of lithography, Prague, 1771. Adolphe Sax, instrument maker, invented the saxophone, Belgium, 1814. Jean Louis Charles Garnier, architect, Paris, 1825. James Abram Garfield, US President, Ohio, 1831. Cesare Lombroso, criminologist, Verona, 1835. Richard Jefferies, essayist and novelist, *The Story of My Heart, Bevis*, Coate, Wiltshire, 1848. John Philip Sousa, bandmaster and composer, *The Stars and Stripes Forever*, Washington D.C., 1854. Thomas Ince, pioneer American film producer, Newport, Rhode Island, 1882. Sir John William Alcock, aviator, 1892.

DIED: Gustavus (II) Adolphus, King of Sweden, Lutzen, near Leipzig, Germany, 1632. Heinrich Schutz, composer, *Daphne* (the first German opera, now lost), Dresden, Germany, 1672. Catherine the Great, Empress of Russia, 1796. John Walter, printer, journalist and founder of *The Times*, Teddington, Middlesex, 1812. Claude Louis Berthollet, chemist, 1822. William Hone, writer and satirist, *Every-Day Book*, Tottenham, Middlesex, 1842. Kate Greenaway, writer and illustrator of children's books, 1901. Sir Johnston Forbes-Robertson, theatrical actor-manager, 1937.

*Revolution Day, Bangladesh (1971). Anniversary of the October
Socialist Revolution, Hungary. Anniversary of the October Socialist
Revolution, USSR (and 8 November). Feasts of SS: Herculanus, bishop
and martyr; Florentius, bishop; Willibrord, bishop; Engelbert, archbishop and martyr.*

The *London Gazette* published for the first time, 1665. ¶ The last spike of the
Canadian Pacific Railway main line is driven in at Craigallachie, British Columbia,
1885. ¶ Bolsheviks led by Lenin overthrow Kerensky's government in Petrograd;
the 'October Revolution' (known thus as the Old Style date is 26 October), 1917.
¶ The search for Lord Lucan begins in London after the discovery of the battered
body of his children's nanny, 1974.

BORN: Marie Curie, French chemist, researched radioactivity, Warsaw, 1867.
Lise Meitner, physicist, co-discovered nuclear fission with Otto Hahn, Vienna,
1878. Sir Chandrasekhara Venkata Raman, physicist, Nobel Prize for Physics,
Trichinopoly, India, 1888. Herman Mankiewicz, scenarist, collaborated with
Orson Welles on *Citizen Kane*, New York City, 1897. Konrad Lorenz, psycho-
logist, Nobel Prize winner, Vienna, 1903. Albert Camus, novelist, *The Outsider*,
Algeria, 1913. Billy Graham, evangelist, Charlotte, North Carolina, 1918. Joan
Sutherland, operatic singer, Australia, 1926.

DIED: Jean Nattier, portrait painter, Paris, 1766. Count Leo Tolstoy, novelist and
philosopher, *War and Peace*, *Anna Karenina*, Astapovo, Russia, 1910. Alfred
Wallace, naturalist and explorer, *Travels on the Amazon and Rio Negro*, *Contributions to the Theory of Natural Selection*, Broadstone, Dorset, 1913. Richard Sorge,
German spy for the Soviet Union; executed, Tokyo, 1944.

NOVEMBER 8

Anniversary of the October Socialist Revolution, USSR (and 7 November).
The Feast of the Four Crowned Ones, a feast in commemoration of the four
(possibly five) masons who were martyred by the Emperor Diocletian after
refusing to sculpt a pagan god for him; their memory has also been kept by
some English Freemasons. Feasts of SS: Cybi, or Cuby, abbot; Deusdedit, pope;
Tysilio, or Suliau, abbot; Willehad, bishop; Godfrey of Amiens, bishop.

The King of Bohemia is defeated at the battle of Prague, 1620. ¶ Euterpe (Asteroid 27) discovered by J. R. Hind, 1853. ¶ Charles Wilkes seizes the Confederate commissioners, John Slidell and James M. Mason, from the *Trent*, a British ship, 1861. ¶ Abraham Lincoln is re-elected President of the US, 1864. ¶ Scylla (Asteroid 155) discovered by J. Palisa, 1875. ¶ Civil war begins in Samoa, 1880. ¶ Montana made a US state (41st), 1889. ¶ End of the Anglo–French offensive in the Somme (began 1 July), 1916. ¶ V. I. Lenin becomes chairman of the Council of People's Commissions, 1917. ¶ Anti-Semitic pogroms begin in Germany, 1938. ¶ The United Nations General Assembly demands that Russian troops be taken out of Hungary, 1956. ¶ A cease-fire is announced between the Royalists and the Republicans in the Yemen, 1964. ¶ London's vegetable and fruit market, Covent Garden, closed for the last time, 1974.

BORN: Edmond Halley, mathematician and astronomer, a comet whose return he predicted bears his name, Haggerston, London, 1656. Gheorghe Gheorghiu-Dej, Rumanian Premier, Rumania, 1901. Katharine Hepburn, film actress, *Adam's Rib*, *The African Queen*, Connecticut, 1909. Christian Barnard, surgeon, South Africa, 1922.

DIED: John Milton, poet and polemicist, *Paradise Lost*, *Paradise Regained*, *Areopagitica*, Chalfont St Giles, Buckinghamshire, 1674. Thomas Bewick, engraver, 1828. Charles Francis Hall, American Arctic explorer; Thank God Harbour, Greenland, 1871. César Auguste Franck, organist and composer, 1890. Francis Parkman, historian, *The Oregon Trail*, *The Jesuits in North America*, Massachusetts, 1893. Anton Rubenstein, pianist and composer, near St Petersburg, 1894. Victorien Sardou, dramatist, *A Scrap of Paper*, *Fedora*, Paris, 1908. Ivan Alexeyvich Bunin, Russian writer, *The Village*, 1953. Edgar Varèse, composer, *Deserts*, *Offrandes*, *Arcana*, New York City, 1965.

The Birthday of Iqbal, Pakistan (Sir Muhammad Iqbal, national poet, 1877–1938).
The Feast of the Dedication of the Basilica of St John Lateran, 'The Mother
and Head of all Churches of the City and of the World', in Rome. Feasts of SS:
Theodore Tiro, martyr; Benignus, or Benen, bishop; Vitonus, or Vanne, bishop.

Moses Montefiore becomes the first Jew to be knighted in England, 1837.
¶ Virtual abolition of flogging in the British army, 1859. ¶ Proclamation of
Bavarian republic, 1918. ¶ Failure of Hitler's attempted *coup d'état* in Munich,
1923. ¶ Shanghai taken by the Japanese, 1937. ¶ Great power failure in New
York and New England, 1965.

BORN: Edward VII of Great Britain, London, 1841. Herbert Kalmus, inventor of
Technicolour, 1881. Anthony Asquith, film director and producer, *The Way to
the Stars*, London, 1902. Spiro T. Agnew, US Vice-President, Baltimore, 1918.

DIED: Thomas Shadwell, dramatist, *The Sullen Lovers*, London, 1692. Guillaume
Apollinaire, poet and writer, *Alcools*, 1918. James Ramsay MacDonald, first
Labour Party Prime Minister of Britain, 1937. Neville Chamberlain, Prime
Minister, signatory of the Munich Agreement, 1940. Chaim Weizmann, Jewish
biochemist and first President of Israel, Rehovot, Israel, 1952. Dylan Thomas,
poet, *Deaths and Entrances, Under Milk Wood*, New York City, 1953. Charles de
Gaulle, soldier and President of France, 1970.

NOVEMBER 10

Anniversary of Potosi, a department of Bolivia. Feasts of SS: Andrew Avellino;
Theoctista, virgin; Trypho, Respicius and Nympha, martyrs;
Aedh MacBrice, bishop; Justus of Canterbury, archbishop.

The Turks defeat the Hungarians at Varna, 1444. ¶ Christopher Columbus discovers Antigua in the New World on his second expedition, 1493. ¶ Huguenots defeated at the battle of St Denis, 1567. ¶ Henry M. Stanley meets Dr Livingstone at Ujiji near Unyanyembe, 1871. ¶ End of the third battle of Ypres (Passchendaele), 1917. ¶ Anti-semitic legislation enacted in Italy, 1938. ¶ Muggsy Spanier records *Blueing the Blues* in New York, 1939. ¶ In Londonderry, Northern Ireland, a Roman Catholic girl who had intended to marry a British soldier is shorn, tarred and feathered, 1971.

BORN: Martin Luther, theologian and reformer, Germany, 1483. Paracelsus, alchemist and physician, Einsiedeln, Switzerland, 1493. Robert Devereux, 2nd Earl of Essex, English soldier and statesman, 1566. François Couperin, composer and harpsichordist, Paris, 1668. William Hogarth, artist and engraver, *A Rake's Progress*, London, 1697. Oliver Goldsmith, author, *The Vicar of Wakefield*, Ireland, 1730. Sir John Thompson, Canadian Prime Minister, Halifax, Nova Scotia, 1844. Vachel Lindsay, poet, Springfield, Illinois, 1879. Sir Jacob Epstein, British sculptor, New York City, 1880. Moise Tshombe, politician, Premier of Katanga, Belgian Congo, 1919.

DIED: Richard Chancellor, navigator, began trade between England and Russia, 1556. Joseph François, Marquis de Dupleix, French administrator in India, 1763. Joseph Black, chemist, 1799. Gideon Algernon Mantell, geologist, London, 1852. Isidore Geoffrey St Hilaire, zoologist, France, 1861. Arthur Rimbaud, poet, *Le Bâteau Ivre, Une Saison en Enfer*, Marseilles, 1891.

The Roman Vinalia, a feast honouring Bacchus the god of wine.
St Martin's Day, BCP; also known as Martinmas, a Quarter Day in Scotland;
traditionally the day English farmers slaughtered those animals that
could not be sustained through winter. Armistice Day,
honouring the signing of the Armistice in 1918 that ended the Great War,
observed by most of the Allied countries and in some it is a legal holiday;
known also as Victory Day and, latterly, Remembrance Day.
Victory Day, Monaco. Independence Day, Rhodesia. Veterans Day,
USA (known as Armistice Day until 1954; a legal holiday in most states).
Feasts of SS: Martin of Tours, bishop; Mennas, martyr;
Theodore the Studite, abbot; Bartholomew of Grottaferrata, abbot.

Indians led by William Butler massacre inhabitants of Cherry Valley in New York, 1778. ¶ The Jacobin Club in Paris is closed, 1794. ¶ Edison's carbon 'loud speaking' telephone demonstrated between London and Norwich, 1878. ¶ Washington is made a US state (42nd), 1889. ¶ Allies and Germany sign Armistice, 1918. ¶ The first 2-minutes' silence is observed in Britain to commemorate those who died in the Great War, 1919. ¶ Ian Smith announces declaration of independence in Rhodesia, 1965. ¶ US launch *Gemini 12* spacecraft into orbit, 1966. ¶ Israel and Egypt sign a ceasefire agreement, 1973. ¶ Sir John Kerr, the Australian Governor-General, dismisses Gough Whitlam and his Labour government, 1975.

BORN: Paul Signac, Neo-Impressionist painter, Paris, 1863. Antoinne Meillet, linguist, France, 1866. Edouard Vuillard, painter, Ciuseaux, France, 1868. George Patton, military commander, led US troops in Sicily (1943) and France (1944), San Gabriel, California, 1885. Alger Hiss, US government employee, accused of aiding the Communist cause, Baltimore, Maryland, 1904.

DIED: Johann Zoffany, portrait painter and artist, Strand Green, Middlesex, 1810. Sören Kierkegaard, philosopher and theologian, *Either-Or*, Denmark, 1855. Ned Kelly, outlaw and bushranger; hanged, Melbourne, Australia, 1880. Fred Niblo, film director, *The Sign of Zorro*, New Orleans, 1948.

Feasts of SS: Martin I, pope and martyr; Nilus the Elder;
Emilian Cucullatus, abbot; Machar, bishop; Cunibert, bishop;
Cumian, abbot; Livinus, bishop and martyr; Lebuin, or Liafwine;
Benedict and his Companions, martyrs; Astrik, or Anastasius, archbishop.

Great flooding of the River Liffey causes much damage to Dublin, 1787. ¶ A dazzling display of meteors is observed by Alexander von Humboldt at Cumana in South Africa, 1799. ¶ Frigga (Asteroid 77) discovered by C. H. F. Peters, 1862. ¶ Great eruption by Mount Vesuvius, 1867. ¶ Annexation of the Gilbert and Ellice Islands by Britain, 1915. ¶ Sinking of the HMS *Ark Royal*, 1941. ¶ The German battleship *Tirpitz* is sunk, 1944. ¶ A salmon is caught in the River Thames, the first since the 1840s, at West Thurrock, 1974.

BORN: Richard Baxter, Puritan scholar, Shropshire, 1615. Jacques Charles, physicist, France, 1746. Gerhard Johann von Scharnhorst, Prussian officer and soldier, reformed and remodelled the Prussian army, Hanover, 1755. Lord Rayleigh, physicist, Witham, Essex, 1842. Sun Yat-sen, Chinese nationalist and revolutionary, founded the Kuomintang party, near Canton, China, 1866.

DIED: Canute II, Danish King of England, 1035. Sir John Hawkyns, Elizabethan admiral and naval commander, Puerto Rico, 1595. Thomas Fairfax, commander of the Parliamentarian army in the English Civil War, 1671. Mrs Elizabeth Gaskell, novelist, *Cranford*, 1865. Percival Lowell, astronomer, *Mars and its Canals*, Flagstaff, Arizona, 1916.

Feasts of SS: Didacus, or Diego; Arcadius and his Companions, martyrs;
Brice, bishop; Eugenius of Toledo, archbishop; Maxellendis, virgin and martyr;
Kilian; Nicholas I, pope; Abbo of Fleury, abbot; Homobonus; Stanislaus Kostka.

Massacre of Danes in the southern counties of England by order of Ethelred II, 1002. ¶ Malcolm is slain and the Scots are defeated at Alnwick, 1093. ¶ The Rebels are defeated at Preston, 1715. ¶ London–Paris telegraph opened, 1851. ¶ The legislature of South Carolina calls a special convention to discuss possible secession from the Union, 1860. ¶ 'Bloody Sunday' in Trafalgar Square, London, with serious casualties amongst the Socialist and Irish demonstrators, 1887. ¶ The first metal dirigible, flown from the Tempelhof Field in Berlin, it was powered by a 16hp Daimler engine, 1897. ¶ Over 60 young children are killed, and many more become seriously ill after drinking from an insecticide-polluted river in Venadillo, Colombia, 1969. ¶ A state of emergency is proclaimed in Britain after coal and electricity workers continue a ban on overtime, 1973. ¶ The United Nations in New York is addressed by Yasser Arafat of the Palestine Liberation Organization, 1974.

BORN: St Augustine of Hippo, theologian, 354. Edward III of England (reigned 1327–77), 1312. Philip of Hesse, Landgrave of Hesse, Marburg, 1504. Maurice of Nassau, Prince of Orange, Dillenburg, 1567. James Clerk Maxwell, physicist, Edinburgh, 1831. Robert Louis Stevenson, novelist, essayist and poet, *Treasure Island, Dr Jekyll and Mr Hyde*, Edinburgh, 1850.

DIED: Ludwig Uhland, Romantic poet, *Old South and North German Folk-Songs*, Tübingen, Germany, 1862. Gioacchino Antonio Rossini, composer, *The Barber of Seville*, Paris, 1868. Camille Pissarro, Impressionist painter, Paris, 1903. Francis Thompson, poet, *The Hound of Heaven, Sister Songs*, London, 1907. Enrico Ceccetti, ballet teacher and director, 1928. Vittorio De Sica, film director, *Umberto D*, 1974.

The Birthday of HM King Hussein, Jordan. Feasts of SS:
Josaphat of Polotsk, archbishop and martyr;
Dubricius, or Dyfrig, bishop; Laurence O'Toole, archbishop.

Severe earthquake in England, great shocks throughout the country, 1318. ¶ Lieutenant Eugene Ely of the US Navy becomes the first man to take off in an aeroplane from the deck of a ship; he flew from the *Birmingham* at Hampton Roads, off Virginia, to Norfolk, 1910. ¶ The Red Army captures Sebastopol, 1920. ¶ *Hello Lola* recorded by Red McKenzie and the Mound City Blue Blowers in Chicago, 1929. ¶ US launches *Apollo 12* spacecraft from Cape Kennedy, 1969. ¶ The marriage at Westminster Abbey of HRH Princess Anne and Captain Mark Philips, 1973.

BORN: Lucas von Hildebrandt, architect, Genoa, 1668. Robert Fulton, inventor of the first steam boat, Pennsylvania, 1765. Sir Charles Lyell, geologist, *Principles of Geology*, Scotland, 1797. Claude Monet, Impressionist painter, Paris, 1840. Leo Hendrik Baekeland, inventor of Bakelite, Ghent, 1863. Jawalharlal Nehru, first Prime Minister of India, Allahabad, India, 1889. Sir Frederick Banting, joint discoverer of a treatment for diabetes, Ontario, 1891. Aaron Copland, composer, *Billy the Kid*, New York, 1900. Senator Joseph McCarthy, prominent anti-communist, Wisconsin, 1908. King Hussein of Jordan, Jordan, 1935. HRH Charles, Prince of Wales, first son of Queen Elizabeth II, 1948.

DIED: Justinian (Flavius Anicius Justinianus), Roman Emperor, 565. Alexander Nevsky, Russian ruler, 1263. Nell Gwynn, actress, King Charles II's mistress, London, 1687. Gottfried Leibniz, philosopher, Hanover, Germany, 1716. Georg Wilhelm Friedrich Hegel, philosopher, *The Phenomenology of the Spirit*, Berlin, 1831. Robert Whitehead, engineer, invented the naval torpedo, Berkshire, 1905. Saki (Hector Hugh Munro), short-story writer, *The Chronicles of Clovis*, killed in action, France, 1916. Manuel de Falla, composer, *The Three-Cornered Hat*, 1946.

Anniversary of the Proclamation of the Republic, Brazil. Feasts of SS: Albert the Great, bishop and doctor; Gurias, Samonas and Abibus, martyrs; Desiderius, or Didier, of Cahors, bishop; Malo, bishop; Fintan of Rheinau; Leopold of Austria.

Confederation Articles for perpetual union of the United States of America are adopted by Congress, 1777. ¶ Lutetia (Asteroid 21) discovered by H. Goldschmidt, 1852. ¶ General Sherman begins his march from Atlanta to the sea, 1864. ¶ Great flooding in London by the Thames which is said to have risen over 28 feet, 1875. ¶ The River Thames overflows between Oxford and Windsor and considerable damage ensues, 1894. ¶ Omsk is taken by the Red Army, 1919. ¶ Inauguration of the Commonwealth of the Philippines, 1935. ¶ Norman Craig Breedlove achieves a speed of 613mph in the jet-powered *Spirit of America* on the Bonneville Salt Flats in Utah, 1965. ¶ The *Queen Elizabeth* ends her final voyage, 1968. ¶ Heavy fighting between Indian and Pakistan troops on the border regions north of Calcutta, 1971.

BORN: William Pitt ('the Elder'), Earl of Chatham, Secretary of State, London, 1708. Sir William Herschel, British astronomer, organist, discovered the planet Uranus, Hanover, Germany, 1738. August Krogh, physiologist, Nobel Prize winner, Denmark, 1874. Marianne Moore, poet, *Observations, The Pangolin and Other Verse*, St Louis, Missouri, 1887. William Averell Harriman, diplomat and ambassador, New York City, 1891. Erwin Rommel, Commander of the Afrika Korps, Heidenheim, Germany, 1891. Aneurin Bevan, British Labour Party politician, Wales, 1897. Sacheverell Sitwell, poet and writer, *All Summer in a Day*, Scarborough, Yorkshire, 1897. Count Claus von Stauffenberg, officer, attempted to assassinate Hitler in 1944, Jettingen, Germany, 1907.

DIED: Albertus Magnus, theologian, 1280. Johannes Kepler, astronomer, Ratisbon, Germany, 1630. Christoph von Gluck, German operatic composer, *Alcestis*, 1787. George Romney, portrait painter, Kendal, Westmorland, 1802. Tz'u Hsi, empress-dowager of China, Peking, 1908. Henryk Sienkiewicz, novelist, *Quo Vadis?*, Switzerland, 1916. Emile Durkheim, French sociologist, 1917. Alfred Werner, chemist, Zurich, Germany, 1919. Lionel Barrymore, actor, 1954. Rudolf Ivanovich Abel, Russian master-spy, 1971.

NOVEMBER 16

Feasts of SS: Gertrude the Great and Mechtildis, virgins; Eucherius of Lyons, bishop; Afan, bishop; Edmund of Abingdon, archbishop; Agnes of Assisi, virgin.

Jack Sheppard, popular thief, executed at Tyburn, London, 1724. ¶ Westminster Bridge is formally opened, 1750. ¶ Calliope (Asteroid 22) discovered by J. R. Hind, 1852. ¶ British Bechuanaland became part of the Crown Colonies, 1895. ¶ Oklahoma is made a US state (46th), 1907. ¶ Georges Clemenceau becomes the Premier of France, 1917. ¶ The Russian Counter-Revolution ends, 1920. ¶ Battle at Derna, 1942. ¶ Probably the greatest meteor shower of historic times, visible in the northern latitudes of the Pacific Ocean (on the night of 16/17 November), 1966.

BORN: Tiberius Claudius Nero, Roman Emperor, Rome, 42BC. John Bright, statesman and reformer, Lancashire, 1811. Anton Rubinstein, pianist and composer, Jassy, Moldavia, 1829. Alphonse Leon Daudet, French humorous writer, 1867. Aleksandr Aleksandrovich Blok, Symbolist poet, *Verses about Russia*, 1880. Paul Hindemith, composer, *Funeral Music for Viola and Strings*, *The Four Temperaments*, Germany, 1895. Sir Oswald Mosley, politician, founded the British Union of Fascists, London, 1896. Eddie Condon, jazz guitarist and bandleader, Indiana, 1905.

DIED: Henry III, King of England, Westminster, 1272. Perkin Warbeck, pretender to the English throne; executed, London, 1499. Lucas von Hildebrandt, architect, Austria, 1745. Louis Riel, Canadian insurgent, executed, Regina, 1885. Carl von Linde, chemist and engineer, Munich, 1934. Charles Maurras, writer and philosopher, founded Action Française, Tours, 1952. Clark Gable, film actor, *The Misfits*, 1960.

*Queen Elizabeth's Day, celebrating the accession of Queen Elizabeth I of England,
observed until the early 18th century. National Army Day, Zaire. Feasts of SS:
Gregory the Wonderworker, bishop; Dionysius of Alexandria, bishop;
Alphaeus and Zachaeus, martyrs; Acisclus and Victoria, martyrs:
Anianus, or Aignan, of Orleans, bishop; Gregory of Tours, bishop;
Hilda, virgin; Hugh of Lincoln, bishop.*

Accession of John Baliol, King of Scotland, 1292. ¶ Johann Gutenberg, the German printer, is granted a loan by the dean and chapter of St Thomas's Church in Strasbourg, 1442. ¶ Accession of Queen Elizabeth I of England, 1558. ¶ The Church of England is re-established, 1558. ¶ Defeat of Austrians at Arcole by Napoleon, 1796. ¶ Relief of Lucknow by Colin Campbell, 1857. ¶ Camilla (Asteroid 107) discovered by Norman Pogson, 1868. ¶ The Suez Canal is formally opened, 1869. ¶ Dahomey is made a French protectorate, 1893. ¶ First ship sails through the Panama Canal, 1913. ¶ Franz von Papen resigns as German Chancellor, 1932. ¶ Colonel Nasser is made Egyptian premier, 1954. ¶ First synthetic diamonds manufactured, by De Beers in South Africa, 1959. ¶ The Soviet *Luna 17* unmanned spacecraft touches down on the Moon, 1970.

BORN: Agnolo Bronzino, Florentine painter, Italy, 1503. Sieur de la Vérendrye, explorer in Canada and the US, Trois-Rivières, Quebec, 1685. Jean le Rond d'Alembert, philosopher, *encyclopédist*, Paris, 1717. Louis XVIII of France, Versailles, 1755. August Ferdinand Möbius, astronomer and mathematician, Germany, 1790. Louis Hubert Lyautey, soldier and colonial governor, Nancy, 1854. Alan Charles Mackerras, Australian conductor, 1925.

DIED: Sir John de Mandeville, traveller, Belgium, 1372. John Picus, Prince of Mirandola, scholar, Florence, 1494. Mary Tudor, Queen of England, London, 1558. Alain Réné le Sage, novelist, *Gil Blas*, Boulogne, France, 1747. Richard Norman Shaw, architect, London, 1912.

The Feast of the Dedication of the Basilicas of St Peter and of St Paul;
St Peter's in Rome was consecrated on this day in 1626, St Paul-outside-the-Walls
on 10 December, 1854. Anniversary of Beni, a department of Bolivia.
Army Day and Anniversary of the Battle of Vertières, Haiti (Army Day since 1938 only;
Vertières was the final battle against the French, 1803).
Independence Day, Morocco. National Day, Sultanate of Oman. Feasts of SS:
Romanus of Antioch, martyr; Mawes, or Maudez, abbot; Odo of Cluny, abbot.

The Dictes or Sayengis of the Philosophhres is completed on the presses of William Caxton at Westminster, it is the first printed book in England bearing a date, 1477. ¶ Dedication of St Peter's Church in Rome, 1626. ¶ The town of Bronte is destroyed by the eruption of Mount Etna in Sicily, 1832. ¶ The Duke of Wellington's funeral at St Paul's Cathedral, 1852. ¶ General Franco's government recognized by Germany and Italy, 1936.

BORN: Pierre Bayle, philosopher and writer, *Dictionnaire historique et critique*, France, 1647. Sir David Wilkie, Scottish artist, Fife, Scotland, 1785. Carl von Weber, operatic composer, *Oberon*, Eutin, Germany, 1786. Louis Jacques Mandé Daguerre, artist and photographic inventor, near Paris, 1789. Nils Eric Nordenskjöld, Arctic explorer, discovered the North East Passage, Helsinki, 1832. Sir William Schwenck Gilbert, librettist, London, 1836. Ignacy Jan Paderewski, piano virtuoso, composer and first Prime Minister of Poland, Podolia Province, Poland, 1860. Percy Wyndham Lewis, painter and novelist, a founder of Vorticism, *The Apes of God*, Nova Scotia, 1882. George Gallup, pioneer of 'scientific' public opinion polls, Iowa, 1901. Johnny Mercer, composer and arranger, Savannah, Georgia, 1909.

DIED: Chester Arthur, US President, 1886. Gustav Fechner, neurophysicist, 1887. Marcel Proust, novelist, *Remembrance of Things Past*, Paris, 1922. Walter Hermann Nernst, chemist, Nobel Prize winner, Germany, 1941. Niels Bohr, atomic physicist, Nobel Prize winner, 1962. Joseph P. Kennedy, US diplomat and financier, 1969.

National Day, Sultanate of Oman. Feasts of SS: Elizabeth of Hungary, widow;
Pontian, pope and martyr; Nerses I, bishop and martyr; Barlaam, martyr.

Blackfriars Bridge in London is opened, 1769. ¶ French invade Portugal, 1807.
¶ President Lincoln's Gettysburg Address, 1863. ¶ Great 'City Fire' in London
causes considerable damage and burns for two days, 1897. ¶ The murder of Sir
Lee Stack in Cairo, 1924. ¶ *Artistry in Rhythm* recorded by Stan Kenton and his
Orchestra, 1943. ¶ Lunar module from US *Apollo 12* spacecraft touches down on
the Moon, 1969.

BORN: Charles I, King of Great Britain, Scotland, 1600. Leopold Auenbrugger,
physician, Austria, 1722. Bertel Thorwaldsen, sculptor, Copenhagen, 1770.
René Auguste Caillie, explorer, reached Timbuktu, France, 1799. Vicomte
Ferdinand Marie de Lesseps, diplomat, promoter of the Suez Canal, Versailles,
1805. Hiram Bingham, explorer and archaeologist in South America, Honolulu,
1875. Indira Ganghi, politician, Prime Minister of India, India, 1917.

DIED: Theobald Wolfe Tone, Irish nationalist, Dublin, 1798. Claude-Nicolas
Ledoux, French architect, 1806. Franz Peter Schubert, composer, Vienna, 1828.
Sir William Siemens, inventor, scientist and industrialist, London, 1883. Thomas
Ince, pioneer American film producer, California, 1924. Edward Tolman,
psychologist, Berkeley, California, 1959.

NOVEMBER 20

Garifuna Settlement Day, Belize. Holiday for the Prince of Monaco, Monaco.
National Day, Sultanate of Oman. Anniversary of the Discovery of Puerto Rico,
Puerto Rico (1493). Feasts SS: Felix of Valois; Dasius, martyr;
Nerses, bishop, and other martyrs; Maxentia, virgin and martyr;
Edmund the Martyr; Bernward, bishop.

Edward I *proclaimed* King of England, 1272. ¶ The British fleet under Admiral Hawke defeat the French under Admiral Conflans in Quiberon Bay, 1759. ¶ Britain declares war on Holland, 1780. ¶ Simon Bolivar declares Venezuela independent of Spain, 1818. ¶ Beginning of the trials of Nazi war criminals at Nuremberg, 1945. ¶ The marriage of Princess Elizabeth (the future Queen Elizabeth II) to Philip, Duke of Edinburgh in Westminster Abbey, 1947. ¶ Assassination of the Spanish Prime Minister Admiral Luis Carrero Blanco in Madrid, 1973. ¶ President Sadat of Egypt visits Israel for peace talks, 1977.

BORN: Otto von Guericke, physicist, demonstrated the vacuum, Magdeburg, Germany, 1602. Nikolai Ivanovich Lobachevsky, mathematician, Russia, 1792. Mocher Mendele, Jewish writer, *The Travels and Adventures of Benjamin the Third*, Russia, 1835. Sir Wilfred Laurier, Canadian Prime Minister, Quebec, 1841. Josiah Royce, philosopher and teacher, *The Religious Aspect of Philosophy*, Grass Valley, California, 1855. Edwin Powell Hubble, astronomer, Missouri, 1889. Jean Painlevé, documentary film maker, *Les Oursins*, Paris, 1902. Henri-Georges Clouzot, film director, *Wages of Fear*, Niort, France, 1907.

DIED: Marcus Aurelius Numerianus, Roman Emperor; murdered, 284. Sir Christopher Hatton, Lord Chancellor, London, 1591. Abraham Tucker, writer, *Light of Nature Pursued*, Dorking, Surrey, 1774. Henry Draper, American astronomer, 1882. Francisco Franco, Spanish dictator, 1975.

NOVEMBER 21

The Feast of the Presentation of the Blessed Virgin Mary, commemorating Mary being given by her parents to the Temple at Jerusalem where she was brought up; the feast is of 6th century origin, formally recognized in 1585.
Feasts of SS: Gelasius I, pope; Albert of Louvain, bishop and martyr.

The first free-flight ascent in a balloon, by Jean de Rozier and the Marquis d'Arlandes, to a height of over 500 feet, in Paris, 1783. ¶ The state of North Carolina ratifies the Constitution of the United States of America, 1789. ¶ Michael Faraday reads the first series of his 'Experimental Researches on Electricity' at the Royal Society in London, 1831. ¶ Suffragette rioting in White-hall and Westminster, 1911. ¶ End of the first battle of Ypres, 1914. ¶ Final surrender at sea of the German fleet, 1918. ¶ *Revolutionary Blues* recorded by Mezz Mezzrow in New York, 1938. ¶ I.R.A. bomb outrages in the centre of Birmingham, England, result in the deaths of twenty people, and serious injury to 187 others, 1974.

BORN: Voltaire (François-Marie Arouet), philosopher, historian, poet, dramatist and novelist, *Candide*, *Micromégas*, *Lettres Philosophiques*, Paris, 1694. Friedrich Ernst Daniel Schleiermacher, philosopher and Protestant theologian, *Introduction to Plato's Dialogues*, Breslau, Germany, 1768. Lewis Morgan, anthropologist and lawyer, Aurora, New York, 1818. René Magritte, Belgian Surrealist painter, Lessinges, Belgium, 1898. Coleman Hawkins, jazz tenor saxophonist, Missouri, 1904.

DIED: Henry Purcell, Baroque composer, *Dido and Aeneas*, London, 1695. Francis Joseph I, Emperor of Austria, 1916. James Barry Munnik Hertzog, Prime Minister of South Africa, 1942. Norman Lindsay, Australian artist and novelist, *Age of Consent*, 1969. Sir Chandrasekhara Venkata Raman, physicist, Nobel Prize for Physics, Bangalore, India, 1970.

[354]

NOVEMBER 22

Anniversary of Portuguese Aggression, Republic of Guinea.
Feasts of SS: Cecilia, or Cecily, virgin and martyr; Philemon and Apphis, martyrs.

The Austrians defeat the Prussians at Breslau (Seven Years War), 1757. ¶ Xanthippe (Asteroid 156) discovered by J. Palisa, 1875. ¶ President John F. Kennedy is assassinated in Dallas. L. B. Johnson is sworn in as President, 1963. ¶ Juan Carlos de Bourbon is sworn in as King of Spain, in the Cortes, Madrid, 1975.

BORN: Richard Neville, Earl of Warwick ('Warwick the Kingmaker'), soldier and statesman, 1428. Robert Cavelier de La Salle, explorer of the Mississippi, Rouen, France, 1643. George Eliot (Mary Ann Evans), novelist, *Middlemarch*, Warwickshire, 1819. George Gissing, novelist, *New Grub Street*, Wakefield, Yorkshire, 1857. Cecil James Sharp, folklorist, London, 1859. Jean Baptiste Marchand, soldier and explorer, France, 1863. Wassily Kandinsky, abstract artist, Moscow, 1866. André Gide, novelist and critic, *L'Immoraliste*, Paris, 1869. Charles de Gaulle, soldier and President of France, France, 1890. Hoagy Carmichael, pianist and song-writer, *Stardust*, Indiana, 1899. Benjamin Britten, composer, *Billy Budd*, *War Requiem*, Lowestoft, 1913.

DIED: Sir Martin Frobisher, English explorer, Plymouth, 1594. Edward Teach, the English pirate 'Blackbeard'; off the coast of North Carolina, 1718. Robert Clive (Clive of India), statesman and soldier, 1774. Sir Arthur Sullivan, composer, *The Mikado*, *Ruddigore*, London, 1900. Jack London, novelist, *Call of the Wild*, *The Iron Heel*, California, 1916. Lorenz Hart, song-writer and composer, 1943. Sir Arthur Eddington, astronomer and physicist, 1944. Andrei Yanuarevich Vyshinsky, Soviet representative at the United Nations, New York City, 1954. Aldous Huxley, novelist, essayist and critic, *Antic Hay*, *Brave New World*, California, 1963. John Fitzgerald Kennedy, US President; assassinated, Dallas, Texas, 1963. Clive Staples Lewis, critic and novelist, *The Screwtape Letters*, Oxford, 1963.

Labour Thanksgiving Day, Japan. Feasts of SS: Clement I, pope and martyr; Amphilochius, bishop; Gregory of Girgenti, bishop; Columban, abbot; Trudo, or Trond.

John Hancock of Massachusetts elected for the second time as President of the Continental Congress, 1785. ¶ Arethusa (Asteroid 95) discovered by R. Luther, 1867. ¶ The Halifax fisheries are awarded to Canada, 1877. ¶ Separation of Luxembourg from the Netherlands, 1890. ¶ 2,300 tons of bombs were dropped on Berlin, 1943.

BORN: Alfonso X (the Wise), King of Castile and Leon, Spain, 1221. John Wallis, mathematician, Ashford, Kent, 1616. Carolus Linnaeus, botanist and taxonomist, Sweden, 1707. François Emile Babeuf, revolutionary socialist, France, 1760. Feodor Ivanovich Tyutchev, poet and translator, *Nature is not what you think, Dream at Sea*, Russia, 1803. Franklin Pierce, fourteenth President of the US, Hillsboro, New Hampshire, 1804. James Thomson, poet and writer, *The City of Dreadful Night*, Port Glasgow, Scotland, 1834. Valdemar Poulsen, inventor of the modern tape-recorder, Copenhagen, 1869. Manuel de Falla, composer, *The Three-Cornered Hat*, Cádiz, Spain, 1876. Boris Karloff, actor, London, 1887. Klement Gottwald, Czech Communist dictator, Czechoslovakia, 1896.

DIED: Agnolo Bronzino, Florentine painter, 1572. Thomas Tallis, organist and composer, Greenwich, London, 1585. L'Abbé Prévost, novelist, journalist and translator, *Manon Lescaut*; Chantilly, France, 1763. Johann Bode, astronomer, 1826. Wilhelm von Struve, astronomer, St Petersburg, 1864. Sir Arthur Wing Pinero, playwright, *The Second Mrs Tanqueray*, *Trelawney of the 'Wells'*, London, 1934. Francis Webb, Australian poet, 1973. André Malraux, novelist and states-man, *Man's Fate*, 1976.

NOVEMBER 24

New Regime Day, Zaire. Feasts of SS: John of the Cross, doctor;
Chrysogonus, martyr; Colman of Cloyne, bishop; Flora and Mary, virgins and martyrs.

The River Thames freezes over, 1434. ¶ The first transit of Venus across the Sun observed, by William Crabtree and the Rev Jeremiah Horrocks, in England, 1639. ¶ Abel Jansen Tasman discovers Van Dieman's Land (known as Tasmania since 1853), 1642. ¶ A fair is held on the River Thames which had frozen over, oxen were roasted, 1715. ¶ A great eruption by Mount Vesuvius, 1759. ¶ Erskine Childers is executed by the Irish in Dublin, 1922. ¶ Hitler rejects Hindenburg's request to assume Chancellorship, 1932. ¶ (Sir) Vivian Fuchs and a British team attempt a crossing of the Antarctic, 1957. ¶ Lee Harvey Oswald is shot by Jack Ruby, while in police custody in Dallas, 1963.

BORN: Laurence Sterne, novelist and clergyman, *The Life and Opinions of Tristram Shandy, A Sentimental Journey through France and Italy,* Clonmel, Tipperary, Ireland, 1713. Zachary Taylor, military general, President of the US, Orange County, Virginia, 1784. Henri de Toulouse-Lautrec, painter, lithographer and graphic designer, Albi, Tarn, France, 1864. Konstantin Aleksandrovich Fedin, novelist, *Cities and Years,* Russia, 1892.

DIED: John Knox, Scottish religious and political reformer, 1572. William Lamb, 2nd Viscount Melbourne, Prime Minister, near Welwyn, Hertfordshire, 1848. Sir Hiram Stevens Maxim, inventor, perfected the machine gun, London, 1916. Robert Erskine Childers, Irish nationalist, writer, *The Riddle of the Sands,* executed, 1922. Georges Clemenceau, statesman, French Prime Minister, 1929. Lee Harvey Oswald, shot by Jack Ruby, Dallas, Texas, 1963.

Independence Day, Surinam. Feasts of SS: Catherine of Alexandria, virgin and martyr;
Mercurius, martyr; Moses, martyr.

Biblical scholars long asserted that it was upon this day that the Great Deluge, or Flood, began in 2348BC. ¶ The English defeat the Scots at Solway Moss, 1542. ¶ New York is evacuated by the British ('Evacuation Day'), 1783. ¶ Union army wins the battle of Chattanooga, Tennessee, 1863. ¶ Nemesis (Asteroid 128) discovered by J. C. Watson, 1872. ¶ Khedive of Egypt sells over 170,000 shares in the Suez Canal to Britain, 1875. ¶ President Kasavubu of the Congolese Republic is deposed by General Mobutu, 1965. ¶ President Papadopoulos is deposed in a Greek military *coup*, 1973.

BORN: Lope de Vega, dramatist and poet, *Fuenteovejuna, Las almenas de Toro*, Madrid, 1562. Joseph Lancaster, educationalist, London, 1778. Andrew Carnegie, industrialist and philanthropist, Scotland, 1835. Carl Benz, pioneer of early motor cars, Germany, 1844. José Maria de Eça Queirós, novelist, *The Relic*, Portugal, 1845. Felix Klein, mathematician, Germany, 1849. Pope John XXIII, Italy, 1881. Anastas Mikoyan, Soviet politician, Tiflis Province, Russia, 1895. Tsung-Dao Lee, physicist, Nobel Prize winner, Shanghai, China, 1926.

DIED: Andrea Doria, Genoese admiral and statesman, 1560. John Lockhart, essayist and critic, *Life of Scott*, 1854. Heinrich Barth, explorer in North Africa, 1865. Dame Lilian Baylis, theatrical manager, 1937. Johannes Jensen, Danish poet and novelist, *The Long Journey*, 1950. Sir Ernest Oppenheimer, mining industrialist and philanthropist, Johannesburg, 1957. Dame Myra Hess, pianist, London, 1965. Upton Sinclair, novelist and reformer, *The Jungle, King Coal*, Bound Brook, New Jersey, 1968. Yukio Mishima, novelist, *Confessions of a Mask*, ritual suicide, Tokyo, 1970.

NOVEMBER 26

Independence Day, Lebanon (1941). Feasts of SS: Silvester Gozzolini, abbot;
Peter of Alexandria, bishop and martyr; Siricius, pope; Basolus, or Basle;
Conrad of Constance, bishop; Nikon 'Metanoeite';
John Berchmans; Leonard of Port Maurice.

The 'Great Storm' rages throughout most of England, there is immense damage and over 8,000 people are reckoned to have lost their lives, 1703. ¶ The Jesuit order is suppressed in France, 1764. ¶ Serfdom abolished in Austria by Joseph II, 1781. ¶ British fleet captures the Dutch possession of St Eustacius in the West Indies, 1781. ¶ Encke's Comet observed throughout Europe, 1818. ¶ *Thriving on a Riff, Ko Ko, Now's the Time* and *Billie's Bounce* recorded by Charlie Parker (with Dizzy Gillespie and Miles Davis) in New York City, 1945. ¶ State of Emergency is proclaimed in Cyprus, 1955. ¶ The French launch their first orbiting satellite, 1965.

BORN: William Cowper, poet and writer, Berkhampstead, Hertfordshire, 1731. Georg Forster, explorer, scientist and writer, Poland, 1754. John Alexander Newlands, chemist, London, 1837. Sir Aurel Stein, archaeologist, Budapest, Hungary, 1862. Willis Haviland Carrier, air-conditioning engineer, New York, 1876. Nikolai Ivanovich Vavilov, geneticist and horticulturist, Moscow, 1887. Emlyn Williams, actor and dramatist, *Night Must Fall*, Mostyn, Wales, 1905. Eugene Ionesco, dramatist, *The Bald Prima Donna*, *Rhinoceros*, Rumania, 1912.

DIED: Isabella I, Queen of Castile and Aragon, Spain, 1504. Niels Stensen, anatomist and physiologist, Schwerin, Denmark, 1686. John McAdam, inventor and engineer, Dumfrieshire, Scotland, 1836. Adam Mickiewicz, Polish Romantic poet and writer, Constantinople, 1855. Coventry Kersey Dighton Patmore, poet and critic, *The Betrothal*, *Faithful Forever*, Lymington, Hampshire, 1896. Sir Leander Starr Jameson, soldier and governor in South Africa, 1917. Cyril Connolly, critic and essayist, *Enemies of Promise*, 1974.

Feasts of SS: Barlaam and Josaphat; James Intercisus, martyr;
Secundinus, or Sechnall, bishop; Maximus of Riez, bishop; Cungar, abbot;
Fergus, bishop; Virgil of Salzburg, bishop.

Formation of the triumvirate in Rome of Octavian, Antony and Lepidus, 43BC.
¶ Biela's Comet observed for the second time, 1832. ¶ Alcemene (Asteroid 82)
discovered by R. Luther, 1864. ¶ Great meteor showers observed in Britain and
Europe, 1872. ¶ President de Gaulle of France opens a tidal power station near
St Malo, the first in the world, 1966. ¶ A man attempted to knife the Pope at
Manila Airport, 1970.

BORN: Anders Celsius, astronomer, devised the centigrade temperature scale,
Sweden, 1701. Sir Charles Sherrington, neurologist and physician, London,
1857. Juho Kusti Paasikivi, President of Finland, Finland, 1870. Chaim Weizmann,
Jewish biochemist and statesman, first President of Israel, Motol, Poland, 1874.
Alexander Dubček, statesman, Slovakia, 1921.

DIED: Jacopo Tatti Sansovino, Florentine sculptor, Venice, 1570. Sir John Eliot,
parliamentarian; of consumption in the Tower of London, 1632. Andrew Meikle,
agricultural engineer, built the first fully-operational threshing machine, Dunbar,
Scotland, 1811. Eugene O'Neill, dramatist, *All God's Chillun Got Wings*,
Mourning Becomes Electra, Boston, Massachusetts, 1953. Arthur Honegger, composer, *King David, Pacific 231*, 1955.

NOVEMBER 28

Dies Mala or 'Egyptian Day', considered unlucky in the Middle Ages.
Anniversary of the Proclamation of the Republic, Burundi (declared by Michael
Micombero in 1966). Anniversary of the Proclamation of the Republic,
Republic of Chad (1958). Anniversary of the Independence from Spain, Panama (1821).
Feasts of SS: Stephen the Younger, martyr; Simeon Metaphrastes;
James of the March; Joseph Pignatelli; Catherine Labouré, virgin.

The Dutch under Admiral Van Tromp surprise the British in the Downs and capture and sink many vessels, 1652. ¶ The Covenanters are defeated in the Pentland Hills outside Edinburgh, 1666. ¶ Retreat through New Jersey to Pennsylvania by George Washington, 1776. ¶ Murat leads French forces into Warsaw, 1806. ¶ Panama becomes independent, 1821. ¶ Independence of Hawaii recognized by Britain and France, 1843. ¶ Violent eruptions of Mount Etna in Sicily, 1868. ¶ Mandalay is occupied by British forces, 1885. ¶ The Sinn Fein is founded in Dublin, 1905. ¶ Lady Astor becomes the first woman Member of Parliament in Britain, 1919. ¶ Churchill, Stalin and Roosevelt meet at Teheran, 1943.

BORN: Jean-Baptiste Lully, composer, Florence, 1632. William Blake, writer and artist, *Songs of Innocence, The Marriage of Heaven and Hell*, London, 1757. John Lloyd Stephens, diplomat and archaeologist, Shrewsbury, New Jersey, 1805. William Froude, naval architect, Devonshire, 1810. Friedrich Engels, political writer, co-author with Karl Marx of the *Communist Manifesto*, Germany, 1820. John Wesley Hyatt, inventor, discovered celluloid, New York, 1837. Andrei Yanuarevich Vyshinsky, Soviet representative at the United Nations, Odessa, 1883. Jose Iturbi, pianist and actor, Valencia, Spain, 1895. Alberto Moravia, novelist and short-story writer, *The Woman of Rome, Two Women*, Rome, 1907. Claude Lévi-Strauss, anthropologist, *A World on the Wane*, Brussels, 1908.

DIED: Gian Lorenzo Bernini, sculptor, *Ecstasy of St Theresa*, 1680. Cesare Beccariam, jurist and economist, 1794. Washington Irving, essayist and historian, *A History of New York*, Tarrytown, New York, 1859. Karl von Baer, embryologist, 1876. Dwight Davis, American tennis enthusiast, founder of the Davis Cup, 1945. Enrico Fermi, physicist, developed the atomic bomb, 1954. Richard Wright, novelist and essayist, *Native Son, Black Boy*, Paris, 1960. Havergal Brian, British composer, *Gothic Symphony*, 1972.

NOVEMBER 29

Liberation Day, Albania. William Tubman's Birthday, Liberia (President, 1895–1971).
Day of the Republic, Yugoslavia (1945). Feasts of SS: Saturninus, martyrs;
Saturninus, or Sernin, bishop and martyr; Radbod, bishop.

Cheyenne and Arapahoe Indians are massacred at Sand Creek in Colorado by troops under the command of Colonel Chivington, 1864. ¶ Proclamation of Hussein as King of the Arab states, 1916. ¶ First Labour Government formed in New Zealand, under Michael Savage, 1935. ¶ Independence of Barbados proclaimed, 1966.

BORN: Christian Doppler, physicist (the 'Doppler effect'), Austria, 1803. Louisa May Alcott, novelist, Pennsylvania, 1832. Tz'u Hsi, empress-dowager of China, Peking, 1834. Gertrude Jekyll, gardener and writer, London, 1843. Sir John Ambrose Fleming, electrical engineer, Lancashire, 1849. Georgy Plekhanov, Marxist theorist and revolutionary, Russia, 1859. Busby Berkeley, film choreographer, *Gold-diggers of 1933, 42nd Street*, Los Angeles, 1895. Clive Staples Lewis, critic and novelist, *The Screwtape Letters*, Belfast, 1898. Carlo Levi, painter and novelist, *Words are Stones*, Torino, 1902.

DIED: Philip IV, King of France, Fontainebleau, 1314. Thomas Wolsey, Cardinal, diplomat and Lord Chancellor, Leicester Abbey, England, 1530. Prince Rupert, Royalist commander in the English Civil War, London, 1682. Maria Theresa, Queen of Hungary and Bohemia, Vienna, 1780. Giambattista Bodoni, printer and type designer, 1813. Horace Greeley, journalist and editor, New York City, 1872. Giacomo Puccini, composer, *La Bohème, Madame Butterfly*, Brussels, 1924. Vladimir Nikolaievich Ipatieff, petro-chemist, New York, 1952. Graham Hill, racing driver, plane-crash, Arkley, Hertfordshire, 1975.

NOVEMBER 30

St Andrew's Day in Scotland, the patron saint. Independence Day, Barbados (1966). National Heroes Day, Philippines. Independence Day, Republic of Yemen (1974). Feasts of SS: Andrew the Apostle; Sapor and Isaac, bishops and martyrs.

Seats were regained in the House of Lords by bishops, 1661. ¶ Charles XII defeats the Russians at Narva, 1700. ¶ Great earthquakes in China; contemporary estimates reckon the deaths to have been in excess of 100,000, 1731. ¶ William of Orange returns to Holland, 1813. ¶ War is declared on France by Mexico, 1838. ¶ The remains of Napoleon Bonaparte arrive in France, 1840. ¶ Finland invaded by the USSR, 1939.

BORN: Casimir IV, King of Poland, 1427. Andrea Doria, Genoese admiral, statesman, Italy, 1466. Andrea Palladio, Renaissance architect, Padua, 1508. Sir Philip Sidney, poet, courtier and soldier, *Arcadia, Astrophel and Stella*, Penshurst, Kent, 1554. Jonathan Swift, satirist and writer, *Gulliver's Travels, The Tale of a Tub*, Dublin, 1667. Theodor Mommsen, historian and classical scholar, *Corpus Inscriptionum Latinarum*, Gardling, Sleswick, 1817. Cyrus West Field, financier, Massachusetts, 1819. Mark Twain (Samuel Langhorne Clemens), writer, journalist and lecturer, *Tom Sawyer, Huckleberry Finn*, Hannibal, Missouri, 1835. Sir Winston Churchill, statesman and historian, 1874.

DIED: St Gregory of Tours, bishop and chronicler, Tours, France, 539. Marcello Malpighi, physiologist, microscopist, Rome, 1694. Oscar Wilde, dramatist, poet, novelist and critic, *The Importance of Being Earnest, The Ballad of Reading Gaol*, Paris, 1900. Edward John Eyre, explorer, Governor of Australia, 1901. Ernst Lubitsch, film director, *Ninotchka, That Uncertain Feeling*, California, 1947. Wilhelm Furtwängler, conductor and musician, 1954. Patrick Kavanagh, Irish poet, *A Soul for Sale*, 1967. Sir Terence Rattigan, dramatist, *French Without Tears, The Winslow Boy*, 1977.

DECEMBER

THIRTY-ONE DAYS

In the old Roman calendar this was the tenth
month of the year, hence its derivation from the
Latin *decem* meaning ten.

DECEMBER 1

Independence Day, Azores. National Holiday, Central African Republic.
Matilda Newport Day, Liberia (national heroine). Independence Day, Madeira.
Independence Restoration Day, Portugal. Feasts of SS: Ansanus, martyr;
Agericus, or Airy, bishop; Tudwal, bishop; Eligius, or Eloi, bishop.

Non-Importation of British goods, as resolved by the Continental Congress, comes into force, 1774. ¶ The Republic of San Domingo is established, 1821. ¶ Rupert's Land is formally transferred to the Canadian government by the Hudson Bay Company, 1869. ¶ Dejanira (Asteroid 157) discovered by Alphonse Borelly, 1875. ¶ Iceland proclaims its sovereignty, 1918. ¶ The first helium-filled balloon, a US Navy dirigible, flies from Hampton Roads, Virginia, to Washington D.C., 1921. ¶ The treaties formulated by the Locarno Conference are signed in London, 1925. ¶ Chiang Kai-shek becomes President of the Chinese Executive, 1935. ¶ President Ford of the US begins an official visit to China, 1975.

BORN: Princess Anna Comnena, Byzantine historian and writer, Constantinople, 1083. John Keill, philosopher and mathematician, Edinburgh, 1671. Martin Klaproth, chemist, Germany, 1743. Ernst Toller, Expressionist playwright, *The Change, Man and the Masses*, Samotschin, East Prussia, 1893. Dame Alicia Markova, ballerina, London, 1910.

DIED: Magnus II, Eriksson, King of Sweden and, as Magnus VII, King of Norway, Sweden, 1374. Lorenzo Ghiberti, Florentine sculptor, 1455. Edmund Campion, scholar and Jesuit; hanged at Tyburn in London, 1581. Alfred Mahan, naval commander and historian, *The Influence of Sea Power Upon History, 1660–1783*, New York, 1914. Paul D'Indy, composer and teacher, 1931. John Burdon Haldane, Marxist biochemist and geneticist, 1964. David Ben Gurion, Israeli statesman and Prime Minister, 1973.

DECEMBER 2

National Day, United Arab Emirates (commemorating the foundation of the country in 1971). Feasts of SS: Bibiana, or Viviana, virgin and martyr; Chromatius, bishop.

Christopher Wren's rebuilt St Paul's Cathedral in London is formally opened, 1697. ¶ Napoleon Bonaparte crowned Emperor by Pope Pius VII in Paris, 1804. ¶ The combined Austro-Russian forces are defeated at Austerlitz by Napoleon, 1805. ¶ The Second Empire is proclaimed in France with Napoleon III as the Emperor, 1852. ¶ The world's first patent for a disposable safety-razor, by King Gillette in New York, 1901. ¶ US Supreme Court ruling that Puerto Ricans cannot be regarded as US citizens, 1901. ¶ US Senate censures Senator Joseph McCarthy, 1954. ¶ A Dutch train is seized by a gang of South Moluccan terrorists and the 70 occupants held hostage, 1975.

BORN: Francis Xavier Quadrio, Jesuit and scholar, Valtellina, Spain, 1695. Henry Galley Knight, illustrator, 1786. Georges Seurat, pointillist painter, Paris, 1859. George Minot, physician and medical researcher, Nobel Prize winner, Boston, Massachusetts, 1885. Peter Carl Goldmark, American engineer, inventor of the long-playing record, Budapest, 1906.

DIED: Hernando Cortes, Spanish conqueror of Mexico, 1547. Gerhardus Mercator, cartographer, Duisburg, Germany, 1594. Philippe Lebon, chemist, developed gas illumination, France, 1804. The Marquis de Sade, writer, philosopher and revolutionary, *Justine, Juliette*, Charenton Asylum, near Paris, 1814. John Brown, anti-slavery campaigner; hanged in Charleston, Virginia, 1859. Jay Gould, financier and railway developer, New York, 1892. Edmond Rostand, dramatist, *Cyrano de Bergerac, L'Aiglon*, Paris, 1918. Sir Peter Buck, New Zealand Maori politician, 1951.

DECEMBER 3

Feasts of SS: Francis Xavier; Lucius; Claudius, Hilaria, and their Companions, martyrs; Cassian, martyr; Sola.

Capitulation of Mauritius, 1810. ¶ Illinois made a US state (21st), 1818. ¶ W. E. Gladstone's first ministry, 1868. ¶ Kut-el-Amara is reached by General Townsend, 1915. ¶ The Indian Prime Minister, Mrs Gandhi, declares a national state of emergency after increased border fighting with Pakistan, 1971. ¶ Laos is proclaimed a People's Democratic Republic after the abdication of King Vatthana, 1975.

BORN: Samuel Crompton, inventor of the spinning mule, Lancashire, 1753. Joseph Conrad, English novelist, *Lord Jim*, Poland, 1857. Anton von Webern, composer, Vienna, 1883. Rajendra Prasad, Indian politician and nationalist leader, India, 1884. Nino Rota, film composer, *La Strada*, Milan, 1911. Jean-Luc Godard, film director, *Jules et Jim*, Paris, 1930.

DIED: Francis Xavier, Jesuit missionary, Shang-ch'uan Tao, China, 1552. Alexander Farnese, Duke of Parma, Spanish soldier, 1592. Robert Louis Stevenson, novelist, essayist and poet, *Treasure Island, Dr Jekyll and Mr Hyde*, Samoa, 1894. Mary Baker Eddy, founder of Christian Science, 1910. Pierre Renoir, Impressionist painter, Cagnes-sur-Mer, France, 1919. Dame Mary Gilmore, Australian poet and writer, 1962.

DECEMBER 4

Feasts of SS: Peter Chrysologus, archbishop and doctor;
Barbara, virgin and martyr; Clement of Alexandria; Maruthas, bishop;
Anno, archbishop; Osmund, bishop; Bernard of Parma, bishop.

Accession of Alexander II of Scotland (reigns until 8 July 1249), 1214. ¶ First
publication of *The Observer*, the second oldest British Sunday newspaper, 1791.
¶ War is declared on Naples by France, 1798. ¶ Queensland in Australia is given
provincial status, 1859. ¶ US Senate agrees to America playing a part in the
United Nations, 1945. ¶ US launch *Gemini VII* into space for link-up with
Gemini VI while orbiting, 1965.

BORN: John Cotton, religious and political leader in America, Derby, England,
1585. Thomas Carlyle, historian and essayist, *The French Revolution*, Dumfries-
shire, 1795. Samuel Butler, novelist and satirist, *Erewhon*, *The Way of All Flesh*,
Nottinghamshire, 1835. Edith Cavell, nurse in the First World War, Norfolk,
1865. Rainer Maria Rilke, poet and writer, *The Sonnets to Orpheus*, *The Notebooks
of Malte Laurids Brigge*, Prague, 1875. Katharine Susannah Prichard, Australian
novelist, *Black Opal*, 1883. Francisco Franco, Spanish dictator, Spain, 1892. Sir
Herbert Read, poet, literary and art critic, *Poetry and Anarchism*, *A Concise History
of Modern Art*, Kirbymoorside, Yorkshire, 1893.

DIED: Duc de Richelieu, cardinal and statesman, Paris, 1642. Thomas Hobbes,
philosopher, *Leviathan*, Hardwick Hall, near Chesterfield, 1679. John Gay,
dramatist, *The Beggar's Opera*, London, 1732. Luigi Galvani, anatomist, 1798.
Robert Banks Jenkinson, Earl of Liverpool, British Prime Minister (1812–27),
London, 1828. William Sturgeon, physicist, built the first electromagnet,
Prestwich, Lancashire, 1850. Stefan George, poet, *The Year of the Soul*, 1933.
Thomas Morgan, genetic biologist, Nobel Prize for Medicine, Pasadena,
California, 1945. Benjamin Britten, composer, *Billy Budd*, *War Requiem*, 1976.

DECEMBER 5

Day of the King's Birthday, Thailand. Feasts of SS: Sabas, abbot;
Crispina, martyr; Nicetius of Trier, bishop; Birinus, bishop;
Sigiramnus, or Cyran, abbot.

Great earthquake in Naples and surrounding region, many thousands of lives lost, 1456. ¶ Phi Beta Kappa is the first fraternity to be founded in the US, at William and Mary College, 1776. ¶ The trial of Louis XVI of France begins, 1792. ¶ Napoleon leaves the French forces in Russia under the command of Murat, 1812. ¶ 21st Amendment (Article XXI) to the Constitution of the US becomes effective, repealing Prohibition, 1933. ¶ The Loyalist offensive begins in Teruel, Spain, 1937. ¶ US–USSR agreement for pacific use of outer space, 1962.

BORN: Martin van Buren, lawyer and senator, US President, Kinderhook, New York, 1782. Christina Rossetti, poet, *The Prince's Progress, The Convent Threshold*, London, 1830. George Armstrong Custer, soldier, Ohio, 1839. Józef Pilsudski, Polish soldier and revolutionary, Zulów, 1867. Fritz Lang, film director, *Metropolis, M, The Ministry of Fear*, Vienna, 1890. Walt Disney, film producer, created Mickey Mouse, *Fantasia*, Chicago, 1901. Werner Heisenberg, physicist, Nobel Prize for Physics, Germany, 1901. Otto Preminger, film director and producer, *Anatomy of a Murder*, Vienna, 1906.

DIED: Sieur de la Vérendrye, explorer in Canada and the US, Montreal, 1749. Giovanni Morgagni, physician, a pioneer of pathology, Padua, Italy, 1771. Wolfgang Amadeus Mozart, harpsichordist and composer, *The Marriage of Figaro, Don Giovanni, The Magic Flute*, Vienna, 1791. Alexandre Dumas, novelist and dramatist, *The Three Musketeers*, 1870. Claude Monet, Impressionist painter, France, 1926. Vachel Lindsay, poet, Springfield, Illinois, 1931. Joseph Erlanger, neuro-physiologist, 1965.

DECEMBER 6

Election of the Boy Bishop who reigned until 28 December, an English custom of the Middle Ages. Independence Day, Finland (1917). Anniversary of the Discovery of Haiti, Haiti (Christopher Columbus, 1492). Feasts of SS: Nicholas of Myra, bishop; Dionysia, Majoricus, and other martyrs; Abraham of Kratia, bishop.

Christopher Columbus discovers Haiti (then named Hispaniola), 1492. ¶ Colonel Pride conducted 'Pride's Purge', 1648. ¶ Cawnpore in India taken by the British, 1857. ¶ Republic proclaimed in Finland, 1917. ¶ Cologne is occupied by the Allies, 1918. ¶ Britain and Ireland sign peace declaration, 1921. ¶ The Irish Free State is proclaimed officially, 1922. ¶ Bangladesh (formerly East Pakistan) is recognized by India, 1971. ¶ Members of the 'Angry Brigade' are each sentenced to ten years' imprisonment in London for bomb outrages, 1972. ¶ Gerald Ford is sworn-in as US Vice-President, 1973.

BORN: Henry VI, King of England, Windsor, Berkshire, 1421. Baldassarre Castiglione, aristocrat and courtier, Italy, 1478. George Monck, 1st Duke of Albemarle, military commander, Devon, 1608. Sir Edmund Andros, diplomat, Governor of Virginia, London, 1637. Warren Hastings, first Governor-General of India, Churchill, Oxfordshire, 1732. Joseph Gay-Lussac, chemist, France, 1778. Paul Emile Botta, archaeologist in Mesopotamia, Italy, 1802. Charles Martin Hall, chemist, pioneered the manufacture of aluminium, Ohio, 1863. Sir Osbert Sitwell, poet and writer, *Laughter in the Next Room, Noble Essences,* London, 1892. Ira Gershwin, composer, New York City, 1896. Dave Brubeck, jazz pianist and composer, *Take Five,* California, 1920.

DIED: Jean Baptiste Chardin, painter, 1779. Jean Charles Louis Blanc, socialist and writer, 1882. Anthony Trollope, novelist, *Barchester Towers, Phineas Finn,* London, 1882. Ernst Werner von Siemens, electrician and engineer, Berlin, 1892.

DECEMBER 7

Dies Mala or 'Egyptian Day', considered unlucky in the Middle Ages.
Independence Day, Ivory Coast Republic (1960, formerly French West Africa).
Feasts of SS: Ambrose, bishop and doctor; Eutychian, pope; Josepha Rossello, virgin.

Henry VI of England crowned King of France in Paris, 1431. ¶ The state of Delaware ratifies the Constitution of the United States of America, 1787. ¶ Thomas Alva Edison demonstrates the first gramophone, 1877. ¶ Italian forces are defeated at Amba Alagi by Ethiopians, 1895. ¶ Pigtails are abolished and the calendar reformed in China by edict, 1911. ¶ David Lloyd George becomes British Prime Minister, 1916. ¶ Formal declaration of war on Austria–Hungary by US, 1917. ¶ Pearl Harbor and Hawaii are bombed by Japanese planes, 1941. ¶ *Apollo 17* launched from Cape Kennedy, 1972.

BORN: Gian Lorenzo Bernini, sculptor, *Ecstasy of St Theresa*, Naples, 1598. Theodor Schwann, physiologist, Neuss, Germany, 1810. Leopold Kronecker, mathematician, Germany, 1823. Willa Cather, novelist, *My Antonia*, Virginia, 1873. Stuart Davis, American modern painter, 1894. Eli Wallach, actor, Brooklyn, New York, 1915. Noam Chomsky, linguist, *Syntactic Structures*, Philadelphia, 1928.

DIED: Sir Peter Lely, painter, London, 1680. Meindert Hobbema, landscape painter, Holland, 1709. Michel Ney, Napoleonic military commander, executed, Paris, 1815. William Bligh, captain of the *Bounty*, 1817. Edward Irving, clergyman, the Catholic Apostolic Church grew from his teachings, Glasgow, 1834. Vicomte Ferdinand Marie de Lesseps, diplomat, promoter of the Suez Canal, 1894. Kirsten Flagstad, soprano, 1962. Thornton Wilder, novelist, *The Bridge of San Luis Rey*, 1975.

DECEMBER 8

The Feast of the Immaculate Conception of the Blessed Virgin Mary,
celebrating not the conception of Christ,
but that of Mary herself within the womb of her mother, Anne;
originally known as the Conception of St Anne, the present name was adopted in 1854.
Mother's Day, Panama. Beach Day, Uruguay. Feast of St Romaric, abbot.

Astroea (Asteroid 5) discovered by K. C. Hencke, 1845. ¶ The dogma of the Immaculate Conception of the Blessed Virgin Mary is declared to be an article of faith by Pope Pius IX, 1854. ¶ The Clifton Suspension Bridge is opened at Bristol, 1864. ¶ Foundation of the American Federation of Labour, 1886. ¶ Inauguration of the London–Australia air mail service, 1934. ¶ War declared on Japan by Britain and Australia and US, 1941. ¶ Martial law declared in Hungary, arrests begin, 1956.

BORN: Mary Stuart, Queen of Scots, Linlithgow Palace, Scotland, 1542. Eli Whitney, inventor, perfected the cotton gin, Westborough, Massachusetts, 1765. Bjørnstjerne Bjørnson, novelist and dramatist, *The Newly-Married Couple*, Norway, 1832. Georges Feydeau, writer of theatrical farces, Paris, 1862. Jean Sibelius, composer, *Finlandia, Tapiola*, Finland, 1865. Aristide Maillol, sculptor, France, 1866. Norman Douglas, Scottish writer, *Siren Land*, Austria, 1868. Padraic Colum, poet, Longford, Ireland, 1881. James Thurber, humorous writer and artist, *The Secret Life of Walter Mitty*, Columbus, Ohio, 1894. Richard Fleischer, film director, *The Vikings, Compulsion*, New York City, 1916. Sammy Davis, Jr, singer and entertainer, New York City, 1925.

DIED: Adriaan Willaert, composer and choralist, Venice, 1562. John Pym, statesman and politician, led the opposition in Parliament to James I and Charles I, London, 1643. Gerard Terborch, painter, Deventer, Netherlands, 1681. Comtesse du Barry, mistress of Louis XV of France, 1793. Herbert Spencer, philosopher and social scientist, *Principles of Psychology, Principles of Sociology*, Brighton, Sussex, 1903. Odessa, 1917. Gertrude Jekyll, English gardener and writer, 1932.

DECEMBER 9

Independence Day, Tanzania (1961). Feasts of SS: The Seven Martyrs of Samosata; Leocadia, virgin and martyr; Gorgonia, matron; Budoc, or Beuzec, abbot; Peter Fourier.

Accession of William I of Scotland, 1165. ¶ First execution in Newgate Prison in London, 1783. ¶ First steam voyage from England to India, 1825. ¶ Hoare-Laval proposals favouring Italy in the Abyssinian conflict are rejected in Britain and France, 1935. ¶ The British offensive in North Africa begins with the Eighth Army attacking Sidi Barrani, 1940.

BORN: Gustavus (II) Adolphus, King of Sweden, Stockholm, 1594. John Milton, poet and polemicist, *Paradise Lost, Paradise Regained, Areopagitica*, London, 1608. Johann Joachim Winckelmann, German art historian and early archaeologist, *Geschichte der Kunst des Alterthums*, Stendal, Prussian Saxony, 1717. Karl Wilhelm Scheele, chemist, discovered oxygen and chlorine, Stralsund (then Sweden), 1742. Claude Louis Berthollet, chemist, France, 1749. Prince Peter Kropotkin, anarchist and geographer, *Mutual Aid*, Moscow, 1842. George Grossmith, humorist, *The Diary of a Nobody* (with Weedon Grossmith), London, 1847. Joel Chandler Harris, journalist and author, *Uncle Remus: His Songs and His Sayings*, Eatonton, Georgia, 1848. Joseph Stalin, Soviet dictator, Georgia, Russia, 1879. Clarence Birdseye, industrialist, inventor of a process for deep-freezing foodstuffs, New York, 1886. John Osborne, dramatist, director and actor, *Look Back in Anger, Hotel in Amsterdam*, London, 1929.

DIED: Said (Sheikm Muslih Addin), poet and teacher, *Gulistan*, Shiraz, Persia, 1292. Ezra Cornell, founder of Cornell University, 1874. Natsume Soseki, novelist and critic, *I am a Cat*, Japan, 1916. Dame Edith Sitwell, poet and writer, *Clowns' Houses, The English Eccentrics*, London, 1964. Karl Barth, theologian and writer, 1968. Ralph Johnson Bunche, diplomat, Nobel Prize for Peace, 1971.

DECEMBER 10

*Human Rights Day, observed by members of the United Nations since
the promulgation of the Universal Declaration of Human Rights in 1948.
Feasts of SS: Miltiades, pope and martyr; Mennas, Hermogenes, and Eugraphus;
Eulalia of Mérida, virgin and martyr; Gregory III, pope;
The London Martyrs of 1591.*

C. Gracchus's first tribunate begins in Rome, 124BC. ¶ This day in France became 20 December when the Gregorian calendar is introduced in 1582. ¶ Newark burned by US forces, 1813. ¶ Mississippi made a US state (20th), 1817. ¶ War declared against Argentina by Brazil, 1825. ¶ President Woodrow Wilson is awarded the Nobel Peace Prize, 1920. ¶ Abdication of Edward VIII, who then becomes the Duke of Windsor, 1936. ¶ The first US domestic jet passenger service inaugurated, between New York and Miami by National Airlines, 1958. ¶ The Federation of Rhodesia and Nyasaland is dissolved, 1963. ¶ First scheduled flight of *Concorde* from London to Singapore, 1977.

BORN: Giovanni Battista Guarini, poet and playwright, *The Faithful Shepherd*, Ferrara, Italy, 1538. Felice Orsini, Italian nationalist, Meldola, Italy, 1819. César August Franck, organist and composer, Belgium, 1822. Emily Dickinson, poetess, Massachusetts, 1830. Melvil Dewey, librarian, inventor of the library classification system that bears his name, New York, 1851. Olivier Messiaen, composer and organist, Avignon, France, 1908.

DIED: Alfred Nobel, industrialist, inventor of dynamite and cordite, instituted the Nobel Prizes, San Remo, Italy, 1896. Sir Joseph Dalton Hooker, botanist and zoologist, London, 1911. Charles Rennie Mackintosh, Art Nouveau architect, London, 1928. Theobold Smith, pathologist, New York City, 1934. Luigi Pirandello, dramatist, *Six Characters in Search of an Author, Each in His Own Way*, Rome, 1936. Henry Cowell, American composer, 1965.

DECEMBER 11

Feasts of SS: Damasus, pope; Barsabas, martyr;
Fuscian, Victoricus, and Gentian, martyrs; Daniel the Stylite.

Llewelyn, last independent prince of the Welsh is defeated at Aber Edw in South Radnorshire, 1282. ¶ James II flees from England, 1688. ¶ Indiana made a US state (19th), 1816. ¶ Annexation of Nagpur by Britain, 1853. ¶ Accession of King George VI of Great Britain, 1936. ¶ Italy leaves the League of Nations, 1939. ¶ War declared on Italy and Germany by US, 1941.

BORN: Sir David Brewster, physicist, *Letters on Natural Magic*, Scotland, 1781. Hector Berlioz, composer, *Harold in Italy*, France, 1803. Alfred de Musset, poet, novelist and dramatist, *Les Nuits,* Paris, 1810. Robert Koch, bacteriologist, discovered the tuberculosis bacillus, Klausthal, Germany, 1843. Fiorello Henry La Guardia, Mayor of New York, New York City, 1882. Pare Lorentz, documentary film director, *The River*, 1905. Aleksandr Solzhenitsyn, novelist, *A Day in the Life of Ivan Denisovich, Cancer Ward*, Roskov, Russia, 1918.

DIED: Bernardino Pintoricchio, painter, Siena, Italy, 1513. The Duke of Alba, Spanish military commander, 1582. Prince de Condé, Louis II de Bourbon, military commander, Fontainebleau, 1686. Colley Cibber, dramatist and stage manager, *The Careless Husband*, 1757. Olive Schreiner, novelist, *The Story of an African Farm*, Capetown, 1920. Edward Murrow, journalist and broadcaster, Director of the US Information Agency, New York, 1965.

DECEMBER 12

Independence Day, Kenya (1963). Constitution Day, Thailand.
Feasts of SS: Epimachus and Alexander and other martyrs;
Finnian of Clonard, bishop; Corentin, or Cury, bishop;
Edburga, virgin. Vicelin, bishop.

The state of Pennsylvania ratifies the Constitution of the United States of America, 1787. ¶ Spain declares war on Britain, 1804. ¶ Immigration Bill passed by US Senate, 1916. ¶ War declared on Japan by Chiang Kai-shek and Chinese, 1936. ¶ The office of Governor-General of Ireland is formally abolished, 1936. ¶ The first hovercraft patented, by (Sir) Christopher Cockerell, 1955. ¶ Greece withdraws from the Council of Europe, 1969.

BORN: Tancred, King of Sicily, crusader, Antioch, 1112. William Lloyd Garrison, slave abolitionist, Massachusetts, 1805. Gustave Flaubert, novelist, *Madame Bovary*, France, 1821. Jan Kasprowicz, poet and folklorist, Poland, 1860. Edvard Munch, painter and lithographer, Löten, Norway, 1863. Alfred Werner, chemist, Mulhouse, France, 1866. Edward G. Robinson, actor, Rumania, 1893. Frank Sinatra, singer and actor, Hoboken, New Jersey, 1917.

DIED: Paolo Uccello, Florentine painter, trained as a goldsmith, Florence, 1475. Stephen Bathory, King of Poland, near Grodno, Poland, 1586. Albrecht von Haller, botanist, anatomist and poet, Berne, Switzerland, 1777. Robert Browning, poet and writer, *The Ring and the Book*, 1889. Sir John Thompson, Canadian Prime Minister, Windsor Castle, England, 1894. Douglas Fairbanks, film actor and producer, 1939. Tallulah Bankhead, actress, New York City, 1968.

DECEMBER 13

*Republic Day, Malta. Feasts of SS: Lucy, virgin and martyr;
Eustratius and his Companions, martyrs; Judoc, or Josse;
Aubert of Cambrai, bishop; Odilia, or Ottilia, virgin.*

Pope Celestine is forced to abdicate, 1294. ¶ New Zealand is discovered by Abel Tasman, 1642. ¶ Oliver Cromwell dissolves the 'Barebone's Parliament' and is made Lord Protector, 1653. ¶ Madrid falls to Napoleon, 1808. ¶ The battle of Fredericksburg won by the Confederacy, 1862. ¶ Russian forces occupy Port Arthur, 1897. ¶ US Marshall Aid to Britain comes to an end, 1950. ¶ Republic of Malta proclaimed, 1974.

BORN: Duc de Sully, soldier and statesman, a supporter and friend of Henry of Navarre (Henry IV), near Mantes, France, 1560. Heinrich Heine, poet, journalist and satirist, *Travel Sketches, On the History of Religion and Philosophy in Germany*, Dusseldorf, Germany, 1797. Ernst Werner von Siemens, electrician and engineer, Lenthe, Prussia, 1816. Talcott Parsons, sociologist, Colorado Springs, Colorado, 1902. Balthazar Johannes Vorster, Afrikaan extremist nationalist, South African Prime Minister, Jamestown, Cape Province, 1915.

DIED: Maimonides, Jewish philosopher, *Guide of the Perplexed*, Egypt, 1204. Donato di Niccolo Donatello, Florentine sculptor, 1466. Niccola Fontana Tartaglia, mathematician, Venice, 1557. Konrad von Gesner, physician, writer, *A Catalogue of Animals*, 1565. François Viète, advocate and mathematician, Paris, 1603. Dr Samuel Johnson, essayist, lexicographer and critic, London, 1784. Wassily Kandinsky, abstract artist, founded the *Blaue Reiter* group, Paris, 1944.

DECEMBER 14

Beginning of the Halcyon Days; in Greek mythology Alcyone and
her husband were changed into kingfishers by the gods, and it was
thought at the time that these birds built their nests upon the
sea during a period of extended calm, usually considered as a
week either side of the winter solstice. Feasts of SS: Spiridion, bishop;
Nicasius, bishop, and his Companions, martyrs; Venantius Fortunatus, bishop.

Accession of Mary of Scotland, 1542. ¶ Alabama made a US state (22nd), 1819. ¶ A Norwegian team led by Captain Roald Amundsen arrives at the South Pole, 1911. ¶ Relations between China and USSR are severed, 1927. ¶ Women's suffrage is introduced in Turkey, 1934. ¶ The League of Nations expels the USSR, 1939.

BORN: Nostradamus (Michel de Nostre-Dame), astrologer and prophet, *Centuries*, Saint-Remy, France, 1503. Tycho Brahe, astronomer and mathematician, Denmark, 1564. James Bruce, African explorer, rediscovered the source of the Blue Nile, 1730. Pierre Puvis de Chavannes, mural painter, Lyons, France, 1824. Paul Eluard, poet, member of the Surrealist movement, Paris, 1895. Kurt von Schuschnigg, Chancellor of Austria in the 1930s, Riva, Austria, 1897.

DIED: Carl Philipp Emanuel Bach, German composer, a son of J. S. Bach, 1788. George Washington, first US President, Mount Vernon, Washington, D.C., 1799. John Loudon, gardener and horticulturist, *Arboretum et Fruticetum Britannicum, or the Trees and Shrubs of Great Britain, Native and Foreign*, 1843. Albert, Prince Consort, husband of Queen Victoria of England, 1861. Jean Louis Agassiz, geologist and naturalist, 1873. Stanley Baldwin, British Prime Minister, 1947. Juho Kusti Paasikivi, President of Finland, Helsinki, 1956. Sir Stanley Spencer, artist, Taplow, Buckinghamshire, 1959.

DECEMBER 15

A Halcyon Day (see 14 December). The Roman festival of Consus,
originally a corn god but later associated with good counsel (also 21 August).
Statute Day, Netherlands Antilles (autonomy granted in 1954).
Constitution Day, Nepal. Feasts of SS: Nino, virgin;
Valerian and other martyrs in Africa; Stephen of Surosh, bishop;
Paul of Latros; Mary di Rosa, virgin.

Cola di Rienzi compelled to abdicate (after founding a Republic in Rome on 20
May), 1347. ¶ Amendments I to X (the 'Bill of Rights') to the Constitution of
the United States of America become effective, 1791. ¶ Napoleon enters Warsaw,
1806. ¶ The Emperor Napoleon's remains are deposited in Les Invalides, Paris,
1840. ¶ Thalia (Asteroid 23) discovered by J. R. Hind, 1852. ¶ General Redvers
Buller is defeated by the Boers at Colenso in Natal, 1899. ¶ The *Thomas W. Lawson*
lost in the English Channel, it was the only seven-masted schooner ever built,
1907. ¶ *The Man I Love* is recorded by Billie Holiday and her Orchestra in New
York, 1939. ¶ US *Gemini 6* and *Gemini 7* spacecraft rendezvous in space over 170
miles above Earth's surface, 1965. ¶ Tanzania severs diplomatic relations with
Britain but remains within the Commonwealth, 1965.

BORN: Nero Claudius Caesar Drusus Germanicus, the Roman Emperor Nero,
Antium, 37. George Romney, portrait painter, Dalton-in-Furness, Lancashire,
1734. Janos Bolyai, mathematician, Hungary, 1802. Alexandre-Gustave Eiffel,
engineer and inventor, Dijon, 1832. Antoine Henri Becquerel, early researcher
into radioactivity, Paris, 1852. Niels Finsen, physician, Nobel Prize winner,
Denmark, 1860. Josef Hoffman, architect, Czechoslovakia, 1870. Maxwell
Anderson, dramatist, Pennsylvania, 1888. Charles Cori, American biochemist,
Nobel Prize in 1947, Prague, 1896. Ahmed Ben Bella, Algerian politician and
Premier, 1918.

DIED: Georg Friedrich Grotefend, classical scholar, Frankfurt, Germany, 1853.
Sir George Cayley, engineer, founder of the study of aerodynamics, 1857. Sitting
Bull, Amerindian chief of the Sioux tribes, South Dakota, 1890. Wolfgang Pauli,
physicist, Nobel Prize winner, Zurich, 1958. Walt Disney, film producer,
creator of Mickey Mouse, *Fantasia*, 1966.

DECEMBER 16

A Halcyon Day (see 14 December). National Day, Bahrain.
National Day, Bangladesh (celebrating the Constitution of 1972).
Day of the Inauguration of the Sultan, Trengganu state, Malaysia.
Day of the Covenant, Republic of South Africa. Feasts of SS:
Eusebius of Vercelli, bishop; Adelaide, widow.

Oliver Cromwell made protector, 1653. ¶ Boston Tea Party, 1773. ¶ By Act of the Senate Napoleon is divorced from Joséphine, 1809. ¶ Zulus defeated by the Boers at Blood River, Natal, 1838. ¶ The first immigrant vessel for the Canterbury settlement, the *Charlotte Jane*, arrives at Lyttelton, New Zealand, 1850. ¶ Santa Anna is declared dictator of Mexico, 1853. ¶ Marthinius Pretorius organizes the South African Republic (Transvaal), 1856. ¶ Haig is made British Commander-in-Chief for France and Flanders, 1915. ¶ End of the battle of Verdun, 1916. ¶ *Doctor Jazz* is recorded by Jelly Roll Morton and his Red Hot Peppers in Chicago, 1926. ¶ Non-intervention protocol regarding Spain is signed in London, 1936. ¶ Beginning of the 'Battle of the Bulge', the major German offensive in the Ardennes, 1944.

BORN: Catherine of Aragon, wife of Henry VIII, Spain, 1485. John Selden, lawyer and legal historian, *History of Tithes*, Worthing, Sussex, 1584. Gebhard von Blücher, Prussian military commander, 1742. Jane Austen, novelist, *Pride and Prejudice*, *Emma*, Hampshire, 1775. Edward Emerson Barnard, astronomer, Nashville, 1857. Zoltan Kodály, composer, *The Peacock*, Hungary, 1882. Sir Noel Coward, actor, entertainer, playwright, Teddington, near London, 1899. Margaret Mead, anthropologist and sociologist, *Coming of Age in Samoa*, Philadelphia, 1901. Arthur C. Clarke, science-fiction novelist and writer, *Rendez-vous with Rama*, Somerset, 1917.

DIED: Richard Bright, physician, Bright's Disease is named after him, 1858. Wilhelm Grimm, historian and folklore collector, *Fairy Tales* (with his brother Jacob), Berlin, 1859. Charles Camille Saint-Saëns, composer, *Carnival of Animals*, Algiers, 1921. Somerset Maugham, novelist and dramatist, *Of Human Bondage*, *Cakes and Ale*, Nice, 1965. Harold Holt, Liberal politician, Prime Minister of Australia; drowned, near Victoria, Australia, 1967.

DECEMBER 17

A Halcyon Day (see 14 December). Feasts of SS: Lazarus;
Olympias, widow; Begga, widow; Sturmi, abbot; Wivina, virgin.

Ochákov taken by the Russian army under Potemkin, 1788. ¶ Simon Bolivar becomes President of Republic of Colombia, 1819. ¶ Egyptian protectorate proclaimed by Britain, 1914. ¶ George II of Greece deposed by army rebellion, 1923. ¶ The battle of the River Plate ends with the scuttling of the German *Graf Spee* near Montevideo, 1939. ¶ Petrol rationing begins in Britain and elsewhere as a result of the closing of the Suez Canal, 1956.

BORN: Prince Rupert, Royalist commander in the English Civil War, Prague, 1619. Domenico Cimarosa, composer, *The Secret Marriage*, Italy, 1749. Jean-Baptiste Girard, priest and educator, Switzerland, 1765. Ludwig van Beethoven, composer, Bonn, 1770. Sir Humphry Davy, chemist, inventor of a safety lamp for miners, Cornwall, 1778. Joseph Henry, physicist, made discoveries in electro-magnetism and acoustics, Albany, New York, 1797. John Greenleaf Whittier, Quaker poet and essayist, *At Sundown, Legends of New England in Prose and Verse*, near Haverhill, Massachusetts, 1807. Jules de Goncourt, writer, author with his brother Edmond of the *Journal*, France, 1830. Ford Maddox Ford, novelist, *Parade's End*, Surrey, 1873. W. L. Mackenzie King, Prime Minister of Canada, Ontario, 1874. Erskine Caldwell, popular novelist, Georgia, 1903. Willard Libby, chemist, discoverer of radio-carbon dating, Grand Valley, Colorado, 1908.

DIED: Simon Bolivar, revolutionary leader in South America, 1830. Lewis Morgan, anthropologist and lawyer, Rochester, New York, 1881. Lord Kelvin, physicist and inventor, 1907. Grigori Efimovich Rasputin, Russian monk, assassinated, St Petersburg, 1916.

DECEMBER 18

A Halcyon Day (see 14 December). Beginning of the Yule period celebrated by
the Goths, Saxons and others in honour of the winter solstice,
it lasted until 7 January and was known as the 'Yule Girth'.
National Day, Republic of Niger. Feasts of SS: Rufus and Zosimus, martyrs;
Gatian, bishop; Flannan, bishop; Winebald, abbot.

The Scots are defeated at Clifton Moor, 1745. ¶ The state of New Jersey ratifies the Constitution of the United States of America, 1787. ¶ Napoleon Bonaparte arrives in Paris after abandoning the French forces in Russia, 1812. ¶ Treaty between US and Panama results in Canal Zone being held by US for annual rent, 1903. ¶ *Atlas I* launched by US at Cape Canaveral, 1958. ¶ The death penalty for murder is abolished in Britain, 1969.

BORN: Abraham Viktor Rydberg, Swedish philosopher and poet, Jönköping, Sweden, 1828. Sir Joseph John Thomson, physicist, discovered the electron, Nobel Prize for Physics, Manchester, 1856. Francis Thompson, poet, *The Hound of Heaven, Sister Songs*, Preston, Lancashire, 1859. Saki (Hector Hugo Munro), British short-story writer, *The Chronicles of Clovis, Beasts and Super-Beasts*, Burma, 1870. Paul Klee, artist, Berne, Switzerland, 1879. Christopher Fry, dramatist, *The First Born*, Bristol, 1907. Jules Dassin, film director, *Naked City*, Middletown, New York, 1912. Willy Brandt, West German statesman, Lübeck, 1913. Mohammed Ali (Cassius Clay), champion boxer, Louisville, Kentucky, 1942.

DIED: Abu Mohammed al-Ghazali, Islamic theologian and mystic, 1111. Antonio Stradivari, violin maker, Cremona, Italy, 1737. Johann Herder, critic, theologian and poet, *Outlines of a Philosophy of the History of Man*, Germany, 1803. Jean Baptiste de Lamarck, naturalist, Paris, 1829. Sir Richard Owen, biologist and palaeontologist, *History of British Fossil Reptiles*, Newtown, Montgomeryshire, 1858. Sir John William Alcock, aviator, 1919. Bobby Jones, American champion golfer, 1971.

DECEMBER 19

A Halcyon Day (see 14 December). The Roman Saturnalia, a feast honouring Saturnus, the god of sowing and seed corn (the festival was later extended to seven days). 'Yule Girth' (see 18 December). Feasts of SS: Nemesius and other martyrs; Anastasius I, pope.

Accession of Henry I of England, 1154. ¶ Toulon recaptured from Alexander Hood by Napoleon Bonaparte, 1793. ¶ Fort Niagara taken by the British, 1813. ¶ Independence of Hawaii recognized by US, 1842. ¶ *Stompy Jones* and *Caravan* recorded in New York City by Barney Bigard and his Jazzopators (a Duke Ellington unit), 1936. ¶ British evacuate Penang, 1941.

BORN: Philip V, King of Spain, Versailles, France, 1683. Albert Abraham Michelson, American physicist, Prussia, 1852. Sir Ralph Richardson, actor, Cheltenham, Gloucestershire, 1902. Leonid Ilyich Brezhnev, Soviet statesman, Ukraine, 1906. Jean Genet, novelist and dramatist, *The Balcony*, 1910.

DIED: Matteo Maria Boiardo, Italian poet, *Canzoniere*, 1494. Vitus Jonassen Bering, Dutch navigator and explorer (Bering Straits), 1741. Emily Brontë, novelist, *Wuthering Heights*, 1848. Joseph Mallord William Turner, landscape painter, etcher and water-colourist, Chelsea, London, 1851. Robert Andrews Millikan, physicist, San Francisco, 1953.

DECEMBER 20

A Halcyon Day (see 14 December). 'Yule Girth' (see 18 December).
Feasts of SS: Ammon and his Companions, martyrs; Philogonius, bishop;
Ursicinus, abbot; Dominic of Silos, abbot.

Cicero's third *Philippic* proclaimed in Rome, 44BC. ¶ The first General Assembly of the Church of Scotland was held, 1560. ¶ The Gregorian calendar introduced by France, 1582. ¶ South Carolina secedes from the Union, 1860. ¶ Creation in Washington of the Joint Committee on the Conduct of the War (American Civil War), 1861. ¶ The Chinese Nanking government is recognized by Britain, 1928. ¶ Harold Wilson tells the House of Commons that there will be no independence for Rhodesia before majority rule, 1966. ¶ Last Australian troops arrive home from Vietnam, 1972.

BORN: John Wilson Croker, Tory politician and writer, Galway, Ireland, 1780. Thomas Graham, chemist, Glasgow, 1805. Harvey S. Firestone, US industrialist, 1868. Sir Robert Menzies, Prime Minister of Australia, Victoria, 1894. Robert Van de Graaff, physicist, inventor of the Van de Graaff nuclear accelerator, Tuscaloosa, Alabama, 1901.

DIED: Ambroise Paré, surgeon, Paris, 1590. Emile Loubet, statesman, France, 1929. Erich Ludendorff, soldier and early member of the Nazi party, Munich, 1937. John Steinbeck, novelist, *The Grapes of Wrath*, New York City, 1968.

DECEMBER 21

Winter Solstice (or 22 or 23 December). A Halcyon Day (see 14 December).
The main day of the Yule festival fell on or about this day, observed by
the Goths and Saxons (see 18 December). Feasts of SS: Thomas
the Apostle; Anastasius II of Antioch, bishop and martyr.

France issues paper money (Assignats), 1789. ¶ Turkish army routed by Egypt at Battle of Konieh, 1832. ¶ Savannah in Georgia, occupied by the Confederacy, falls to General Sherman, 1864. ¶ First appearance of a crossword puzzle in a newspaper, the *New York World*, 1913. ¶ Walt Disney's *Snow White and the Seven Dwarfs* opens in Los Angeles, the world's first full-length, colour, sound, animated cartoon, 1937. ¶ Launching of *Apollo 8* from Cape Kennedy, 1968. ¶ Dr Kurt Waldheim succeeds U Thant as Secretary-General of the United Nations, 1971.

BORN: Masaccio, Florentine painter, Italy, 1401. Mathurin Régnier, satirical poet, Chartres, France, 1573. Leopold von Ranke, historian, *History of the Popes*, Germany, 1796. Sir Joseph Whitworth, industrialist and engineer, Stockport, Cheshire, 1803. Benjamin Disraeli, statesman and novelist, London, 1804. Mily Alexeyvich Balakirev, Russian composer, *Tamara*, 1837. Anthony Powell, novelist, *The Music of Time*, London, 1805. Heinrich Böll, writer, Nobel Prize for Literature, Cologne, 1917. Kurt Waldheim, Secretary-General of the United Nations, Austria, 1918.

DIED: Giovanni Boccaccio, Italian writer and poet, *The Decameron*, 1375. Catherine of Braganza, wife of Charles II of England, Lisbon, 1705. F. Scott Fitzgerald, novelist, *The Great Gatsby*, 1940. George Patton, military commander, led US troops in Sicily (1943) and France (1944), Heidelberg, Germany, 1945. Lewis Terman, psychologist, pioneered the devising of intelligence tests, Palo Alto, California, 1956.

DECEMBER 22

Winter Solstice (or 21 or 23 December). A Halcyon Day (see 14 December).
'Yule Girth' (see 18 December). Dies Mala or 'Egyptian Day',
considered unlucky in the Middle Ages. Feasts of SS:
Frances Xavier Cabrini, virgin; Chaeremon, Ischyrion, and other martyrs.

For Swiss Catholics and the Catholic States of Germany this day became
1 January with the introduction of the Gregorian calendar, 1583. ¶ Mungo Park
returns after his first voyage to Africa, 1797. ¶ Savannah in Georgia is occupied
by Unionist forces under the command of General Sherman, 1864. ¶ After conviction by a court-martial held *in camera* Alfred Dreyfus is sent to Devil's Island
in French Guiana, 1895. ¶ The exiled government of Bangladesh is established in
Dacca, 1971.

BORN: Roger II, King of Sicily, 1095. Hermann Reimarus, philosopher,
Hamburg, 1694. James Oglethorpe, British colonist of the US state of Georgia,
London, 1696. James Wolfe, military commander, conqueror of Quebec,
Westerham, Kent, 1726. John Crome, landscape painter, Norwich, 1768. Jean
Henri Fabre, entomologist and naturalist, 1823. Giacomo Puccini, composer, *La
Bohème, Madame Butterfly*, Lucca, Italy, 1858. Edgar Varèse, composer, *Deserts,
Offrandes, Arcana*, Paris, 1883.

DIED: Aulus Vitellius, Roman emperor; Rome, 69. Duc de Sully, soldier and
statesman, Villebon, France, 1641. George Eliot (Mary Ann Evans), novelist,
Middlemarch, Chelsea, London, 1880. Baron Richard von Krafft-Ebing, neuro-
psychiatrist, *Psychopathia Sexualis*, Vienna, 1902. Nathanael West (Nathan
Wallenstein Weinstein), novelist, *Miss Lonelyhearts, The Day of the Locust*, near
El Centro, California, 1940. Franz Boas, anthropologist, 1942. Beatrix Potter,
children's writer, created Peter Rabbit, Lancashire, 1943. Harry Langdon, silent
film comedian, California, 1944.

DECEMBER 23

Winter Solstice (or 21 or 22 December). A Halcyon Day (see 14 December).
The Roman festival of Larentalia, celebrating the Etruscan earth-goddess Acca
Larentia who nursed Romulus and Remus. 'Yule Girth' (see 18 December).
Feasts of SS: The Ten Martyrs of Crete; Victoria and Anatolia, virgins and martyrs;
Servulus; Dagobert II of Austrasia; Thorlac, bishop.

Marcus Aurelius returns to Rome with his son, Lucius Aelius Aurelius Commodus, and holds triumph, 176. ¶ First appearance of the Asiatic cholera in Scotland, at Haddington, 1831. ¶ Great storms in the North Atlantic result in over 60 vessels being lost, 1890. ¶ Main offensive began in Catalonia by rebel forces under General Franco, 1938. ¶ The captain and crew of the *Pueblo* are released by the North Koreans at Panmunjon, 1968. ¶ The Shah of Persia announces that the Gulf States will increase the price of oil by 100%, 1973.

BORN: James Gibbs, architect, Scotland, 1682. Sir Richard Arkwright, inventor, Lancashire, 1732. Jean François Champollion, Egyptologist, deciphered the Rosetta Stone, France, 1790. Joseph Smith, founder of the Church of Jesus Christ of Latter-Day Saints (Mormons), Sharon, Vermont, 1805. Karl Richard Lepsius, Egyptologist, *Monuments of Egypt and Ethiopia*, Saxony, 1810. J. Arthur Rank, businessman, Methodist and sometime film producer, Hull, Yorkshire, 1888.

DIED: John Cotton, religious and political leader in America, 1652. Thomas Robert Malthus, economist, *An Essay on the Principles of Population*, Haileybury, Hertfordshire, 1834. Anthony Herman Fokker, aeronautical engineer, 1939. Hideki Tojo, Japanese Prime Minister, executed by the Allies, Tokyo, 1948. Lavrenti Beria, Soviet secret-police chief under Stalin; executed, 1953. Edward, Lord Halifax, statesman, 1959.

Eve of the Nativity of Christ, Christmas Eve. A Halcyon Day (see 14 December).
'Yule Girth' (see 18 December). Feasts of SS: Gregory of Spoleto, martyr;
Delphinus, bishop; Tharsilla and Emiliana, virgins; Irmina, virgin, and Adela, widow.

Attempted assassination of Napoleon I by an 'infernal machine', 1800. ¶ The Treaty of Ghent: end of war between US and Britain, 1814. ¶ Part of the Capitol and the whole of the Library of Congress destroyed by fire, Washington, D.C., 1851. ¶ First public radio broadcast in the world, by Professor Fessenden in the US, 1906. ¶ Albania is declared a Republic, 1924. ¶ Fall of a large meteorite in Leicestershire; it is estimated to have weighed over 100 lbs and is probably the largest to have fallen in Britain in modern times, 1965. ¶ Darwin in Australia is devastated by Cyclone Tracy, 1974.

BORN: John Lackland, King of England, Oxford, 1167. George Crabbe, poet and writer, *Tales of the Hall*, Suffolk, 1754. Kit Carson, frontiersman, Madison County, Kentucky, 1809. James Prescott Joule, physicist, the measure of a unit of energy bears his name, Salford, Lancashire, 1818. Matthew Arnold, poet and critic, *Culture and Anarchy*, Middlesex, 1822. Juan Ramón Jiménez, poet, *Silver and I*, Nobel Prize for Literature, Moguer, Spain, 1881. Louis Jouvet, theatrical actor and director, France, 1887. Michael Curtiz, American film director, *The Charge of the Light Brigade, Casablanca*, Budapest, Hungary, 1888. Howard Hughes, aircraft manufacturer, film director and industrialist, Texas, 1905. Adam Rapacki, Polish politician, Poland, 1909.

DIED: John Dunstable, English astrologer and composer, 1453. Andreas von Karlstadt, German Protestant preacher and reformer, 1541. William Makepeace Thackeray, novelist and satirist, *Vanity Fair, The Book of Snobs*, London, 1863. Clarence King, geologist, 1901. Léon Bakst, painter and stage designer, 1924. Alban Berg, composer, *Wozzeck*, 1935.

DECEMBER 25

The Feast of the Nativity (or Birthday) of our Lord Jesus Christ;
first observed in Rome in the 4th century; known as Christmas Day throughout the world.
A Halcyon Day (see 14 December).
The Roman festival of the Winter Solstice (Dies Natalis Solis Invicti).
'Yule Girth' (see 18 December).
Regarded as New Year's Day in most Catholic countries until the 12th century.
Commonly called Midwinter Day. Family Day, Angola.
Day of the Creation of the Mauritanian People's Republic, Mauritania.
Feasts of SS: Eugenia, virgin and martyr; The Martyrs at Nicomedia: Anastasia, martyr.

Charlemagne is crowned emperor of the West at Rome by Pope Leo III, 800.
¶ William I of England crowned, 1066. ¶ The Pilgrim Fathers land at Plymouth
Rock after crossing the Atlantic, 1620. ¶ 'Great Frost' of London begins (lasts
until 8 February 1740), 1739. ¶ Ice hockey supposedly invented by the Royal
Canadian Rifles at Kingston, 1855. ¶ Hankow was occupied by Japanese forces,
1938. ¶ Japanese troops force surrender of Hong Kong, 1941.

BORN: Sir Isaac Newton, mathematician, physicist and astronomer, *Philosophiae
Naturalis Principia Mathematica*, Woolsthorpe, Lincolnshire, 1642. Julien Offray
de La Mettrie, army surgeon and philosopher, St Malo, France, 1709. William
Collins, poet, 'To the Passions', Chichester, Sussex, 1721. Alexander Scriabin,
composer and pianist, *Prometheus*, Moscow, 1872. Mohammed Ali Jinnah,
Governor-General of Pakistan, 1876. Maurice Utrillo, painter, Paris, 1883.
Conrad Hilton, founder of the Hilton Hotels, New Mexico, 1887. Dame
Rebecca West, novelist and critic, *The Meaning of Treason*, Edinburgh, 1892.
Humphrey Bogart, film actor, *The Maltese Falcon, Casablanca*, New York, 1899.
Cab Calloway, jazz singer and bandleader, Rochester, New York, 1907. Anwar
Sadat, President of Egypt, al Minūfiyuh Governorate, Egypt, 1918.

DIED: Joseph Fouché, revolutionary, head of French secret police, 1820. Karel
Capek, dramatist, *Rossum's Universal Robots*, 1938. W. C. Fields, film comedian,
Never Give a Sucker an Even Break, 1946. Otto Loewi, physician and neuro-
physiologist, Nobel Prize winner, New York, 1961. Charlie Chaplin, actor and
comedian, *The Gold Rush, Modern Times*, 1977.

DECEMBER 26

A Halcyon Day (see 14 December). 'Yule Girth' (see 18 December).
St Stephen's Day, BCP; known as Offering or Boxing Day in England since the early
19th century, possibly as it was the custom to give 'boxes', or presents,
Handsel Day in Scotland. Feasts of SS: Stephen, martyr;
Archelaus, bishop; Dionysius, pope; Zosimus, pope.

Dedication of the first Westminster Abbey building, 1065. ¶ Accession of King Stephen of England (reigns until 25 October 1154), 1135. ¶ Hessians defeated by George Washington at the battle of Trenton, 1776. ¶ Signing of the Treaty of Pressburg, 1805. ¶ Independence of Belgium, 1830. ¶ The German battleship *Scharnhorst* is sunk, 1943.

BORN: Thomas Gray, poet and scholar, 'Elegy Written in a Country Churchyard', *Pindaric Odes*, London, 1716. Lord George Gordon, Protestant extremist, London, 1751. Charles Babbage, inventor of 'difference engines' and calculating machines, Devon, 1792. Dion Boucicault, actor and dramatist, Dublin, 1822. Henry Miller, novelist, *Tropic of Cancer*, *Tropic of Capricorn*, New York City, 1891. Mao Tse-tung, Chairman of the Central Committee of the Chinese Communist Party, Hunan Province, China, 1893.

DIED: Claude Helvetius, philosopher and encyclopedist, Voré, France, 1771. John Wilkes, parliamentarian and political reformer, published *The North Briton*, London, 1797. Heinrich Schliemann, a pioneer of modern archaeology, Naples, 1890. Melvil Dewey, librarian, inventor of the library classification system that bears his name, 1931. James Stephens, novelist and poet, *Insurrection*, London, 1950. Charles Pathé, pioneer film producer and director, Monte Carlo, 1957. Harry S. Truman, US President, Kansas City, 1972.

DECEMBER 27

*A Halcyon Day (see 14 December). 'Yule Girth' (see 18 December).
Feasts of SS: John the Evangelist; Fabiola, matron; Nicarete, virgin;
Theodore and Theophanes.*

French troops invade Holland, 1794. ¶ Foundation stone of the Cathedral of St John the Divine laid in New York City, 1892. ¶ Josef Stalin and his supporters triumph over Trotsky at the All-Union Congress, 1927. ¶ The International Monetary Fund (IMF) established, 1945. ¶ Assassination of Premier of Egypt, Nokrashy Pasha, 1948.

BORN: Johannes Kepler, astronomer, Württemberg, Germany, 1571. Jakob Bernoulli, mathematician, Switzerland, 1654. Sir George Cayley, engineer, founder of the study of aerodynamics, Yorkshire, 1773. Alexander Gordon Laing, explorer and officer, Edinburgh, 1793. Louis Pasteur, chemist and bacteriologist, France, 1822. Sir Mackenzie Bowell, Canadian Prime Minister, Rickinghall Superior, Suffolk, England, 1823. Carl Zuckmayer, dramatist, *The Captain of Kopenick*, *The Devil's General*, Nackenheim, Germany, 1896. Marlene Dietrich, actress and singer, Berlin, 1904.

DIED: Pierre de Ronsard, poet, *Odes, Amours de Cassandre*, Tours, France, 1585. Charles Martin Hall, chemist, pioneered the manufacture of aluminium, 1914. Sergey Yesenin, poet, *Black Man*; suicide, Leningrad, 1925. Anatoli Lunacharsky, Soviet dramatist, 1933. Max Beckmann, German Expressionist painter, 1950. Lester Pearson, Prime Minister of Canada, Nobel Prize for Peace, Ottawa, 1972.

DECEMBER 28

*The Feast of the Holy Innocents, commemorating the children massacred
in Bethlehem by King Herod; observed on this day since the 6th century;
Innocents' Day in BCP; known also as Childermas (Day), and long
considered to be the unluckiest day of the year. 'Yule Girth' (see 18 December),
The Dethroning of the Boy Bishop who was elected on 6 December,
an English custom of the Middle Ages. Proclamation Day,
Australia (certain states only). Birthday of the King, Nepal.
Feasts of SS: Theodore the Sanctified, abbot; Antony of Lérins.*

With the death of Queen Mary II on this day, William III of England reigned alone, 1694. ¶ Independence of Mexico recognized by Spain, 1836. ¶ Iowa made a US state (29th), 1846. ¶ The Tay Bridge disaster, 1879. ¶ Formation of the National India Congress, 1886. ¶ The 38th Parallel is crossed by advancing Chinese forces in Korea, 1950.

BORN: Sir John Lawes, agriculturalist, Rothamsted, Hertfordshire, 1814. Thomas Woodrow Wilson, US President, a founder of the League of Nations, Staunton, Virginia, 1856. Pio Baroja, novelist, *Struggle for Life*, Spain, 1872. Sir Arthur Eddington, astronomer and physicist, 1882. Roger Sessions, composer, Brooklyn, New York, 1896.

DIED: Pierre Bayle, philosopher and writer, *Dictionnaire historique et critique*, 1706. Robert Macgregor, Scottish clan chief, known as Rob Roy, Perthshire, 1734. Emerich de Vattel, diplomat and jurist, Neuchâtel, Switzerland, 1767. Thomas Macaulay, statesman and historian, *Lays of Ancient Rome*, London, 1859. George Gissing, novelist, *New Grub Street*, London, 1903. Alexandre-Gustave Eiffel, French engineer and inventor, 1923. Maurice Ravel, composer, *Boléro*, *Daphnis et Chloé*, Paris, 1937. Theodore Dreiser, novelist, *An American Tragedy*, 1945. Jack Lovelock, New Zealand athlete, 1949. Paul Hindemith, composer, *Funeral Music for Viola and Strings*, *The Four Temperaments*, 1963.

DECEMBER 29

'Yule Girth' (see 18 December). Feasts of SS: Thomas of Canterbury, archbishop and martyr; Trophimus, bishop; Marcellus Akimetes, abbot; Ebrulf, or Evroult, abbot.

Murder of Thomas à Becket at Canterbury Cathedral, 1170. ¶ Buffalo burnt by British forces, 1813. ¶ Insurrection of troops in Moscow is suppressed after the death of Czar Alexander I, 1825. ¶ Texas is made a US state (28th), 1845. ¶ Canton taken by the British and French, 1857. ¶ HMS *Warrior*, the first British ironclad, is launched, 1860. ¶ Johannesburg is raided by Starr Jameson, 1895. ¶ First German incendiary bombs are dropped on the City of London, 1940. ¶ Heavy Allied bombing raids on Berlin, 1943.

BORN: Marquise de Pompadour, the mistress of Louis XV, Paris, 1721. Charles Macintosh, chemist, pioneer of the water-proofing of fabrics, Glasgow, 1766. Christian Thomsen, archaeologist, Copenhagen, 1788. Charles Goodyear, inventor of vulcanized rubber, Connecticut, 1800. Andrew Johnson, US President, Raleigh, North Carolina, 1808. William Ewart Gladstone, Liberal Prime Minister, Liverpool, 1809. Karl Ludwig, physiologist, Germany, 1816. Pablo Casals, cellist, Spain, 1876. Klaus Emil Julius Fuchs, Soviet spy in Britain, Germany, 1911.

DIED: Thomas à Becket, 1170. Thomas Sydenham, physician, wrote widely on medicine and disease, London, 1689. Jacques David, French Neo-classical artist, murdered, 1825. Charles Lamb, essayist and writer, *Essays of Elia*, Edmonton, Middlesex, 1834. Christina Rossetti, poet, *The Prince's Progress*, *The Convent Threshold*, London, 1894. Rainer Maria Rilke, poet and writer, *The Sonnets to Orpheus*, *The Notebooks of Malte Laurids Brigge*, Valmonte, Switzerland, 1926. Fletcher Henderson, American jazz arranger and band-leader, 1952.

DECEMBER 30

'Yule Girth' (see 18 December). Rizal Day, Philippines (José Rizal, national hero, 1863–1896). Feasts of SS: Sabinus and his Companions, martyrs; Anysia, martyr; Anysius, bishop; Egwin, bishop.

Abdication of King Michael of Rumania, 1947. ¶ Sovereignty of Vietnam proclaimed after French renounce their claims, 1949. ¶ Formation of a federation by the states of French West Africa, 1958.

BORN: Titus Flavius Sabinus Vespasianus, Roman Emperor, Rome (?), 39. Theodor Fontane, novelist, *Before the Storm*, Germany, 1819. Rudyard Kipling, novelist and poet, *The Jungle Book*, Bombay, 1865. Stephen Leacock, economist and humorous writer, *Moonbeams from the Larger Lunacy*, Hampshire, 1869. Hideki Tojo, Japanese Prime Minister, responsible for the attack on Pearl Harbour, Tokyo, 1884. Sir Carol Reed, film director, *The Fallen Idol*, London, 1906.

DIED: Jean Baptiste von Helmont, chemist and natural scientist, coined the word *gas*, near Brussels (?), 1644. Robert Boyle, chemist and physicist, 1691. John Needham, scientist and cleric, Brussels, 1781. Sir William White Baker, explorer, discovered Lake Albert, 1893. Amelia Bloomer, American campaigner for women's rights, popularized 'bloomers', 1894. Romain Rolland, novelist and biographer, Nobel Prize for Literature, *Jean Christophe*, Switzerland, 1944. Alfred North Whitehead, philosopher and mathematician, *Science and the Modern World*, *Principia Mathematica* (with Bertrand Russell), Cambridge, Massachusetts, 1947. Trygve Lie, the first Secretary-General of the United Nations, Norway, 1968.

DECEMBER 31

*New Year's Eve. 'Yule Girth' (see 18 December). In Scotland the
New Year festivity is known as Hogmanay and is greatly celebrated
(the word Hogmanay is of unknown derivation, possibly from the
Scandinavian Hogenat, 'Hogg-night', a Yule-tide feast when animals
were ritually slaughtered). Restoration Day, Genève canton,
Switzerland. Feasts of SS: Silvester I, pope;
Columba of Sens, virgin and martyr; Melania the Younger, widow.*

The Yorkists are defeated by the Lancastrians at Wakefield, 1460. ¶ The Protestant League of Smalcalde in Germany, 1531. ¶ The first ship left France carrying Huguenots bound for South Africa, 1687. ¶ A Window Tax was imposed in England, 1695. ¶ Benedict Arnold's attack on Quebec fails, 1775. ¶ Ottawa is chosen to be the capital of Canada by Queen Victoria, 1857. ¶ German attack on Cambrai, 1917. ¶ Prohibition enacted in Canada, 1917. ¶ *Bugle Call Rag* is recorded by Spike Hughes and his Orchestra in New York City, 1930. ¶ International Geophysical Year comes to an end, 1958. ¶ Beginning of the 'three day week' in Britain brought about by disputes in the coal and electricity industries, 1973.

BORN: Hermann Boerhaave, physician and teacher, Netherlands, 1668. Charles Edward Stuart, 'Bonnie Prince Charlie', leader of the Jacobite Rebellion to depose George II of England, Rome, 1720. Charles Marquis Cornwallis, military commander, London, 1738. Ismail Pasha, Khedive of Egypt, Cairo, 1830. Emile Loubet, statesman, France, 1838. Giovanni Pascoli, poet, *Myricae, Canti di Castelvecchio*, Italy, 1855. Henri Matisse, painter, Picardy, 1869. George Catlett Marshall, directed American war efforts in the Second World War, formulated the Marshall Aid Plan, Pennsylvania, 1880.

DIED: Lucius Aelius Aurelius Commodus, Roman Emperor, 192. Thomas Erastus, theologian, Basel, Germany, 1583. Giovanni Borelli, mathematician and astronomer, 1679. John Flamsteed, the first Astronomer Royal, 1719. Gustave Courbet, French painter and revolutionary, 1877. Miguel de Unamuno, philosopher, essayist and poet, *The Tragic Sense of Life, Mist*, Salamanca, Spain, 1936. Sir Malcolm Campbell, winner of land and water speed records, 1948. Maxim Litvinov, Soviet statesman, Moscow, 1951.

APPENDIX

I

Easter and other movable feasts and customs

To deal adequately with the subject(s) of this section would require a work many times the length of the present volume; the problems and complexities of Easter alone have spawned a vast literature. All I have attempted is to give a general note about the most important and to present a selection of their alternative names – names frequently encountered in history and folk-lore.

As this list is relatively short I have not cross-referenced the entries, to do so would have been to swamp the text with *sees* or qvs.

A very full list of names used in dating is given in *The Handbook of British Chronology*, edited by F. M. Powicke, Royal Historical Society, London, 1939, pp. 403–19.

For British calendar customs and related folk-lore see the volumes detailed under the names of Banks, Paton and Wright in Section IV of the Bibliography.

ADVENT SUNDAY is the Sunday nearest to 30 November (St Andrew's Day) that allows three Sundays between it and Christmas Day. From Latin *adventus*, the coming (of Christ).

ASCENSION DAY falls on the Thursday following the fifth Sunday after Easter. It is commonly called Holy Thursday and it celebrates Christ's Ascension into Heaven forty days after his Resurrection. A legal holiday in some Catholic countries.

ASH WEDNESDAY is the first day of Lent, since the 6th century. It falls on the Wednesday before Quadragesima Sunday, the sixth Sunday before Easter. In about 590 Pope Gregory is said to have introduced the custom of sprinkling ashes, the day then being known as *Dies Cinerum*.

BLACK MONDAY, Easter Monday.

CARE SUNDAY, Passion Sunday, the second Sunday before Easter.

CHARE THURSDAY, Maundy Thursday.

COLLOP MONDAY, the day before Shrove Tuesday.

CONFESSION TUESDAY, Shrove Tuesday.

CORPUS CHRISTI, a feast honouring the doctrine of transubstantiation and deriving from the Lord's Supper. It is observed on the Thursday after Trinity Sunday, that is the Thursday following the eighth Sunday after Easter. The observance was instituted by Pope Urban IV in 1264 and subsequently confirmed by the Council of Vienne in 1311. A legal holiday in many Catholic countries.

CROSS WEEK, Rogation Week.

EASTER DAY/SUNDAY commemorates and celebrates the death and Resurrection of Jesus Christ. It was first observed as a special festival about the year AD68, and is now the most important date in the Christian calendar. The rules for its computation were drawn up by the fathers of the Council of Nicaea in AD325: Easter Day is the first Sunday after the full moon which happens upon, or next after, the 21st day of March; and if the full moon happens upon a Sunday, Easter Day is the Sunday after. But the full moon mentioned is not the real moon, the Paschal Full Moon, but a hypothetical one, and special tables drawn up from certain lunar cycles need to be consulted. For further information see the preliminary matter in *The Book of Common Prayer* and Part III of Alexander Philip's *The Calendar*, Cambridge, 1921.

There have been several proposals to fix Easter, most recently by the World Council of Churches, but it appears very unlikely that any will be adopted in the near future – tradition and inertia will see to it.

It may seem strange that a word of pagan origin is retained for so important a Christian feast. The best explanation is that given by the Venerable Bede in the 8th century when writing about April: 'Eosturmonath, which is now rendered the Paschal month, and formerly received its name from a goddess (worshipped by the Saxons and other ancient nations of the North) called Eostre, in whose honour they observed a festival in this month. From the name of this goddess they now design the Paschal season, giving a name to the joys of a new solemnity from a term familiarized by the use of former ages.' (Quoted by Gillian Edwards in *Hogmanay and Tiffany*, London, 1970, p. 128).

Governed by the date of Easter are the following movable feasts (in order of their occurrence): Septuagesima Sunday, Sexagesima Sunday, Quinquagesima Sunday, Shrove Tuesday, Ash Wednesday, Quadragesima Sunday, Mid-Lent or Mothering Sunday, Passion Sunday, Palm Sunday, Maundy Thursday, Good Friday, EASTER, Low Sunday, the Rogation Days, Ascension Day, Pentecost or Whit Sunday, Trinity Sunday, and Corpus Christi.

EGG SATURDAY, the Saturday before Shrove Tuesday.

EMBER WEEKS were introduced by Pope Callixtus I (217–222) to seek God's blessing, by fasting and prayer, for the produce of the earth. It was then customary for the penitents to sprinkle the ashes or embers of humiliation upon their heads.

The Ember Days in the Anglican Church are the Wednesday, Friday and Saturday after the first Sunday in Lent, Whit Sunday, 14 September (Holy Cross Day), and 13 December (St Lucia's Day).

FASTMAS, Shrove Tuesday.

GANG WEEK, Rogation Week.

GOOD FRIDAY commemorates the Crucifixion of Christ and falls on the Friday before Easter Sunday.

GRASS WEEK, Rogation Week.

GREAT WEEK, Holy Week, the week before Easter.

HOCK-TIDE, the second Monday and Tuesday after Easter. It was the custom in England to publicly collect money that would be 'laid out for pious uses.' The name is of unknown derivation.

HOLY WEEK, the week preceding Easter.

INDULGENCES, WEEK OF, Holy Week, the week preceding Easter.

LENT is the forty day fast, exclusive of Sundays which are feast days, that precedes Easter. The first day of Lent is Ash Wednesday, and the day before that, Shrove Tuesday.

LONG FRIDAY, Good Friday, the Friday before Easter.

LOW SUNDAY, the first Sunday after Easter. 'Low' probably because of its relative unimportance in comparison.

MAUNDY THURSDAY, the day before Good Friday. The name comes from either *mande*, a hand-basket in which alms were given to the poor by the king or queen, or, and this seems the more likely, from Christ's *dies mandati*, the commandment given to the disciples at the Last Supper that they should love one another.

The English custom of giving alms to the poor on this day was begun by Edward III in the 14th century. Nowadays the alms are limited to specially minted coins. The number of recipients is regulated by the sovereign's age.

MID-LENT SUNDAY, the fourth Sunday in Lent, the third before Easter. Known also as Mothering Sunday.

MOTHERING SUNDAY, Mid-Lent Sunday.

PALM SUNDAY celebrates Christ's triumphal entry into Jerusalem for the Feast of the Passover. He was greeted by a crowd bearing palms in his honour, and it is the custom in many countries to carry them on this day, in England goat willow is substituted. Palm Sunday is the last Sunday before Easter, the sixth in Lent.

PANCAKE TUESDAY, Shrove Tuesday.

PASCHAL FEAST, the Eastern Church's name for Easter Day.

PASSION SUNDAY, the fifth Sunday of Lent, the second before Easter. Sometimes called Care Sunday. The week following is Passion Week.

PENTECOST, the seventh Sunday after Easter, otherwise known as Whit Sunday.

PLOUGH MONDAY, the first Monday after 6 January, Epiphany. Traditionally, the day work in the fields was resumed.

PROCESSION WEEK, Rogation Week.

QUADRAGESIMA SUNDAY is the first Sunday in Lent, the sixth before Easter. The name comes from it being about forty days before Easter.

QUINQUAGESIMA SUNDAY is the seventh Sunday before Easter; so named as it is about the fiftieth day before Easter. Known also as Shrove Sunday.

RELICK SUNDAY is the third Sunday after Midsummer Day, 24 June (the Feast of the Nativity of St John the Baptist), and was observed only in those churches that possessed relics of a saint, eg Canterbury Cathedral.

RESURRECTION SUNDAY, Easter Day.

ROGATION SUNDAY, the Sunday preceding the Rogation Days.

ROGATION WEEK is the week containing the Rogation Days, the Monday, Tuesday and Wednesday preceding Ascension Day (the Thursday following the fifth Sunday after Easter). From the Latin *rogare*, meaning to beseech, as 'extraordinary prayers and supplications' were appointed in preparation for the observance of Christ's coming Ascension.

ROPE MONDAY, the first day of Hock-Tide, the second Monday after Easter.

SEPTUAGESIMA SUNDAY is the third Sunday before Lent, the ninth before Easter. Called Septuagesima as it is about seventy days before Easter.

SEXAGESIMA SUNDAY is the second Sunday before the beginning of Lent, the eighth before Easter. The name arises from it being around sixty days before Easter.

SHROVE MONDAY, the day before Shrove Tuesday.

SHROVE SUNDAY, the Sunday before Shrove Tuesday, Quinquagesima Sunday.

SHROVE THURSDAY, the Thursday following Shrove Tuesday.

SHROVE TUESDAY, Pancake Day, the day before the first day of Lent (Ash Wednesday).

TRINITY SUNDAY is the eighth Sunday after Easter, the Sunday that follows Whit Sunday. It celebrates the Trinity of the Father, Son and Holy Ghost, and was begun by Thomas Becket, Archbishop of Canterbury, in commemoration of his consecration on that day in 1164.

WEEK OF INDULGENCES, Holy Week, the week preceding Easter.

WHIT MONDAY, the day after Whit Sunday.

WHIT SUNDAY is the seventh Sunday after Easter and celebrates the descent of the Holy Ghost upon the Apostles. Pentecost in the Roman Church. It was earlier known as White Sunday from the custom of dressing the newly-baptized in white robes. Whit Monday and Tuesday follow.

WHITSUNTIDE, Whit Sunday, Monday and Tuesday.

II

The French Republican Calendar

In France on 24 November 1793 the Christian Era was abolished and a new one begun. It was to be known as the Era of the Republic and Year I would date from midnight of 21/22 September 1792. Along with the point of the beginning of the year, all of the names and most of the styling associated with the Gregorian Calendar were thrown out, though its basic calendrial principles were retained (not even the French Revolution could alter the movement of the heavenly bodies). Weeks were replaced with *Decades*, the 'months' began at new times and were awarded fresh names, and Leap Years henceforth were to be known as Olympic Years.

The Republican Calendar was used throughout France from 26 November 1793 until the Gregorian Calendar's restoration on 1 January 1806. It is the only modern instance of a revolutionary government altering the calendar that was in use before it came to power (the introduction of the Gregorian calendar by Russia and other countries in the present century were merely reforms long overdue). It has much to recommend it both in its ease of use and logicality, and it demands our respect.

From the Calendar's inauguration in November 1793 until the year 1800 the 1 *Vendémiaire* corresponded with the Gregorian 22 September. After 28 February

1800 and until it was abolished the Republican Calendar was one day 'ahead' of the Gregorian, that is the 1 *Vendémiaire* then corresponded with 23 September.

In tabular form the correspondences until 1800 were as follows:

22 Sept to 21 Oct	*Vendémiaire* (Vintage month)	AUTUMN
22 Oct to 20 Nov	*Brumaire* (Foggy month)	
21 Nov to 20 Dec	*Frimaire* (Sleety month)	
21 Dec to 19 Jan	*Nivose* (Snowy month)	WINTER
20 Jan to 18 Feb	*Pluviose* (Rainy month)	
19 Feb to 20 Mar	*Ventose* (Windy month)	
21 Mar to 19 Apr	*Germinal* (Budding month)	SPRING
20 Apr to 19 May	*Floréal* (Flowery month)	
20 May to 18 Jun	*Prairal* (Pasture month)	
19 Jun to 18 July	*Messidor* (Harvest month)	SUMMER
19 July to 17 Aug	*Thermidor* or *Fervidor* (Hot month)	
18 Aug to 16 Sep	*Fructidor* (Fruit month)	

The names of the months were ridiculed in England, as one would expect, and the following lines, a supposed translation, became an oft-recited refrain:

AUTUMN – wheezy, sneezy, freezy.
WINTER – slippy, drippy, nippy.
SPRING – showery, flowery, bowery.
SUMMER – hoppy, croppy, poppy.

The twelve months of the Republican Calendar, as will have been noticed, each contained thirty days only. The five further days needed to complete a year were placed at the end of *Vendémiaire* and were known as the *Jours complémentaires*, these were the Festival days, the *Sansculottides*:

17 Sep	*Primidi*, dedicated to Virtue
18 Sep	*Duodi*, dedicated to Genius
19 Sep	*Tridi*, dedicated to Labour
20 Sep	*Quartidi*, dedicated to Opinion
21 Sep	*Quintidi*, dedicated to Rewards

This account is based largely on that of John J. Bond's, and for additional information and a set of corresponding almanacs the reader is directed to that writer's *Handy-Book of Rules and Tables for Verifying Dates Within the Christian Era*, London, 1869.

III

The Calendar of The Book of Common Prayer

The Book of Common Prayer: And Administration of The Sacraments and Other Rites and Ceremonies of the Church, according to the Use of the Church of England, aside from being one of the glories of the English language, is also used, with only minor changes, by many overseas episcopal churches.

The edition now in use is that of 1662, Charles II's book, and its ancestry is traceable back through the Prayer Books of James I and Queen Elizabeth to the *King's Primer* of 1545.

Certain 'Additions and Deviations' were proposed in 1928 and, although the Royal Assent has not yet been given, owing to defeat of the Measure in the House of Commons, they are included in present editions, but noted as such. The 1928 'Alternative Calendar' makes several changes in the existing calendar and these I have noted at the end.

The *State Services* formerly annexed to the *Book*, for 5 November (Gunpowder Plot), 30 January (Charles I's execution), and 29 May (Charles II's Restoration), were ordered to be discontinued in January, 1859.

For the history of the *Book*, its origins, sources and revisions see the volumes by Brightman, and Frere and Proctor in Section II of the Bibliography.

JANUARY
1. Circumcision of Our Lord 6. Epiphany of Our Lord 8. Lucian, Priest and Martyr 13. Hilary, Bishop and Confessor 18. Prisca, Roman Martyr and Virgin 20. Fabian, Bishop of Rome and Martyr 21. Agnes, Roman Virgin and Martyr 22. Vincent, Spanish Deacon and Martyr 25. Conversion of St Paul

FEBRUARY
2. Purification of Mary the Blessed Virgin 3. Blasius, an Armenian Bishop and Martyr 5. Agatha, a Sicilian Virgin and Martyr 14. Valentine, Bishop and Martyr 24. St Matthias, Apostle and Martyr

MARCH
1. David, Archbishop of Menevia 2. Cedde, or Chad, Bishop of Lichfield 7. Perpetua, Mauritan. Martyr 12. Gregorius Magnus, Bishop of Rome and Confessor 18. Edward, King of the West Saxons 21. Benedict, Abbot 25. Annunciation of the Virgin Mary

APRIL
3. Richard, Bishop of Chichester 4. Ambrose, Bishop of Milan 19. Alphege, Archbishop of Canterbury 23. St George, Martyr 25. St Mark, Evangelist and Martyr

MAY
1. SS Philip and James, Apostles and Martyrs 3. Invention of the Cross 6. St John the Evangelist *ante Portam Lat* 19. Dunstan, Archbishop of Canterbury 26. Augustine, the first Archbishop of Canterbury 27. Venerable Bede, Presbyter

JUNE
1. Nicomede, Roman Priest and Martyr 5. Boniface, Bishop of Mentz and Martyr 11. St Barnabas, Apostle and Martyr 17. St Alban, Martyr 20. Translation of Edward, King of the West Saxons 24. Nativity of St John the Baptist 29. St Peter, Apostle and Martyr

JULY
2. Visitation of the Blessed Virgin Mary 4. Translation of St Martin, Bishop and Confessor 15. Swithun, Bishop of Winchester, Translation 20. Margaret, Virgin

and Martyr at Antioch 22. St Mary Magdalen 24. Fast 25. St James, Apostle and Martyr 26. St Anne, Mother to the Blessed Virgin Mary

AUGUST

1. Lammas Day 6. Transfiguration of Our Lord. 7. Name of Jesus 10. St Laurence, Archdeacon of Rome and Martyr 24. St Bartholomew, Apostle and Martyr 28. St Augustine, Bishop of Hippo, Confessor and Doctor 29. Beheading of St John the Baptist

SEPTEMBER

1. Giles, Abbot and Confessor 7. Evurtius, Bishop of Orleans 8. Nativity of the Blessed Virgin Mary 14. Holy Cross Day 17. Lambert, Bishop and Martyr 21. St Matthew, Apostle, Evangelist and Martyr 26. St Cyprian, Archbishop of Carthage and Martyr 29. St Michael and All Angels 30. St Jerome, Priest, Confessor and Doctor

OCTOBER

1. Remigius, Bishop of Rhemes 6. Faith, Virgin and Martyr 9. St Denys, Areopagite, Bishop and Martyr 13. Translation of King Edward, Confessor 17. Etheldreda, Virgin 18. St Luke, Evangelist 25. Crispin, Martyr 28. SS Simon and Jude, Apostles and Martyrs

NOVEMBER

1. All Saints' Day 6. Leonard, Confessor 11. St Martin, Bishop and Confessor 13. Britius, Bishop 15. Machutus, Bishop 17. Hugh, Bishop of Lincoln 20. Edmund, King and Martyr 22. Cecilia, Virgin and Martyr 23. St Clement I, Bishop of Rome and Martyr 25. Catherine, Virgin and Martyr 30. St Andrew, Apostle and Martyr

DECEMBER

6. Nicolas, Bishop of Myra in Lycia 8. Conception of the Blessed Virgin Mary 13. Lucy, Virgin and Martyr 16. *O Sapientia* [an anthem sung on each day until Christmas Eve] 20. Fast 21. St Thomas, Apostle and Martyr 24. Fast 25. Christmas Day 26. St Stephen, the first Martyr 27. St John, Apostle and Evangelist 28. Innocents' Day 31. Silvester, Bishop of Rome.

The 1928 'Alternative Calendar'

JANUARY

Discontinued: Lucian, Prisca. *Introduced*: 17. Antony of Egypt, Abbot. 19. Wulfstan, Bishop of Worcester 26. Polycarp, Bishop of Smyrna and Martyr 27. John Chrysostom, Bishop of Constantinople and Doctor

FEBRUARY

Discontinued: Blasius, Agatha, Valentine. *Introduced*: 3. Anskar of Sweden, Bishop

MARCH

Discontinued: Edward. *Introduced*: 17. Patrick, of Ireland, Bishop 20. Cuthbert, Bishop of Lindisfarne

APRIL

Introduced: 11. Leo the Great, Bishop of Rome and Doctor 21. Anselm, Archbishop of Canterbury and Doctor 30. Catherine of Siena, Virgin

MAY

Discontinued: Invention of the Cross. *Introduced*: 2. Athanasius, Bishop of Alexandria and Doctor 4. Monnica, Matron 25. Aldhelm, Bishop of Sherborne

JUNE

Discontinued: Nicomede, Translation of King Edward. *Introduced*: 9. Columba, Abbot of Iona 14. Basil, Bishop of Caesarea in Cappadocia, and Doctor 28. Irenaeus, Bishop of Lyons and Doctor

JULY

Discontinued: Translation of St Martin

AUGUST

Introduced: Oswald, King of Northumbria and Martyr 20. Bernard of Clairvaux, Abbot 31. Aidan, Bishop of Lindisfarne

SEPTEMBER

Discontinued: Evurtuis, Lambert. *Introduced*: 16. Ninian, Bishop in Galloway 19. Theodore of Tarsus, Archbishop of Canterbury

OCTOBER

Introduced: 4. Francis of Assisi 26. Alfred, King of the West Saxons

NOVEMBER

Discontinued: Britius, Machutus. *Introduced*: 2. Commemoration of All Souls 8. Saints, Martyrs, and Doctors of the Church of England 17. Hilda, Abbess of Whitby

DECEMBER

Discontinued: Lucy, Silvester *Introduced*: 4. Clement of Alexandria, Doctor 17. Ignatius, Bishop of Antioch and Martyr in Rome

Note: St Alban is changed to 22 June and St Cyprian to 13 September. Crispinian is now included with his brother, Crispin, on 25 October. And St Hugh is moved back a day to 16 November.

IV

The Earth was Created on 10 September

Reducing the entire history of the Universe to a single year has been a popular method of dramatizing cosmic time scales and highlighting the comparatively late arrival of Man. The 1950s was the great Age of the Cosmic Likening, when, to grasp distances and sizes, the popularizers of science asked us to imagine that the dome of St Paul's Cathedral was the Sun, that a golf-ball in Luton or thereabouts was the Earth, that –

Well, those writers vied with one another for more striking (and usually complex) similes until one's head was awhirl with footballs in Edinburgh, oranges in Liverpool, apple pips just outside of Birmingham, and glass marbles encircling the Orkneys or wherever (the topography was changed to suit the place of publication, usually).

But the year reduction has always fascinated me and it *is* striking, I therefore offer no excuses in subjoining a more detailed 'year', common not leap, than has usually been presented.

Lastly, I am surprised but not unhappy that no self-appointed seer or visionary, coughed-up by the occult revival, has yet got around to drawing Cosmic Parallels and Hidden Meanings from this exercise. Like the measurements of the Great Pyramid, the cosmic year can offer hours of entertainment and amusement to a mind that would otherwise be unoccupied.

1 January 00.00 hours, nothing. In the first 0.0000000122 of a second, 'The First Three Minutes', everything or nearly everything is created in the Big Bang and flung asunder, the Cosmic Diaspora (15,000 million years ago).

10 September, 1.36am, the creation of the Earth (4,600 million years ago).

29 September, 1.48pm, the creation of the oldest known rock (3,800 million years ago).

11 October, a few seconds before 8.41am, the first life appears on Earth (about 3,355 million years ago).

16 December, 4.04am, the first crustaceans appear (650 million years ago).

20 December, just before 7.41am, the first vertebrates (480 million years ago).

27 December, a little after 9.03am, mammals have evolved (190 million years ago).

30 December, 7.07am (and 12 seconds), appearance of the first primates (70 million years ago).

31 December: at nearly a minute past 10.00pm the first true man is about (3,400,000 years ago); and at 4.2 seconds before midnight the Christian Era begins. The Atomic Age, dating from the dropping of the bomb on Hiroshima in 1945, commenced at 0.074 seconds before midnight.

On this scale the Universe has another year or so ahead of it. Its expansion will stop, it will begin to contract and steadily get ever more dense until – it 'pops', disappears. Then nothing, again. Eventually it will re-appear and the cycle, in Hindu cosmology known as the *kalpa*, will begin again. All in the twinkling of an eye of Zeus.

V

The Days of the Week

Latin	Saxon	English	French	Spanish	German
Dies Solis	Sun's Day	Sunday	Dimanche	domingo	Sonntag
Dies Lunae	Moon's Day	Monday	Lundi	lunes	Montag
Dies Martis	Tiw's Day	Tuesday	Mardi	martes	Dienstag
Dies Mercurii	Woden's Day	Wednesday	Mercrédi	miércoles	Mittwoch
Dies Jovis	Thor's Day	Thursday	Jeudi	jueves	Donnerstag
Dies Veneris	Friga's Day	Friday	Vendredi	viernes	Freitag
Dies Saturni	Seater's Day	Saturday	Samedi	sabado	Sonnabend

Day of the month	Jan Oct	Apr **July** *Jan*	Sept Dec	Jun	Feb Mar Nov	Aug *Feb*	May	
1 8 15 22 29	A	B	C	D	E	F	G	Mon
2 9 16 23 30	G	A	B	C	D	E	F	Tues
3 10 17 24 31	F	G	A	B	C	D	E	Wed
4 11 18 25	E	F	G	A	B	C	D	Thur
5 12 19 26	D	E	F	G	A	B	C	Fri
6 13 20 27	C	D	E	F	G	A	B	Sat
7 14 21 28	B	C	D	E	F	G	A	Sun

Jan Oct	Apr **July** *Jan*	Sept Dec	Jun	Feb Mar Nov	Aug *Feb*	May
		1800	1801	1802	1803	
1804	1805	1806	1807		*1808*	1809
1810	1811		*1812*	1813	1814	1815
	1816	1817	1818	1819		*1820*
1821	1822	1823		*1824*	1825	1826
1827		*1828*	1829	1830	1831	
1832	1833	1834	1835		*1836*	1837
1838	1839		*1840*	1841	1842	1843
	1844	1845	1846	1847		*1848*
1849	1850	1851		*1852*	1853	1854
1855		*1856*	1857	1858	1859	
1860	1861	1862	1863		*1864*	1865
1866	1867		*1868*	1869	1870	1871
	1872	1873	1874	1875		*1876*
1877	1878	1879		*1880*	1881	1882
1883		*1884*	1885	1886	1887	
1888	1889	1890	1891		*1892*	1893
1894	1895		*1896*	1897	1898	1899
1900	1901	1902	1903		*1904*	1905
1906	1907		*1908*	1909	1910	1911
	1912	1913	1914	1915		*1916*
1917	1918	1919		*1920*	1921	1922
1923		*1924*	1925	1926	1927	
1928	1929	1930	1931		*1932*	1933
1934	1935		*1936*	1937	1938	1939
	1940	1941	1942	1943		*1944*
1945	1946	1947		*1948*	1949	1950
1951		*1952*	1953	1954	1955	
1956	1957	1958	1959		*1960*	1961
1962	1963		*1964*	1965	1966	1967
	1968	1969	1970	1971		*1972*
1973	1974	1975		*1976*	1977	1978
1979		*1980*	1981	1982	1983	
1984	1985	1986	1987		*1988*	1989
1990	1991		*1992*	1993	1994	1995
	1996	1997	1998	1999		*2000*

The Romans dedicated one day of the week to each of the planets (deities) then known, *and* the sun and the moon, also regarded as planets. The Saxon names bear an obvious correspondence, and, in fact, are little more than a 'translation', and from them we derive the names now in use. The French and Spanish are straight from the Latin (and in Spain are not initially capitalized), whilst the German come also from the Saxon with only two exceptions: Wednesday is *Mittwoch*, 'Middle of the Week', and Saturday is *Sonnabend*, 'Sunday Eve'.

VI

Calendar AD 1800–2000

To find the day of the week.
Example: 24 March 1878
In the March column opposite 24 (Day of the month) is C. Find 1878 in the list of years, look above and find C, across on the right indicated as a Sunday.

To find the day of the month.
Example: Monday,——June 1904
Find 1904. Above it, opposite Monday, is F. Under June F, in the left hand column, gives 6, 13, 20 and 27 as the days of June 1904 upon which Monday fell.

To find the months.
Example: Saturday, 8 —— 1898
Above 1898 and facing Saturday is A. Opposite 8 in the first column (Day of the month) A gives January and October (as the only months in 1898 which contain an '8th' falling on a Saturday).

To find the years.
Example: Friday, 18 December ——
Below December and opposite 18 (Day of the month) is G. Find G across from Friday and the years in the column below are those which contain a Friday, 18 December.

*The January and February in italic are to be used only for Leap Years. Years in italic are Leap Years.

Bibliography

I. The Calendar, Chronology, Dating, etc.
II. Church Festivals and Customs
III. Saints and Their Days
IV. Popular and Other Festivals and Customs
V. Some 'Day Books'

I have not listed here the 400 or so works of history, biography, and related subjects that were consulted in the preparation of entries for the present book. To do so would have proved lengthy and essentially redundant. Information about what to read on, say, the French Revolution or Ypres is not difficult to come by *and* in a classified and annotated form that I could not have equalled.

Instead, what I have done is to list a good selection of works on the underlying assumptions of *A Book of Days*, studies that explain how a book like this is possible, together with suggestions for pursuing matters of associated interest like chronology in general, time scales, dating, etc.

The importance of feasts and festivals, both religious and secular, is not neglected – there are three slightly over-lapping sections.

Finally, I have appended a list of some other day books, all of which are well worth tracking down.

I

The Calendar, Chronology, Dating, etc.

ARCHER, P. *The Christian Calendar and the Gregorian Reform*. 1941.

BENEDICTINES. *L'Art de Vérifier les Dates*. 8 volumes, Paris, 1783.

BERRY, WILLIAM B. N. *The Growth of a Prehistoric Time Scale*. London, 1968.

BICKERMAN, ELIAS J. *Chronology of the Ancient World*. London, 1968. A work of great scholarship and elucidation that 'answers a simple question: how are we able to date the events of ancient history?'

BLACK, F. A. *The Calendar and its Reform*. 1932.

BOLTON, L. *Time Measurement*. 1924.

BOND, JOHN J. *Handy-Book of Rules and Tables for Verifying Dates Within the Christian Era*. London, 1869.

BOSANQUET, EUSTACE F. *English Printed Almanacs and Prognostications*. Bibliographical Society Illustrated Monographs, No. xvii, London, 1917.

BROWNE, SIR THOMAS. *The Works of Sir Thomas Browne*. Edited by Simon Wilkin. 3 volumes, London, 1835–6, 1852.
Volume 2, Book VI of *Pseudodoxia Epidemica*: Chapter 1, Concerning the beginning of the world, that the time thereof is not precisely known, as commonly it is presumed. Chapter 2, Of men's enquiries in what season or point of the Zodiack it began, that, as they are generally made, they are in vain, and as

particularly, uncertain. Chapter 3, Of the divisions of the seasons and four quarters of the year, according unto astronomers and physicians; that the common compute of the ancients, and which is still retained by some, is very questionable. Chapter 4, Of some computation of days, and deductions of one part of the year unto another.

Calendar Reform Committee Report. Indian Government, 1955.

CLAVIUS, CHRISTOPHER. *Kalendarium Gregorianum perpetuum cum privilegio summi Pontificis et aliorum Principum.* Rome, 1582. Appended to the Bull issued by Pope Gregory XIII that introduced the Gregorian Calendar in 1582.

CLINTON, HENRY FYNES. *Fasti Hellenici: The Civil and Literary Chronology of Greece, from the Earliest Accounts to the Death of Augustus.* 3 volumes, Oxford, 1824–34. *Fasti Romani: The Civil and Literary Chronology of Rome and Constantinople, from the Death of Augustus to the Death of Heraclius.* 2 volumes, Oxford, 1845–50.

COLSON, F. H. *The Week: An Essay on the Origin and Development of the Seven-Day Cycle.* Cambridge, 1926. An interesting essay containing much information not easily obtainable elsewhere.

COMTE, AUGUSTE. *System of Positive Polity.* 4 volumes, London, 1877. The fourth volume contains a folding chart of Comte's proposed 'Positivist Calendar.'

DE MORGAN, AUGUSTUS. *The Book of Almanacs.* London, 1851, 1907.

DE VAUX, R. *Ancient Israel.* London, 1961.

DINSMOOR, W. B. *The Archons of Athens in the Hellenistic Age.* 1931.

DOW, S. and HEALEY, R. F. *Sacred Calendars of Eleusis.* 1965.

DRAKE, MILTON. *Almanacs of the United States.* 2 volumes, New York, 1962.

DUBBERSTEIN, WALDO H. and PARKER, RICHARD A. *Babylonian Chronology 626BC–AD75.* London and New York, 1956.

EHRICH, R. W. *Chronologies in Old World Archaeology.* 1965.

EICHER, D. *Geologic Time.* New York, 1968.

EISENBERG, AZRIEL. *The Story of the Jewish Calendar.* New York, 1958.

Explanatory Supplement to the Astronomical Ephemeris and the American Ephemeris and Nautical Almanac. HMSO, London, 1961, 1968.

FINEGAN, JACK. *Handbook of Biblical Chronology.* Princeton, 1964.

FREEMAN-GRENVILLE, GREVILLE. *Muslim and Christian Calendars, being Tables for the Conversion of Muslim and Christian Dates from the Hejira to the Year 2000 (AD).* Oxford, 1963.

FRY, EDWARD ALEXANDER. *Almanacks for Students of English History.* London, 1915. Amongst the tables, a set of almanacks for every day upon which Easter can fall.

HALES, WILLIAM. *A New Analysis of Chronology.* London, 1809.

HART, RABIE J. *Chronos: A Handbook of Comparative Chronology.* London, 1912.

HERTZ, J. H. *Changing the Calendar.* London, 1931.

HEYWOOD, ABEL. *Three Papers on English Printed Almanacs.* London, 1904.

HODGE, FREDERICK W. (editor). *The Handbook of American Indians North of Mexico.* 3 volumes, Washington, 1907. The third volume includes an article on the calendrial concepts of the Amerindians.

HOOD, PETER. *How Time is Measured.* London, 1955.

LANGDON, S. *Semitic Menologies.* 1935. *Babylonian Menologies.* 1935.

LEACH, E. R. 'Primitive Time Reckoning' in *A History of Technology*, edited by Hall, Holmyard and Singer. Oxford, 1956.

MARSHACK, ALEXANDER. *The Roots of Civilization.* London, 1970. A study of the lunar and solar bone tallys of earliest man.

MOMMSEN, THEODOR. *Römische Chronologie.* Berlin, 1859. The most important single study of the calendars and chronology of Rome. No English translation has yet appeared.

MICHELS, AGNES K. *The Calendar of the Roman Republic.* Princeton, 1967.

MERITT, B. D. *The Athenian Year.* 1961.

National Commission on Calendar Simplification. US Government Printing Office, Washington, 1929.

NEEDHAM, JOSEPH and LING, WANG. *Science and Civilization in China.* The third volume, 1959, contains a discussion of the Chinese calendar.

NEUGEBAUER, O. *The Exact Sciences in Antiquity.* 1957.

NEWTON, SIR ISAAC. *The Chronology of Ancient Kingdoms Amended.* 1728.

NICOLAS, SIR HARRIS. *The Chronology of History.* London, 1833.

NILSSON, M. P. *Primitive Time-Reckoning.* 1920.

NINEHAM, DENNIS E. *Historicity and Chronology in the New Testament.* New York, 1965.

O'BEIRNE, T. H. *Puzzles and Paradoxes.* Oxford, 1965. Chapter Ten is a lively essay on the problems of fixing Easter from a mathematician's point of view.

PARKER, RICHARD A. *The Calendars of Ancient Egypt.* 1950.

PHILIP, ALEXANDER. *The Calendar: Its History, Structure and Improvement.* Cambridge, 1921. After fifty years this still remains the best introduction to the subject.

POOLE, R. L. *Medieval Reckonings of Time.* London, 1921. *Studies in Chronology and History.* Edited by Austin Lane Poole. Oxford, 1934. Includes an essay on 'The Beginning of the Year in the Middle Ages.'

POWICKE, F. M. *Handbook of British Chronology.* Royal Historical Society, London, 1939, 1972. An invaluable compilation of regnal years, saints' days, etc.

PRAKKEN, D. W. *Studies in Greek Genealogical Chronology.* 1943.

PRITCHETT, W. K. *Ancient Athenian Calendars on Stone.* 1963.

SAMUEL, A. E. *Ptolemaic Chronology.* 1962. *Greek and Roman Chronology.* 1972.

SMILEY, TERAH L. and STOKES, MARVIN A. *An Introduction to Tree-Ring Dating.* Chicago, 1968.

SPIER, ARTHUR. *Comprehensive Hebrew Calendar.* New York, 1952.

SPINDEN, H. J. *The Reduction of Maya Dates.* 1924.

STAMP, A. E. *Methods of Chronology.* London, 1933.

THOM, ALEXANDER. *Megalithic Sites in Britain.* Oxford, 1967. *Megalithic Lunar Observatories.* Oxford, 1971. Two pioneer studies of man's earliest attempts at computing and predicting lunar, solar and other cycles.

VAN DER MEER, P. *The Chronology of Ancient Western Asia and Egypt.* 1955.

WILSON, P. W. *The Romance of the Calendar.* London, 1937.

WORMALD, FRANCIS. *English Kalendars before 1100.* London, 1934.
ZEUNER, F. E. *Dating the Past.* London, 1958. Concerned principally with the methods and techniques available to the archaeologist in dating early and prehistoric remains and in fixing relative chronologies.

II

Church Festivals and Customs

ANDREWS, WILLIAM. *Church History, Customs and Folklore.* London, 1881. *Curious Church Customs.* 1895. *Curious Church Gleanings.* 1896.
AUBREY, JOHN. *Remaines of Gentilisme and Judaisme.* Edited by J. Britten. Folk-Lore Society, London, 1881.
BRIGHTMAN, F. E. *The English Rite: Being a Synopsis of the Sources and Revisions of the Book of Common Prayer.* 2 volumes, London, 1915.
CAULDWELL, I. *Ceremonies of Holy Church.* London, 1948.
DAWSON, W. F. *Christmas and its Associations.* London, 1901.
FRERE, W. H. and PROCTER, FRANCIS F. *A New History of the Book of Common Prayer.* London, 1901.
HOLE, CHRISTINA. *Christmas and its Customs.* London, 1939.
POLHILL, C. C. *Christmas in Ritual and Tradition.* London, 1925.
SCHUSTER, CARDINAL ILDEFONSO. *The Sacramentary (Liber Sacramentorum):* *Historical and Liturgical Notes on the Roman Missal.* Translated by Arthur Levelis-Monke. 5 volumes, London, 1924. A magisterial work on the origin and development of the Catholic Church's customs and rituals, the manner of their observance, and much else.
TILLE, A. *Yule and Christmas.* London, 1899.
TYRER, J. W. *An Historical Survey of Holy Week.* London, 1932.
VAUX, J. E. *Church Folk Lore.* London, 1902.

III

Saints and Their Days

ATTWATER, DONALD. *The Penguin Dictionary of Saints.* Harmondsworth, 1965.
BARING-GOULD, SABINE. *Curious Myths of the Middle Ages.* London, 1869. and FISHER, J. *The Lives of the British Saints.* 4 volumes, London, 1907–13.
Bibliotheca Sanctorum. Institutio Giovanni XXIII/Pontificia Universita Lateranense. 12 volumes, Rome, 1961–9.
BOLLANDISTS. *Acta Sanctorum.* 'The Acts of the Saints.' 67 folio volumes to date, from 1643 onwards.
BOND, FRANCIS. *Dedications and Patron Saints of English Churches.* London, 1914.

BUTLER, ALBAN. *The Lives of the Saints.* Second edition, London, 1779. There have been many revisions, enlargements and new editions since. The most comprehensive and historically reliable are those by, principally, Herbert Thurston S. J., 12 volumes, London, 1926–38, and Donald Attwater, 4 volumes, London, 1956. As low on biographical detail as it is high on exhortations is the 4 volume edition prepared by Father F. C. Husenbeth, Dublin, 1928.

DELEHAYE, HIPPOLYTE. *Legends of the Saints.* Translated by Donald Attwater. London, 1962.

FORBES, A. P. *Kalendars of Scottish Saints.* 1872.

ROEDER, HELEN. *Saints and Their Attributes.* London, 1955.

URLIN, E. *Festivals, Holy Days and Saints' Days.* London, n.d.

IV

Popular and Other Festivals and Customs

ASHTON, J. A. *A Righte Merrie Christmas.* London, 1894.

AULD, W. M. *Christmas Traditions.* London, 1931.

BANKS, M. MACLEOD. *British Calendar Customs: Scotland, Movable Festivals.* 1937. *British Calendar Customs: Scotland, Fixed Festivals, January to March.* (inclusive) 1939. *British Calendar Customs: Scotland, Fixed Festivals, June to December.* (inclusive) 1942. *British Calendar Customs: Orkney and Shetland.* 1946. All published by the Folk-Lore Society, London. Reprinted, New York and Liechtenstein, 1975–6.

BRAND, JOHN. *Observations on Popular Antiquities.* First published in 1777. Editions by Sir H. Ellis, 1813, and W. Carew Hazlitt, 1905.

DITCHFIELD, P. H. *Old English Customs.* London, 1896.

DYER, T. T. *British Popular Customs.* London, 1911.

EDWARDS, GILLIAN. *Hogmanay and Tiffany: The Names of Fasts and Feasts.* London, 1970. An entertaining collection of essays on etymology.

ERSKINE, W. H. *Japanese Festivals and Calendar Lore.* London, 1933.

FOWLER, W. WARDE. *Roman Festivals.* London, 1899.

GRANET, M. *Festivals and Songs of Ancient China.* London, 1932.

HOLE, CHRISTINA. *A Dictionary of British Folk Customs.* London, 1978.

LI-CH'EN, TUN. *Annual Customs and Festivals in Peking.* 1936.

LONG, GEORGE. *The Folklore Calendar.* London, 1930.

MELLER, W. C. *The Boy Bishop.* London, 1923.

MILES, C. A. *Christmas in Ritual and Tradition.* London, 1912.

PATON, C. I. *Manx Calendar Customs.* Folk-Lore Society, London, 1943.

PROCTOR, L. A. *The Seasons Pictured.* London, 1885.

RADFORD, E. and M. A. *The Encyclopedia of Superstitions.* London, 1948. Revised and enlarged edition by Christina Hole, London, 1961.

SANDYS, W. *Christmastide.* London, 1852.

WHISTLER, LAWRENCE. *The English Festivals.* London, 1947.

WRIGHT, A. R. *British Calendar Customs: England, Movable Festivals.* 1936. *British Calendar Customs: England, Fixed Festivals, January to May.* (inclusive) 1938. *British Calendar Customs: England, Fixed Festivals, June to December.* (inclusive) 1940. All three volumes edited by T. East Lones and published by the Folk-Lore Society, London. Reprinted, New York and Liechtenstein, 1975–6.

V
Some 'Day' Books

BRADY, JOHN. *The Clavis Calendaria: or, A Compendious Analysis of the Calendar Illustrated by Ecclesiastical, Historical and Classical Anecdotes.* London, 1805 (?), third edition, 1822.

CHAMBERS, ROBERT. *A Book of Days: A Miscellany of Popular Antiquities in Connection with the Calendar, including Anecdote, Biography & History, Curiosities of Literature, and Oddities of Human Life and Character.* 2 volumes, London and Edinburgh, 1863.

DARLING, SIR WILLIAM. *A Book of Days.* London, 1951. Draws largely on the work of Chambers above.

FORSTER, T. *Perennial Kalendar and Companion to the Almanack.* London, 1824. A useful work containing much original information.

HONE, WILLIAM. *The Every-Day Book: or, Everlasting Calendar of Popular Amusements, Sports, Pastimes, Ceremonies, Manners, Customs, and Events, incident to each of the Three Hundred and Sixty-Five Days, in Past and Present Times.* 2 volumes, London, 1826–7. *The Table Book.* 2 volumes, London, 1827–8. Illustrations by George Cruikshank and others. Compiled on the same principles as *The Every-Day Book. The Year-Book of Daily Recreation and Information concerning Remarkable Men and Manners, Times and Seasons.* London, 1832. Illustrations by George Cruikshank and others.

JONES-BAKER, DORIS. *Old Hertfordshire Calendar.* Chichester, 1974. A 'day book' devoted to the customs, folk-lore and popular and social history of one English county. A delightful work in every way, but so messily designed it should win an award.

L'ENVOI

Imagine God, as the Poet saith, *Ludere in Huamnis*, to play
but a game at Chesse with this world; to sport Himself with
making little things great, and great things nothing;
Imagine God to be at play with us, but a gamester . . .
JOHN DONNE, *An Anatomy of the World* (1611)

A NOTE ON THE TYPEFACE

This book was composed on the Monotype in Bembo, Series 270, a face originally cut by Francesco Griffo for the great Venetian printer Aldus Manutius who first used it for a short Latin tract written by Cardinal Bembo and published in 1495. It is the earliest and undoubtedly the most beautiful of all old face designs in the history of typography. The companion italic is based upon a chancery hand perfected by Giovanni Tagliente (1524). The re-cutting undertaken by the Monotype Corporation dates from 1929.